Tests and Measurements
in Child Development

A Handbook

ORVAL G. JOHNSON
JAMES W. BOMMARITO

Tests and Measurements in Child Development: A Handbook

Jossey-Bass Inc., Publishers

615 Montgomery Street · San Francisco · 1971

TESTS AND MEASUREMENTS IN CHILD DEVELOPMENT
A Handbook
Orval G. Johnson and James W. Bommarito

Jossey-Bass, Inc., Publishers
615 Montgomery Street
San Francisco, California 94111

Library of Congress Catalog Card Number 78-110636

International Standard Book Number ISBN 0-87589-090-3

Manufactured in the United States of America
Composed and printed by York Composition Company, Inc.
Bound by Chas. H. Bohn & Co., Inc.

JACKET DESIGN BY JANE OKA

FIRST EDITION

Code 7112

The Jossey-Bass
Behavorial Science Series

General Editors

WILLIAM E. HENRY, *University of Chicago*

NEVITT SANFORD, *Wright Institute, Berkeley*

Preface

The collection and description of the measures in *Tests and Measurements in Child Development* have involved long hours of searching and many days of attempting to capture the essence of someone else's work. Our belief that this source book would prove helpful to many professionals whose work involves children was our chief reinforcer. We received additional reinforcement from colleagues—sometimes as they responded to our requests for measures, sometimes as they heard of our compilation of measurements.

We are convinced of the need to continue this project by updating *Tests and Measurements in Child Development,* perhaps at five-year intervals. We encourage feedback from colleagues about the utility of the source book as it is presently organized and about measures that should be included in future editions. We are interested in hearing of both new and old measures that should be included.

In our opinion, the research worker himself is in the best position to determine the maximum usefulness of a measure for his purposes. Because of this belief we have made no attempt to pass judgments on the value of each measure. We have simply described them. Nonetheless, we cannot resist discussing two interrelated advantages of *Tests and Measurements in Child Development.* First, it describes measures with some unique advantages. For example, measures are available to test the child's perceptions of his parents' child-rearing practices, the parental reports of the same events, and the realism and accuracy of the child's perceptions. Second, the availability of measures for diverse variables encourages numerous research ideas and facilitates the verification or refutation of theories that have formerly rested on assumption. This potential of the text provides a distinct and exciting advantage for the imaginative research worker. For example, the measures just described make it feasible to test the validity of the phenomenological point of view that the child's perception of events is as important as, if not more significant than, the events themselves. This view could be contrasted with the behavioristic position that the experiences themselves are more crucial in shaping a child's behavior than is his perception of them.

We gratefully acknowledge the support of the National Institute of Mental Health under Grant No. 1 R11 MH02347-01 and of the Office of Economic Opportunity under Contract No. OEO-2452 in the execution of this project. We are indebted to Corinne Hawkins, Sharon Kilby, and Betty White for the enthusiastic contribution of their library skills and the systematic search procedure that evolved from their efforts; to Nina, Kristin, and Lisa Johnson, and to Martha Bommarito for timely help in proofreading or typing sections of the manuscript; and to the Graduate Office of Southern Illinois University (Edwardsville) for assistance with the preparation of the manuscript. William E. Henry, general editor of the Jossey-Bass Behavioral Science Series, helped us when we could not see the forest for the trees. We are particularly grateful to the hundreds of colleagues, the authors of the measures we have described, who answered our numerous (and sometimes overly persistent) requests for additional information.

We dedicate the book to Nina and Marty.

Boulder   ORVAL G. JOHNSON
April 1971   JAMES W. BOMMARITO

Contents

Tests and Measurements in Child Development

A Handbook

P<small>ART</small> ONE

LOGIC AND STRUCTURE

CHAPTER 1

Criteria and Coverage

A fast-growing number of researchers are planning and carrying out research with young children. The rigorousness of the research depends on the quality of the overall design and the extent to which the terminology of the study can be made operational. Many of the variables with which researchers deal in studies of young children are operationalized in the form of scores on tests, rating scales, frames of reference for observation, structured interviews, checklists, and self-report forms. Objective measures, in particular, lend themselves to use from a number of theoretical approaches. When variables are made operational through standardized procedures (of which tests are one special type), the researcher is protected in part from his own biases.

For purposes of this discussion we may classify measures as published or unpublished. We define a published measure as one that is or has been published for sale by an established publisher, one who usually publishes more than one measure and whose measures are reviewed in the *Mental Measurements Yearbooks*. Guides for the user are ordinarily provided, often in the form of a test manual, and norms are generally given. By unpublished measures we mean those that have appeared in a journal, research report, book, or other publication, but which are not produced commercially for sale by an established publisher. The entire measure frequently is not presented but may be available from the author.

Heretofore, there has been no central source to which researchers could go for specialized information on unpublished measures suitable for children. The

3

value of a central source of information about unpublished measures appears manifold. First, since these measures are so widely scattered in various sources, there is vast duplication of effort from study to study in ferreting out of the literature the data-gathering instruments or techniques that are pertinent to each investigation. Much of that duplication of effort can be eliminated by centralizing the information on unpublished measures. Second, the individual evaluator or researcher is unlikely to cover a very wide segment of the literature in his search because of time limitations so is almost sure to miss measures that would be useful to him. Third, a central source has heuristic value. It may stimulate the planning of evaluation phases of research by increasing the number of measurement options available to the researcher. He may thus find measures more specific to his research or evaluation needs. It was our impression that there were possibly hundreds of unpublished measures in the literature. We found, in fact, over a thousand measures, of which about one third met the selection criteria described below. Common sense told us that most professionals working with children were unaware of the bulk of these measures. The many letters we received from researchers and evaluators in support of this compilation constitute evidence of a need for a central source of information on unpublished measures.

SEARCH PROCEDURE

The major effort to find measures was concentrated in the professional journals. We asked ourselves how we could be assured of a broad enough screening procedure to find most of the useful measures. The references researchers usually consult in similar circumstances, such as abstracts, reviews, and indexes, are not adequate to the task. While they are useful in providing leads, they are not appropriate as the basic document from which to work because they are not specific enough. An abstract or review of an article may mention the variables dealt with but seldom names the measure used. Indexes are only slightly more specific. Our choice, in retrospect a happy one, was to search the journals in the fields of psychology, psychiatry, and education that appeared to offer the likeliest return in the form of numbers of measures. We found that the table of contents of a journal seldom rendered enough information to determine whether an acceptable measure was there. Consequently, we went through all the journals, page by page, looking for measures or mention of measures.

We chose the ten-year period from 1956 through 1965 on the assumption that most of the measures of lasting value would have appeared in the literature within that period. The journals we searched are listed in Appendix A. When we found a measure or a reference to one, we checked the *Mental Measurements Yearbooks* to see whether the measure was described there. If it was, we excluded it from further consideration since it was already described in a source book. If it was not, we looked in the journal article or in some of the related references for the measure itself. The ideal situation occurred when the complete measure was presented in the article since it would thus be readily available to the reader. If the measure was not included with the article, we ordinarily wrote to the author for a copy of his measure, unless he gave some other source. It was occasionally necessary to send a follow-up letter to an author or to ask for further information, but in general the response to our initial request was excellent.

The page-by-page search of the journals yielded at least two types of information: the measures that we were looking for and leads to other measures. The leads took us into sources other than journals—mostly books, research reports, and unpublished papers. Leads came to us also from colleagues who were aware of our project and suggested measures that we might want to include.

There is no clear line of demarcation between what should be considered a test and what is not a test. It is in large part a function of one's definition. A case in point is the Kreezer-Dallenbach Meaning of Opposition Test. The researcher can usually work up such a test in a short time. The test would probably have high reliability, and there is certainly considerable face validity. This measure, constructed in 1929, is not in the strictest sense an opposites test. The purpose was to determine whether the subjects understood the relation of opposition, not to test their knowledge of specific opposites. As the authors point out, the answers *not smooth* or *unsmooth* to the word *smooth,* for example, were considered correct. The main value of a measure like this to the student and researcher is twofold: First, knowing that someone else has constructed a measure of the relation of opposition may suggest that other kinds of concepts may be measured in a similar way. It may, in other words, be thought-provoking and suggestive of possible alternatives. Second, the norms that have been developed for different age groups are certainly suggestive of the age at which this ability becomes predominant.

On a few occasions we felt the item type was of more significance than the specific items used by the author. In such cases we did not make a particular effort to procure the author's complete test, especially if considerable difficulty and expense were involved. We did this only when we felt that the researcher would be able, using the model for items given by the author, to formulate his own specific items. Any reliability or validity statistics computed on the basis of the author's items would not necessarily apply to the items made up by other persons, of course.

One type of measure that frequently appeared in the literature was the laboratory apparatus, which in many instances was set up for a particular research project. This apparatus presented tasks to the subject and measured the speed or some other indication of success in accomplishing the tasks. In most cases such tasks were not included as measures of child behavior, although for the specific piece of research in which they appeared, they were exactly that. The task was included, however, if there were data on norms, reliability, and validity, and if the measure met the criterion of usability.

SELECTION OF MEASURES

Six criteria governed the selection of measures to be included. The first three are relatively objective, while the others involve greater degrees of judgment. The six criteria are: (1) The measure must be suitable for use with children between birth and age 12, the latter being the modal age of children in the last year of elementary school. (2) The measure must be available to other professionals. On occasion we received measures which the author said would not be generally available. These were not included. (3) The measure must be an unpublished, noncommercial one, as previously defined. (4) There must be enough information to enable others to use the measure effectively. Particularly necessary were instructions for administering and scoring. A surprising number of measures were presented without scoring criteria for the items. These measures were often used in exploratory studies and were frequently questionnaires. Data on norms, reliability, and validity were considered desirable but not crucial. (5) The measure must be long enough so that norms and meaningful reliability and validity data could be developed by the user if they did not exist. (6) The measure must be usable, in the technical sense of the term. For example, a measure involving much heavy, expensive laboratory equipment was not included.

We have attempted to describe as accurately as possible the measures included. We do not anticipate that our success in doing so will be complete in any sense. One reason is that our data were not always as complete as we would have liked, even after we had read all the material that we could find on the measure. Limitations on the amount of information we could collect were set by limitations on the quantity of material published about the measure; inability to get authors to send additional material; inability to contact a few authors; and, in a few cases, our unwillingness to impose further on prolific researchers who had already supplied us with reprints, unpublished papers, and personal correspondence. A second reason involves the usual communication gaps, personal blindspots, and idiosyncratic interpretations that must invariably occur in an effort such as this.

We tried to maintain an objective view in writing the test descriptions. For the most part, we have succeeded at least in suppressing the feelings we may have had about some of the measures. The novelty of some aroused our interest, but we leave the judgment of novelty to the reader. The potential usefulness of some measures, especially the adaptation to specific research uses, was continually suggested by the measures and our own experience. Most of the time we withheld comments on possible applications of measures on the assumption that the comments might channel and restrict the reader's thinking about them.

SUGGESTIONS FOR FUTURE AUTHORS

We could not examine hundreds of journal articles, books, reports, and theses as we did, with an eye to the measures used, without developing our own conception of what information researchers should ideally provide. If a measure is to be maximally useful to other researchers, its creator should concern himself with the following general rules: (1) Give the measure a title. It should be appropriate in reflecting the variable to be measured, but any name is better than none. Name it after yourself, if you wish, but name it. It is less likely to be referred to thereafter as "that measure that Smith made" or by seven different names, as in the case of one widely used measure. (2) Identify the variable that the instrument is designed to measure. A surprising number of measures, and the studies using them, were lacking in this respect. There are at least two advantages in specifying the variable: The researcher is likely to sharpen his research focus when he verbalizes the nature of the variables. And communication about the research is enhanced when the nature of the variables is made as clear as possible. (3) Make the measure available to other researchers. Shared knowledge is one of the essences of science. The researcher who in the process of reporting his study brings a new measure to the attention of his colleagues should at the same time commit himself to provide the measure to interested colleagues or to provide them with information about where it is available. (4) Provide colleagues with any data necessary or useful for applying the measure. Instructions for administration and scoring, in addition to data on reliability and validity, should be available to other researchers.

OTHER RESOURCES

Published resource books providing information on measuring instruments, particularly those instruments not available commercially, are few in number. This section provides summaries of other sources that cover different sections of the measurement picture. While none of them deals exclusively with child and child-related measures, as does this work, they constitute most of the centralized information on measurement instruments in this country.

The standard reference for information on published tests is O. K. Buros' *Sixth Mental Measurements Yearbook* (1965). It is the tenth in a series of publications providing test users with the basic data they need for choosing from among hundreds of tests. Critical reviews of tests, plus extensive bibliographies, constitute the bulk of the *Yearbook*. It lists 1,219 tests, 795 critical reviews, ninety-seven excerpts from test reviews appearing in thirty journals, and 8,001 references for specific tests. A section on books and reviews lists 527 books. Buros' companion volume, *Tests in Print,* is a comprehensive bibliography of tests available as of its publication date (1961).

A resource for researchers who are looking particularly for indications that a measure has been used and is thus supposedly time-tested is Bonjean, Hill, and McLemore (1967). The 579-page book is the result of a survey done by the authors of twelve years of four sociological journals. They have 3,609 uses and citations for 2,080 scales and indices. They used seventy-eight classes in an attempt to find a useful and integrated classification system, and provide extensive bibliographies on commercially published and experimental measures. Some measures that are judged by the authors to have been used over a period of time are described in detail.

The Cattell and Warburton (1967) volume entitled *Objective Personality and Motivation Tests* culminates years of effort by the authors. This large volume, subtitled *A Theoretical Introduction and Practical Compendium,* includes descriptions of 412 tests, many of which are designed for adults or older children (beyond elementary school level). While the book is not restricted to child measures, separate child forms exist for a number of the tests. The tests are described according to a prescribed format, providing information on the name of the test, the age for which the measure is appropriate, testing time required, availability of different forms, and type of test. The variables measured by the test are given, plus the age range and the length of the test (in terms of time). The tests are classified in one of twelve categories, of which the following are examples: ability tests, performance tests, perceptual tests, questionnaires, opinionnaires. Techniques used to prevent faking of responses are described, as are the theory, rationale, and design of the instrument. Examples of items are given, in addition to details of administration and scoring. Six separate indexes are provided, including indexing by test title, variable title, and manifest content.

The Cornell University Testing and Service Bureau publishes each year a list of the measures available at the Bureau. Most of them are published commercially and are reviewed in Buros' *Mental Measurements Yearbooks,* but a few of them are in the experimental stage. The test list is organized with the names of the tests first, followed by a list of publishers and an index, making it feasible to associate a measure with its publisher.

The Educational Testing Service maintains a test collection and has published bimonthly since 1968 the *Test Collection Bulletin*. The following description of the test collection comes from the July 1968 *Bulletin:*

The test collection of the Carl Campbell Brigham Library contains an extensive collection of standardized tests as well as some experimental tests in education and psychology. It also includes publishers' catalogs and descriptive materials, information on scoring services and systems, test reviews, and reference volumes on testing. The tests are indexed by title, author, number (an accession number assigned when the test was indexed), and subject. Qualified persons, both inside and outside of Educational Testing Service, may have access to the materials in the Test Collection. Publishers' restrictions regarding access to test materials are carefully observed.

The publication that appears to come closest to this volume with respect to purpose and method is the collection of attitude scales compiled by Shaw and Wright (1967). They have described and reprinted 176 scales for the measurement of attitudes, although they have not specialized in measures concerning children. Their organization of test descriptions is similar to ours, although the two were derived independently, and it includes the following major topics: description, subjects, response mode, scoring, reliability, validity, and special comments. The scales are grouped into eight categories, including scales concerned with the following topics: social practices, social issues and problems, international issues, abstract concepts, political and religious attitudes, ethnic and national groups, significant others, and social institutions. The entire scale is included in the description in each case.

Simon and Boyer (1967) have compiled "an anthology of classroom observation instruments." Twenty-six systems for analyzing classroom interaction are described in sufficient detail for the researcher to evaluate their applicability to his measurement task. Each system is described, the categories for classification of behavior are given in detail, procedures for determining reliability are outlined and reliability figures given where they have been determined, and a bibliography is provided.

The observation instruments are classified according to system focus (affective domain, cognitive domain, work process, and behavior); type of communication recorded (verbal, nonverbal); and subject of observation (teacher only, student only, teacher and student). A system summary for each system is helpful in pulling together most of the significant information needed by the researcher who is shopping for an observation system suited to his interests and to his facilities.

Webb and others (1965) describe a large number of nonreactive measures useful in sociological and psychological research. The purpose is to call attention to research data that are not derived from tests, interviews, or questionnaires. While these techniques are not designed specifically for the study of children, they can be applied to a variety of subject populations. The measurement techniques are classified as follows: (1) Physical traces: Erosion and accretion. An example is measuring museum exhibit popularity by counting the frequency with which the floor tiles around it were worn out and had to be replaced. Another example, based on accreting data, is the evaluation of various aspects of a culture by studying its refuse.

(2) The running record. This section describes the use of records, government and other, and mass media in research on human behavior. (3) The episodic and private record. This section is concerned with sales records, institutional records, and personal documents as possible substitutes for direct observation of behavior. (4) Simple observation has been applied in a number of areas to several classes of variables: exterior physical signs (such as clothing, presence or absence of tattoos); expressive movement (such as studies relating emotion to gesture); physical location (for example, spontaneous seating arrangements in interracial settings); language behavior (for example, conversation sampling); and time duration (such as measuring attractiveness of a museum exhibit by the amount of time the average viewer spends at it). (5) Contrived observation—hidden hardware and control. This section describes many ingenious observation techniques and strategies.

Researchers interested in measures of self-concept should consult Wylie's (1961) book. She lists eighty-three "questionnaires, adjective check lists, rating schemes for indexing self-regard" and fourteen self-evaluative rating scales made specifically for experimental purposes. While there is no indication that any of them are particularly suitable for use with children, some of them could undoubtedly be modified for purposes of child research.

The researcher interested in Q-technique should consult the Stephenson (1953) book. The semantic differential is described by Osgood, Suci, and Tannenbaum (1957). A book of readings edited by Snider and Osgood (1969) treats the theoretical basis, methodology, uses, and validity of the technique.

FORMAT FOR DESCRIPTION

In order to be maximally useful, the descriptions of the measures must give the essentials in easily understood form. The potential user of a measure should know from reading the description if it is likely to meet his specific needs. The data we provide will in most cases be sufficient basis for the decision to eliminate or select research and evaluation instruments.

The format on which we finally settled provided for the following information, in the order given: name of measure, author, age of children, variable, type of measure, source from which the measure may be obtained, description of measure, reliability and validity, bibliography. Each section of the description format is discussed below, with the rationale for some sections where it is needed and some of the problems and issues that we encountered.

Name: The name used in our description is whenever possible one provided by the creator of the instrument. Occasionally the author used more than one name from article to article for the same measure. In such cases we selected the title given in the latest reference we had. When no title was attached by the author we coined one, using whenever possible some of the author's words from his writing about the measure. Sometimes the author referred to a measure as, for example, the time conception test, without capitals. In such cases our practice was to capitalize his terms into a proper name. Widely used measures, if not christened early by their authors, appear to accumulate names. Obviously, this situation complicates the problem of storing and retrieving information on these measures.

Author: This section entailed few problems. For most measures there was a single author. Multiple authors were listed in the order given in what we considered the basic document for the measure. Sometimes the same group wrote several articles reporting research in which the measure was used, with senior authorship changing with each article. This made it difficult to establish the senior author of the instrument. We customarily used the order of authorship given for the article in which the measure was first introduced.

Another minor problem was the adaptation or revision of an instrument. Whether we described a measure as Smith's adaptation of the Jones Preschool Intelligence Test or as Smith's Intelligence Test depended on our judgment of the extent of the revision and on what the revising author called it. If he gave it a new title, we used that.

Age: This item refers to the age of child for whom the measure is appropriate. For several reasons, the designation of age appropriateness for a measure should be interpreted as simply a rough guideline. The age figures that we reported are not in any sense restrictive. The age or age range tells the reader that use of the measure with the designated age group is appropriate; it does not mean that extending the range above or below the given age or age span is inappropriate. The figures we used sometimes came from the author's instructions. Frequently, however, the author did not specify any age range, but the study or studies using the instrument were done with subjects of a specific age range. In such cases, we indicated the age appropriateness of the measure to be the age of subjects used in the research. Another reason for interpreting the age designation loosely is that norms for many of the instruments are based on very small samples, and the setting of age limits may be premature. Finally, if one is working with exceptional populations (for example, retarded adolescents or gifted kindergartners) he may need measures that are not designed for the age group with which he is working but that are appropriate for his special population. In a few instances the author gave no age level for the measure, and there was no other indication of the appropriate age. In those cases we made a judgment of the appropriate age level.

Variable: This item designates the dimension along which the instrument is designed to measure. It should have been one of the simplest items to determine for each measure but was in fact one of the most difficult. We preferred to derive a clear author's statement of the variable for which his instrument was constructed. In a surprising number of instances, we could not find any straightforward designation of the variable, particularly in some of the older research. When the variable was not named by the author, we gave it an appropriate name.

Type of Measure: The prospective user of a measure is interested in the instrument because it entails some practical considerations. What level of training is necessary to administer the measure? How much time does it take to administer and score? Can the data be collected by group administration or by mail? What is the cost of equipment? Of duplication? While a word or short descriptive phrase cannot give specific answers to these questions, it may tell the individual whether to eliminate or to pursue any one measure. The information in this section, more than the others, is augmented in the section entitled "Description of Measure."

Source from Which the Measure May Be Obtained: After reading a description of a measure, the reader may wish to examine the measure itself. The source listed in this section will provide him with the complete measure. Sometimes the entire instrument is published in a journal article, in which case we have referred to that item in the bibliography (see below). "See Jackson, 1963" means that the entire measure appears in the bibliographic reference by Jackson in 1963. If a name with address is given as the source, it is usually the author; he has either stated in the literature that he would provide copies of the measure or has agreed through correspondence with us to honor requests for a copy.

Description of Measure: The items up to this point have, of course, been descriptive of the measure. This section, however, augments in narrative style the demographic information provided in the first six sections. We covered the following points whenever the information was available to us: (1) A further detailing of the variable or variables. Many of the instruments were designed to measure along several dimensions, and these dimensions are detailed in this section. (2) The procedure for administration of the measure, which should help the potential user decide the suitability of the measure for his population. (3) The method of scoring and ways of summarizing the results of the measure. The way in which the author derived summary scores and subscores is described here. (4) The length of the measure, in terms either of number of items or of administration time. (5) Samples of the items, just as they appear in the measure. Whenever a measure was constituted of different item types, examples of each were included in the description. Our item samples were chosen to give what we felt was a representative view of the items and also to point up the special flavor of the measure. (6) Special considerations for the potential user, such as skills necessary for administration and scoring, special equipment needed, restrictions on use imposed by the author of the measure, cost, and precautions and suggestions for using the measure. (7) Comments, usually by the author and sometimes by researchers, about the usability or other features of the measure.

Reliability and Validity: In our initial letter to the originator of the measure we asked for evidence of reliability and validity. We usually received one or more publications or reprints reporting research done with the measure. From these we extracted and summarized the evidence for validity and reliability. Sometimes the information was so limited we could report everything we found, while with other measures we had to cut out substantial portions of useful data. Studies specifically designed to investigate the validity of a measure were abstracted in this section whenever they were accessible to us. Many measures, however, have never been researched in this way. Typically, a measure was used in a study where the validity was assumed, but the hypotheses in the study were supported and construct validity of the measure used could be inferred from the results. Data on reliability were infrequently provided by the originators of the measure.

Bibliography: The bibliography represents a sample of the use of the measure and is not meant to be comprehensive. In going through the journals, when we came upon a measure that seemed to fit our criteria, we asked the author of the article for a reprint of his article, a copy of the measure, and any other reprints or reports of studies or bibliographic references that would contribute to our knowledge of the measure. We felt that, with this procedure, we would be very likely to hear from the people who have the most experience with the measure. To review all the literature on all the measures would be an enormous task, the net value of which is questionable.

BIBLIOGRAPHY

BONJEAN, C. M., HILL, R. J., and MC LEMORE, S. D. *Sociological Measurement: Inventory of Scales and Indices*. San Francisco: Chandler Publishing Company, 1967.

BUROS, O. K. (Ed.). *The Sixth Mental Measurements Yearbook*. Highland Park, N.J.: Gryphon Press, 1965.

BUROS, O. K. *Tests in Print*. Highland Park, N.J.: Gryphon Press, 1961.

CATTELL, R. B., and WARBURTON, F. W. *Objective Personality and Motivation Tests*. Urbana, Ill.: University of Illinois Press, 1967.

Cornell University Testing and Service Bureau. *Cornell University Test List*. Ithaca, N.Y.: 1960.

Educational Testing Service. *Test Collection Bulletin*, Vol. 2, No. 4, Princeton, N.J.: 1968.

OSGOOD, C. E., SUCI, G. J., and TANNENBAUM, P. H. *The Measurement of Meaning*. Urbana, Ill.: University of Illinois Press, 1957.

SHAW, M. E., and WRIGHT, J. M. *Scales for the Measurement of Attitudes*. New York: McGraw-Hill, 1967.

SIMON, A., and BOYER, E. G. (Eds.). *Mirrors for Behavior: An Anthology of Classroom Observation Instruments*. Philadelphia: Research for Better Schools, Inc., 1967.

SNIDER, J. G., and OSGOOD, C. E. *Semantic Differential Techniques: A Sourcebook*. Chicago: Aldine Publishing Company, 1969.

STEPHENSON, W. *The Study of Behavior: Q-technique and Its Methodology*. Chicago: University of Chicago Press, 1953.

WEBB, E. J., CAMPBELL, D. T., SCHWARTZ, R. D., and SECHREST, L. *Unobtrusive Measures*. Chicago: Rand McNally and Company, 1965.

WYLIE, R. C. *The Self Concept*. Lincoln: University of Nebraska Press, 1961.

CHAPTER **2**

Classification System

There is no generally accepted classification system for measures of human characteristics. Probably everyone who has collated a number of measures for publication has felt some need for organizing and classifying the measures. The basis for categorization goes beyond the personal compulsion to infuse order into an amorphous mass of data. It is based on the assumption that unorganized data are less useful than organized data. Thus, the author or editor imposes on the data the organization that he would find most useful and that he feels others would find useful. Sometimes the organization may conform with some articulated theoretical system, but typically the dominant theme of classification is that of usefulness.

There are several possible bases for classification of measures, all of which have been employed by various authors. (1) Frequently measures are categorized according to the content or area measured. Tests, for example, are frequently classified as tests of intelligence or academic aptitude, achievement, personality, aptitude, and interest (personal or vocational). They may also be classed more broadly as verbal versus performance or language versus nonlanguage. (2) A second classificatory mode involves the manner of administration of the measure. A distinction is made between tests that can be administered to more than one individual and tests involving a one-to-one testing situation. Closely related to the group-versus-individual dimension is the response mode dimension, where measures are classed as paper-and-pencil, oral-verbal response, automated-response (button-pressing), and other less often used response modes. (3) Another classification scheme that has been employed primarily for tests is based on the scoring method and is usually referred to as objective versus subjective. This system sets up a specious dichotomy, considering the subjectivity frequently involved in determining the objectively "right" answer and the objectivity that intrudes into the scoring of essay-type questions. (4) Classification is sometimes concerned with the format of the measure, which may be a test, checklist, rating scale, observation schedule, situational task, or other. This classification is closely related to (2) and (3) above since differences in measures are in large part a function of differences in administration and scoring. (5) For some purposes, measures are classified according to the subject population for whom they are designed. These include infant measures, preschool and adult measures, measures of teacher attitudes, and measures of social institutions (for example, family status characteristics). (6) Sometimes the system that appears to be most helpful is the empirically tested alphabetical system.

These are all different ways of looking at the data-gathering process, and their value as classification systems must be determined by the usefulness of perceiving measures in any particular one of these frames of reference. The different classifications described above are not in any sense clearly separable ways of looking at measures. The following are examples of how the different category systems for measures are related to each other: We only give paper-and-pencil tests (response mode classification) to people who can read and write (subject population classification); infant and preschool child measures (subject population) are probably never group administered (administration method); intelligence (content classification) is usually measured by tests rather than rating scales or checklists (format classification). We did not find any established system to be most useful for this project. It seemed to us that a system developed empirically and based in part on the systems described above would have maximum usefulness.

The classification system that is used herein for the measures we have described is an empirical one. It is empirical in the sense that we looked at the data we had and, with the criterion of usefulness to the researcher in mind, set up categories that appeared to us to accommodate the data in the usefulness context. Ten categories of measures appeared to include all the data. Some of the categories are subdivided into groups, so that there are twenty-three classes in all, the last one being a miscellaneous category. As in any situation where one imposes an organization on unstructured data, there are many cases where measures may fall into either of two and occasionally three classes. Usually, these cases could be resolved in favor of one category, with close scrutiny of the measure and the category.

The measures described in this book have been organized into ten categories, and the larger categories have been subdivided into groups. The categories and groups are listed below, with the names of the measures included in each classification unit.

CATEGORY 1. Measures of different aspects of cognition constitute the largest category. The measures in this category are classified into five groups as follows:

Group 1-a. *Intelligence and school readiness.* These measures generally sample broad spectra of common experiences and are designed to derive an overall intellectual functioning level of the child.

ABC Inventory
Bender Development Scoring System
Bereiter-Engelmann Pre-School Evaluation Form
Denver Developmental Screening Test
Draw-A-Scene Test
Experimental Group Version of Progressive Matrices
Face-Hand Test
Five-Point Rating Scale for the Young Trainable Child
Hammond-Skipper Pre-School Achievement Rating Scale
Hildreth's Checklist for Gifted Children

Koppitz Drawing Scale of Developmental Maturity
Preschool Educational Attainment Scale (EAD)
Probst Test
Riggs-Rain Classification System
Rutgers Drawing Test
Scale of Real-Life Ability
Social Opinions Inventory (SOI)
Teacher's Rating Questionnaire (TRQ)
Tests of Mental Ability
T. M. R. Performance Profile for the Severely and Moderately Retarded
Wang Mental Ability Test

GROUP 1-b.   *Language and number skills.*   While these skills often constitute parts of intelligence and school readiness measures, they are important enough to warrant measures devoted exclusively to them.

Composite Scale of Language
Discrimination, Seriation, and Numeration Test
Dodwell's Number Concept Test
Irwin-Hammil Abstraction Test
Number Facility Scale
Objective Language Scale
Observational Rating Scale of Language
Pacific Number Test (PNT)
Parsons Language Sample (PLS)
Picture Vocabulary Test for Deaf Children

Preschool Preposition Test
Receptive, Expressive, and Phonetic Language Scale
Revision of the Smith Vocabulary Test
The Scrambled Sentence Test for Deaf Children
Semantic Habits
Syntactical Relations Test for Deaf Children
Verbal Scale
Word Association Test

GROUP 1-c.   *Specific achievements.*   These measures focus on a relatively narrow aspect of the child's experience, such as his experience with money.

Bible Knowledge Test
Coin Test 1 and Coin Test 2
Dramatic Acting Test: A Role Playing Test for Children
Experience with Money Test
Financial Knowledge Test
Hunter Science Achievement Test
Hunter Science Aptitude Test

MacLatchy Test of the Pre-School Child's Familiarity with Measurement
Physical Causality Test
Pupil Musical Rating Scale
Sequentially Scaled Achievement Test
Tonal Configuration Test

GROUP 1-d.   *Cognitive style and cognitive processes.*   Measures of curiosity are also included in this group.

Children's Reactive Curiosity Scale
Conceptual Style Test

Deductive Reasoning Test
Fruit Distraction Test

Generalization-Discrimination Test
Matching Familiar Figures
Maw and Maw Curiosity Scale for
   Elementary School Children
Maw and Maw Curiosity Scale for
   Elementary School Children:
   Picture and Story Satisfaction Items
   Code Test (Battery A)
   Foolish Sayings Test (Battery B)
   Hidden Pictures Test (Battery A)
   Path Puzzles Test (Battery B)

The-Trip-to-the-Zoo Test
   (Independent Test)
What Do You Know Test
What Would You Do Test
   (Battery A)
Which Saying Do You Believe Test
Which to Discuss Test
   (Independent Test)
Object Curiosity Test
Stroop Color-Word Test
   (Modified Form)
Test of Solving Puzzles

GROUP 1-e. *Miscellaneous.* A few cognitive measures could not be classified logically in any of the four groups above. This group includes, for example, measures of memory, reciprocity, animism, and space conceptualization.

Adjective-Noun Paired Associates Test
Meaning of Opposition
A Measure of Piaget's
   "Reciprocity" Concept
Memory for Objects

Memory for Word Forms
Prognostic Reading Test
Safier's Animism Test
Space Conceptualization Scale

CATEGORY 2. This category includes measures of personality and specific emotional characteristics, classified into four groups.

GROUP 2-a. *Personality—general.* The measures in this group are designed to sample across several or many aspects of personality. This group is composed of a large proportion of rating scales, projective tests, and checklists.

Children's Insight Test
Classroom Behavior Inventory
Columbus Sentence Completion Scale
Despert Fables
Follow-up Letters
Identification Figures
Koppitz Human Figure Drawing as
   Emotional Indicators
Lerner-Murphy Frustration Test
Life Situation Perception Test
Miniature Situations Test
Minnesota Personality Profile II
Modified, Nonverbal Administration
   of the MAPS Test

Mooseheart Wishes and
   Fears Inventory
Nurse's Scale for Rating Neonates
Peterson Problem Checklist
Projective Interview Technique
Rabin Adaptation of Sacks & Levy
   Sentence Completion Test
Rating-Ranking Scales for
   Child Behavior
School Observation Schedule
School TAT
Sonoma Check List
Strauss-Kephart Behavior Rating Scale
The Structured Interview Technique

GROUP 2-b. *Personality variables.* Each of these measures focuses on one aspect of personality. In most cases, the name of the measure indicates the variable involved.

Achievement Motivation
Affectivity Interview Blank
Barber Suggestibility Scale

Behavior Unit Observations
Borke Categories for Quantifying the
   Play Therapy Process

Campos Story Completion Technique
Checklist of Child's Nervous
  Mannerisms and Fears
Child Conflict Scale
Child Transition Test
Children's Opinion Scale
Children's Social Desirability
  Questionnaire
Defensiveness Scale
Dependence Proneness Scale
Impulsivity Scale
Index of Graphic Constriction-
  Expansiveness
Intolerance of Ambiguity Scale
Kooker's Achievement-Boredom Scale

Kooker's Security-Insecurity Scale
  (SI Scale)
The Modified Luchins Rigidity Test
Morale Scale for Handicapped
  Children
Mummery Scale of
  Ascendant Behavior
Parent-Child Need Assessment
Peer Rating Aggression Instrument
Permissive Doll-Play Test
Playfulness Scale
Problem Situations Test
SD Scale for Children
Story Completion Test (Form B)

GROUP 2-c. *Personality adjustment.* The interaction of the child with his environment, the methods he uses to cope with it, and the effectiveness of his efforts to adjust are measured by these instruments. The measures are concerned with the impact of the individual on his surroundings, rather than with the predominantly intrapsychic variables dealt with in group 2-a.

Adapted Bills, Vance, and McLean
  Index of Adjustment
Adjustment Inventory for the Deaf
Behavior Checklist
Behavior Description Chart
Draw-A-Group Test
Mitchell's Guess Who Questionnaire
Pittsburgh Adjustment Survey Scales
Psychiatric Follow-up Coding

St. Louis Symptom Inventory
Secret Stories Test
Teacher Rating Scale
Toronto Infant Security Scale
Ullmann's Forced-Choice Pupil
  Adjustment Scale
Visiting Teacher Rating Scale
Zeligs' Annoyance Test

GROUP 2-d. *Anxiety.* These measures could be classified logically in Group 2-b, but we judged that they warranted a separate group because of their number and because of the important role of the anxiety construct in research.

The Anxiety Scale
Children's Anxiety Pictures
Children's Manifest Anxiety Scale
General Anxiety Scale for Children

Palmar Sweat Prints
Teacher's Rating Scale
Test Anxiety Scale for Children

CATEGORY 3. The measures in this category are concerned with the way children feel about several aspects of their environment.

GROUP 3-a. *Attitudes toward Adults.* These measures concentrate on children's feelings about parents and teachers and their reactions to the behavior of these adults. Several measures concerned with the process of identification are included.

About My Teacher Inventory
Adult-Child Interaction Test
Attitudes toward Authority
Bronfenbrenner Parent Behavior
  Questionnaire

Children's Reports of
  Parental Behavior Inventory
Emmerich's Child Nurturance-Control
  Scale
Imitation Schedule

Index of Overcritical Perception
  by the Child
Louis-Hawkes Scale
My Teacher Scale
Pals and Pen Pals Test
Parental Punitiveness Scale
Perception of Parents
Role Taking Questionnaire

Sears' Observer Rating Scale
Sechrest's Structured Interview
  Schedule with Children
Sex-Role Attitude Test (Child Form)
Sexual Differentiation Scale for the
  D-A-P Test
Structured Doll-Play Test

GROUP 3-b. *Attitudes toward peers.* All but one of these are sociometric-type measures. There are several similar measures in Group 2-c, but they focus one step beyond these measures on social adjustments.

Children's Perception of
  Their Classmates
Classroom Social Distance Scale
Forced-Choice Sociometric Interview
Picture Sociometric Interview

Questionnaire on the Abilities of
  Blind Children
Social Discrimination Questionnaire
Who Are They Test

GROUP 3-c. *Other factors.* Here the focus is away from other persons and toward other environmental forces and phenomena.

Attribution of Responsibility
  Questionnaire (Form E)
Check Sheet of Opportunity in
  Human Relations
Children's Locus of Control Scale
Conceptions of Religious
  Denominations

Elementary Social Causality Test
Intellectual Achievement
  Responsibility
A Scale for the Content and Temporal
  Dimensions of Life Space
Uses Test

CATEGORY 4. Self-concept. These instruments are designed to measure the child's feelings about himself. Some of them are concerned with the general self-concept, while others focus on specific aspects or components of the self-concept, such as body image and capacity for responsibility.

Adjective Check List
Children's Responsibility Inventory
  (Children's Form)
Children's Self Conception Test
Children's Somatic Apperception Test
Elementary School Index of
  Adjustment and Values
Inside-of-the-Body Test

Lipsitt Self-Concept Scale for Children
Morgan Punishment-Situations Index
Perception Score Sheet
Self-Concept Inventory
The Self-Concept—Self Report Scale
Self-Other Orientation Tasks
Self-Social Symbols Tasks
Zeligs' Test on New Year's Resolutions

CATEGORY 5. Characteristics of the child's environment. Many of these measures are concerned with the attitudes and practices of parents and teachers in their relationships with children. Other instruments in this category are designed to measure the breadth and richness of the cognitive experiences open to young children.

GROUP 5-a. *Quality of mothering.* These measures fit also into Group 5-b, but the importance of the concept of mothering warrants a special group of measures.

Child-Rearing Practices Interview
Fifteen Rating Scales of
    Maternal Behavior
Levy's Maternal Interest Interview
Maternal Attitude toward
    Independence Training
Maternal Care Checklist
Maternal Values Questionnaire

Mother-Child Interaction Method
    Scale
A Scale to Measure Social Class
    Differences in Maternal Attitudes
Shoben's Parent-Attitude Survey
Teachers' Rating Scale of
    Parental Nurturance-Control

GROUP 5-b. *Child-rearing practices.* Measures of social class status are included here.

Children's Responsibility Inventory
    (Parental Form)
Conditions of Child Rearing
Educational Attitude Survey
Farm Family Socioeconomic Status
    Scale (Short Form)
Home Index Inventory
Home Rating Scale
Index of Parental Dissatisfaction with
    Social-Emotional Behavior
Indices of Level of Parents'
    Dissatisfaction and Child's
    Perception of Parents' Dissatisfaction
    with Child's Behavior
Minnesota Scale of Parent's Opinions
Multiple Rating Scale
Observational Record of Discipline
Parental Attitude Research Instrument

Parental Attitude Scale
Parental Development Timetable
Parental Nurturance-Control
    Attitude Scale
Parental Practices Inventory
Parent Attitude Inventory
Parent Interview Schedule
Porter Parental Acceptance Scale
Questionnaire for Parents of
    Pre-School Handicapped Children
Scale of Parental Dissatisfaction with
    Instrumental Behavior
Sex-Role Attitude Test (Adult Form)
Social Deprivation Scale
Stanford Parent Questionnaire
Stouffer Parental Attitude Scale
Structured Parental Interview
The Traditional Family Ideology Scale

GROUP 5-c. *Attitudes, primarily of parents, toward school.*

Attitude Scale toward the Gifted
Blatt's Evaluation Check List for
    Classes

Parent Attitude toward
    Education Scale
The Teacher as Seen by His Colleagues

CATEGORY 6. This category includes measures of motor skills, brain injury, and sensory perception and discrimination.

GROUP 6-a. *Motor skills.* This group includes physical fitness, laterality, and speech articulation.

Boston University Speech Sound
    Discrimination-Picture Test
Compact Picture Articulation Test
Daily Activity Record
Impulse-Scale

Irwin Articulation Test
Physical Fitness Tests
Predictive Screening Test of
    Articulation
Right-Left Discrimination

GROUP 6-b. *Brain injury.* This group includes measures designed to aid in the diagnosis of brain injury in children.

Burks' Behavior Rating Scale
Child Rating Scale (Activity Level)
Ellis Visual Design Test
   (Goldenberg version)
Graham Behavior Test for Neonates
Graham-Ernhart Block-Sort or
   Concepts Test

Graham-Ernhart Copy-Forms Test
Graham-Ernhart Parental
   Questionnaire
Perceptual-Motor Battery
Strauss-Werner Marble Board Test
   (Goldenberg version)

GROUP 6-c. *Sensory perception*. This group includes discrimination of visual, auditory, and tactual stimuli.

Auditory-Visual Pattern Test
Children's Visual Achievement Form
Elkind's Ambiguous Pictures
Finger Localization Test

Hidden Figures Test
Irwin-Jensen Sound Discrimination
   Test
Stereognostic Test

CATEGORY 7. Physical attributes. This category includes several measures of physical characteristics to be used with neonates, body measurements, and one measure of bicycle skill.

Apgar Scale
Bicycle Safety—Performance and
   Skills Test
Body Measurements of American Boys
   and Girls
Irritability Scale

Maturation Scale
Measurement of Height and Weight
Muscle Tension Scale
Pain Threshold Test
School Survey Form

CATEGORY 8. Attitudes and interests not otherwise classified. These include children's attitudes toward sex roles, ethnic groups, problem solving, and other aspects of their experience.

A Child Attitude Inventory for
   Problem Solving
Children's Knowledge about
   Occupations Test
Doll-Play Interview
Games and Activities Preference List
Gough, Harris, Martin, and Edwards
   Prejudice Index

How Would You Finish It?
Interview Schedule
Kutner's Ethnic Attitude Test
Role Distribution (Children's Series)
Social Attitudes Scale
Things I Like to Do
Thurstone Sentence Completion Form

CATEGORY 9. Measures of social behavior. This category includes measures of interaction, particularly between children and the adults in their environment. Measures of aggressive behavior are included here because aggression is usually defined as involving others, so is in that sense social behavior. Several of the measures are frames of reference for observing social behavior.

Affectional and Aggressive
   Observation Check Sheet
Aggression Scale
Beller's Child Dependence on
   Adult Scale

Beller's Scale of Independence or
   Autonomy among Children
Categories for Measuring Interaction
   Behavior in Nonverbal Psychotic
   Children

Categories of Interpersonal Cognition Child Scale

Children's Behavior Check List

Children's Minimal Social Behavior Scale

Crispin System of Interactional Analysis

Feeding Rating Scale

First Order Coding Manual

"Guess Who" Technique

G-W Method of Paired Direct and Projective Questionnaire

Impulse Control Categorization Instrument

Index of Effectiveness of Parent-Child Communication

Medinnus First Grade Adjustment Scale

Mother-Child Interaction Test

Objective Method for the Analysis of Child-Adult Interaction

Slobodian Reading Observation Record

Social Analysis of the Classroom

Social Reaction Interview

Socialization Scale

Stevenson's Behavioral Unit Observational Procedure

Test Reaction Scale

Wrightstone's Controlled Observation Scale

CATEGORY 10. Unclassified. These measures did not fit into any of the first nine categories.

Colorado Braille Battery

Dale-Chall Readability Formula

Facts about Mental Deficiency Test

Spatial Characteristics Test

Tri-Modal Imagery Scale

Visual Imagery Index

PART TWO

MEASURES OF
CHILD BEHAVIOR

Category 1. Cognition

Category 2. Personality and Emotional Characteristics

Category 3. Perceptions of Environment

Category 4. Self-Concept

Category 5. Environment

Category 6. Motor Skills, Brain Injury, and Sensory
             Perception

Category 7. Physical Attributes

Category 8. Miscellaneous Attitudes and Interests

Category 9. Social Behavior

Category 10. Unclassified

C<small>ATEGORY</small> **1**

COGNITION

Group 1-a: Intelligence and School Readiness

Group 1-b: Language and Number Skills

Group 1-c: Specific Achievements

Group 1-d: Cognitive Style and Cognitive Processes

Group 1-e: Miscellaneous

Group I-a

Intelligence and School Readiness

ABC INVENTORY

AUTHORS: Normand Adair and George Blesch

AGE: 4 years 9 months through 4 years 11 months

VARIABLE: School readiness

TYPE OF MEASURE: Individually administered paper-and-pencil test

SOURCE FROM WHICH THE MEASURE MAY BE OBTAINED: Educational Studies and Development, 1357 Forest Park Road, Muskegon, Michigan 49441

DESCRIPTION OF MEASURE: The ABC Inventory is a school readiness test consisting of a series of tasks comprising four sections which are orally administered to the child. The responses and skills required of the child consist of naming tests, common knowledge, simple drawings, and elementary counting skill (Adair and Blesch, 1965a). Detailed instructions are provided for administering the test, scoring the responses, and interpreting the results (Adair and Blesch, 1965b).

Sample items from the scale follow (Adair and Blesch, 1965a):

What has (*a*) *wings* (*any winged insect, bird, or machine*); (*b*) *four wheels* (*any four-wheel object or device*)
Tell me the color of (*a*) *grass* (*green*); (*b*) *an apple* (*red*); (*c*) *a banana* (*yellow*)
Which is larger: (*a*) *a dog or a cat;* (*b*) *cow or a pig;* (*c*) *man or boy*

RELIABILITY AND VALIDITY: The test has been administered to two separate samples of children ranging in age from 4 years 9 months through 4 years 11 months. The earlier sample in 1962 included 166 children; the later group in 1964 consisted of 314 children. Scores were not separated according to sex groups, nor were efforts made to determine the influence of socioeconomic class status on results. The authors, however, have contended that the possibility of a selective and biased sampling group was diluted because of the large sample and the restricted age range.

Reliability data for the scale are based on the high similarity from measures of location and dispersion for the two separate samples in 1962 and 1964. A cut-off score of 68 divided the original sample ($N = 166$) into upper and lower halves of the distribution. Validity of the scale was then determined on the basis of the first grade pass-fail record of children in each half. In this connection, 86 per cent of the failures were correctly identified. Seventy-seven, or 63 per cent of those passing, scored above 68 (tetrachoric correlation $= .70$).

A ready scale has also been constructed for the ABC Inventory. In the development of this scale, a frequency curve was plotted from the combined results over a three year period ($N = 619$). A test for kurtosis and skewness from the normal curve indicated no significant deviation of results. Percentile ranks were then calculated for deviation scores from the mean and assigned an age index. This index constitutes the readiness age and roughly approximates mental age functions of other tests. As a partial validity check on this readiness age, the correlation coefficient between age indices and Stanford-Binet mental ages was calculated on a small sample (N = 14). The resulting product moment correlation was .78.

BIBLIOGRAPHY:

ADAIR, N., and BLESCH, G. *The ABC Inventory.* Muskegon, Michigan: Educational Studies and Development, 1965a.

ADAIR, N., and BLESCH, G. *The ABC Inventory—Administration and Scoring Procedures for Examiners and Teachers.* Muskegon, Michigan: Educational Studies and Development, 1965b.

BENDER DEVELOPMENTAL SCORING SYSTEM

AUTHOR: Elizabeth M. Koppitz

AGE: 5 through 10

VARIABLE: Intelligence, neurological functioning, and emotional adjustment

TYPE OF MEASURE: Perceptual and projective test

SOURCE FROM WHICH THE MEASURE MAY BE OBTAINED: See Koppitz (1964)

DESCRIPTION OF MEASURE: The Bender Developmental Scoring System is an objective measurement of responses children make to the Bender Visual-Motor Gestalt Test. The test is administered in the usual way, but the drawings are examined for the presence or absence of certain characteristics on the basis of thirty mutually exclusive scoring items subsumed under seven categories: distortion of shape, notations, circles for dots, perseveration, integration of parts, angles and curves, and incorrect angles. Examples of the errors and instructions for administering and scoring the test are given in detail. For interpreting the scores, normative data are provided to compare the child's performance to that of others who are similar in chronological age, maturation in visual-motor perception, and grade level.

RELIABILITY AND VALIDITY: Normative data rest on average performances of 1,104 public school children in grades kindergarten through five and ranging in age between 5 and 10 years 11 months. The distribution of the data, moreover, is in terms of age, sex, and grade. Means and standard deviations have been provided for chronological age groups, mental age groups, and grade levels.

The author contends that the Developmental Scoring System can be used with considerable confidence in that it is quite reliable. Statistics to support her conclusion include interrater reliabilities ranging between .88 to .96 for raw scores, and test-retest reliability coefficients over a four month interval ranging between .55 to .66 (Kendall's tau). All these statistics were significant at the .001 level.

Validating support for the scale comes from a number of sources: the validation of the seven categories of errors against school achievement; the sharp differentiation between low and high school achievers (p of .02 or less) on the basis of composite scores; cross-validation of this differentiation; statistically significant correlations of composite scores with results of achievement tests on a short-term basis (coefficients between −.46 to −.60) and a long-term basis (coefficients between −.46 to −.60); significant correlations between scores on the Bender and results on the Binet and WISC (−.48 to −.70); close associations between scores and M. A. levels (average r of −.70); and significantly higher scores for controls than for brain-injured children (p < .001) at all age levels of the sample. The coefficients of correlation are in a negative direction because the scores representing the number of errors on the Bender are compared with other results.

On the basis of the foregoing evidence, Koppitz has concluded that for children between 5 and 10 years her scoring system may be used to measure readiness, to predict school achievement, to assess intelligence roughly, to study specific learning problems, to detect neurological impairment, and to identify mental retardation.

BIBLIOGRAPHY:

KOPPITZ, E. M. *The Bender Gestalt Test for Young Children*. New York: Grune & Stratton, 1964.

BEREITER-ENGELMANN PRE-SCHOOL EVALUATION FORM

AUTHORS: Carl Bereiter and Siegfried Engelmann

AGE: Preschool

VARIABLE: Academic achievement

TYPE OF MEASURE: Objective evaluation sheet measuring achievement

SOURCE FROM WHICH THE MEASURE MAY BE OBTAINED: See Bereiter and Engelmann (1966)

DESCRIPTION OF MEASURE: The Evaluation Checklist of Achievement by Bereiter and Engelmann consists of a series of cognitive skills related to fifteen minimum goals of academic achievement which a preschool child must possess if he is to succeed in the formal academic work of the first grade. According to these authors, the success of a preschool program can be gauged by the extent to which the children attain these goals. As these workers also point out, the culturally deprived child is notably lacking in these cognitive skills.

Nine of the goals pertain to linguistic attainments, while six relate to numerical and reading skills. In the authors' estimation, the latter set of achievements are more likely to require concerted, systematic, and special effort. Samples of the minimum goals, as these authors describe them, are given below.

Ability to use both affirmative and not statements in reply to the question "What is this?" "This is a ball. This is not a book."

Ability to use both affirmative and not statements in response to the command "Tell me about this ——— ball, pencil, etc." "This pencil is red. This pencil is not blue."

Ability to handle polar opposites (If it is not ———, it must be ———) for at least four concept pairs, e.g., big-little, up-down, long-short, fat-skinny.

Ability to distinguish printed words from pictures.

Ability to rhyme in some fashion to produce a word that rhymes with a given word, to tell whether two words do or do not rhyme, or to complete unfamiliar rhyming jingles like "I had a dog, and his name was Abel; I found him hiding under the ———."

RELIABILITY AND VALIDITY: The authors provide no statistical data in support of the evaluation checklist. The goals are stated in such objective terms that reliability and validity studies could easily be conducted.

BIBLIOGRAPHY:

BEREITER, C., and ENGELMANN, S. *Teaching Disadvantaged Children in the Preschool.* Englewood Cliffs, N.J.: Prentice-Hall, 1966.

DENVER DEVELOPMENTAL SCREENING TEST

AUTHORS: William K. Frankenburg and Josiah B. Dodds

AGE: Infants and preschool children

VARIABLE: Development (gross motor, fine motor—adaptive, language, and personal-social)

TYPE OF MEASURE: Test—individually administered

SOURCE FROM WHICH THE MEASURE MAY BE OBTAINED: See Frankenburg and Dodds (1966)

DESCRIPTION OF MEASURE: This measure is, as the title implies, a screening instrument designed to identify "children with serious developmental delays." It can be used by individuals without training in administering psychological tests. Typically a child is administered only about twenty of the 142 items, some of which the examiner observes without formal testing. The test measures four aspects of functioning: gross motor; fine motor—adaptive, involving the use of the hands and solving nonverbal problems; language (hearing, talking); and personal-social, including self-care and relationships with others.

The authors selected 240 items from infant developmental and preschool intelligence tests and administered them to 200 infants and preschoolers. The number of items was reduced to 142, using the criteria of ease of administration, clarity of scoring, and narrow spread of the item along the age continuum. The authors have developed what appears to be a convenient, efficient scoring sheet. Age norms are provided, based on 1,036 children, for each item and for blue-collar and white-collar family children.

Examples of items are given below. Gross motor—thirty-one items:

Head up 90°. *Administration: Place baby prone on flat surface. Scoring: Pass if baby lifts head and chest up so that face makes a 90° angle with the table.*
Gets to sitting. *Administration: Note if child gets himself from prone to a sitting position. Scoring: Pass if observed or reported.*
Pedals trike. *Administration: Ask parent how child rides tricycle. Scoring: Pass any report of child pedaling ten feet or more on the level.*

Fine motor, adaptive—thirty items:
Equilateral activity. *Administration: While the baby is on his back or held in his mother's arms, note the spontaneous activity of the child's arms and legs. Scoring: Pass if spontaneous activity with arms and legs is symmetrical. Inactivity of one limb would result in a fail.*
Transfers cube. *Administration: Place a block in the child's hand and encourage him to transfer it to the other hand. Scoring: Pass if the child transfers the cube from one hand to the other without assistance of his mouth, body, or table. May pass by report.*
Copies cross. *Administration: The examiner shows the child a picture of a cross in*

the test book and asks the child to copy it. Three trials are permitted. Scoring: A pass is given to any two more or less straight lines which intersect at any point.

Language—twenty-one items:

Vocalizes. *Administration: During the examination listen for vocalization other than crying, such as cooing, throaty sounds, etc. Scoring: Pass if child makes any vocal sounds other than crying. May pass by report.*

Points one body part. *Administration: Ask child, "show me your ———" (eye, nose, foot, etc.). Scoring: Pass if child correctly points to one body part. May pass by report.*

Three prepositions. *Administration: Caution the mother not to move. Give the child a block and ask him to place it in succession on the table, under the table, in front of mommy's chair, and behind her chair. An incorrect response may not be corrected by the examiner. Scoring: Pass if the child executes three of the four commands correctly.*

Personal-social—twenty-three items:

Smiles responsively. *Administration: Smile or talk to infant. Do not touch him. Scoring: Pass if infant smiles back. May pass by report.*

Removes coat. *Administration: Ask mother if child removes any of his clothing, such as coat, shoe, sock, or underpants. Scoring: Pass if child removes a garment other than his hat.*

Wash and dry hands. *Administration: Ask if child can do so by himself. Scoring: Pass only if child is able to manage all aspects of the two tasks without help, except turning on faucets that are out of his reach.*

RELIABILITY AND VALIDITY: When each of four examiners tested twelve children (four in common with each of the other three examiners), interexaminer agreement on pass or fail ranged from 77 per cent to 97 per cent, with a mean of 89 per cent. Validity of the measure may be inferred from the age progression of the items as shown by the norms, where age is related to the percentage of children passing each item.

BIBLIOGRAPHY:

FRANKENBURG, W. K., and DODDS, J. B. *Denver Developmental Screening Test.* Denver: University of Colorado Medical Center, 1966. (Mimeographed)

DRAW-A-SCENE TEST

AUTHOR: Viktor Lowenfeld

AGE: 2 to 17

VARIABLE: Growth (intellectual, emotional, social, perceptual, physical, esthetic, creative)

TYPE OF MEASURE: Free drawing

SOURCE FROM WHICH THE MEASURE MAY BE OBTAINED: See Lowenfeld (1952)

DESCRIPTION OF MEASURE: The author provides a framework that can be used to evaluate the spontaneous drawings of children to get measures of growth in the areas mentioned above. He provides several evaluation charts at different age levels. The first evaluation chart is formulated to provide an evaluation method for growth of children aged 2 to 4. This is called the scribbling stage. For each area of growth, there are items that must be checked. For example, under the emotional growth area, the first question is, "Does the child enjoy his scribbling?" The scorer or evaluator is then to check either "none," "some," or "much." In the book in which the evaluation charts are given, the author elaborates on the question and gives some suggestions and rather loose criteria that the scorer can use in making his judgment. The next evaluation chart is set up to measure growth at the pre-schematic stage, between the ages of 4 and 7. Again, there is a limited number of items within each category, the numbers ranging from three (in intellectual growth) to six (in emotional growth). The scoring criteria are very loose, which would lead one to expect the reliability of the measure to be relatively low.

Growth during the schematic stage (ages 7 to 9) and the gang stage (ages 9 to 11) is assessed with the use of evaluation charts that are separate but similar to those for other levels mentioned above. A generalized evaluation chart is given that, according to Lowenfeld, could be used at any age level.

With careful training of scorers a respectable reliability level might be achieved for this evaluation method. The measure has the advantage of being usable with drawings that have already been made.

RELIABILITY AND VALIDITY: None.

BIBLIOGRAPHY:

LOWENFELD, V. *Your Child and His Art*. New York: The Macmillan Company, 1955.

LOWENFELD, V. *Creative and Mental Growth*. New York: The Macmillan Company, 1952.

WEST, J. H. "Correlates of the Draw-A-Scene." *Journal of Clinical Psychology*, 1960, *16*(1).

EXPERIMENTAL GROUP VERSION OF PROGRESSIVE MATRICES

AUTHORS: Read D. Tuddenham, Louis Davis, Leslie Davison, and Richard Schindler

AGE: Grades one through six

VARIABLE: Intelligence

TYPE OF MEASURE: Experimental group version of individually administered intelligence test

SOURCE FROM WHICH THE MEASURE MAY BE OBTAINED: An extended report of this study may be obtained without charge from Read D. Tuddenham, Department of Psychology, University of California, Berkeley, California, or for a fee from the American Documentation Institute. Order Document No. 5429, remitting $1.75 for microfilm or $2.50 for photocopies.

DESCRIPTION OF MEASURE: The experimental group version of Raven's Progressive Matrices Test consists of both the 1947 form (Set A, AB, and B), appropriate for the first four grades, and the 1938 form, suitable for fifth and sixth graders. The tests are dittoed and stapled in throwaway black and white booklets. In most instances, testing time is less than thirty minutes, though the students are allowed forty minutes to complete the test. The group version is designed to circumvent the disadvantages of the individually administered form, such as a lack of American norms. Both the advantages of the present scale and the disadvantages of the individual form are described in full. The two forms of the test have been administered to 423 children in grades one through six.

RELIABILITY AND VALIDITY: Kuder Richardson reliability coefficients for separate grade levels on the 1947 form or the 1938 version or both ranged from .87 to .94. On the individual sets within the scales, the coefficients were somewhat lower, within age levels, ranging between .33 (Set A, grade six) to .88 (Set D, grade five). The several indices of concurrent validity, moreover, included the expected progression of performance between grades, normative data closely resembling Raven's original results with Scottish children, and substantial correlations with group tests of intelligence clustering around .40 or .45, though as long as two or three years elapsed between the administration of the two tests correlated.

BIBLIOGRAPHY:

TUDDENHAM, R. D., DAVIS, L., DAVISON, L., and SCHINDLER, R. "An Experimental Group Version for School Children of the Progressive Matrices." *Journal of Consulting Psychology*, 1958, 22, 30.

FACE-HAND TEST

AUTHOR: M. B. Bender

AGE: Normal, disturbed, retarded, and/or organically impaired adults and children

VARIABLE: Intelligence

TYPE OF MEASURE: Performance test

SOURCE FROM WHICH THE MEASURE MAY BE OBTAINED: See Bender (1952); Pollack and Gordon (1960).

DESCRIPTION OF MEASURE: The Face-Hand Test is a simple, brief, non-verbal measure of intelligence based on a subject's accuracy in designating simultaneous tactual stimulation applied to him by the examiner. Fourteen trials of tactual stimulation given simultaneously in pairs are presented to the child. The procedure recommended is that the test be given first with the child's eyes closed and then repeated with the eyes open. Swanson (1957) presents specific details for administering the scale, while Pollack and Gordon (1960) provide a detailed discussion on the interpretation of test results. In general, the interpretation of the results is based on the consistency of findings on the two administrations (eyes open and closed) and the types of errors made. Illustrative presentations of simultaneous face and hand stimuli which these authors (Pollack and Gordon, 1960) recommend are right cheek–left hand, left cheek–right hand, right cheek–right hand, left cheek–left hand, right cheek–left cheek.

RELIABILITY AND VALIDITY: In a sample of 124 children between the ages of 6 and 15, consisting of retarded subjects as well as emotionally disturbed subjects with normal intelligence, both the number and pattern of errors were related to mental age as determined by such individually administered psychometric tests as the Merrill-Palmer and the Stanford-Binet (Pollack and Gordon, 1960). Performance reportedly relates highly to the mental age norms for both adults and children unaffected by the psychiatric diagnosis and severity of the behavior disorder (Pollack and Gordon, 1960).

BIBLIOGRAPHY:

BENDER, M. B. *Disorders in Perception*. Springfield, Ill.: Charles C Thomas, 1952.

COHN, R. "On Certain Aspects of Sensory Organization of the Human Brain." *Neurology*, 1951, *1*, 119–122.

FINK, M., and BENDER, M. B. "Perception of Simultaneous Tactile Stimuli in Normal Children." *Neurology*, 1953, *3*, 27–34.

FINK, M., GREEN, M. A., and BENDER, M. B. "Perception of Simultaneous Tactile Stimuli by Mentally Defective Subjects." *Journal of Nervous and Mental Disease*, 1953, 117, 43–49.

FINK, M., GREEN, M. A., and BENDER, M. B. "The Face-Hand Test as a Diagnostic Sign of Organic Mental Syndrome." *Neurology*, 1952, *2*, 48–56.

POLLACK, M., and GOLDFARB, W. "The Face-Hand Test in Schizophrenic Children." *American Medical Association Archives of Neurology and Psychiatry*, 1957, *77*, 635–642.

POLLACK, M., and GORDON, E. "The Face-Hand Test in Retarded and Non-Retarded Emotionally Disturbed Children." *American Journal of Mental Deficiency*, 1960, *64*, 758–760.

SWANSON, R. "Perception of Simultaneous Tactual Stimulation in Defective and Normal Children." *American Journal of Mental Deficiency*, 1957, *61*, 743–752.

FIVE-POINT RATING SCALE FOR THE YOUNG TRAINABLE CHILD

AUTHORS: John R. Peck and C. Lucille Sexton

AGE: Young trainable children under 12

VARIABLE: Social, health, and academic achievement

TYPE OF MEASURE: Rating scale

SOURCE FROM WHICH THE MEASURE MAY BE OBTAINED: Texas Education Agency, Department of Special Education, 201 E. 11th Street, Austin, Texas

DESCRIPTION OF MEASURE: The purpose of this rating scale is to provide an instrument whereby a pupil's progress may be evaluated over a period of one school year in the following areas: social adjustment, self-care, economic usefulness, language development, music, arts and crafts, and physical development. It may be used as a basis for a report of progress to parents, to forward to a receiving school or institution when a child is transferred, and to determine the point at which the pupil (on a basis of overall progress) is to move to another class. The scale may also be used to determine progress for an individual and to ascertain areas of training necessary for class groups.

Each of the areas above has a range of four to nine items. The items themselves are rated in inverse order with 1 denoting the highest level of behavior and 5 the lowest level of skill. Examples of items are given below from the area of social adjustment—participation.

Sharing: *(1) initiates sharing, (2) shares willingly, (3) shares when reminded, (4) shares with repeated urging, (5) does not share, even when urged.*

For the area of self-care—grooming:

Washing: *(1) washes and dries well and leaves room neat, (2) usually washes and dries well but leaves room untidy, (3) attempts to wash and dry (without supervision), (4) attempts to wash with little success (with supervision), (5) does not wash.*

RELIABILITY AND VALIDITY: Correlations for the scale on the basis of two independent ratings range between .70 and .80 (Peck, 1960).

BIBLIOGRAPHY:

PECK, J. R., and SEXTON, C. L. *A Comparative Investigation of the Learning and Social Adjustment of Trainable Children in Public School Facilities, Segregated Community Centers, and State Residential Centers.* U. S. Office of Education Cooperative Research Branch, Project SAE-6430, 1960.

PECK, J. R. Personal Communication, March 29, 1966.

PECK, J. R., and SEXTON, C. L. *Five Point Rating Scale for the Young Trainable Child.* Texas Education Agency, Austin, Texas (no date).

HAMMOND-SKIPPER PRE-SCHOOL ACHIEVEMENT RATING SCALE

AUTHORS: Sarah L. Hammond and Dora Skipper

AGE: 3 to 5

VARIABLE: Cognitive and social development

TYPE OF MEASURE: Rating scale

SOURCE FROM WHICH THE MEASURE MAY BE OBTAINED: Dora Skipper, The Florida State University, Dept. of Elementary Education, Tallahassee, Florida 32306

DESCRIPTION OF MEASURE: This measure consists of a list of items for assessing achievement. Items were selected from the literature and judged by specialists to be appropriate for the early childhood years. The checklist is intended to be used in helping the teacher gain a picture of the child's status as a basis for planning and guidance and as a means of assessing a child's progress. The measure consists of seventy-one items on which the rater evaluates each child. Examples of items are eats with spoon, puts on coat alone, pedals tricycle, follows simple directions, looks at page from top to bottom, counts rationally 1 to 5, speaks in sentences (of at least five words), and listens and identifies sounds of different instruments. Each of the seventy-one items is checked in one of four columns headed "always," "sometimes," "never," and "does not apply."

RELIABILITY AND VALIDITY: None.

BIBLIOGRAPHY: None

HILDRETH'S CHECKLIST FOR GIFTED CHILDREN

AUTHOR: Gertrude Hildreth

AGE: 10 and over; an abbreviated version of this checklist has been prepared for younger children in the 5- to 10-year age range

VARIABLE: Giftedness

TYPE OF MEASURE: Teacher checklist

SOURCE FROM WHICH THE MEASURE MAY BE OBTAINED: See Hildreth (1966)

DESCRIPTION OF MEASURE: The checklist consists of sixty-five items based on research reports of the traits of the gifted. Fifteen of the points relate to the child's background and early experiences. The items are grouped into five categories: mental traits, intellectual qualities; command of language; academic skills and attainments; special interests, aptitudes, talents; and personal and social traits, character qualities.

In using the checklist, Hildreth directs teachers to rate all pupils whom they consider to be in the upper 5 per cent in aptitude, and then to collect test information and other data as they check on their ratings. This procedure gives teachers a part in identification procedures and focuses their attention on points to be used in school and home guidance of these pupils.

RELIABILITY AND VALIDITY: The author provides no data regarding reliability, validity, and standardization. Content validity, however, may be inferred from the fact that the checklist is based on research reports of the traits of the gifted.

BIBLIOGRAPHY:

HILDRETH, G. H. *Introduction to the Gifted.* New York: McGraw-Hill, 1966.

KOPPITZ DRAWING SCALE OF DEVELOPMENTAL MATURITY

AUTHOR: Elizabeth Munsterberg Koppitz

AGE: Kindergarten through sixth grade

VARIABLE: Intelligence

TYPE OF MEASURE: Performance test

SOURCE FROM WHICH THE MEASURE MAY BE OBTAINED: See Koppitz (1967)

DESCRIPTION OF MEASURE: The Koppitz Drawing Scale for Developmental Maturity rests on the premise that the mental maturity of the child can be deduced by the absence of items commonly found in drawings or by the presence of indicators rarely found. Thus, the absence of expected items (those found in 16 to 85 per cent of all human figure drawings [HFDs] and called common or not unusual) would reveal mental immaturity or retardation. In contrast, the presence of items found in less than 16 per cent of all HFDs (called exceptional items) would only occur in HFDs of children with above average mental maturity. HFDs were scored for expected and exceptional items, each with a value of 1. Omission of an expected item was scored as −1, and the presence of an exceptional item was +1. To avoid negative scores, the value of 5 was added. Further details on the scoring system are given by Koppitz. The total possible score range is between 0 and 7, or possibly 8 for young children. The number of exceptional items decreases with age, and the scoring system differentiates less well at the upper end of mental ability.

RELIABILITY AND VALIDITY: The scoring system was applied to 347 boys, age 6 to 12, who had been seen for clinical help. As a means of evaluating protocols, normative data have been developed on the basis of findings from 1856 public school children in grades kindergarten through sixth. These data are subdivided according to age and sex of each child. At each age level, product-moment correlations were computed between the HFD scores and the WISC and Stanford-Binet IQ scores respectively. At the nine age levels, the correlations range between .45 and .80. In each case, the coefficients were significant at the .005 level. Koppitz states that the findings offer support for the hypothesis that expected and exceptional items on HFDs are diagnostically significant and can be used as a quick and easy way of assessing mental maturity.

Koppitz concluded that the HFD scores could be interpreted for both sex groups within the 6 to 12 age range in terms of seven classifications of mental maturity. These range between high average to superior and retarded. For example, an HFD score of 9 or 7 denoted high average to superior intelligence (IQ 110 and up); whereas an HFD score of 6 denoted average to superior intelligence (IQ 90 to 135).

The author has defended these broad categories of mental functioning as preferable to an IQ or mental age score because such grouping is more meaningful and reliable for HFD scores than specific IQ scores would be. This is particularly true, she feels, when the HFD test is administered to a whole class of school beginners in a screening program. The considerable overlap in the categories (see above examples), however, possibly should be carefully considered in the use of this classification system.

BIBLIOGRAPHY:

KOPPITZ, E. M. "Expected and Exceptional Items on Human Figure Drawings and IQ Scores of Children Age 5 to 12." *Journal of Clinical Psychology,* 1967, XXIII, 81–83.

PRESCHOOL EDUCATIONAL ATTAINMENT SCALE

AUTHORS: Edgar A. Doll and Edward L. McKnight

AGE: Preschool and first-grade children

VARIABLE: Achievement (educational attainment)

TYPE OF MEASURE: Structured interview

SOURCE FROM WHICH THE MEASURE MAY BE OBTAINED: Edgar A. Doll, 2373 Chuckanut Drive, Bellingham, Washington. At present, an experimental form of the scale will be released for experimental use. This will be done for those professional students of child development who will submit projects for experimental use of this instrument and the sharing of the experimental data gained through such experimental use. Before the scale will be released to any research worker a letter will be required to provide a statement of the problem and a description of the sample to which the scale is to be administered. In all probability, a small charge will be made to cover the cost of printing and distribution of the material on a non-profit basis (Doll, 1966).

DESCRIPTION OF MEASURE: The EAD contains 130 items encompassing eight categories of behavior, including ambulation, manipulation, rapport, communications, responsibility, information, ideation, and creativity. An example of progressive scaling within one of the more easily specified categories, "ambulation," is as follows (the numbers on the right are the age locus).

Sits	.5	Climbs	3.0	Skips	5.0
Stands	1.0	Jumps (1)	3.5	Jumps (2)	5.5
Walks	1.5	Hops	4.0	Follows	6.0
Runs	2.0	Circles	4.5	Dances	6.5
Balances	2.5			Rides	7.0

For each category there is one item for each age level. The age levels are by half-year intervals from birth to 84 months (7.0 years) or approximately to first-grade schooling. The purpose of the measure is to provide an assessment of children not readily accessible to direct examination because of sensory impairments, speech or language difficulties, emotional disturbances, neuromuscular handicaps, resistance to examination, cultural problems, and other impediments to communication. The assessment provides a measure of what the child can do and also of what he does do in his usual state.

The scale follows the general design of the Vineland Social Maturity Scale. It calls for a system of standardized interview reporting with an informant who knows the child's usual behavior. The examiner may also observe most of the performances that are reported. The insight gained from the informant's participation in the appraisal is frequently very helpful. The scoring follows the plan used for the Vineland Maturity Scale.

RELIABILITY AND VALIDITY: As the senior author has pointed out, the scale has not been standardized; nor have there been any noteworthy studies of reliability and practicability except that "a considerable range of experience has been developed indicating that the scale is practicable and has very real and immediate usefulness."

BIBLIOGRAPHY:

DOLL, E. A. *Manual for EAD Preschool Attainment Scale* (Research Edition, 1966).

DOLL, E. A., and MC KNIGHT, E. L. "A Preschool Educational Attainment Scale." *Cerebral Palsy Journal*, 1965, *26*, 3–5.

DOLL, E. A., and MC KNIGHT, E. L. *Record Booklet for the Preschool Educational Attainment Scale* (no date, mimeographed).

PROBST RANGE OF INFORMATION TEST

AUTHOR: Cathryn A. Probst

AGE: Preschool and primary school

VARIABLE: General information

TYPE OF MEASURE: Test, individually administered

SOURCE FROM WHICH THE MEASURE MAY BE OBTAINED: See Probst (1931)

DESCRIPTION OF MEASURE: The items on this measure are similar to the information items on the Wechsler Scales. There are two forms of the test, each consisting of sixty-six items. These items are divided into eleven areas or topics and six items measuring knowledge about the topic. The topics or areas measured are local points of interest; time and number; current topics; natural phenomena; literature and music; animals, birds, and insects; plants and flowers; occupations and industries; household arts; simple mechanics; and games and amusements. Local points of interest and current topics obviously need to be modified for both the time and locales where the test is to be used. For example, Rosen's adaptation of the items in local points of interest for use in Milwaukee contains the following items:

Tell me the name of a Milwaukee newspaper.
What is the name of a lake in Milwaukee?
What is the Mississippi?
What is Wisconsin Avenue?
What is the North Shore? What is WOKY?

Similarly, for current topics, some modifications must be made according to the time. Rosen has modified the Probst Test in this way for his Milwaukee version:

Who is Freddy?
Who is Khrushchev?
Who was the first president?
Who is Mickey Mantle?
Who is Beaver?
Who is Dwight Eisenhower?

Examples of other items in the test are the following:

What colors are the keys on the piano?
What was Cinderella's coach or carriage made of?
Who makes money by cutting hair?
What is a shoe made of?

The items are scored right or wrong, and the two forms of the test may be combined to increase reliability. This test, like any other information-measuring test, may be considered in large part a measure of opportunity to learn.

The test is administered individually, in either one or two sessions. Probst administered it in two sessions and reported a mean administration time of seventeen minutes for Form A and nineteen minutes for Form B. Templin (1958) administered it in a single session and found the mean time to be approximately thirty minutes.

RELIABILITY AND VALIDITY: Probst (1931) reported an uncorrected equivalent forms reliability of .94 and a corrected reliability of .97. She found that corrected reliabilities for the eleven topics or areas range from .45 to .89 with a median of .76. The equivalent forms data reported above were based on one hundred kindergarten children. Templin (1958) reported an equivalent form corrected reliability of .94.

BIBLIOGRAPHY:

PROBST, C. A. "A General Information Test for Kindergarten Children." *Child Development,* 1931, 2, 81–95.
TEMPLIN, M. C. "General Information of Kindergarten Children: A Comparison with the Probst Study after 26 Years." *Child Development,* 1958, 29(1), 87–96.

RIGGS-RAIN CLASSIFICATION SYSTEM

AUTHORS: Margaret M. Riggs and Margaret E. Rain

AGE: Almost any age from birth to maturity

VARIABLE: Type of mental retardation

TYPE OF MEASURE: Check scale

SOURCE FROM WHICH THE MEASURE MAY BE OBTAINED: Riggs and Rain (1952); Riggs and Cassell (1952)

DESCRIPTION OF MEASURE: The Riggs-Rain System is a formal method of diagnosing mental retardation according to the degree of information available in the records. Six major categories are used: familial, organic, unexplained, mixed, mongoloid, nonclassifiable. Each category has several subdivisions representing levels of certainty in terms of the amount of information available.

Specifically, the Classification System enables one to classify the etiology of a case as familial or organic according to "definite positive evidence" or "a slight suspicion" for each category. An example of definite evidence follows for classifying cases as familial:

At least one parent or sibling (not half sib, not twin, not putative parent) is diagnosed as "backward," "dull," "retarded," "mentally deficient," or "borderline intelligence or less," on the basis of an intelligence test, or by an individual or institution known to base diagnoses only on intelligence tests; such deficiency not accompanied by a possible organic cause or symptomatology indicative of such a cause, as these are defined in this paper.

Examples of definite evidence for classifying cases as organic:

Diagnosis by a neurologist or endocrinologist on the basis of objective examination that a recognized organic syndrome is responsible for the child's retardation, e.g., cerebral palsy, megalencephaly, Froelich's syndrome, hydrocephalus. If equally competent authorities in the same field have given conflicting opinions disregard the evidence entirely.

One or more of the following are in the case history: (a) severe falls or injuries to the mother during pregnancy; (b) German measles (rubella) in first three months of pregnancy; (c) mother had severe anemia during pregnancy.

Two helpful aids in the use of this system have also been provided: a complete guide to indicate levels of certainty in the diagnosis and a data sheet for recording all the necessary information that will enable one to make a diagnosis.

RELIABILITY AND VALIDITY: In specifying the causes and symptoms the authors were willing to accept as evidence of organic damage, they included only those actually found in a series of about 300 cases, and those well recognized as being significant for the etiology and diagnosis of damage to the central nervous system.

The authors accepted agreement of at least three or four judges as the criterion for reliability in the classification of any given case. On this basis, agreement was found in 85 of the one hundred cases. "This means that we may expect between 76 and 91 per cent agreement of this sort at or beyond the .05 level of confidence, and between 74 and 93 per cent at or beyond the .01 level of confidence." (Riggs and Cassell, 1962).

BIBLIOGRAPHY:

RIGGS, M. M., and RAIN, M. E. "A Classification System for the Mentally Retarded. Part I: Description." *Training School Bulletin,* 1952, *49,* 75–84.

RIGGS, M. M., and CASSELL, M. E. "A Classification System for the Mentally Retarded. Part II: Reliability." *Training School Bulletin,* 1952, *49,* 151–168.

RUTGERS DRAWING TEST

AUTHOR: Anna Spiesman Starr

AGE: 4 to 7 years

VARIABLE: Intelligence

TYPE OF MEASURE: Paper-and-pencil performance test

SOURCE FROM WHICH THE MEASURE MAY BE OBTAINED: See Starr (1952)

DESCRIPTION OF MEASURE: The Rutgers Drawing Test consists of fourteen geometric figures drawn to scale and arranged in order of difficulty with ample space beneath each figure for the child's copy. These figures make up the series: cross, circle, square, square with extended sides, oblique cross, Indian swastika, triangle, baseball, block cross, straight line star, diamond, double rectangle interlaced star, and Maltese cross.

As part of the procedure, the child is expected to copy a figure directly beneath the geometric form on a single sheet of paper. Details on administering the test and the material necessary are provided. Responses are scored as 2 for success, 1 as partial credit, or 0 for failure. As an aid to scoring, complete and extensive scoring samples are provided for all figures. By means of a table for the derivation of scoring norms, raw scores may then be converted to an equivalent drawing age in months.

The Rutgers Drawing Test is usually given individually but may be used with small groups of children already familiar with each other. No time limit is necessary, but Starr has concluded that about five minutes are required for the average child. Further, she has emphasized that the test should be limited to children between the 4 to 7 year levels.

A study was made of 277 normal children within the age range of 3 to 6 who had had individual examinations at the Rutgers Clinic. A comparison of their MA scores on Binet and the MA of the Drawing Test showed a product-moment correlation of .72, with a probable error of .019. A study of fifty-seven mentally deficient children under 12 years of age (no IQ over 60) showed the correlation between their Binet and Drawing scores to be .61, P.E. .05.

BIBLIOGRAPHY:

STARR, A. S. "The Rutgers Drawing Test." *Training School Bulletin,* 1952, *49,* 45–64.
STEVENS, M. C. "A Drawing Test for the Preschool Child." Unpublished Master's thesis, Rutgers University, 1937.

SCALE OF REAL-LIFE ABILITY

AUTHORS: Denis H. Stott and L. H. Duncan

AGE: Retarded children

VARIABLE: Social competence

TYPE OF MEASURE: Rating scale

SOURCE FROM WHICH THE MEASURE MAY BE OBTAINED: D. H. Stott, University of Guelph, Guelph, Ontario, Canada

DESCRIPTION OF MEASURE: This measure, composed of eighty-two items, is designed to measure the social competence of mentally retarded children. Ten separate areas of functioning are measured: managing own clothes (seven items); doing classroom jobs (eleven items); understanding pictures (five); drawing (seven); powers of observation (twelve); general alertness (nine); counting and money (ten); telling time, etc. (nine); general competence (seven); hobbies and specialized accomplishments (five).

A teacher or other person acquainted with the child answers each item either yes, no, or barrier. The teacher uses the barrier option when in his opinion the child may be capable of the behavior but for some motivational barrier, which he designates from a checklist of thirteen. Examples of items are given below:

Takes off overcoat
Puts own chair up to desk or table
Can point to familiar objects in a classroom picture
Draws some kind of recognizable picture of a person or of a thing
Can count mechanically up to 10; up to 20; up to 100
Knows when clock indicates time to go, put on radio, etc.
Has been known to act with considerable common sense

A profile of a child's ability and his motivational barriers may be plotted from the scores for each area of functioning. The competency score for each area is derived by counting the yes responses, and the motivational barrier score is obtained by counting the barrier responses. The senior author states that the measure can be completed in fifteen minutes.

RELIABILITY AND VALIDITY: The senior author is conducting a validation study comparing the predictive value of this scale with that of standard intelligence tests.

BIBLIOGRAPHY:

STOTT, D. H. "The Assessment of Mentally Handicapped Children." *The Medical Officer*, 1963, *110*, 235–239.

SOCIAL OPINIONS INVENTORY (SOI)

AUTHOR: Cecile Finley

AGE: Sixth grade through adulthood

VARIABLE: Social maturity

TYPE OF MEASURE: Objective opinionnaire

SOURCE FROM WHICH THE MEASURE MAY BE OBTAINED: Cecile Finley, Board of Education, Rockville, Maryland

DESCRIPTION OF MEASURE: The SOI attempts to make direct measures of the social maturity level of an individual by the extent to which he participates in certain cooperative activities with persons in his environment or indirectly by the way he evaluatively perceives others in their cooperative activities.

The scale, which is orally administered to groups and requires about fifty minutes to complete, consists of four parts. The major portion of the test consists of three parts in which the subject is required to react to the same list of 125 people and social institutions. The list includes individuals of such varying significance for him as mothers, teachers, ministers, friendly neighbors, and Negro artists. The three sets of responses required of him are in terms of three dimensions. In Part I, he is asked to indicate the nouns whose elimination would improve the world. In Part II, he is asked to indicate names on the list that would improve the world. Finally, in Part III, he checks words naming someone or something that has no personal concern for him. Part IV comprises a Social Distance Scale consisting of five sets. These include three lists of people, one list of ethnic groups, and one list of countries.

Since the scoring system for the scale is very involved, Finley (1955) should be consulted for details. As an aid in the use of the scale, however, complete directions for administering the test and a comprehensive scoring key are provided.

RELIABILITY AND VALIDITY: Preliminary norms for grade six through adulthood in terms of medians and probable errors have been provided. These normative groups range in size from thirty-five (adult criterion) to 154 (grade six). The reliability coefficients that have been provided, however, relate only to a single college class. For this group the test-retest reliability over a six-month interval was .84. Finley (1955) should be consulted for full details concerning the validating support for the scale. The author, however, has indicated that the validity of the scale is demonstrable through at least three different lines of evidence: comparisons of the scores of criterion groups of adults—social, unselected, and antisocial; comparisons of student election scores with Social Opinions Inventory scores; and comparisons of the scores of city children who have engaged successfully in many cooperative activities and rural children who have had very limited social experiences.

BIBLIOGRAPHY:

FINLEY, C. B. "The Social Opinions Inventory as a Measure of Social Maturity." *Child Development*, 1955, *26*, 81–90.

TEACHERS' RATING QUESTIONNAIRE (TRQ)

AUTHOR: E. M. Wright

AGE: Junior kindergarten through the elementary grades

VARIABLE: Achievement and development of children

TYPE OF MEASURE: Rating scales

SOURCE FROM WHICH MEASURE MAY BE OBTAINED: Research Department, Board of Education, Toronto, Canada

DESCRIPTION OF MEASURE: In using the Teacher's Rating Questionnaire, teachers rate their students on several aspects of development on a Likert Scale. The questionnaire is conceived as a method of getting at diverse properties of "achievement" and also ascertaining the degree and character of the teacher-child interaction. The rating scale, which has been given in three roughly equivalent forms, consists of five subsections with varying numbers of items in each section. In its latest form, the subsections have a total of twenty-four items. The subsections with the total number of items in each include English language (five items); social interaction (three items); emotional (nine items); mental (four items); and physical (three items). The meanings of the subsections are self-explanatory with the possible exceptions of the ones entitled mental and physical. The items on the former primarily assess scholastic work habits; those on the latter rate skills in motor coordination. A sample item from the emotional section follows:

Rate 0—no ability to get along with other children (does not talk; very shy; cannot share; cannot take turns; cannot refrain from bossing; pushing; snatching; disturbing; always irritable, etc.)

Rate 2—needs a great deal of teacher help to get along with others, or can only get along with a few "special" friends, or can only get along with others when engaged in a few specific activities, or is very inconsistent from day to day in ability to get along with others

Rate 4—acts as described in question

Rate 6—frequently displays friendly attitude and ability to get along with others reasonably well

Rate 8—consistently displays ability to get along with others reasonably well in any situation

Means and standard deviations, based on large numbers of children, are available for senior kindergarten through grade two. A manual with complete directions for administering the test is also available. An IBM card system procedure has been developed for scoring the teachers' ratings. There are two forms of the measure. The Fall Questionnaire provides assessment of skills at the beginning of the school year; the June Questionnaire provides a check point for progress.

RELIABILITY AND VALIDITY: Roughly equivalent forms have been administered over an interval of time by different teachers to the same children. The reliability data obtained in this fashion were, in effect, coefficients of stability and equivalence, though strict equivalence is somewhat questionable since the three forms of the scale included different numbers of items. These coefficients were primarily derived from three separate groups: children in kindergarten and the first grade (N of 2,762), those in grade one and two (N of 5,847), and those in senior kindergarten and later in grade two (N of 2,574). The respective ranges for the reliability coefficients were .371 (physical) to .577 (mental); .362 (mental) to .587 (language); and .310 (emotional) to .462 (language). All coefficients were significant at or beyond the .01 level of significance.

Validity appears to rest primarily on concurrent validation from the correlations between the various items of the language and mental subscales of the TRQ with five subtests of the Metropolitan Achievement Test (MAT): word knowledge, word discrimination, reading, spelling, and arithmetic. Children's scores on the MAT in grade one were correlated with their scores on the Kindergarten Rating Questionnaire. These reliability coefficients ranged between .37 (spelling on the MAT vs. language on the TRQ) to .678 (reading on the MAT vs. language on the TRQ).

Intercorrelations among the subscales of TRQ have been rather high but, for the most part, appear to be sharply reduced after the effects of language and mental scores have been partialed out. Since a few intercorrelations remain rather high even after partial correlation, these data should probably be studied rather closely by potential users of the scale. Since large collections of data are still being analyzed, the study of the test is far from complete.

BIBLIOGRAPHY:

Research Department. *Study of Achievement: An Outline of a Longitudinal Study from Junior Kindergarten through the Elementary Grades*. Toronto, Canada: Board of Education, 1964.

TESTS OF MENTAL ABILITY

AUTHORS: Gerald S. Lesser, Gordon Fifer, and Donald H. Clark

AGE: 6 years, 2 months through 7 years, 5 months

VARIABLE: Verbal ability, reasoning ability, numerical ability, and space ability

TYPE OF MEASURE: Test—individually administered

SOURCE FROM WHICH THE MEASURE MAY BE OBTAINED: Lesser et al. (1964) give examples of items

DESCRIPTION OF MEASURE: This measure is designed for the study of class or ethnic group differences along the variables mentioned above. It is an adaptation of the Hunter College Aptitude Scales for Gifted Children (Davis, Lesser, and French, 1960), eliminating and modifying many of the scales in the Hunter test. There are four scales composed of fourteen subtests and a total of 206 items. The scales and subtests making them up are as follows, with number of items:

Verbal scale		Numerical scale	
Picture vocabulary	30	Enumeration	6
Word vocabulary	30	Addition	10
		Subtraction	10
Reasoning scale		Multiplication	10
Picture analogies	18	Division	10
Picture arrangement	16		
Jump peg	12	Space scale	
		Object completion	16
		Estimating path	12
		Jigsaw puzzles	16
		Perspective	10

The interested scholar may consult Lesser, Fifer, and Clark (1964) for item examples of some of the subtests.

RELIABILITY AND VALIDITY: Reliabilities (corrected for attenuation) were as follows: The r for the entire sample (N = 320) was .92. The range was from .79 to .94. Jewish (.84) and Negro children (.85) showed somewhat lower reliabilities on the reasoning scale than they did on other scales. The reliabilities for these scales were lowest for both middle-class Negro and Jewish children (r = .79). Reliabilities for lower-class Negro children (r = .94) and lower-class Jewish children (r = .88) were distinctly superior to those for their middle-class counterparts. Reliability for boys (r = .92) surpassed that for girls (r = .84).

Reasoning (median r of .62) correlated highest with the other scales.

BIBLIOGRAPHY:

LESSER, G. S., FIFER, G., and CLARK, D. H. *Mental Abilities of Children in Different Social and Cultural Groups.* Comparative Research Project No. 1635, 1964, Office of Education, Department of Health, Education, and Welfare, Washington, D.C.

DAVIS, F. B., LESSER, G. S., FRENCH, E. G., *et al.* "Identification and Classroom Behavior of Gifted Elementary-School Children." Cooperative Research Monographs, 1960, No. 2, 19032. In "The Gifted Student," OE 35016, Monograph No. 2, Office of Education, Department of Health, Education, and Welfare, Washington, D.C.

T. M. R. PERFORMANCE PROFILE FOR THE SEVERELY AND MODERATELY RETARDED

AUTHORS: Alfred J. DiNola, Bernard P. Kaminsky, and Allan E. Sternfeld

AGE: School-age, trainable mentally retarded

VARIABLE: Daily living activities (see description of measure)

TYPE OF MEASURE: Rating scale

SOURCE FROM WHICH THE MEASURE MAY BE OBTAINED: Reporting Service for Exceptional Children, 563 Westview Avenue, Ridgefield, New Jersey

DESCRIPTION OF MEASURE: This measure was developed to meet the need for an instrument more sensitive than the standard measures of intellectual functioning for use with trainable mentally retarded children. It is designed for use as an evaluation instrument in the area of skills of living. The six areas measured are social behavior, self-care, communication, basic knowledge, practical skills, and body usage. Each of the six major areas is divided into four topics, and each topic is measured by ten items. Thus, the total measure consists of 240 items. Examples of items for the area of social behavior, topic of self-control are the following:

Stability: *(0) becomes upset without apparent cause, (1) becomes upset when mildly provoked or reprimanded, (2) occasionally exhibits control even when mildly provoked or reprimanded, (3) usually exhibits control even when provoked or reprimanded, (4) maintains stability unless seriously provoked.*

Temper Control: *(0) displays temper tantrums without obvious cause, (1) displays temper tantrum whenever annoyed or frustrated, (2) occasionally displays temper outburst when responding to physical control, (3) rarely displays temper and responds well to verbal control, (4) has reasonable control, verbalizes his feelings.*

For the area of communication, topic of modes of communication:

Eye Contact as a Speaker: *(0) does not look at listener, (1) looks at listener only when directed to do so, (2) looks at listener with occasional appropriate eye contact, (3) looks at listener with appropriate eye contact, (4) can maintain eye contact with more than one person in group conversation.*

Each item has a score range of 0 to 4. The scores are cumulated by topic and area, and area scores may be plotted on a yearly comparative chart. The sum of the six area scores is converted into a habile index, which is a percentage of a norm or goal score for the 240 items. The goal is set as 720, so that, with possible scores of 0 to 960, the habile index may range 0 to 133.

RELIABILITY AND VALIDITY: No data on reliability or validity are reported.

BIBLIOGRAPHY:

DI NOLA, A. J., KAMINSKY, B. P., and STERNFELD, A. E. *T. M. R. Performance Profile for the Severely and Moderately Retarded: Teachers Manual and Record Booklet.* Reporting Service for Exceptional Children, Ridgefield, New Jersey, 1965.

WANG MENTAL ABILITY TEST

AUTHOR: James D. Wang

AGE: Fourth, fifth, and sixth grades

VARIABLE: Mental ability

TYPE OF MEASURE: Group test

SOURCE FROM WHICH THE MEASURE MAY BE OBTAINED: See Wang (1941)

DESCRIPTION OF MEASURE: This measure consists of twenty multiple-choice questions, objectively scored, which can, according to the author, be administered in six minutes. Some sample items of the test are as follows:

Which one of the five words below means the opposite of south?
  (1) west, (2) sunset, (3) north, (4) equator, (5) left.
A toe is to a foot the same as a finger is to what?
  (1) head, (2) arm, (3) glove, (4) hand, (5) elbow.

RELIABILITY AND VALIDITY: The test was correlated with the Hemmon-Nelsom Tests of Mental Ability, Form A, for grades 3 to 8. The correlation between the two tests was .80. The partial correlation between the two tests, holding chronological age constant, was .81.

BIBLIOGRAPHY:

WANG, J. D. "A Study of Certain Factors Associated wth Children's Play Interests." Unpublished doctoral dissertation, George Peabody College for Teachers, 1941.

Group 1-b

Language and Number Skills

COMPOSITE SCALE OF LANGUAGE

AUTHOR: Oliver P. Kolstoe

AGE: Mongoloid children between the chronological ages of 5½ years and 13 years 11 months

VARIABLE: Language development

TYPE OF MEASURE: Structured observation

SOURCE FROM WHICH THE MEASURE MAY BE OBTAINED: See Kolstoe (1958)

DESCRIPTION OF MEASURE: The Composite Scale uses selected items from the Kuhlmann tests and the Revised Stanford-Binet, Form L, and involves measurement of the child's ability to follow instructions in a candy game. An example of an item from the procedures for stimulated situations for the Composite Scale is presented below (used for language understanding). The following were suggested steps for the "stimulator" to follow. *X* denotes items to be scored.

    a. "Do you want another piece of candy?"
    b. "This time I am going to hide it."
    c. "I want you to find the candy."
    d. Pantomime—sotto voce—"Where shall I hide it?" Looking around the room.
x *e. "Stand with your back to me."*
x *f. "You turn around."*
x *g. "Close your eyes."*
x *h. "Put your hands over your eyes."*
    i. Hide the candy in an obvious place so that the child can find it easily.
x *j. "You can look now." If necessary, add:*
x *k. "Open your eyes."*
x *l. "Turn around."*
x *m. "See if you can find the candy." If necessary, pantomime looking for the candy, drawing the child in to help look.*
    n. "Where is it? Where is the candy? Can you find the candy?" etc.
    o. "You may eat the candy."

The scoring for the scale consists of the number of items answered correctly and the administration of the test requires two observers and a "stimulator" to initiate activities.

RELIABILITY AND VALIDITY: No data on reliability have been presented. Kolstoe's subjects were thirty Caucasian mongoloid children, divided into two groups of fifteen. The experimental group received intensive instruction in language. Though the differences are not statistically significant, nine out of the fifteen experimental cases showed superiorities over the control pair. Also, the scores tended to be more discriminative between those of higher and lower abilities.

BIBLIOGRAPHY:

KOLSTOE, O. P. "Language Training of Low-Grade Mongoloid Children." *American Journal of Mental Deficiency*, 1958, *63*, 17–30.

DISCRIMINATION, SERIATION, AND NUMERATION TEST

AUTHOR: David Elkind

AGE: 4 to 6

VARIABLE: Number conception

TYPE OF MEASURE: Performance test

SOURCE FROM WHICH THE MEASURE MAY BE OBTAINED: See Elkind (1964) for a description of the materials and procedure for administering the test

DESCRIPTION OF MEASURE: The materials used in the test are sets of blocks, slats, and sticks representing respectively three-dimensional, two-dimensional, and one-dimensional materials. There are two sets of size-graded blocks, nine blocks to a set, the first set beginning with a 1 inch cube with succeeding blocks ½ inch larger progressively, while in the second set the smallest block is a ¾ inch cube with the succeeding blocks increasing by ½ inch each. The two sets of blocks are painted different colors.

The slats are ½ and ¼ inch thick, but vary in length. The first set of slats starts with the shortest at 1½ inches and each succeeding slat increases by ½ inch. As with the blocks, the second set of slats is made to interlock with the first set, that is, the shortest slat is 1¾ inches and succeeding slats are each ½ inch longer than the preceding one. The slats are painted the same way as the blocks. Two sets of sticks, ¼ inch in diameter, make up the one-dimensional materials. The length of the two sets of sticks is the same as the length of the slats, and the sticks are painted the same color as the blocks and slats.

The discrimination section of the test consists of four problems each on the sticks, the slats, and the blocks. The four sets of items are the same, regardless of the materials used. The child is asked to find the smallest (stick, block, or slat), then to find the largest, and then to find the smallest and largest when they are camouflaged in such a way as to make them look different, that is, to look larger if it is smaller and vice versa. The total possible score on the discrimination section of the test is 12 points.

The seriation part of the test consists also of twelve items, four using each of the three materials. Again, the items are the same regardless of the materials used. The child is first asked to make a stairway with the sticks or slats or blocks, using four or seven or nine elements. These differing number of elements make up the first three items, wheras in the fourth item the child is asked to take five additional items picked at random from the second set and to put them in their proper place in the "stairway."

The numeration test is made up also of twelve items, all of them again the same four with the three different types of materials. When the elements are made into a stairway, the examiner requests the child to count the number of stairs. The child is then asked how many steps a doll would have to climb to reach a designated stair. Again, as with the discrimination and seriation tests, the two sets of each type of material are mixed together to make the item additionally difficult.

RELIABILITY AND VALIDITY: No direct evidence was given on the reliability of the measures. Elkind found an increase in mean discrimination, seriation, and numeration scores as age increased. Elkind formulated various hypotheses based on the work of Piaget about the relationship between age of child, type of material, and type of test. In general, his hypotheses were supported.

BIBLIOGRAPHY:

ELKIND, D. "Discrimination, Seriation, and Numeration of Size and Dimensional Differences in Young Children: Piaget Replication Study VI." *The Journal of Genetic Psychology,* 1964, *104,* 275–296.

DODWELL'S NUMBER CONCEPT TEST

AUTHOR: P. C. Dodwell

AGE: 5 to 8

VARIABLE: Understanding of number concepts

TYPE OF MEASURE: Semistructured interview

SOURCE FROM WHICH THE MEASURE MAY BE OBTAINED: See Dodwell (1960)

DESCRIPTION OF MEASURE: The Dodwell Number Test is a practical application of Piaget's age-maturational theory concerning the development of number concepts among children. As such, it uses a variety of materials which involve the subjects in making judgments about quantities of numbers. The tasks also allow the child to manipulate the materials.

The scale consists of a semistructured interview that is conducted individually with the child and includes the following five situations: relation of perceived size to number (conservation); provoked correspondence; unprovoked correspondence; seriation; and cardination and ordination. In the conservation task, the child is required to perceive the constancy of a number of objects (beads) placed in differently shaped containers. In the correspondence tasks, the child is asked to determine the number of objects in two sets of materials where perceptual correspondence is destroyed, though the sums in each case are identical. In seriation, the child is required to match two rows of objects in order of increasing size, such as matching dolls from smallest to largest with canes in the same order of size progression. Finally in cardination and ordination, the child is queried for his grasp of the relationship between ordinal and cardinal numbers.

The meaning of the terms, the materials required, and the exact details of administering the test are described in full. Fifty-four questions are listed on the test blanks as standard questions and are always used except in a few cases. The blank containing these questions can be obtained from Dodwell upon request.

Two patterns of scoring are used for the test blanks. First, a score on the number of items answered correctly can be obtained. Second, the number of A responses can be determined. An A response is one in which the child makes his judgment of size or number on the basis of perceived characteristics alone.

RELIABILITY AND VALIDITY: Dodwell's tests have been administered to 250 children of normal intellectual ability in kindergarten, grade one, and grade two. The reliability of the total scores, however, is based on samples principally from kindergarten and grade one. These correlations were short (one-week interval) and long (three-month intervals) test-retest coefficients. The coefficients range between .56 (total A scores) and .78 (total point scores) for Ns of 50 and between .73 (A scores) and .87 (point scores) for Ns of 60.

According to Dodwell, validity of the test is supported by the correlation of

.59 obtained between scores on a teacher-made number concept test emphasizing understanding and the results on the author's test. Since the scalogram analysis of the test scores yielded a coefficient of reproducibility of only .690, however, Dodwell has concluded that the items form at best a quasiscale.

Dodwell (1961) has also developed a group version of the number test based essentially on the same materials and procedures. Both the point scores (r of .68) and the A score (r of .73) appear to correlate highly with the results of the individual test.

BIBLIOGRAPHY:

DODWELL, P. C. "Children's Understanding of Number and Related Concepts." *Canadian Journal of Psychology,* 1960, *14,* 191–205.

DODWELL, P. C. "Children's Understanding of Number Concepts: Characteristics of an Individual and of a Group Test." *Canadian Journal of Psychology,* 1961, *15,* 29–36.

DODWELL, P. C. "Relations between the Understanding of the Logic of Classes and of Cardinal Number in Children." *Canadian Journal of Psychology,* 1962, *16,* 152–160.

IRWIN-HAMMILL ABSTRACTION TEST

AUTHORS: Donald D. Hammill and Orvis Irwin

AGE: Mentally retarded and cerebral palsied children between 6 and 17

VARIABLE: Language development

TYPE OF MEASURE: Test, individually administered

SOURCE FROM WHICH THE MEASURE MAY BE OBTAINED: Hammill and Irwin (1966)

DESCRIPTION OF MEASURE: The Irwin-Hammill Abstraction Test consists of two forms with twenty-five items in each form. The items are administered individually to the children. Complete instructions for administering the test have been provided (Irwin and Hammill, 1964). The items themselves illustrate three forms of categorization and abstraction: sequential, coordinate, and mixed. As an example of the sequential category, the subject is required to give the number between 3 and 5. As an illustration of the coordinate category, the subject is required to select the one dissimilar category from the following nouns: cat, dog, horse, tree. Finally, as an illustration of the mixed category, the subject is requested to match the proper adjective describing the noun rabbit: tall, furry, feathery, prickly.

In addition to the verbal and individual administration of the test, the directions allow handicapped subjects, such as the cerebral palsied, to respond manually or in any manner possible for them. Sample items from the revised form of the test are given below.

A baseball is: *ROUND, sour, hot, mushy.*
A light is: *what you hear, what you feel, WHAT YOU SEE, what you eat.*
A pony is: *a small wagon, A SMALL HORSE, a small tiger, a small car.*

The test has been administered to 122 cerebral palsied children ranging in age from 6 to 17 (Irwin and Hammill, 1964) and to 109 mentally retarded children within the same age range (Hammill and Irwin, 1966).

Though the authors do not explicitly describe the scoring system, it appears that the score consists simply of the number of items answered correctly by the child.

RELIABILITY AND VALIDITY: The final forms of the test for cerebral palsied children reduced the initial pool of fifty items to twenty-five on the basis of three criteria: significant correlations between items and the total score, very low phi coefficients mostly between items to indicate independence of test functioning, and the difficulty level of the items. In the two final forms of the test, reliability data refer to reliability of the observer and to the reliability of the abstraction test. In the first instance, the overall agreement between observers for fifty-five children with speech problems was 98.6 per cent. In the latter case, reliability coefficients for both split-half and parallel forms were .95. When the Kuder-Richardson Formula No. 20 was applied to the data of Form X, the coefficient of reliability was .95; for Form Y, the coefficient was .96. The two forms of the abstraction test also correlated highly with scores of the WISC Similarity Test and the Peabody Test, the correlations ranging between .72 and .74. Statistical results similar to those found with cerebral palsied children have been obtained with mentally retarded subjects (Hammill and Irwin, 1966).

BIBLIOGRAPHY:

HAMMILL, D. D., and IRWIN, O. C. "An Abstraction Test Adapted for Use with Mentally Retarded Children." *American Journal of Mental Deficiency*, 1966, *70*, 866–72.

IRWIN, O. C., and HAMMILL, D. D. "An Abstraction Test for Use with Cerebral Palsied Children." *Cerebral Palsy Review*, 1964, *25*, 3–9.

NUMBER FACILITY SCALE

AUTHORS: Gerald Lesser, Gordon Fifer, and Donald H. Clark

AGE: 6 years, 2 months through 7 years, 5 months

VARIABLE: Number facility

TYPE OF MEASURE: Test

SOURCE FROM WHICH THE MEASURE MAY BE OBTAINED: See Lesser et al. (1964)

DESCRIPTION OF MEASURE: The authors' purpose is to measure numerical concepts prior to formal training. The numerical test consists simply of two pictures: the first one is for the enumeration, addition, and subtraction subtests, and the second is for the multiplication and division subtests. The first shows houses, trees, autos, and other objects in quantity. The second shows a fruit and vegetable stand with some children. The test items require the subject to enumerate, add, subtract, multiply, and divide the objects in the scenes. In enumerating, the subject is permitted to count with his fingers touching the picture since the purpose of the enumerating test is to determine the subject's ability to count. Touching is not permitted on the other subtests. The names of objects to be manipulated, the phrasing of the questions, and the test directions were all put in the simplest possible language, and the wording producing the least confusion was adopted. The directions for giving these tests appear in Appendix A (Lesser et al., 1964), and Appendix B shows the test blank with the specific enumerations and answers required.

RELIABILITY AND VALIDITY: The reliability coefficient for the entire sample was .96. All ethnic groups showed consistently high reliabilities (.94–.96). The range of intercorrelation for this scale with other scales was .28 (lower-class) to .58 (Puerto Rican and Negro) on the verbal scale; .52 (middle-class) to .74 (Puerto Rican) on the reasoning scale; and .40 (Jewish) to .54 (Negro) on the space test (Lesser et al., 1964, pp. 86–101).

BIBLIOGRAPHY:

LESSER, G. S., FIFER, G., and CLARK, D. H. *Mental Abilities of Children in Different Social and Cultural Groups.* Comparative Research Project No. 1635, 1964. Office of Education, U. S. Department of Health, Education, and Welfare, Washington, D.C.

DAVIS, F. B., LESSER, G. S., FRENCH, E. G., ET AL. "Identification and Classroom Behavior of Gifted Elementary-School Children." *Cooperative Research Monographs,* 1960, No. 2, 19032. In "The Gifted Student," OE-35016, Monograph No. 2, Office of Education, Department of Health, Education, and Welfare, Washington, D.C.

OBJECTIVE LANGUAGE SCALE

AUTHOR: W. G. Williams

AGE: 5 to 12

VARIABLE: Language development

TYPE OF MEASURE: Observation of behavior and individual test items

SOURCE FROM WHICH THE MEASURE MAY BE OBTAINED: See Williams (1960). Definition of the language scale items and other explanatory data may be obtained by writing the author at Speech and Hearing Clinic, Purdue University, Lafayette, Indiana.

DESCRIPTION OF MEASURE: This measure is a language scale and is a modification of one developed earlier by M. J. Mecham. The items were taken primarily from Doll's Vineland Social Maturity Scale, Gesell's Developmental Schedules, Terman and Merrill's revision of the Binet Scale, Poole's Maturation Scale of Articulation, and the works of McCarthy. All the items are listed in the Williams article, and each item is designated by category: reading, writing, speaking, and listening.

RELIABILITY AND VALIDITY: "Scores on the language scale and metropolitan results were tested by means of rank-order correlation. A significant relationship was found, except in three grades" (Williams, 1960). Analysis of variance showed significant difference between successive grade levels. A significant relationship was found between the scores of speech-delayed children and the evaluations of speech clinicians. The split-half reliability was significant. "The scores obtained by teachers and clinician, all using the language scale, were tested by t-ratio and rho correlation. A significance of difference was found with t; a significant relationship was found with rho for most grades. The teachers' subjective evaluation and use of the language scale were correlated by using rho and the sign test. No significant relationship was found with most grades" (Williams, 1960).

BIBLIOGRAPHY:

WILLIAMS, W. G. "The Adequacy and Usefulness of an Objective Language Scale When Administered to Elementary School Children." *Journal of Educational Research*, 1960, *54*, 30–33.

OBSERVATIONAL RATING SCALE OF LANGUAGE

AUTHOR: Oliver P. Kolstoe

AGE: Mongoloid children between the chronological age of 5½ years and 13 years 11 months

VARIABLE: Language development

TYPE OF MEASURE: Structured observation

SOURCE FROM WHICH THE MEASURE MAY BE OBTAINED: See Kolstoe (1958)

DESCRIPTION OF MEASURE: Kolstoe's Observational Rating Scale of Language is a structured measuring instrument using two concepts as follows: "a. *Vertical* language development means growth in complexity of language functioning. For example, the child who says 'ba'; later, 'me ba'; and still later 'give me ba' is developing vertically in the sense in which the term is used in this study. b. *Horizontal* language development refers to the broadening of the child's ability to comprehend and verbalize at a given stage of development. For example, the child who knows only four words and later learns new words is developing horizontally . . ." (Kolstoe, 1958).

The scale is used in three different situations of one-half hour duration. These periods are free play, with two children of the same sex; free play with a different playmate; and a structured situation in which the child is asked specific questions relating to various pictures. In the free play situations, an observer attempted to elicit verbalizations if none were forthcoming.

Finally, the observers rate the language of the subjects in terms of five levels of competency, depending on the number of responses the children emit. These ratings range from a score of 1 for barely emerging language (one response) to a score of 5 for proficient language (five or more responses). Complete directions have been described for all possible contingencies of linguistic behavior in terms of this observational rating system. Two sample items from the scale are cries communicatively and laughs or smiles communicatively.

RELIABILITY AND VALIDITY: The Observational Rating Scale is part of a battery of tests given to thirty Caucasian mongoloid subjects, subdivided into experimental and control groups. The experimental group was so designated because it was placed in an intensive planned program of instruction for language development. The program and the materials used for instruction are described in detail.

The average chronological age for both groups ranged between 9 years 1 month to 9 years 6 months; mean mental ages were 2 years 2 months, average IQ scores were in the middle twenties, and the chronological age spread was from 5 years 6 months to 13 years 11 months.

There was only moderate agreement between two observers as reflected by a rank correlation coefficient of .53 for their recordings of vertical language development. The discriminating power of the scale was not great. The experimental group showed very little difference between the fall and spring ratings and the gains they made were not any greater than those of the control group. On the basis of these results, Kolstoe has concluded that the discriminating value of the scale was questionable. Nevertheless, the scale constitutes a test of language ability that extends downward to the beginning stages of linguistic skills.

BIBLIOGRAPHY:

KOLSTOE, O. P. "Language Training of Low-Grade Mongoloid Children." *American Journal of Mental Deficiency,* 1958, *63,* 17–30.

PACIFIC NUMBER TEST (PNT)

AUTHORS: Anna M. Shotwell, Harvey F. Dingman, and George Tarjan

AGE: Mental retardates with mental ages from 3 to 9 years

VARIABLE: Development of arithmetical skills

TYPE OF MEASURE: Objective achievement test

SOURCE FROM WHICH THE MEASURE MAY BE OBTAINED: Anna M. Shotwell, Soc. Education, 900 E. Harrison Avenue, G-6, Pomona, California 91767

DESCRIPTION OF MEASURE: The PNT includes sixty-eight items ranging in difficulty level from mental ages of 3 to 9. Each mental age level has six or more items, and scoring follows the Binet procedure of establishing basal and ceiling ages and expressing the total scores as an arithmetic age. Though the test usually requires individual examinations, it can be administered on a group basis with retardates who have a minimum mental age of 6 provided that seven specified items are individually administered at another time. As a group test, the required time of administration is approximately fifteen minutes.

The intent of the scale is to circumvent the errors retardates make on typical achievement tests due to deficiencies in reading and writing or inability to follow complex verbal directions. The items within the test itself involve coin recognition and counting, weight discrimination, recognition of certain numbers of objects, and understanding of positional terms, such as middle and most. Items from Year III follow (each item counts two months):

Recognizing two blocks. Procedure: *Take two blocks and put them in front of the subject. Ask, "How many?" Score: 1 point for correct performance.*

Recognizing two beads. Procedure: *Take two beads and put them in front of the subject. Ask, "How many?" Score: 1 point for correct performance.*

Recognizing two fingers. Procedure: *Hold two fingers in front of the subject. Ask, "How many?" Score: 1 point for correct performance.*

Counting. Procedure: *Say "Count like this: 1 . . . now go on." If necessary, say "What comes next: 1 . . . ." Score: 1 point if child counts to 2 or more.*

Giving two buttons. Procedure: *Empty box of eight buttons before the subject, and say "Put two buttons in the box." Give only one trial. Score: 1 point for correct performance.*

Giving two sticks. Procedure: *Put four sticks and an uncovered box before the subject and say, "Put two sticks into the box." Score: 1 point for correct performance.*

RELIABILITY AND VALIDITY: The test has been administered to 175 mental retardates ranging in mental ages between 3 and 9 years and in chronological ages between 9 and 27 years. The split-half reliability for these cases was .99 when corrected by the Spearman-Brown formula. The same group yielded a validity co-efficient of .93 between mental ages and the scores on the scale. Finally, only those items have been retained which statistical analyses have proven to be appropriate to their mental age levels of placement, according to percentage passing, and progression in percentage passing at successive mental age levels.

BIBLIOGRAPHY:

MC INTYRE, R. B., and DINGMAN, H. F. "Mental Age vs. Learning Ability: An Investigation of Transfer of Learning between Hierarchical Levels." *American Journal of Mental Deficiency,* 1963, *68,* 396–403.

SHOTWELL, A. M., DINGMAN, H. F., and TARJAN, G. "A Number Test for Mental Defectives." *American Journal of Mental Deficiency,* 1956, *61,* 589–594.

SILVERSTEIN, A. B., ANGER, R., and KRUDIS, B. R. "The Meaning of Indefinite Number Terms for Mentally Retarded Children." *American Journal of Mental Deficiency,* 1964, *69,* 419–424.

PARSONS LANGUAGE SAMPLE

AUTHOR: Joseph E. Spradlin

AGE: Retardates age 6 to 15

VARIABLE: Language development

TYPE OF MEASURE: Test, individually administered

SOURCE FROM WHICH THE MEASURE MAY BE OBTAINED: See Spradlin (1963)

DESCRIPTION OF MEASURE: This measure is administered individually and consists of 139 items divided into subtests as follows with item examples:

Tact—*twenty-eight objects or pictures which the child names. There is a four-step sequence from the real to the symbolic, involving first seven real objects, then seven miniature objects, then seven colored pictures, and finally seven black and white pictures. The experimenter shows the subject the stimulus and says, "What is it?" or "What do you call it?" Examples are a ball, a pencil; a miniature car, miniature pliers; a colored picture of a motherly type woman; a black and white picture of a puppy. The subject must give the name of the object; responses are scored as appropriate, unappropriate, unintelligible, and no response.*

Echoic—*there are twenty-two words, sentences, or digits which the child is to repeat. This does not need exemplifying.*

Echoic gesture—*the child is asked to mimic thirteen gestures. Example: The examiner points at the light and says, "Do this." The examiner places a block on the table, taps it with his finger, and says, "Do this."*

Comprehension—*eighteen items, some of which involve vocal, some gestural, and some vocal and gestural instructions. Examples: (vocal only) The examiner says "Put your finger on your nose." Credit is given if child places finger on his nose.*

Intraverbal—*twenty-nine questions are open-end sentences. Example: "What do we do when we are hungry?" "We smile when we are happy, we cry when we are ————."*

Intraverbal gesture—*twenty-four questions that can be answered with a verbal or a gestural response. Examples: "Where is your ear?" "What do you do with a key?"*

Maud—*five items, arranged so the subject will request an object either verbally or gesturally. Example: The examiner pounds a peg in the pegboard, then he hands the board to the child and says, "You do it." The examiner retains the mallet. A maud response is recorded if the child requests the mallet vocally.*

RELIABILITY AND VALIDITY: The maud subtest was eliminated from the battery as a result of very low reliability. Split-half reliability r's were .90 and over for verbal subtests, and .84 and over for nonvocal subtests. When twenty subjects were retested after two to five months, reliability coefficients for vocal tests were .86 to .99, and .64 to .92 for nonverbal tests. Another test-retest study of thirty-two children ages 9 to 12, with a seven-month interval, resulted in coefficients ranging from .82 to .96 on vocal tests, and .59 to .89 on nonverbal tests.

The PLS verbal and nonverbal were correlated with Wechsler Intelligence Scale for Children (WISC) verbal and performance scales. Correlation coefficients were: PLS verbal and WISC verbal subtests, range .68 to .75; PLS total and WISC full scale IQ scores, range .41 to .51; nonverbal subtest r's were essentially zero.

Psychiatric aides were asked to rank children in their cottages for speech and nonverbal communication, and these results were correlated with PLS vocal scores. For five cottages, these correlations ranged .33 to .86, median .64. For PLS nonvocal scores, the r's ranged .18 to .80, median .40.

BIBLIOGRAPHY:

SPRADLIN, J. E. "Assessment of Speech and Language of Retarded Children: The Parsons Language Sample." *Journal of Speech and Hearing Disorders,* Monograph Supplement No. 10, January, 1963.

PICTURE VOCABULARY TEST FOR DEAF CHILDREN

AUTHORS: Howard L. Roy, Jerome D. Schein, and D. Robert Frisina

AGE: Deaf children between the ages of 3 and 7

VARIABLE: Language development

TYPE OF MEASURE: Nonverbal test

SOURCE FROM WHICH THE MEASURE MAY BE OBTAINED: See Roy et al. (1964)

DESCRIPTION OF MEASURE: The Picture Vocabulary Test for Deaf Children used at Gallaudet College consists of four parts: nouns, verbs (present perfect), adjectives (color), and verbs (past tense). The nouns are printed on 5 × 5 inch photographs with three distractors. In Part II, each item is printed with a phrase correctly identifying what is occurring in an 8 mm. motion picture and three incorrect responses. In Part III (the colors), 3 × 6 inch colored papers are presented and a card is printed with the names of four colors, one of which is the name of the color shown. Finally, in Part IV (past tense verbs), a number of cards contain a correct verb and three distractors relating to an 8 mm. motion picture that had been presented.

Sample items and alternatives from each part are presented below. Part I— nouns.

Car: *cow, cat, dog, car.*
Ball: *boat, ball, bird, bear.*

Part II—verbs (present tense).

Dog running: *is Sailing, is Working, is Running, is Walking.*

Part III—adjectives (colors).

Black: *red, brown, black, green.*

Part IV—verbs (past tense).

A ball rolling: *ate, flew, read, rolled.*

The score is the number of correct responses. Complete details on materials and procedures are provided.

RELIABILITY AND VALIDITY: No data on reliability and validity were presented. Nevertheless the reviewer considers this test sufficiently objective in its scoring to facilitate the procurement of statistical data.

BIBLIOGRAPHY:

ROY, H. L., SCHEIN, J. D., and FRISINA, D. R. *New Methods of Language Development for Deaf Children.* Washington, D.C.: Gallaudet College, Cooperative Research Project No. 1383, 1964. (Mimeographed)

PRESCHOOL PREPOSITION TEST

AUTHORS: May Aaronson and Earl Schaefer

AGE: 3 to 5

VARIABLE: Knowledge of prepositions; verbal comprehension

TYPE OF MEASURE: Test, individually administered

SOURCE FROM WHICH THE MEASURE MAY BE OBTAINED: A few of the test boards are available for research purposes from the authors at the Center for Studies of Child and Family Mental Health, National Institute of Mental Health, 5454 Wisconsin Ave., Chevy Chase, Maryland 20015.

DESCRIPTION OF MEASURE: This is a measure of the young child's knowledge of prepositions, which the authors believe is related to verbal comprehension. This test can be administered by nonprofessional personnel, and can be scored later by a professional examiner. The equipment for the test is a yellow metallized board with the figures of a green automobile and a red boy. The figures are raised slightly; the boy is colored red to minimize racial identification. The test items are divided into two parts: Part I is designed to determine whether the subject understands the essential terminology of the test, and includes these and similar items (ten items in all):

Show me the car.
Show me the boy.
Show me the board *that the car and the boy are on.*
Show me the wheels *of the car.*

If Part I indicates that the child does not know some of the terms, he is taught them.
Part II constitutes the test proper. Samples of the twenty-three items are:

Put the ball into *the boy's hands,* into *the boy's hands.*
Put the ball up *as* high *on the board as you can,* up *as* high *on the board as you can.*
Put the ball under *the car,* under *the car.*
Put the ball inside *the window of the car,* inside *the window of the car.*

The child's responses may be scored directly on the Individual Test Record as right or wrong, or they may be recorded on Picture Score Sheets and scored later. The authors provide detailed rules for scoring.

RELIABILITY AND VALIDITY: Preliminary data provided by the authors on children ages 2 to 8 indicate a regular progression of scores with age up to age 5½ or 6, at which age most of the subjects reach the ceiling of the test. When the PPT scores of 28 Afro-American lower socioeconomic status males, age 3 years, were correlated with their scores on the Stanford-Binet, Johns Hopkins Perceptual Test, and Peabody Picture Vocabulary Test, the resulting coefficient of correlation in each case was .57.

BIBLIOGRAPHY:

AARONSON, M., and SCHAEFER, E. *Preschool Preposition Test: Manual of Instructions, 1968* (unpublished).

RECEPTIVE, EXPRESSIVE, AND PHONETIC LANGUAGE SCALE

AUTHORS: Michael J. D'Asaro and Vera John

AGE: 6 weeks to 68 months

VARIABLE: Language development

TYPE OF MEASURE: Combination of semistructured observation schedule and questionnaire

SOURCE FROM WHICH THE MEASURE MAY BE OBTAINED: See D'Asaro and John (1961)

DESCRIPTION OF MEASURE: The R-E-P scale allows the observation of receptive, expressive, and phonetic skills, A sample item for 21 months follows:

Receptive: *Points to parts of doll on request—finds one part at 18 months and an additional part for each succeeding month up to 22 months.*

Expressive: *Has twenty words. Combines two or three words that express two or more different ideas, e.g., "daddy go byebye," not just "go byebye."*

Phonetic: *Echoes two or more last words.*

The R-E-P combines interviews with the mother and direct observation of the child. In the maternal interview, the mother is questioned about the child's development in the three linguistic components. In addition, structured information is obtained from Doll's Vineland Social Maturity Scale. At the same time, the child's behavior is observed and recorded.

Details of scoring have not been provided. However, the items are sufficiently explicit so they can be scored for presence or absence. For this reason, it would not be too difficult to develop a scoring system for this scale.

RELIABILITY AND VALIDITY: The standardization population consists of 108 children covering an age range from 6 weeks to 68 months. Since less than ten children represent each age level, however, the authors caution that the results of the standardization reflect only trends. Nevertheless, the data show the expected age progression for item differentiation.

No statistics on the reliability of the scale have been presented; the validity data rest on an additional standardization study of thirty-four language handicapped children. In the latter group, quotients were obtained for receptive language (R scores) and expressive language (E scores). These scores were then correlated with the Vineland or V scores. The Spearman Rank Correlation Coefficients were .641 for V and R, and .664 for V and E. In both cases, the correlations attained are statistically significant at the 1 per cent level. Also, the prediction that severely retarded children would show the smallest R-E differences in comparison to the rest of the diagnostic population was substantiated.

BIBLIOGRAPHY:

D'ASARO, M. J., and JOHN, V. "A Rating Scale for Evaluation of Receptive, Expressive, and Phonetic Language Development in the Young Child." *Cerebral Palsy Review*, 1961, 22, 3–4, 17–19.

REVISION OF THE SMITH VOCABULARY TEST

AUTHORS: H. M. Williams and M. L. McFarland

AGE: Preschool children

VARIABLE: Language development (word knowledge)

TYPE OF MEASURE: Test, individually administered

SOURCE FROM WHICH THE MEASURE MAY BE OBTAINED: See Williams and McFarland (1937)

DESCRIPTION OF MEASURE: The Revision of the Smith Vocabulary Test consists of two equivalent forms (Forms I and II) that include representative words from Thorndike's list of 10,000 common words. In testing the child, each acceptable response to a word receives full credit. The responses expected from the child are recognition (A questions) and recall (B questions). The test is presented on two sets of cards with a picture in the front and a question to be read aloud by the examiner in the back. An individual score sheet is also used. The manual is sufficiently explicit to enable the research worker to use the test without the pictures or to develop his own set of pictorial material. The test is administered on an individual basis and requires a minimum mental age of 3 to serve as an adequate instrument of assessment. Examples of A and B questions from Form I are given below:

Pocket: *"What is this that we carry things in?"*

Take: *Hand child pencil. "Now I give you the pencil, and, now, [taking back the pencil] what do I do?"*

Dish: *Picture of dishes. "What are these?" Gesture across all dishes.*

Pocket: *"Show me your pocket. Do you have a pocket?"*

Take: *Hand child small car. "Now give it to me. Now take it."*

Dish: *"What is a dish for?"*

RELIABILITY AND VALIDITY: On a sample of 117 preschool Iowa City children, the parallel form reliability was .96, with a probable error of .79 test words. On a sample of forty children ranging in age between 4 years 4 months and 6 years 6 months, the correlation between scores on the new revised form and the original Smith test was .98, an index of concurrent validity.

Two additional noteworthy features of the scale are as follows: First, by computing the per cent of words passed on each test item by a large sample of children (278 subjects ranging in age between 2 years 3 months and 6 years 2 months) and rearranging the items in order of difficulty, the two forms are now quite equivalent. Second, mean vocabulary scores have been described for both chronological and mental ages on two separate samples ranging in age from approximately 2 years 3 months to 6 years 2 months. One sample consisted of 242 superior children (average IQ 124); the other included a group of sixty-four orphanage children (average IQ 84).

BIBLIOGRAPHY:

WILLIAMS, H. M., and MC FARLAND, M. L. "A Revision of the Smith Vocabulary Test for Preschool Children." Part III of *Development of Language and Vocabulary in Young Children*. Iowa City: University of Iowa Studies in Child Welfare, 1937, *13*, 35–46.

WILLIAMS, H. M., and MC FARLAND, M. L. "A Revision of the Smith Vocabulary Test for Preschool Children." Part III of *Development of Language and Vocabulary in Young Children*. "Appendix A: A manual for revised vocabulary scale." Iowa City: University of Iowa Studies in Child Welfare, 1937, *13*, 79–94.

SCRAMBLED SENTENCE TEST FOR DEAF CHILDREN

AUTHORS: Howard L. Roy, Jerome D. Schein, and D. Robert Frisina

AGE: Deaf children between the ages of 3 and 7

VARIABLE: Language development

TYPE OF MEASURE: Test, individually administered

SOURCE FROM WHICH THE MEASURE MAY BE OBTAINED: See Roy et al. (1964)

DESCRIPTION OF MEASURE: Like the Syntactical Relations Test, the Scrambled Sentence Test attempts to assess the deaf child's grasp of syntax. However, we consider this test inferior to the Syntactical Relations Test because chance and memory factors play a greater part.

The materials for the test include eleven sets of four or five cards each, one word printed on each card. Each set of words is then presented to the child as a scrambled sentence. The test proper consists of ten scrambled sentences. There is also a sample item administered prior to this test. The score consists of the number of words placed in correct sequence within the ten sentences. The maximum possible score is 45. Two sample items follow:

sleeps the cat white
the boat sails blue

As in the other tests of the Gallaudet battery (Picture Vocabulary, Syntactical Relations), this scale is administered on an individual basis. Gestures and facial expressions are used to indicate that the order of the sentences needs rearrangement.

RELIABILITY AND VALIDITY: Since this scale is part of a battery that includes the Picture Vocabulary and Syntactical Relations tests, the sample is identical in all three cases. Unlike the other scales, however, some support in terms of concurrent validity is available for this test. These data refer to the finding of a significant difference in scores on this test between an experimental group (N = 15) that had undergone a programmed instructional sequence on language development and a control group (N = 15) that had not had the benefit of this program.

As a precautionary note, the authors emphasize that the total battery score yields the most reliable measure because of its broader sampling of behavior. The battery to which they referred included the three tests mentioned above and the Gates Primary Reading Test: Part A, Word Recognition, and Part B, Sentence Reading.

BIBLIOGRAPHY:

ROY, H. L., SCHEIN, J. D., and FRISINA, D. R. *New Methods of Language Development for Deaf Children.* Washington, D.C.: Gallaudet College, Cooperative Research Project No. 1383, 1954. (Mimeographed)

SEMANTIC HABITS INVENTORY

AUTHORS: Jim C. Nunnally, Ronald L. Flaugher, and William F. Hodges

AGE: Elementary school children through adulthood

VARIABLE: Language development (semantic habits)

TYPE OF MEASURE: Forced binary-choice inventory

SOURCE FROM WHICH THE MEASURE MAY BE OBTAINED: See Nunnally et al. (1963)

DESCRIPTION OF MEASURE: The Semantic Habits scale includes 143 items that consist of two components—the stimulus words and the response alternatives for the five subscales of the binary-choice measure. These components are described in full. The alternative choice for each stimulus item may be classified into four verbal response tendencies or semantic habits that include positive evaluations, or the E-plus tendency (e.g., pretty and good); negative evaluations or the E-minus tendency (e.g., ugly and bad); responses in terms of observable, or sensuous denotative qualities, or the D tendency (e.g., long and sharp); and classificatory evaluation of some denotative attribute or the C tendency (e.g., reptile or coed).

The total instrument contains five subscales: E-plus vs. D; E-plus vs. C; E-minus vs. D; E-minus vs. C; and C vs. D. The following item contrasts E-plus and D responses: Orange: ——— sweet ——— round. This item contrasts E-plus and C responses: Orange: ——— sweet ——— fruit. This item contrasts D and C responses: Orange: ——— round ——— fruit. Various other combinations of the scales are possible. The test also has a multiple choice format. The stimulus word *priest*, for example, has the following options or associations: good (E-plus); sin (E-minus); robe (D); minister (C); prayer (F). In addition, a free response form is also available: A baseball is ———.

RELIABILITY AND VALIDITY: The scale has been used with more than 3,000 subjects including small children, elementary- and high-school children, college students, and members of the Armed Forces. Normative data presently exist only for adults. The means and standard deviations for the three major scales have been given for both males and females (Nunnally et al., 1963).

Most of the reliability coefficients provided are of the split-half type corrected by the Spearman-Brown prophecy formula. Reliability coefficients average in the .50's for seventy college students. With $N = 822$, the three major scales (total E-plus, total E-minus, and the C-D balance scale) had reliabilities of approximately .80 (Nunnally et al., 1963). In a later study Nunnally and Hodges (1965) presented some data on the stability of the scale. In their study, test-retest reliabilities over a six-month interval ranged between .69 and .75 for males ($N = 22$) and between .39 and .81 for females ($N = 23$). In a one-year interval, the coefficients ranged between .50 for the C-D to .65 for the E-plus scale for males ($N = 41$) and between .25 (E-plus) and .74 (C-D) for females ($N = 19$).

Validity of the scale rests on three related types of findings. First, the results evidently are not affected by response sets. Second, the results of the scale correlate significantly with corresponding scales (coefficients of about .50). Finally, correlations among the subscales are in the expected direction. For example, "E-plus versus D correlates positively with E-plus versus C, and E-minus versus D correlates positively with E-minus versus C, and so on."

On the basis of these results, Nunnally and his colleagues conclude that "Our working assumption is that semantic habits represent different modes of frequency of usage. If that is so, many hypotheses follow about relations between semantic habits and verbal learning, verbal performance, perception, and personality." As one example in support of these conclusions, they cite evidence that the scales have small but consistent correlations with personality inventories (Nunnally and Flaugher, 1963a).

BIBLIOGRAPHY:

NUNNALLY, J. C., FLAUGHER, R. L., and HODGES, W. F. "Measurement of Semantic Habits." *Educational and Psychological Measurement,* 1963, *XXIII,* 419–434.
NUNNALLY, J. C., and FLAUGHER, R. L. "Correlates of Semantic Habits." *Journal of Personality,* 1963, *31,* 192–202.
NUNNALLY, J. C., and HODGES, W. F. "Some Dimensions of Individual Differences in Word Association." *Journal of Verbal Learning and Verbal Behavior,* 1965, *4,* 82–88.

SYNTACTICAL RELATIONS TEST FOR DEAF CHILDREN

AUTHORS: Howard L. Roy, Jerome D. Schein, and D. Robert Frisina

AGE: Deaf children between the ages of 3 and 7

VARIABLE: Language development

TYPE OF MEASURE: Test, non-verbal, individually administered

SOURCE FROM WHICH THE MEASURE MAY BE OBTAINED: See Roy et al. (1964)

DESCRIPTION OF MEASURE: The Syntactical Relations Test is designed to measure the child's grasp of syntax. According to the authors, the vocabulary is simple and probably known to most deaf children. Selecting the correct response depends upon recognizing the part of speech that is missing.

The materials for the test are twenty-two cards containing sentences with missing words indicated by blank spaces, and three response options. The child is requested to select the word that correctly belongs in the blank space from a group of three alternatives. A sample item follows:

The ——— dog is eating: *red, cow, ate.*

The test, like many other tests developed at Gallaudet College, is administered on an individual basis and the score is simply the total number of correct responses.

RELIABILITY AND VALIDITY: Since the Picture Vocabulary Test for Deaf Children and the Syntactical Relations Test for Deaf Children were part of the same battery of tests, the comments on the reliability, validity, and standardization of the former also apply to the latter.

BIBLIOGRAPHY:

ROY, H. L., SCHEIN, J. D., and FRISINA, D. R. New Methods of Language Development for Deaf Children. Washington, D.C.: Gallaudet College, Cooperative Research Project No. 1383, 1954. (Mimeographed)

VERBAL SCALE

AUTHORS: Gerald S. Lesser, Gordon Fifer, and Donald H. Clark

AGE: 6 years, 2 months through 7 years, 5 months

VARIABLE: Intelligence

TYPE OF MEASURE: Vocabulary test

SOURCE FROM WHICH THE MEASURE MAY BE OBTAINED: Lesser et al. (1964)

DESCRIPTION OF MEASURE: The Verbal Scale consists of thirty Picture Vocabulary items and thirty Word Vocabulary items, the latter subtest being administered in two parallel forms of fifteen words each. The examiner enters on the answer blank the entire response given by each subject unless it is obviously correct. Items were either scored right (+1) or wrong (0).

The authors' definition of verbal ability as significant for intellectual ability should be noted: "This is defined as memory for verbal labels in which reasoning elements, such as those required by verbal analogies, are reduced to a minimum" (Lesser et al., 1964).

RELIABILITY AND VALIDITY: Reliabilities (corrected for attenuation) ranged from .78 to .94. For the entire sample of 320 children, r was .93. Reliabilities were lowest for middle-class Jewish children (r = .78) and highest for middle-class children considered as one sample (r = .94). The 1964 reference should be consulted for details on these reliabilities as they relate to each ethnic group, social-class group, sex group, and each ethnic group subdivided into socioeconomic class components (Lesser et al., 1964).

The items selected for the picture vocabulary were those found in the environments of urban children in the population to be sampled. The artists were instructed to make their drawings of people neutral in tone and to simplify them. Items selected for the word vocabulary test were also representative. Also, the words selected had to have equivalents in another language that were similar in difficulty. A check was also made to see that the original English word was retained in the process of being translated from English to another language or dialect and back to English. Linguistics experts were consulted for criteria to use in retaining words.

BIBLIOGRAPHY:

LESSER, G. S., FIFER, G., and CLARK, D. H. *Mental abilities of children in different social and cultural groups.* Comparative Research Project No. 1635, 1964, Office of Education, U. S. Department of Health, Education, and Welfare, Washington, D.C.

DAVIS, F. B., LESSER, G. S., and FRENCH, E. G., ET AL. "Identification and Classroom Behavior of Gifted Elementary-school Children." *Cooperative Research Monographs,* 1960, No. 2, 19032. Washington, D.C.: Office of Education, Dept. of Health, Education, and Welfare.

WORD ASSOCIATION TEST

AUTHORS: Roger Brown and Jean Berko

AGE: First, second, and third grade elementary school children or adults

VARIABLE: Language development

TYPE OF MEASURE: Semistructured projective test

SOURCE FROM WHICH THE MEASURE MAY BE OBTAINED: See Brown and Berko (1960)

DESCRIPTION OF MEASURE: The Word Association Test includes thirty-six stimulus words—six words representing each of six parts of speech, including count nouns (C.N.), mass nouns (M.N.), adjectives (Adj.), transitive verbs (T.V.), intransitive verbs (I.V.), and adverbs (Adv.). Each part is explicitly defined. For example, count nouns usually name bounded objects (e.g., *table, house*). The complete list of C.N. is table, house, foot, needle, apple, doctor; the complete list of M.N. is milk, water, sand, sugar, air, cheese (p. 5).

The test is individually administered with no definite time limits and the child is simply asked to respond with the first word he thinks of when he hears the individually presented stimulus word from each part-of-speech classification. Each of the thirty-six responses is, in turn, scored as homogeneous (Hmg.) or heterogeneous (Htg.) with reference to its stimulus word. Thus, a homogeneous response to the stimulus words "to send" would be "to receive"; a heterogeneous response would be "away."

The test has been administered to a group of children (N = 20) in each of the first three grades and to an adult group (N = 20).

RELIABILITY AND VALIDITY: On ten protocols of 360 response words on the word association test, independent scoring by two judges yielded perfect agreement except for three instances where the authors felt more information should have been elicited. Accordingly, they conclude that the judgment of the responses as homogeneous or heterogeneous "is an objective scoring procedure with high reliability." Evidence of validity came from at least three findings that were as predicted and expected. First, there was clear confirmation of an increase of homogeneous responses with age. Secondly, the evidence was clear that development in the child of speech for the count noun and adjective function preceded other parts of speech. Finally, highly statistically significant differences in the number of homogeneous responses between adults and children occurred in favor of the former.

BIBLIOGRAPHY:

BROWN, R., and BERKO, J. "Word Association and the Acquisition of Grammar." *Child Development*, 1960, *31*, 1–14.

Group 1-c

Specific Achievements

BIBLE KNOWLEDGE TEST

AUTHOR: H. W. Parshall

AGE: Has been used with children with mental ages from 3 years 6 months to 14 years 3 months

VARIABLE: Knowledge of the Bible

TYPE OF MEASURE: Test

SOURCE FROM WHICH THE MEASURE MAY BE OBTAINED: See Parshall (1960)

DESCRIPTION OF MEASURE: The test is designed to provide a simple scale of questions available to chaplains as a tool in planning Sunday School programs. Twenty-five items were prepared from the Bible, nine from the Old Testament and sixteen from the New Testament. They are arranged in the order in which they appear in the Bible rather than in any order of difficulty.

The test was administered orally on an individual basis although it appears adaptable to group administration.

Examples of the twenty-five items on the measure are the following:

(Yes)   *God made the world.*
(Yes)   *Moses was the name of the baby found in a basket in a river.*
(No)   *Jesus was born in the city of Jerusalem.*
(No)   *The Good Samaritan was one of Jesus' disciples.*
(Yes)   *Following his death, Jesus was placed in a tomb in the side of a hill.*

RELIABILITY AND VALIDITY: Forty-eight subjects with mean age 8 years, 10 months were retested after one to three months. The reliability coefficient was .92. Scores on this test correlated .61 with the mental age of mental defectives and −.12 with the chronological age of the same group.

The Bible Knowledge Test was used as an aid in establishing a religious program of training for institutionalized mental defectives. The author suggests its use with newly admitted patients as an aid to placement in the religious program of the institution. Administration is quick and easy, and it has high face validity.

BIBLIOGRAPHY:

PARSHALL, H. W. "A Bible Knowledge Test for Institutionalized Mental Defectives." *American Journal of Mental Deficiencies,* 1960, *64,* 960–962.

87

COIN TEST 1 AND COIN TEST 2

AUTHORS: Helen R. Marshall and Lucille Magruder

AGE: 7 to 12

VARIABLE: Knowledge of money use

TYPE OF MEASURE: Test, individual

SOURCE FROM WHICH THE MEASURE MAY BE OBTAINED: See Marshall and Magruder (1960)

DESCRIPTION OF MEASURE: This test evaluates children's understanding of the use of money. The subject is shown a penny, nickel, dime, quarter, and half-dollar, and is asked to name them. In the second section of the test, he is asked to tell the examiner what each coin will buy. In this section of the test, the examiner is required to judge whether or not the response is correct, that is, whether the item named by the child is one that can be ordinarily purchased for the coin he assigns to it. In the third part of the test, the child is shown a box of articles bought in a dime store, and his task is to pick out one that can be bought for a penny, one that can be bought for a nickel, and so on. The items used in the original test by Marshall and Magruder are listed in their article. Obviously, these items would change with price levels, and would have to be adapted to changes in the price structure. The items up to this point constitute Coin Test 1. The score on the test was the number of correct answers.

Coin Test 2 includes all of Coin Test 1, plus a fourth portion of the test in which the subject assigns a coin value to each of the eighteen dime store items previously mentioned.

The total possible score for Coin Test 1 is 15, and for Coin Test 2, 28.

RELIABILITY AND VALIDITY: No reliability data are given in the Marshall and Magruder material. Scores on both the short and the long forms of the coin test were shown to increase as chronological age increased.

BIBLIOGRAPHY:

MARSHALL, H. R., and MAGRUDER, L. "Relations between Parent Money Education Practices and Children's Knowledge and Use of Money." *Child Development,* 1960, *31,* 253–284.

MARSHALL, H. R. "Differences in Parent and Child Report of the Child's Experience in the Use of Money." *Journal of Educational Psychology,* 1963, *54*(3), 132–137.

MARSHALL, H. R. "The Relation of Giving Children an Allowance to Children's Money Knowledge and Responsibility and to Other Practices of Parents." *The Journal of Genetic Psychology,* 1964, *104,* 35–51.

DRAMATIC ACTING TEST:
A ROLE PLAYING TEST FOR CHILDREN

AUTHORS: Patricia Bowers and Perry London

AGE: Kindergarten through age 12

VARIABLE: Role playing or empathical skills

TYPE OF MEASURE: Observer rating scale

SOURCE FROM WHICH THE MEASURE MAY BE OBTAINED: The Dramatic Acting Test and its scoring manual have been deposited with the American Documentation Institute. Order Document No. 8260 from ADI Auxiliary Publications Project, Photoduplication Service, Library of Congress, Washington, D.C. 20540. Remit in advance $1.75 for microfilm or $2.50 for photocopies and make checks payable to: Chief, Photoduplication Service, Library of Congress. Copies of the test may also be obtained on request from Perry London, Department of Psychology, University of Southern California, Los Angeles 90007.

DESCRIPTION OF MEASURE: The Dramatic Acting Test is an attempt to measure empathical skill which its authors feel is essential to development of social perspective. The experimenter describes an interpersonal situation to the child, and assigns roles to himself and the child, providing standardized lines for himself while the child invents his own responses. Among the roles for the child are: mother (the experimenter plays a child who has broken a lamp); father (the experimenter is a child whose teacher has complained to the father regarding school behavior and low grades); friend (the experimenter plays a peer who has lost $10); bully (the experimenter is a younger child who desires to play ball with the bully's team); teacher (the experimenter is a whining "tattletale" who complains about the behavior of a classmate); and sheriff (the experimenter plays the robber).

The content of the subject's lines is rated on a four-point scale: no role adoption, lack of plausible sequence or adequate role adoption, moderately plausible sequence, and satisfactory role adoption. Each line is scored, and the average scores for each role are totaled. Only the content of what the child says is scored. The general procedures for scoring the children's responses, however, may occur in either one or two forms. An independent observer may simultaneously observe and score the performance or the child's statements may be recorded on tape for later analysis. Administration time is fifteen minutes.

RELIABILITY AND VALIDITY: Interscorer product-moment correlations between .80 and .87 were found on a sample of forty children subdivided into equal sex groups at ages 5, 7, 9, and 11 (Bowers and London, 1965). In a subsequent study by Madsen and London (1966) who administered the test to twenty-one girls and twenty-one boys between the ages of 7 and 12, the interscorer reliabilities ranged from .84 to .93.

BIBLIOGRAPHY:

BOWERS, P., and LONDON, P. "Developmental Correlates of Role-Playing Ability." *Child Development*, 1965, *30*, 499–508.

LONDON, P., and BOWERS, P. *The Dramatic Acting Test: A Role Playing Test for Children*. Los Angeles: University of Southern California, 1964. (Mimeographed)

MADSEN, C. H., JR., and LONDON, P. "Role Playing and Hypnotic Susceptibility in Children." *Journal of Personality and Social Psychology*, 1966, *3*, 13–19.

EXPERIENCE WITH MONEY TEST

AUTHORS: Helen R. Marshall and Lucille Magruder

AGE: 7 to 12

VARIABLE: Experience with money

TYPE OF MEASURE: Checklist

SOURCE FROM WHICH THE MEASURE MAY BE OBTAINED: See Marshall and Magruder (1960)

DESCRIPTION OF MEASURE: This measure is made up of a total of sixteen items, the first nine being scored 2 points for each one correct and the last seven, 1 point for each correct response. Examples of the two-point items are the following:

The child gave a detailed description of how he had used the spending money in the past week (1 point was given for a partial report).
The child had at least once helped to select an article of his clothing and could describe the article and selection.
The child had at least once participated in family talk about the purchase of expensive family items, such as TV sets or furniture, and could name the item.

Examples of the 1-point items are the following:

The child at some time had bought a movie ticket at the ticket window or had used his spending money or earnings to pay for a ticket.
The child had charged some item at a store at least once.
The child was currently saving an amount of money three times that received as spending money in the past week.

RELIABILITY AND VALIDITY: None of the several publications using this measure report any direct reliability or validity data.

BIBLIOGRAPHY:

MARSHALL, H. R. "Differences in Parent and Child Reports of the Child's Experience in the Use of Money," *Journal of Educational Psychology,* 1963, *54*(3), 132–317.

MARSHALL, H. R. "The Relation of Giving Children an Allowance to Children's Money Knowledge and Responsibility and to Other Practices of Parents." *Journal of Genetic Psychology,* 1964, *104,* 35–51.

MARSHALL, H. R., and MAGRUDER, L. "Relations Between Parent Money Education Practices and Children's Knowledge and Use of Money." *Child Development,* 1960, *31,* 253–284.

FINANCIAL KNOWLEDGE TEST

AUTHOR: Helen R. Marshall

AGE: 7 to 12

VARIABLE: Knowledge of use of money

TYPE OF MEASURE: Test, individual or group administration

SOURCE FROM WHICH THE MEASURE MAY BE OBTAINED: Helen R. Marshall, New Mexico State University, Psychology Department, University Park, New Mexico 88070

DESCRIPTION OF MEASURE: The Financial Knowledge Test is a thirteen-item, four-option, multiple-choice test in which the questions center around the relative cost of clothing, food, and cars, insurance and mortgages, and money management. Examples of items are given below:

Which of these makes of cars is the most *expensive when you purchase a 1959 model:* (a) Dodge, (b) Cadillac, (c) Ford, (d) Studebaker?

Which of these clothing "fad" items usually costs the least *money:* (a) *special sweater,* (b) *special hat,* (c) *fancy belt,* (d) *special T-shirt?*

When a family purchases such things as electrical appliances or furniture, which of these four ways is the least *expensive way to pay for the item:* (a) *cash at time of purchase,* (b) *charge to the family account, to be paid for in future months,* (c) *installment payments made monthly for eight months,* (d) *the lay-away plan, or making installments on purchase before receiving the item?*

Which kind of beef costs the most per pound to buy: (a) *hamburger,* (b) *shortrib roast,* (c) *liver,* (d) *steak?*

This test presents a kind of item to which the researcher may wish to add more items to increase the reliability of the measure. The score on the test is the number of items correct.

RELIABILITY AND VALIDITY: None reported.

BIBLIOGRAPHY:

MARSHALL, H. R. "Differences in Parent and Child Reports of the Child's Experience in the Use of Money." *Journal of Educational Psychology,* 1963, *54,* 132–137.

MARSHALL, H. R. "The Relation of Giving Children an Allowance to Children's Money Knowledge and Responsibility and to Other Practices of Parents." *Journal of Genetic Psychology,* 1964, *104,* 35–51.

MARSHALL, H. R., and MAGRUDER, L. "Relations between Parent Money Education Practices and Children's Knowledge and Use of Money." *Child Development,* 1960, *31,* 253–284.

HUNTER SCIENCE ACHIEVEMENT TEST

AUTHORS: Gerald S. Lesser, Fredrick B. Davis, and Lucille Nahemow

AGE: Gifted children 6 and 7 years old

VARIABLE: Achievement in science

TYPE OF MEASURE: Test, group

SOURCE FROM WHICH THE MEASURE MAY BE OBTAINED: See Davis et al., 1959

DESCRIPTION OF MEASURE: The Hunter Science Achievement Test consists of seven subscales (140 multiple-choice and true-false items) which cover the following topics: related to water—its importance in the world, techniques for purification; how it is used for cleaning purposes, forms in which it appears in air; Archimedes Principle; water pressure, seeks its own level, the Cartesian Diver; surface tension, cohesion and adhesion; and related to sound—vibration and transmission.

The raw scores for each of the seven subscales are weighted according to the amount of classroom time devoted to each. The weighted raw scores are then summed to obtain a single, composite science achievement score. Examples of the items follow:

Water is used for (a) growing plants, (b) cooking, (c) washing. Which one of these do you think is most important?

Water is also used for (a) putting out fires, (b) turning waterwheels, (c) quenching our thirsts. Which one of these do you think is most important?

How much of a vegetable is made of water? (a) most of it, (b) about one-half of it, (c) less than one-half of it.

How much of you is water? (a) 50 per cent, (b) 70 per cent, (c) 90 per cent.

RELIABILITY AND VALIDITY: The identical sampling group described in the Hunter Science Aptitude Test applies here. Data on the actual score ranges, the means, and the standard deviations are provided. With one exception (unit II or test II, r of .74), split-half reliabilities for the scales range from .34 to .53. The reliability of the weighted composite science achievement score was .82.

Correlations between achievement test scores and teachers' rankings for ability to learn science were .76 and .79. The correlation between Binet IQ scores and results on the achievement tests was only .21. Though statistically significant in some cases, intercorrelations among the science subtests range from low (r of .18 between tests or units VI and VII) to moderate (r of .54 between units I and III), suggesting that the subscales measured independent functions.

BIBLIOGRAPHY:

LESSER, G. S., DAVIS, F. B., and NAHEMOW, L. "The Identification of Gifted Elementary School Children with Exceptional Scientific Talent." *Educational and Psychological Measurement*, 1962, 22, 349–363.

DAVIS, F. B., FRENCH, E. G., and LESSER, G. S. *Identification of Classroom Behavior of Elementary-School Children Gifted in Five Different Mental Characteristics.* New York: Hunter College, 1959. (Mimeographed, 83 pages)

HUNTER SCIENCE APTITUDE TEST

AUTHORS: Gerald S. Lesser, Fredrick B. Davis, and Lucille Nahemow

AGE: Gifted children 6 and 7 years old

VARIABLE: Scientific aptitude

TYPE OF MEASURE: Objective test questionnaire

SOURCE FROM WHICH THE MEASURE MAY BE OBTAINED: See Davis et al., 1959)

DESCRIPTION OF MEASURE: The Hunter Science Aptitude Test consists of two forms, each with ninety-one items. The items are presented in groups or serial arrangements so that there are twelve series from three to five items each, in both forms of the measure. Each cluster of items refers to some behavior objective, such as ability to recall information or the ability to assign meanings to observations. The test simultaneously assesses prior knowledge and the ability to learn new material.

The method of scoring and administering the test involves testing-teaching. Each item is scored 2, 1, or 0. Items early in each series thus measure information that the child acquired prior to the test situation. The examiner then explains the item. Success on later items in the series requires the subject to understand the explanation given to the previous items in the series, and then to apply the explanation to a new situation. In general, the items included in this test are designed to measure recall of scientific information, ability to assign meanings to observations, ability to apply scientific principles to prediction, and ability to use the scientific method. Samples of the items, expected answers, and scoring are given below:

"What do we call a space where there is nothing, not even air?" Explanation: "A vacuum. It's a	"a vacuum"	2
place with nothing in it, not even air."	"Space," "hold"	0
Show child two pieces of paper. Give child one. "These pieces of paper are exactly the same. Crumple this one into a ball. Now is one paper		
heavier than the other?" Explanation: "The	"No"	2
paper weigh the same amount. The crumpled		
paper weighs the same amount as it did before	"Yes"	0
you crumpled it. It's still the same piece of paper."		

The child does not need to be able to read, and there are no time limits for the measure.

RELIABILITY AND VALIDITY: The two forms of the test were administered to fifty-eight children in the third grade at Hunter College Elementary School before formal science lessons began in the classroom. The children represented a homogeneous middle-class group, with a range of Stanford-Binet IQ scores (1937 Revision) from 136 to 171, with a mean of 150.4. Normative data for the two forms of the test have not been provided.

The authors describe three forms of reliability data. First, the degree of interjudge agreement in categorizing the items as measured by the Coefficient of Concordance (W) was .80. Second, the parallel-forms reliability coefficient of the Hunter Science Aptitude Test was .64. Third, an estimate was made of the reliability of each form of the test separately from the correlation between the parallel forms and their variances. The reliability coefficients were .61 for Form AX and .67 for Form BX.

Three sources of data support the validity of the scale. The principal predictive validity criterion was performance on seven science achievement tests. The correlation of Form AX with the weighted composite science achievement test score administered three to nine months later was .77; that of Form BX was .71. The correlation between scores on the science aptitude test with teachers' rankings on ability to learn science range from .56 to .77 ($p < .01$). Finally, there was a statistically significant difference ($p < .01$) between the extent to which the Hunter Science Aptitude Test and Stanford-Binet Intelligence Quotient predict science achievement. Thus, the correlation between IQ and achievement test scores was only .21.

BIBLIOGRAPHY:

LESSER, G. S., DAVIS, F. B., and NAHEMOW, L. "The Identification of Gifted Elementary School Children with Exceptional Scientific Talent." *Educational and Psychological Measurement*, 1962, 22, 349–363.

DAVIS, F. B., FRENCH, E. G., and LESSER, G. S. *Identification of Classroom Behavior of Elementary-School Children Gifted in Five Different Mental Characteristics*. New York: Hunter College, 1959. (Mimeographed, 83 pages)

MAC LATCHY TEST OF THE PRE-SCHOOL CHILD'S FAMILIARITY WITH MEASUREMENT

AUTHOR: Josephine H. MacLatchy

AGE: Children 3, 4, and 5 years old

VARIABLE: Measurement

TYPE OF MEASURE: Structured interview

SOURCE FROM WHICH THE MEASURE MAY BE OBTAINED: See Spayde (1953)

DESCRIPTION OF MEASURE: This measure was devised to assess the familiarity of the preschool child with measurement, and has seven inclusive topics: time, liquid measure, weight, long measure, groups of like things (dozens and pairs), money, and miscellaneous items. Most emphasis, however, has been placed on time, including such topics as the days of the week, months, seasons, and specific hours. According to MacLatchy, the children's information on the other topics proved to be rather vague (MacLatchy, 1951).

An item from the topic of time follows:

What time of day is it when you get up and eat breakfast? or When is it dark outside? or When do you go to bed?

When do you have lots of time to play? or When do you (or little children) take your nap (their naps)? or (for children who attend kindergarten in the afternoon) When do you come to kindergarten?

What time comes between morning and afternoon? or What do we call the middle of the day? or When does your mother come to take you home from kindergarten?

The items are reportedly placed in descending order of difficulty. Though the test can be administered on a group basis, not more than three children can usually be interviewed in one session. Administration time is at least twenty minutes. The materials necessary and procedural precautions have been outlined by MacLatchy (1950).

RELIABILITY AND VALIDITY: No direct data on reliability and validity are presented.

BIBLIOGRAPHY:

MAC LATCHY, J. H. "The Test of the Pre-school Child's Familiarity with Measurement." *Educational Research Bulletin*, 1950, *XXIX*, 207–208, 222.

MAC LATCHY, J. H. "The Pre-school Child's Familiarity with Measurement." *Education*, 1951, *71*, 479–482.

SPAYDE, P. E. "Kindergarten Children's Familiarity with Measurement." *Educational Research Bulletin*, 1953, *32*, 234–238.

PHYSICAL CAUSALITY TEST

AUTHOR: Rolf E. Muuss

AGE: Fifth and sixth grades

VARIABLE: Knowledge of physical science

TYPE OF MEASURE: Test

SOURCE FROM WHICH THE MEASURE MAY BE OBTAINED: Rolf E. Muuss, Goucher College, Baltimore, Maryland 21204. The author can provide samples at $.50 per test but not quantity orders.

DESCRIPTION OF MEASURE: The Physical Causality Test is available in two forms (A and B) with thirty items in each scale. The test measures awareness as related to causal factors of phenomena, multiple causation, common scientific procedures, the approximate nature of measurement, the approximate nature of predictions, and the provisional character of scientific knowledge.
   Sample items are:

An awareness of factors that cause a phenomenon.   *What could you do to make the water in the air form in drops on the outside of a glass? (a) set a glass of ice water in a very warm room, (b) set a glass of ice water in the refrigerator, (c) set a glass of warm water in a very warm room, (d) set an empty glass in a very warm room, (e) set a glass of hot water in a very cold room.*

An awareness of the multiplicity of factors that cause a phenomenon.   *Not all people require the same number of food calories or food energies each day because: (a) they do not like to eat the same thing, (b) no two people do the same kind of work, (c) some days a person is hungrier than on other days, (d) people burn up different amounts of calories depending whether they are a boy or girl and where they are, (e) people burn up a different amount of calories depending on what they are doing and how much they weigh.*

RELIABILITY AND VALIDITY: The test-retest reliability of the two test forms over a two-week interval is .74 (N = 72). The correlation with intelligence is .45 (N = 116) for Form A and .44 (N = 116) for Form B. Increases in scores occurred from fifth to sixth grades. Children who had undergone a training program of learning social causality appeared better able to solve problems involving an understanding of causalities and probabilities than controls without the special training (Muuss, 1961).

BIBLIOGRAPHY:

MUUSS, R. E. "The Transfer Effect of a Learning Program in Social Causality on an Understanding of Physical Causality." *Journal of Experimental Psychology,* 1961, *29,* 231–247.

PUPIL MUSICAL RATING SCALE

AUTHOR: Robert G. Petzold

AGE: Upper elementary school age

VARIABLE: Musical accomplishment

TYPE OF MEASURE: Rating scale

SOURCE FROM WHICH THE MEASURE MAY BE OBTAINED: See Petzold (1960)

DESCRIPTION OF MEASURE: This twelve-item rating scale is designed for the use of teachers in rating the musical ability of children in grades four through six. The items are designed to measure four aspects of musical ability: general singing ability (six items); rhythmic responsiveness (two items); musical knowledges and skills (two items); and general interest in musical activities (two items). Examples of the items are given below:

General singing ability. *The pupil is able to match individual tones and intervals: always, usually, occasionally, seldom, never.*

Musical knowledges and skills. *When participating in appropriate music reading activities, the pupil's response shows that he is: a leader, capable of much independent music reading; partially independent, voice always moves in direction of notes and is frequently accurate; occasionally able to control the direction of the voice by using notes; seldom is able to react to the notation, learns by rote most of the time; seems to be unaware of the meaning of the notation, cannot differentiate one symbol from another.*

RELIABILITY AND VALIDITY: The coefficient of correlation between scores on this rating scale and the Kwalwasser Music Talent Test, Form B, for 438 fourth and sixth grade children in three schools, by school, was .34, .39 and .34.

BIBLIOGRAPHY:

PETZOLD, R. G. "The Perception of Music Symbols in Music Reading by Normal Children and by Children Gifted Musically." *Journal of Experimental Psychology,* 1960, *28*(4) (June).

SEQUENTIALLY SCALED ACHIEVEMENT TEST

AUTHORS: Richard C. Cox and Glenn T. Graham

AGE: Kindergarten, first and second grades

VARIABLE: Arithmetic

TYPE OF MEASURE: Test

SOURCE FROM WHICH THE MEASURE MAY BE OBTAINED: Learning Research and Development Center, University of Pittsburgh

DESCRIPTION OF MEASURE: The test is based on the assumption that a specific score indicates whether a student has mastered specified behaviors. The authors extend the concept of reproducibility to achievement testing. Thus, if the behaviors tested can be arranged sequentially, and the tests are scalable, a score of 4 means that S has correctly answered items 1, 2, 3, and four, and no items beyond. The highest score would be similar to the Binet basal score, and would tell the teacher those behaviors the student has mastered and those he has not. These authors attempt to develop such a test. The test was, however, administered to the kindergarten, first, and second grade (Cox and Graham, 1966, p. 5).

RELIABILITY AND VALIDITY: The authors use the Scalogram Analysis by Guttmann in the development of the achievement test. They derive a coefficient of reproducibility that indicates how well an individual's response pattern can be reproduced by knowing his total score. A revised form of the achievement test was administered to kindergarten, first-, and second-grade children. The response pattern yielded a reproducibility coefficient of .970, a scalability coefficient of .792.

BIBLIOGRAPHY:

COX, R. C., and GRAHAM, G. T. "The Development of a Sequentially Scaled Achievement Test." Presentation at the American Educational Research Association, Annual Convention, Chicago, Ill., February, 1966.

TONAL CONFIGURATION TEST

AUTHOR: Robert G. Petzold

AGE: Upper elementary age

VARIABLE: Perception of music symbols

TYPE OF MEASURE: Performance test, individually administered

SOURCE FROM WHICH THE MEASURE MAY BE OBTAINED: See Petzold (1960)

DESCRIPTION OF MEASURE: The author began with an analysis of 326 songs randomly selected from eighteen songbooks used in grades three through six. In this way he identified 558 tonal configurations, of which he selected ten of the most common to make up the ten items of the test. The instructions for the test are taped, recorded, and then played back to the subjects, and their responses are recorded on a second tape recorder. The subject is first shown the stimulus card on which the first item is presented and he is given the starting pitch for that configuration. He sings his response to the visual presentation. The subject is next given the visual configuration combined with an aural presentation (using the piano as the instrument), after which the subject sings what he has heard while looking at the visual configuration. This procedure is followed for the ten items, after which the items are presented a second and third time, but in randomized order. An item is scored correct if the correct response has occurred on two of the three trials. The item is wrong if it is sung incorrectly or if the subject does not try the complete item.

RELIABILITY AND VALIDITY: The test was given to eighty-nine children chosen at random from fourth-, fifth-, and sixth-grade populations. The mean scores for the three grades were not significantly different, although the differences were in the expected direction and N was small (N = 30, 28, 31, respectively, fourth, fifth, and sixth grades). The subjects came from three different schools, and the difference between schools was significant at the .05 level. A sex difference in scores favored the girls but was not significant with this N.

When the configurations were presented aurally there were no significant differences between the sexes or among the different grade levels or different schools. In general the subjects had higher mean scores on the aural part of the test than they did on the visual part. The correlation between the visual and aural scores for all grades (N = 89) was .64.

BIBLIOGRAPHY:

PETZOLD, R. G. "The Perception of Music Symbols in Music Reading by Normal Children and by Children Gifted Musically." *Journal of Experimental Education*, 1960, 28(4) (June).

Group 1-d

Cognitive Style and
Cognitive Processes

CHILDREN'S REACTIVE CURIOSITY SCALE

AUTHORS: R. K. Penney and B. McCann

AGE: Grades four, five, and six

VARIABLE: Reactive curiosity

TYPE OF MEASURE: Group-administered questionnaire

SOURCE FROM WHICH THE MEASURE MAY BE OBTAINED: See Penney and McCann (1964)

DESCRIPTION OF MEASURE: The Children's Reactive Curiosity Scale consists of ninety items that attempt to test the manner in which the child reacts to the curiosity he exhibits toward his environment. The items of the scale, which are orally administered on a group basis, require the child to respond to each one as true or false. Half the items indicate reactive curiosity if answered as true; the remainder indicate this trait if answered as false. In addition to the ninety items, ten items from the lie portion of the Children's Manifest Anxiety Scale constitute an integral part of the scale. Thus, a scorer can determine the degree of falsification by summing the number of lie items answered as true. In the scale proper, the appropriate scoring for each item and the L items are clearly indicated. Samples of the items from the scale are given below.

I almost always play with children my own age.
Sometimes it is fun to be a little bit scared.
I like arithmetic.

The scale has been administered to 433 children in grades four, five, and six from seventeen classes in two elementary schools within the state of Texas.

RELIABILITY AND VALIDITY: The test-retest reliability coefficients for the CRC scale over a two-week period range from .65 to .78 for the different sex by grade classifications. At all grade levels, girls scored higher than boys on the CRC scale. Over the same interval of time, test-retest reliability coefficients for the L scale range between .74 to .85 for the different sex by grade classifications. Test-retest correlation coefficients based on the 40 items that discriminate between extreme groups at statistically significant levels, however, range between .67 and .83 for boys and .80 and .91 for girls.

The authors contend that the lack of relationship between reactive curiosity, falsification, and intelligence (as measured by the California Mental Maturity Scale) constitutes partial evidence for discriminant validation. As a measure of concurrent validity, a positive and significant relationship was found between curiosity and originality for sixth grade children (correlation coefficient was between .25 and .32) but not for fourth-grade pupils (correlation coefficients between —.06 and .09). The measure of originality was Guilford's Unusual Uses Test.

BIBLIOGRAPHY:

PENNEY, R. K., and MC CANN, B. "The Children's Reactive Curiosity Scale." *Psychological Reports*, 1964, *15*, 323–334.

CONCEPTUAL STYLE TEST

AUTHOR: Jerome Kagan et al.

AGE: Elementary school children

VARIABLE: Style of conceptualization

TYPE OF MEASURE: Individually administered picture test

SOURCE FROM WHICH THE MEASURE MAY BE OBTAINED: See Kagan et al. (1963) and Kagan, et al. (1964) for sample items

DESCRIPTION OF MEASURE: This test consists of thirty sets of pictures, each set containing three objects or people or combinations of objects and people. One item, for example, shows a wrist watch, a man, and a ruler. The child is asked to pick out two pictures that are alike or go together in some way (Kagan et al., 1964) and state the basis for his grouping. The stimuli are designed to elicit the two major concept classes of analytic and relational concepts, and, to a lesser extent, inferential-categorical concepts. Analytic concepts are manifested by pairings based on similarity in some objective attribute that is a differentiated part of the total stimulus. Examples of this category are,

The watch and ruler have numbers
The zebra and shirt have stripes
The house and pipe have smoke coming out
People with hats on
Animals with tongues out

The basis of similarity in these examples is in a component part of the total stimulus (e.g., numbers, stripes, smoke, hats, tongues). The relational category involves pairings based on a functional relationship between two stimuli. Examples of relational concepts are,

The man wears the watch
The matches light the pipe
The hat goes on the man
The dog and cat play together

The inferential-categorical class includes pairings based on similarity in some inferred quality or involves a language convention. Examples of inferential concepts are (Kagan et al., 1964):

Inanimate objects
Articles of clothing
Human beings

RELIABILITY AND VALIDITY: The number of analytic responses tends to increase with age, for both boys and girls, although the progression is somewhat erratic for boys. There is moderate stability over a year and increasing stability of an analytic attitude with age. The corrected split-half reliability coefficient (N = 300) in one study was .94 (Kagan et al., 1963). According to Kagan et al. (1964), highly analytic children on the thirty-item CST, as compared with nonanalytic children, produce more differentiated ink blot responses; attach new verbal responses to component parts of a geometric design rather than to its most salient aspect; inhibit impulsive motor behavior.

BIBLIOGRAPHY:

KAGAN, J., MOSS, H. A., and SIEGEL, I. E. "Psychological Significance of Styles of Conceptualization." *Monographs of the Society for Research in Child Development,* 1963, *28* (Ser. No. 86, Whole No. 2), 73–112.

KAGAN, J., ET AL., "Information Processing in the Child." *Psychological Monographs,* 1964, *78,* No. 1 (Whole No. 578).

LEE, L. C., KAGAN, J., and RABSON, A. "The Influence of a Preference for Analytic Categorization upon Concept Acquisition." *Child Development,* 1963, *34,* 433–442.

KAGAN, J. "Reflection-Impulsivity and Reading Ability in Primary Grade Children." *Child Development,* 1965, *36,* 609–628.

DEDUCTIVE REASONING TEST

AUTHOR: Bernard Kutner

AGE: Second grade children

VARIABLE: Cognition

TYPE OF MEASURE: Test

SOURCE FROM WHICH THE MEASURE MAY BE OBTAINED: See Kutner (1958)

DESCRIPTION OF MEASURE: The Deductive Reasoning Test (DRT) consists of nine items—an introductory item to familiarize the subject with the nature of the task, and eight test items. The introductory item and two test items follow:

Electric lights never twinkle. This light is twinkling. Is it an electric light? Why?
It runs but it has no feet; it roars but it has no voice. What is it? Why?
Jane is taller than Jill. Mary is shorter than Jill. Who is the tallest of all?

The author has enumerated the items indicative of the type of problem involved.

RELIABILITY AND VALIDITY: Since the sample was the identical one involved in Kutner's Ethnic Attitude Test the comments referring to this group also apply here. As in the EAT, also, no statistics on reliability have been reported for the DRT. A number of findings, however, point to significant differences between the problem solving approaches of prejudiced and non-prejudiced children. Since these are in the expected direction, the data provide some construct validity for the DRT. Illustrations of these findings follow: (1) The more prejudiced children had much more difficulty in reaching valid conclusions on ambiguous problems than did the less prejudiced students. (2) Less prejudiced children tended to be more flexible in their problem solving. (3) Less prejudiced children more freely admitted ignorance.

BIBLIOGRAPHY:

KUTNER, B. "Patterns of Mental Functioning Associated with Prejudice in Children." *Psychological Monographs,* 1958, 72, 7 (Whole No. 460).

FRUIT DISTRACTION TEST

AUTHOR: Sebastiano Santostefano

AGE: 6 to 13

VARIABLE: Flexibility in cognitive control

TYPE OF MEASURE: Individually administered performance test

SOURCE FROM WHICH THE MEASURE MAY BE OBTAINED: See Santostefano (1964)

DESCRIPTION OF MEASURE: The Fruit Distraction Test measures the degree to which an individual is able to continue concentrating on a central task in the face of intruding stimuli. The test itself consists of two 10 × 15 inch cards, each of which contains fifty drawings of several kinds of fruit in various colors. Card I includes these drawings only; Card II also includes dissimilar non-fruit objects consisting of achromatic line drawings that serve as intruding distractors or stimuli. Before administering the test individually to the subject, preliminary checks are made to determine if he can name the fruits and the colors. Subsequently, his task on each card is to name the fruit as rapidly as possible without skipping. In the last part of the test, the subject is asked for his recall of distracting objects on card II.

The test yields three measures: reading time distractibility score (time to read card 2 minus card 1); reading errors distractibility score (total reading errors with card 2 minus total reading errors with card 1); and the number of intrusive stimuli recalled (Santostefano, 1964).

RELIABILITY AND VALIDITY: Santostefano (1964) found significant differences among three groups (brain damaged children, orphaned children, and public school children) on the variable of reading time differences between "normal" and "distracting" conditions. Differences in number of reading errors between the normal and distracting conditions were not significant for the three groups of children, although they were in the same direction as reading *time* differences. No significant differences were found between the groups on the number of "intrusive object" recalls. Scores on this measure were not significantly related to intelligence.

BIBLIOGRAPHY:

SANTOSTEFANO, S. "Cognitive Controls and Exceptional States in Children." *Journal of Clinical Psychology*, 1964, *20*, 213–218.

GENERALIZATION-DISCRIMINATION TEST

AUTHOR: Perry London

AGE: 4 to 13

VARIABLE: Generalization behavior

TYPE OF MEASURE: Test, individually administered

SOURCE FROM WHICH THE MEASURE MAY BE OBTAINED: See London (1958)

DESCRIPTION OF MEASURE: The test consists of six separate discrimination tests, of which three may be described as "social" tasks and the other three as "non-social." Each item or task consists of a series of fifteen cards on which are shown figures changing gradually over fifteen steps from one percept to another. In the first social task, for example, an ogre holding a club changes to a Santa Claus holding a bag of toys. In the other social tasks, a young man in a suit changes to a young woman, and a little girl standing by a table changes into a cocker spaniel. The three nonsocial tasks show a triangle changing into a circle, a large rectangle changing into a small one, and a blue square changing into a green square. For each task, there is a training set of five cards in which the first and last of the five cards are identical with cards 1 and 15 of the experimental set. The subject's score on each test is the number of the card on which he first reported the difference between that card and the number 1 card. Three scores are derived from the measure: an overall score, being an average score for all six tasks; a social score, the average for the three social tasks, and a nonsocial score, the average for the three nonsocial tasks.

RELIABILITY AND VALIDITY: Thirty normal boys ranging in age from 7 to 13 were retested at intervals from five to eight days. The test-retest correlations were .79 for the social tasks, .90 for the nonsocial tests, and .82 for the overall score.

London (1958) found a significant relationship between age and mean score on this measure. Maladjusted children, as compared with normal children, had higher means on the overall tests and also on the social tests and had significantly higher variances on the overall, the social, and the nonsocial sections of the test. London found further that when his normal and maladjusted groups were divided into subgroups with age spans 4 to 6, 7 to 9, and 10 to 12, the mean differences were considerably larger for the social than for the nonsocial tests, with the maladjusted having consistently higher scores.

BIBLIOGRAPHY:

LONDON, P. "Developmental Aspects of Discrimination in Relation to Adjustment." *Genetic Psychology Monographs,* Teachers College, Columbia University, 1958, 57, 293–336.

MINNICH, R. E., and LONDON, P. "Effects of Differential Instructions and Anxiety Level on Discrimination Learning, Madigan Army Hospital, Tacoma, Washington." *The Journal of Genetic Psychology,* 1959, 95, 283–292.

MATCHING FAMILIAR FIGURES

AUTHOR: Jerome Kagan, et al.

AGE: Pre-school through elementary

VARIABLE: Reflection over alternative-solution hypothesis

TYPE OF MEASURE: Individual Picture Performance Test

SOURCE FROM WHICH THE MEASURE MAY BE OBTAINED: Jerome Kagan, Harvard University, William James Hall, Cambridge, Massachusetts 02138. Cost: $5.00

DESCRIPTION OF MEASURE: This test is designed to measure along the reflection-impulsivity dimensions the extent to which a child takes time to assess the validity of the hypothesis he makes in problem solving. The measure consists of twelve items plus two practice items. Each item is made up of two sheets, one of which has a picture of one object, and the other has six objects resembling the stimulus object, but differing in various detailed ways. The subject is to match the stimulus with the correct object on the second sheet. Examples of items include a house, scissors, telephone, lamp, ship, etc., with a stimulus figure and six options, one of which is exactly like the stimulus figure. Scores are obtained on response time to final selection, total errors, and number of items correct on first choice.

RELIABILITY AND VALIDITY: The MFF response times correlated .44 and .34 with response time of two forms of a design recall test, which is also considered by the author to be a measure of reflection. The MFF was administered a year later than the two design recall tests. The error scores were not correlated significantly between MFF and the design recall test.

BIBLIOGRAPHY:

KAGAN, J., ROSMAN, B. L., DAY, D., ALBERT, J., and PHILLIPS, W. "Information Processing in the Child." *Psychological Monographs,* 1964, *78,* No. 1 (Whole No. 578).

MAW AND MAW CURIOSITY SCALE FOR ELEMENTARY SCHOOL CHILDREN

AUTHORS: Wallace H. Maw and Ethel W. Maw

AGE: Fifth grade

VARIABLE: Curiosity

TYPE OF MEASURE: Test

SOURCE FROM WHICH THE MEASURE MAY BE OBTAINED: U.S. Office of Education, Maw and Maw (1964), Project No. 801, SAE 8519

DESCRIPTION OF MEASURE: The Maw and Maw Curiosity Scale is based on the thesis that differences in curiosity could partially account for the differences in the amount of general information possessed by children of the same tested intelligence. The authors define curiosity as behavior consisting of four types of activity: exploratory and manipulative reactions to strange and incongruous elements in the environment; a desire for additional knowledge about the self and environment; a search for new experiences; and a persistence in searching and exploring stimuli because of an urge for additional knowledge (Maw and Maw, 1964). The items of the scales are predicated upon these definitions.

The test includes two batteries, each with a number of subtests. The batteries, together with the concept each test is thought to measure, consist of the following: Battery A includes What Would You Do (preferred behavior); Which Saying Do You Believe (conservatism, caution); Hidden Pictures (persistence, attention); Code (persistence, desire to know, attention). Battery B includes What Do You Know (breadth of information); Foolish Sayings (attention, detection of absurdities); Path Puzzles (persistence, desire to know, attention); and Chinese Musical Instrument (questions about a picture). The two independently administered tests were the Which to Discuss test, consisting of geometric designs varying in balance and familiarity, and the Zoo Story test involving true and false questions about a story giving little-known facts about animals. Details for each subtest are provided in the individual description of the subscales. Each battery requires only about forty-five minutes to administer, but time estimates necessary to complete each subscale do not appear to be available. The authors provide a comprehensive bibliography of the literature on curiosity and related matters.

RELIABILITY AND VALIDITY: The test-retest reliabilities for Battery A and Battery B respectively were .52 and .66. Validating evidence for the scale comes from a number of sources. Composite scores on Batteries A and B correlated positively and significantly with external criteria of curiosity, as determined by a combination of teacher, peer, and self-judgments of curiosity. However, these correlations were too low to justify the use of either battery alone as a predictor of composite scores. A number of subscales yielded significant differences between high- and low-curiosity groups in the predicted direction. The present forms of the Maw and Maw Curiosity Scale were established after two preliminary studies in which ineffective tests were eliminated, new ones were developed, and others were modified.

The use of the scale may perhaps be limited because the normative group consisted solely of fifth-grade children. A rather large proportion of the paternal occupations, moreover, were in the highly skilled or professional categories.

BIBLIOGRAPHY:

MAW, W. H., and MAW, E. W. *An Exploratory Study into the Measurement of Curiosity in Elementary School Children*. Washington, D.C.: U. S. Office of Education, 1964.

MAW, W. H., and MAW, E. W. "The Differences between the Scores of Children with High Curiosity and Low Curiosity on a Test of General Information." *Journal of Educational Research*, 1963, *57*, 76–79.

MAW, W. H., and MAW, E. W. "Children's Curiosity as an Aspect of Reading Comprehension." *The Reading Teacher*, 1962, *15*, 236–40.

MAW, W. H., and MAW, E. W. "Establishing Criteria for Evaluating Measures of Curiosity." *Journal of Experimental Education*, 1961, *29*, 299–306.

MAW, W. H., and MAW, E. W. "Information Recognition by Children with High and Low Curiosity." *Educational Research Bulletin*, 1961, *40*, 197–201.

MAW, W. H., and MAW, E. W. "Nonhomeostatic Experiences as Stimuli of Children with High Curiosity." *California Journal of Educational Research*, 1961, *12*, 57–61.

MAW, W. H., and MAW, E. W. "The Relationships between Curiosity and Scores on a Test of General Information." *Journal of the Association for Research in Growth Relationships*, 1960, *2*, 27–33.

MAW AND MAW CURIOSITY SCALE FOR ELEMENTARY SCHOOL CHILDREN—Picture and Story Satisfaction Items

AUTHORS: Wallace H. Maw and Ethel W. Maw

AGE: Fifth grade

VARIABLE: Curiosity

TYPE OF MEASURE: Test, Projective

SOURCE FROM WHICH THE MEASURE MAY BE OBTAINED: U.S. Office of Education, Maw and Maw (1964), Project No. 801, SAE 8519

DESCRIPTION OF MEASURE: The picture-and-story-satisfaction items include a train story and a picture of a Chinese Musical Instrument. The main objective of the test is to elicit questions from the children that show a desire for additional information. Scoring is based on the number of questions asked and the number of independent ideas expressed in the questions. The independent ideas are scored on a qualitative basis. An example of one independent idea on the train story is: "Did anyone die? How many people died?" An illustration of two independent ideas on the same story is: " 'What happened to the signal lights?' and 'Did the train reach the station on time?' "

In a preliminary study, a record was also made of the amount of time each child spent in writing questions. By reducing the items from several to these two, however, the average increase in the number of questions asked was 100 per cent.

RELIABILITY AND VALIDITY: In general, the scores of the higher-curiosity groups exceeded those of the lower-curiosity groups on both the number of ideas and independent ideas, but the differences were slight and not statistically significant. On the Picture Story, however, the number of questions asked by the upper third of the higher-curiosity group did exceed those of the lower third of the lower-curiosity group (F of 2.37, p < .05). Statistically significant differences emerged that favored girls on both the productivity of questions asked and the number of independent ideas expressed.

Test-retest reliabilities were computed separately for the Musical Instrument and the Train Story but solely on the basis of the number of questions asked. The coefficients of reliability were respectively .66 and .75 based on an interval of one week between test administrations (Maw and Maw, 1964).

BIBLIOGRAPHY:

MAW, W. H., and MAW, E. W. *An Exploratory Study into the Measurement of Curiosity in Elementary School Children.* Washington, D.C.: U.S. Office of Education, 1964.

MAW, W. H., and MAW, E. W. "Children's Curiosity as an Aspect of Reading Comprehension." *The Reading Teacher,* 1962, *15,* 236–40.

MAW, W. H., and MAW, E. W. "Establishing Criteria for Evaluating Measures of Curiosity." *Journal of Experimental Education,* 1961, *29,* 299–306.

MAW, W. H., and MAW, E. W. "Information Recognition by Children with High and Low Curiosity." *Educational Research Bulletin,* 1961, *40,* 197–201.

MAW, W. H., and MAW, E. W. "Nonhomeostatic Experiences as Stimuli of Children with High Curiosity." *California Journal of Educational Research,* 1961, *12,* 57–61.

MAW, W. H., and MAW, E. W. "The Relationship between Curiosity and Scores on a Test of General Information." *Journal of the Association for Research in Growth Relationships,* 1960, *2,* 27–33.

MAW AND MAW CURIOSITY SCALE FOR ELEMENTARY SCHOOL CHILDREN—Code Test (Battery A)

AUTHORS: Wallace H. Maw and Ethel W. Maw

AGE: Fifth grade

VARIABLE: Curiosity

TYPE OF MEASURE: Test

SOURCE FROM WHICH THE MEASURE MAY BE OBTAINED: U.S. Office of Education, Maw and Maw (1964), Project No. 801, SAE 8519

DESCRIPTION OF MEASURE: The Code Test is another measure of preference for the unusual and unfamiliar. Each code consists of three types of letters: letters from the Roman alphabet, letters in odd positions, and letters from the ancient Ethiopian alphabet. The child's task is to decode the messages.

Two different scoring systems may apply. In one system the authors recommend a score of 1 for each correct letter of the Roman alphabet, a score of 2 for each correct letter in an odd position, and a score of 3 for each correct letter in the ancient Ethiopian alphabet. The solutions to the codes reveal thirty letters in the Roman alphabet, sixty-seven letters in odd positions, and twenty-three letters in the ancient Ethiopian alphabet. Consequently, the range in scores for letters alone is from 0 to 233. The authors also recommend additional credit for each correct word and still more credit for each correct message. Since there are thirty-four words and five messages, 39 additional credits are possible. Under this second scoring system, the scores may range between 0 and 272.

RELIABILITY AND VALIDITY: Statistically significant differences between higher- and lower-curiosity groups occurred in a one-tailed test. These applied to both high and low thirds and high and low halves on external indices of curiosity. Significant sex differences in favor of girls also emerged. Test-retest reliability over a one-week interval was .49 (Maw and Maw, 1964).

BIBLIOGRAPHY:

MAW, W. H., and MAW, E. W. *An Exploratory Study into the Measurement of Curiosity in Elementary School Children.* Washington, D.C.: U.S. Office of Education, 1964.

MAW, W. H., and MAW, E. W. "Children's Curiosity as an Aspect of Reading Comprehension." *The Reading Teacher,* 1962, *15,* 236–40.

MAW, W. H., and MAW, E. W. "Establishing Criteria for Evaluating Measures of Curiosity." *Journal of Experimental Education,* 1961, *29,* 299–306.

MAW, W. H., and MAW, E. W. "Information Recognition by Children with High and Low Curiosity." *Educational Research Bulletin,* 1961, *40,* 197–201.

MAW, W. H., and MAW, E. W. "Nonhomeostatic Experiences as Stimuli of Children with High Curiosity." *California Journal of Educational Research,* 1961, *12,* 57–61.

MAW, W. H., and MAW, E. W. "The Relationships between Curiosity and Scores on a Test of General Information." *Journal of the Association for Research in Growth Relationships,* 1960, *2,* 27–33.

MAW AND MAW CURIOSITY SCALE FOR ELEMENTARY SCHOOL CHILDREN—Foolish Sayings Test (Battery B)

AUTHORS: Wallace H. Maw and Ethel W. Maw

AGE: Fifth grade

VARIABLE: Curiosity

TYPE OF MEASURE: Test

SOURCE FROM WHICH THE MEASURE MAY BE OBTAINED: U.S. Office of Education, Maw and Maw (1964), Project No. 801, SAE 8519

DESCRIPTION OF MEASURE: The test reportedly measures the ability to detect verbal absurdities. The value of the test is based on the premise that children of high curiosity are more aware of their environments than are low-curiosity children, and they should consequently recognize absurdities more readily than low-curiosity children. The test consists of twenty-two items. Some of the items are common absurdities, others are straightforward statements. The children are told to mark the foolish statements with "X" and those that are not foolish with "C." The score is the number of correct items. An example of a foolish saying follows:

Bob said to Jack, "I'll meet you at the lodge. If I get there first, I'll make a chalk mark on the door. If you get there first, rub it out."

RELIABILITY AND VALIDITY: The test-retest reliability for the scale over a one-week interval was .58. Validity rested on several findings. (1) The mean scores of high-curiosity groups were significantly higher than those of low-curiosity groups. These differences in means held for comparisons between upper and lower thirds and higher and low halves. (2) The results of the final study were consistent with the data of the preliminary investigation. (3) Though no data are presented, the authors state that all the subscales were revised on the basis of discriminating items. On this scale, the number of items was reduced from fifty-two to twenty-two (Maw and Maw, 1964).

BIBLIOGRAPHY:

MAW, W. H., and MAW, E. W. *An Exploratory Study into the Measurement of Curiosity in Elementary School Children.* Washington, D.C.: U.S. Office of Education, 1964.

MAW, W. H., and MAW, E. W. "The Differences between the Scores of Children with High Curiosity and Low Curiosity on a Test of General Information." *Journal of Educational Research,* 1963, *57,* 76–79.

MAW, W. H., and MAW, E. W. "Children's Curiosity as an Aspect of Reading Comprehension." *The Reading Teacher,* 1962, *15,* 236–40.

MAW, W. H., and MAW, E. W. "Establishing Criteria for Evaluating Measures of Curiosity." *Journal of Experimental Education,* 1961, *29,* 299–306.

MAW, W. H., and MAW, E. W. "Information Recognition by Children with High and Low Curiosity." *Educational Research Bulletin,* 1961, *40,* 197–201.

MAW, W. H., and MAW, E. W. "Nonhomeostatic Experiences as Stimuli of Children with High Curiosity." *California Journal of Educational Research,* 1961, *12,* 57–61.

MAW, W. H., and MAW, E. W. "The Relationships between Curiosity and Scores on a Test of General Information." *Journal of the Association for Research in Growth Relationships,* 1960, *2,* 27–33.

MAW AND MAW CURIOSITY SCALE FOR ELEMENTARY SCHOOL CHILDREN—Hidden Pictures Test (Battery A)

AUTHORS: Wallace H. Maw and Ethel W. Maw

AGE: Fifth grade

VARIABLE: Curiosity

TYPE OF MEASURE: Test

SOURCE FROM WHICH THE MEASURE MAY BE OBTAINED: U.S. Office of Education, Maw and Maw (1964), Project No. 801, SAE 8519

DESCRIPTION OF MEASURE: In its final form, this test consists of two pictures, the Jungle and Arrowhead. These hidden picture items are based on the premise that curiosity in children is related to their persistence in examining and exploring stimuli, in order to know more about them. The jungle picture is a scene depicting animals so blended with their natural habitat that it is difficult to discern them. The children are asked to circle each wild animal they see. On the arrowhead picture, the children are asked to circle all the Indian arrowheads they perceive. The papers are then scored by assigning one point for each object correctly circled and by subtracting a point for each incorrect circle.

RELIABILITY AND VALIDITY: No significant differences between the scores of high- and low-curiosity groups were found. Boys' mean scores were significantly higher on the arrowhead picture. The test-retest reliability coefficient for the scale over an interval of one week was .70 (Maw and Maw, 1964).

BIBLIOGRAPHY:

MAW, W. H., and MAW, E. W. *An Exploratory Study into the Measurement of Curiosity in Elementary School Children.* Washington, D.C.: U.S. Office of Education, 1964.

MAW, W. H., and MAW, E. W. "Children's Curiosity as an Aspect of Reading Comprehension." *The Reading Teacher,* 1962, *15,* 236–40.

MAW, W. H., and MAW, E. W. "Establishing Criteria for Evaluating Measures of Curiosity." *Journal of Experimental Education,* 1961, *29,* 299–306.

MAW, W. H., and MAW, E. W. "Information Recognition by Children with High and Low Curiosity." *Educational Research Bulletin,* 1961, *40,* 197–201.

MAW, W. H., and MAW, E. W. "Nonhomeostatic Experiences as Stimuli of Children with High Curiosity." *California Journal of Educational Research,* 1961, *12,* 57–61.

MAW, W. H., and MAW, E. W. "The Relationship between Curiosity and Scores on a Test of General Information." *Journal of the Association for Research in Growth Relationships,* 1960, *2,* 27–33.

MAW AND MAW CURIOSITY SCALE FOR ELEMENTARY SCHOOL CHILDREN—Path Puzzles Test (Battery B)

AUTHORS: Wallace H. Maw and Ethel W. Maw

AGE: Fifth grade

VARIABLE: Curiosity

TYPE OF MEASURE: Test

SOURCE FROM WHICH THE MEASURE MAY BE OBTAINED: U.S. Office of Education, Maw and Maw (1964), Project No. 801, SAE 8519

DESCRIPTION OF MEASURE: The test is based on the thesis that peristence in seeking information is an element of curiosity. The scale consists of ten items that require the child to trace a path through a maze of numbers in order to discover whether he has solved the riddle correctly. Because of the time necessary for the children to complete the path puzzles, the test is administered in two parts, with five items in each section.

A sample item, for which the solution is the word "air," is given below in its entirety with its solution (Maw and Maw, 1964).

"A house full, a yard full,
but you can't get a spoonful."
What is it? ———

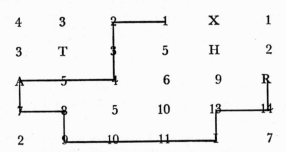

Explicit directions for scoring are not evident. Since the correctness of the paths can be determined objectively, scoring the scale should not prove difficult.

RELIABILITY AND VALIDITY: The test-retest reliability coefficient for the Path Puzzles Test over an interval of one week was .35. On two different samples, high-curiosity groups exhibited statistically significant higher scores than low-curiosity groups.

BIBLIOGRAPHY:

MAW, W. H., and MAW, E. W. *An Exploratory Study into the Measurement of Curiosity in Elementary School Children.* Washington, D.C.: U.S. Office of Education, 1964.

MAW, W. H., and MAW, E. W. "Children's Curiosity as an Aspect of Reading Comprehension." *The Reading Teacher*, 1962, *15*, 236–40.

MAW, W. H., and MAW, E. W. "Establishing Criteria for Evaluating Measures of Curiosity." *Journal of Experimental Education*, 1961, *29*, 299–306.

MAW, W. H., and MAW, E. W. "Information Recognition by Children with High and Low Curiosity." *Educational Research Bulletin*, 1961, *40*, 197–201.

MAW, W. H., and MAW, E. W. "Nonhomeostatic Experiences as Stimuli of Children with High Curiosity." *California Journal of Educational Research*, 1961, *12*, 57–61.

MAW, W. H., and MAW, E. W. "The Relationships between Curiosity and Scores on a Test of General Information." *Journal of the Association for Research in Growth Relationships*, 1960, *2*, 27–33.

MAW AND MAW CURIOSITY SCALE FOR ELEMENTARY SCHOOL CHILDREN—The-Trip-to-the-Zoo Test (Independent Test)

AUTHORS: Wallace H. Maw and Ethel W. Maw

AGE: Fifth grade

VARIABLE: Curiosity

TYPE OF MEASURE: Test

SOURCE FROM WHICH THE MEASURE MAY BE OBTAINED: U.S. Office of Education, Maw and Maw (1964), Project No. 801, SAE 8519

DESCRIPTION OF MEASURE: The-Trip-to-the-Zoo Test is administered in two parts. In the first section, a story filled with little-known facts about animals is read aloud to the children as a group. At the time of the reading, the children also have a copy of the story at their desks. After an interval of time the children are administered a test of forty true and false items testing their recall of facts contained in the story. The score is simply the number of correct responses. Typical of the items are the following (Maw and Maw, 1964):

The zoo-keeper has to give prairie dogs a lot of water or they will die.
Giraffes "talk" with their tails.

The test assumes that children of higher curiosity attend more closely to unusual information and are more likely to recognize statements based on such information when they later encounter them (Maw and Maw, 1964, p. 78).

RELIABILITY AND VALIDITY: Test-retest reliability was .75. Highly significant differences between criterion groups in favor of the highly curious emerged (p < .05 on a one-tail t test for significance). There were significant differences between the means for sex groups (Maw and Maw, 1964).

BIBLIOGRAPHY:

MAW, W. H., and MAW, E. W. *An Exploratory Study into the Measurement of Curiosity in Elementary School Children,* Washington, D.C.: U.S. Office of Education, 1964.

MAW, W. H., and MAW, E. W. "Children's Curiosity as an Aspect of Reading Comprehension." *The Reading Teacher,* 1962, *15,* 236–40.

MAW, W. H., and MAW, E. W. "Establishing Criteria for Evaluating Measures of Curiosity." *Journal of Experimental Education,* 1961, *29,* 299–306.

MAW, W. H., and MAW, E. W. "Information Recognition by Children with High and Low Curiosity." *Educational Research Bulletin,* 1961, *40,* 197–201.

MAW AND MAW CURIOSITY SCALE FOR ELEMENTARY SCHOOL CHILDREN—What Do You Know Test

AUTHORS: Wallace H. Maw and Ethel W. Maw

AGE: Fifth grade

VARIABLE: Curiosity

TYPE OF MEASURE: Test

SOURCE FROM WHICH THE MEASURE MAY BE OBTAINED: U.S. Office of Education, Maw and Maw (1964), Project No. 801, SAE 8519

DESCRIPTION OF MEASURE: The use of general-information items is based upon the assumption that one who is curious about his environment will have gathered a larger store of general knowledge than will one who is not curious, although the tested intelligence of the two may be the same.

The items for this general-information test were written on topics selected at random from the World Book Encyclopedia. Compton's Encyclopedia, Collier's Encyclopedia, and Junior Britannica were then checked to see if the information necessary for the correct answer to each item were contained in each. Items that did not appear in all four encyclopedias were eliminated. The test, which is self-administering, consists of forty-six multiple-choice items. The following item is typical of those used (Maw and Maw, 1964).

Kremlin is: *the fortified part of a Russian City, the place where the American Congress meets, a stiff material to make shirts stand out, a book of fairy stories.*

The score consists of the number of correct items.

RELIABILITY AND VALIDITY: The mean score of the higher-curiosity group, as measured by a one-tailed t test (t of 1.74) was significantly higher with $p < .05$. As is true for all the subscales of the two Maw and Maw curiosity batteries, the criterion groups of curiosity were selected by three methods: teacher ratings, peer ratings, and self-ratings. In the first measure, teachers of seven classes ranked their children on two separate occasions over a period of eight weeks. A mean r of .77 was obtained. In the peer ratings, scores children received by one half of the class were compared with their scores on the remaining portion. The mean rank correlation coefficient was .45. In the self-ratings, the split-half coefficient by the Spearman-Brown formula was .91. These validating data are presented in detail (Maw and Maw, 1964).

A test-retest reliability coefficient over an interval of a week was .77 ($N = 164$).

BIBLIOGRAPHY:

MAW, W. H., and MAW, E. W. *An Exploratory Study into the Measurement of Curiosity in Elementary School Children.* Washington, D.C.: U.S. Office of Education, 1964.

MAW, W. H., and MAW, E. W. "The Differences between the Scores of Children with High Curiosity and Low Curiosity on a Test of General Information." *Journal of Educational Research*, 1963, *57*, 76–79.

MAW, W. H., and MAW, E. W. "Children's Curiosity as an Aspect of Reading Comprehension." *The Reading Teacher*, 1962, *15*, 236–40.

MAW, W. H., and MAW, E. W. "Establishing Criteria for Evaluating Measures of Curiosity." *Journal of Experimental Education*, 1961, *29*, 299–306.

MAW, W. H., and MAW, E. W. "Information Recognition by Children with High and Low Curiosity." *Educational Research Bulletin*, 1961, *40*, 197–201.

MAW, W. H., and MAW, E. W. "Nonhomeostatic Experiences as Stimuli of Children with High Curiosity." *California Journal of Educational Research*, 1961, *12*, 57–61.

MAW, W. H., and MAW, E. W. "The Relationships between Curiosity and Scores on a Test of General Information." *Journal of the Association for Research in Growth Relationships*, 1960, *2*, 27–33.

MAW AND MAW CURIOSITY SCALE FOR ELEMENTARY SCHOOL CHILDREN—What Would You Do Test (Battery A)

AUTHORS: Wallace H. Maw and Ethel W. Maw

AGE: Fifth-grade children only in normative group

VARIABLE: Curiosity

TYPE OF MEASURE: Questionnaire

SOURCE FROM WHICH THE MEASURE MAY BE OBTAINED: U.S. Office of Education, Maw and Maw (1964), Project No. 801, SAE 8519

DESCRIPTION OF MEASURE: The What Would You Do Test or Preferred Behavior Scale is based on the hypothesis that children high in curiosity prefer activities different from those preferred by low-curiosity children. The items of the scale are designed with this assumption in mind. The final form of the test consists of twenty-six situations that provide the child with four options for his choice of behavior. The directions for scoring these items are not altogether clear. Though the directions are to score the item most indicative of curiosity as 1 and the others as 0, no key is provided in the literature. A careful study of the test, however, suggests that the option most indicative of curiosity is apparent, as the following illustrative item shows (Maw and Maw, 1964):

If you could have any of the following for your birthday, would you select: *a phonograph, a badminton set, a checker game, a microscope?*

RELIABILITY AND VALIDITY: The statistical support for the scale rests on a reported revision based on item discrimination, statistically significantly greater mean scores for high-curiosity groups in several studies, and a satisfactory test-retest reliability coefficient of .77 over a one week interval (Maw and Maw, 1964).

BIBLIOGRAPHY:

MAW, W. H., and MAW, E. W. *An Exploratory Study into the Measurement of Curiosity in Elementary School Children.* Washington, D.C.: U.S. Office of Education, 1964.

MAW, W. H., and MAW, E. W. "Children's Curiosity as an Aspect of Reading Comprehension." *The Reading Teacher,* 1962, *15,* 236–40.

MAW, W. H., and MAW, E. W. "Establishing Criteria for Evaluating Measures of Curiosity." *Journal of Experimental Education,* 1961, *29,* 299–306.

MAW, W. H., and MAW, E. W. "Information Recognition by Children with High and Low Curiosity." *Educational Research Bulletin,* 1961, *40,* 197–201.

MAW, W. H., and MAW, E. W. "Nonhomeostatic Experiences as Stimuli of Children with High Curiosity." *California Journal of Educational Research,* 1961, *12,* 57–61.

MAW, W. H., and MAW, E. W. "The Relationships between Curiosity and Scores on a Test of General Information." *Journal of the Association for Research in Growth Relationships,* 1960, *2,* 27–33.

MAW AND MAW CURIOSITY SCALE FOR ELEMENTARY SCHOOL CHILDREN—Which Sayings Do You Believe Test

AUTHORS: Wallace H. Maw and Ethel W. Maw

AGE: Fifth-grade children

VARIABLE: Curiosity

TYPE OF MEASURE: Semi-projective Scale

SOURCE FROM WHICH THE MEASURE MAY BE OBTAINED: U.S. Office of Education, Maw and Maw (1964), Project No. 801, SAE 8519

DESCRIPTION OF MEASURE: This test is designed to test the hypothesis that children of high curiosity tend to select more frequently statements advocating action, change, and risk-taking than do children of low curiosity. Agreement with this tendency on each item is given a score of 1; disagreement is assigned a score of 0. Disagreement refers to the acceptance of the status quo and the avoidance of risk. Each item thus includes a pair of statements, one indicating risk-taking or action, the other favoring inaction or the status quo. The test consists of sixteen items so that a range in score from 0 to 16 is possible. Though no key is provided, the statement favoring risk-taking is quite evident, as the two illustrative items below indicate (Maw and Maw, 1964):

Don't bite off more than you can chew. Anything is possible.
Dare to follow the truth. Don't rock the boat.

RELIABILITY AND VALIDITY: The split-half reliability for the scale was .70. The validating evidence in support of this scale is similar to that provided for the other subscales of the Maw and Maw test batteries. First, the scale has been revised on the basis of preliminary forms in the direction of greater discrimination. Second, mean scores of high-curiosity groups surpassed those of low-curiosity groups at the .025 confidence level (Maw and Maw, 1964).

BIBLIOGRAPHY:

MAW, W. H., and MAW, E. W. *An Exploratory Study into the Measurement of Curiosity in Elementary School Children.* Washington, D.C.: U.S. Office of Education, 1964.

MAW, W. H., and MAW, E. W. "Children's Curiosity as an Aspect of Reading Comprehension." *The Reading Teacher,* 1962, *15,* 236–40.

MAW, W. H., and MAW, E. W. "Establishing Criteria for Evaluating Measures of Curiosity." *Journal of Experimental Education,* 1961, *29,* 299–306.

MAW, W. H., and MAW, E. W. "Information Recognition by Children with High and Low Curiosity." *Educational Research Bulletin,* 1961, *40,* 197–201.

MAW, W. H., and MAW, E. W. "Nonhomeostatic Experiences as Stimuli of Children with High Curiosity." *California Journal of Educational Research,* 1961, *12,* 57–61.

MAW, W. H., and MAW, E. W. "The Relationship between Curiosity and Scores on a Test of General Information." *Journal of the Association for Research in Growth Relationships,* 1960, *2,* 27–33.

MAW AND MAW CURIOSITY SCALE FOR ELEMENTARY SCHOOL CHILDREN—Which to Discuss Test (Independent Test)

AUTHORS: Wallace H. Maw and Ethel W. Maw

AGE: Fifth grade

VARIABLE: Curiosity

TYPE OF MEASURE: Test

SOURCE FROM WHICH THE MEASURE MAY BE OBTAINED: U.S. Office of Education, Maw and Maw (1964), Project No. 801, SAE 8519

DESCRIPTION OF MEASURE: The Which to Discuss Test is one of four measures from the Maw and Maw scales designed to test the hypothesis that high-curiosity children select experiences related to an unbalanced or unfamiliar environment more frequently than do low-curiosity children. The test consists of forty sets of three geometric figures, one of which is usually clearly more unbalanced and unfamiliar than the other two. The children are asked to select the one figure of the three that they would like to hear about if a story accompanied each figure. In order to disguise the purpose of the test and to eliminate the possibility of response set, a few items contain figures with equal familiarity or balance or both. In the scoring, however, only the unbalanced or unfamiliar objects are scored 1; balanced and familiar objects are given no credit. The total score presumably is the sum of correct selections for unbalanced and unfamiliar figures.

RELIABILITY AND VALIDITY: The use of the Kuder-Richardson formula to measure internal consistency resulted in a coefficient of .91. Statistically significant differences in mean scores were found in favor of high-curiosity groups and girls (Maw and Maw, 1964). The items were found to be of approximately equal difficulty.

BIBLIOGRAPHY:

MAW, W. H., and MAW, E. W. *An Exploratory Study into the Measurement of Curiosity in Elementary School Children.* Washington, D.C.: U.S. Office of Education, 1964.

MAW, W. H., and MAW, E. W. "Children's Curiosity as an Aspect of Reading Comprehension." *The Reading Teacher,* 1962, *15,* 236–40.

MAW, W. H., and MAW, E. W. "Establishing Criteria for Evaluating Measures of Curiosity." *Journal of Experimental Education,* 1961, *29,* 299–306.

MAW, W. H., and MAW, E. W. "Information Recognition by Children with High and Low Curiosity." *Educational Research Bulletin,* 1961, *40,* 197–201.

MAW, W. H., and MAW, E. W. "Nonhomeostatic Experiences as Stimuli of Children with High Curiosity." *California Journal of Educational Research,* 1961, *12,* 57–61.

MAW, W. H., and MAW, E. W. "The Relationships between Curiosity and Scores on a Test of General Information." *Journal of the Association for Research in Growth Relationships,* 1960, *2,* 27–33.

OBJECT CURIOSITY TEST

AUTHORS: Paul W. McReynolds, Mary Acker, and Caryl Pietila

AGE: Upper elementary age children

VARIABLE: Curiosity

TYPE OF MEASURE: Situational test with structured observation

SOURCE FROM WHICH THE MEASURE MAY BE OBTAINED: Paul W. McReynolds, Department of Psychology, University of Nevada, Reno, Nevada. Duplicated copies of the rating scales, as well as lists of the objects presented for exploration and the detailed instructions to the subjects, can be obtained from the senior author upon request.

DESCRIPTION OF MEASURE: The author uses the term "objective curiosity" in the interests of scientific accuracy, but suggests that the measure is probably indicative of curiosity generally. The technique involves observation of children's spontaneous exploration when presented with some interesting objects. The materials used in this test are described by McReynolds et al. (1961). The specific objects used are listed in the object box test score sheet provided by the author.

The testing is done in two phases. In the first or "experimental" phase, the experimenter places twelve objects one at a time into an "object box," which is curtained so the subject does not see the object as he manipulates it with his hands and attempts to identify it. After each guess, the subject may take the object out of the box and play with or look at it, until the next item is placed in the object box. The experimenter unobtrusively observes the subject during this time, using a predetermined schedule for observing his object-behavior. For example, in the manipulation of a toy flashlight, the subject gets one point for each of the following: move top to different angle; unscrew top; unscrew bottom; remove bulb; clip onto something; install battery; turn on; read writing on side. Furthermore, one point is given for each question about an object and for each comment implying curiosity. After the twelve objects are presented, the subject is told that the test is over and is then shown to another table with a box containing twenty-three additional objects which he is free to examine. This free play period lasts ten minutes, during which he is observed as in the first phase. The object curiosity score is the sum of the points earned in exploring the thirty-five objects.

Other researchers may find it necessary to use different objects, so that specific scoring criteria (behaviors to be credited as indications of curiosity) would have to be developed. The examples given by McReynolds, et al. (1961) on their object box test score sheet would be useful to the researcher who wishes to use his own objects and establish his own lists of scorable behavior.

RELIABILITY AND VALIDITY: Reliability of the score was estimated by the split-half method, with an attempt made to equate objects in the two halves on the basis of number of possible points that could be earned, on whether the object was used in the first or second phase, and on their interest to boys or girls. The corrected reliability was .87.

The total object curiosity scores for thirty children were compared with the teacher ratings of these children on several variables, with the following results: object curiosity was positively and significantly correlated with overall psychological health, scholastic motivation, and curiosity (as judged by the teacher). Object curiosity was negatively and significantly related to nervous behavior, maladjustment in the classroom, maladjustment to the teacher, and maladjustment to peers.

BIBLIOGRAPHY:

MC REYNOLDS, P., ACKER, M., and PIETILA, C. "Relation of Object Curiosity to Psychological Adjustment in Children." *Child Development*, 1961, *32*, 393–400.

STROOP COLOR-WORD TEST (Modified Form)

AUTHOR: J. R. Stroop

AGE: The Stroop Color-Word Test has been used with a wide group of subjects ranging from 7 to 80 years of age (Rand et al., 1963; Comalli et al., 1962).

VARIABLE: Cognitive style

TYPE OF MEASURE: Psychometric and projective

SOURCE FROM WHICH THE MEASURE MAY BE OBTAINED: Rand et al. (1963); Jensen (1965); and Jensen and Rohwer, Jr. (1966)

DESCRIPTION OF MEASURE: No standardized version of the SC-WT as yet exists, though the need for such standardization and suggestions for its development have been elaborated in detail (Jensen and Rohwer, Jr., 1966). As a start in standardizing the test, Jensen (1965) has outlined with care the nature and the dimensions of the cards needed, the format for administering the scale, and directions for scoring. Despite the lack of standardization, in all versions, the test is individually administered and requires three cards—a color card (card A), a word card (card B), and a color-word card (card C). Each card has one hundred items to be named and the subject's score on each card is the total time (in seconds) he takes to name the items. The color card (A) includes one hundred patches from three to five different colors; card B (the word card) simply has the names of the colors printed in black and white; and the color-word card (card C) has the color words printed in an ink of a conflicting color. Thus, the word RED might be printed in green, yellow, or blue, but never in red. The test takes five to eight minutes to administer. For an exact analysis of the responses, tape recording of the entire testing session is recommended (Rand et al., 1963).

The test has been used for a variety of purposes, but principally as a measure of personality variables and as a measure of cognitive styles. In the former case, it has been used as a projective test with scores for deviant responses to items (e.g., inappropriate color responses, such as red to the stimulus word green), deviant responses to sequence (e.g., inserted linguistic word or phrases, "this is hard"), and total time. The comprehensive review of the literature by Jensen and Rowher (1966) indicates that the Stroop scores "evince most of their relevance in the cognitive realm." Potential consumers of this scale may find many benefits from a careful study of the review by Jensen and Rowher (1966). They make many worthwhile suggestions for future uses of the Stroop Test, needed refinements, scoring variations, psychometric properties, practice effects, theoretical bases of the scale; and the relationships of the scores to other variables, including cognitive styles and personality dimensions. Normative data on responses to all three cards from a wide range of age groups have been developed (Comalli et al., 1962; Jensen, 1965).

RELIABILITY AND VALIDITY: High test-retest reliability of the three basic scores has been found in some studies. Since the reliability coefficients vary with the type of score employed, the data should be studied in detail (Jensen, 1965; Jensen and Rowher, Jr., 1966). Validity is difficult to assess primarily for two reasons. First, no standardized version of the test exists as yet. Second, "though the Stroop has been used in many studies, the procedures employed have not usually contributed much to our understanding of the processes actually measured by the Stroop . . ." (Jensen and Rowher, Jr., 1966). Nevertheless, predictions about outcomes relating to age and cognitive styles have been verified (Comalli et al., 1962; Jensen and Rowher, Jr., 1966). Concurrent validation may be assumed on the basis of the low to moderate but statistically significant correlations between Stroop factors and memory span, personality traits, specific scholastic abilities, and scores on other projective tests (Jensen and Rowher, Jr., 1966).

BIBLIOGRAPHY:

COMALLI, P. E., JR., WAPNER, S., and WERNER, H. "Interference Effects of Stroop Color-Word Test in Childhood, Adulthood, and Aging." *Journal of Genetic Psychology*, 1962, *100*, 47–53.

JENSEN, A. R. "Scoring the Stroop Test." *Acta Psychologica*, 1965, *24*, 398–408.

JENSEN, A. R., and ROWHER, W. D., JR. "The Stroop Color-Word Test: A Review." *Acta Psychologica*, 1966, *25*, 36–93.

STROOP, J. R. "Studies of Interference in Serial Verbal Reactions." *Journal of Experimental Psychology*, 1935, *18*, 643–662.

RAND, G., WAPNER, S., WERNER, H., and MC FARLAND, J. H. "Age Differences in Performance on the Stroop Color-Word Test." *Journal of Personality*, 1963, *31*, 534–558.

TEST OF SOLVING PUZZLES

AUTHOR: Esin Kaya

AGE: 9 to 12, grades 3 to 6

VARIABLE: Cognitive functions related to creativity

TYPE OF MEASURE: Test

SOURCE FROM WHICH THE MEASURE MAY BE OBTAINED: Esin Kaya, 3 Hunters Court, Setauket, New York 11785

DESCRIPTION OF MEASURE: This test consists of forty-two items divided into eight parts or sections. The items vary considerably in format, as indicated by the following examples:

The child is instructed to find as many hidden words as he can in words like "wheat, start, planet," without changing the order of any letters.
Name all the round things you can think of.
Tell all the different ways you can use a newspaper; knife; tire; cork.
Find a third word that means the same as "gift" and "now." (Answer: present.)
Tell a short story using these (and other) four words: job, shy, sand, people.
Match puzzles, in which the subject is instructed to, for example, take away three matches from a design to leave two triangles.
Find the rule for this (and other) progression: mouse, cat, pig, cow, elephant (they become larger).
Five drawings are presented, and the subject must report everything he thinks each might be.

The author provides detailed instructions for administration of the test by teachers. Separate scoring procedures are provided for each of the four factors measured, which are divergent production, convergent production, perceptual analytic thinking, and originality.

RELIABILITY AND VALIDITY: Test-retest reliabilities, over a period of one year, by grade and subtest, are as follows:

Grades	Flexibility	Synthesis	Analysis	Originality	Total
3–4	.71	.66	.69	.48	.82
4–5	.71	.53	.72	.53	.79
5–6	.74	.62	.76	.55	.84
Total	.75	.62	.76	.58	.85

The four factors postulated in the process of developing the measure did not show up in the factor analysis as clear and separate factors, although one general and three specific factors were revealed.

BIBLIOGRAPHY:

KAYA, ESIN. *Creativity: Revised Scoring Instructions.* New York: New York University School of Education, 1962. (Dittoed)

KAYA, ESIN. *Solving Puzzles, Form X.* New York: New York University School of Education, 1960. (Mimeographed)

KAYA, ESIN. *Solving Puzzles, Form X—Teacher's Manual of Instructions.* New York: New York University School of Education, 1960. (Mimeographed)

KAYA, ESIN. *Test of Solving Puzzles: Its Development, Reliability, and Validity.* New York: New York University School of Education, 1965. (Dittoed)

Group 1-e
Miscellaneous

ADJECTIVE-NOUN PAIRED ASSOCIATES TEST

AUTHOR: Allan Paivio

AGE: Fourth and fifth grades

VARIABLE: Verbal learning

TYPE OF MEASURE: Test

SOURCE FROM WHICH THE MEASURE MAY BE OBTAINED: See Paivio (1963)

DESCRIPTION OF MEASURE: The Adjective-Noun Paired Associates Test consists of four lists of sixteen adjective-noun paired associates word groups. The scale attempts to measure linguistic habits that are important determinants of learning and retention of word sequences. The four lists include thirty-two adjectives and equal numbers of concrete and rather general nouns. The items from which the lists are drawn (listed in the order: adjective-concrete noun, abstract noun) are: wooden-box, heap; soft-chair, spot; bright-star, idea; yellow-corn, grain; clean-dress, clothes; gentle-boy, child; pretty-rose, flower; beautiful-queen, lady; proud-Indian, people; heavy-lead, load; loud-shot, noise; sharp-pencil, stick; green-ball, toy; deep-valley, place; equal-half, share; fancy-shoes, things; open-window, space; hungry-bear, animal; early-morning, time; brave-hunter, fellow; hard-iron, metal; sweet-orange, fruit; stone-castle, building; fresh-meat, food; paper-dollar, money; cold-wind, air; soft-music, sound; tall-oak, tree; happy-Christmas, holiday; wise-man, person; busy-bee, bug; large-army, crowd.

Within each list, the pairings include eight adjectives and concrete nouns and eight adjectives and abstract nouns from the master lists presented above. On each list of sixteen paired associates, eight adjectives are paired with concrete nouns and eight with abstract nouns. Since each list can be presented in A-N or N-A order, eight different lists are possible for the entire scale. Though the precise lists used are not discernible from the source of the test, the assignment of the items to different lists was on a random basis. The purpose of the test in the Paivio (1963) study was to measure the effect of noun abstractness on learning adjective-noun paired associates. The interested investigator could develop his own separate lists.

The test is administered orally on a group basis with two seconds allowed between each pairing. On the recall session, only the stimulus words (the first word of each pair) are read with ten seconds allowed between each presentation. On this second administration, the children are required to write down their responses. For group comparison purposes, the sequence of the lists should be presented in counterbalanced fashion for the A-N and N-A lists. It is also recommended that each class receive the same two lists.

RELIABILITY AND VALIDITY: The test has been given to children of both sex groups in the fourth and fifth grades (N = 136). The main source of support for the scale appears to be in the form of construct validity. The results of Paivio's

(1963) study verified several predictive hypotheses. First, within the paired words presented, recall was greater for noun stimuli in the N-A order than for adjective stimuli in the A-N sequence (p < .001). Second, learning under noun-adjective pairs was significantly superior for concrete nouns than for abstract nouns (p < .001). Third, the N-A order was learned more easily with concrete nouns than with abstract nouns. Finally, recall was not found to be related to the meaningfulness of the words, such as their familiarity to the child. The fact that these findings were consistent with previous results lends more substance to the construct validity of the scale.

BIBLIOGRAPHY:

LAMBERT, W. E., and PAIVIO, A. "The Influence of Noun-Adjective Order on Learning." *Canadian Journal of Psychology,* 1956, *10,* 9–12.

PAIVIO, A. "Learning of Adjective-Noun Paired Associates as a Function of Adjective-Noun Word Order and Noun Abstractness." *Canadian Journal of Psychology,* 1963, *17,* 370–379.

THORNDIKE, E. L., and LORGE, I. *The Teacher's Workbook of 30,000 Words.* New York: Bureau of Publications, Teachers College, 1944.

MEANING OF OPPOSITION

AUTHORS: G. Kreezer and K. M. Dallenbach

AGE: 5 to 7½

VARIABLE: Concept of opposition

TYPE OF MEASURE: Test, individually administered

SOURCE FROM WHICH THE MEASURE MAY BE OBTAINED: See Kreezer and Dallenbach

DESCRIPTION OF MEASURE: This test is made up of a twenty-five-item word list as follows: white, short, fat, wet, glad, hard, in, slow, weak, open, heavy, up, smooth, little, sleep, shut, strong, quick, out, soft, sad, dry, thin, long, black. The subject is given some examples of opposites, gets feedback and limited instruction about opposition, and is then presented with the stimulus words one at a time. The scoring system does not require that antonyms be given, but simply that the subjects demonstrate by their replies that they understand the nature of opposition. Thus, the answers "not smooth," or "unsmooth," to the word "smooth," were as correct as the response "rough." The test is therefore designed and scored to measure understanding of the concept or relation of opposition, rather than as an opposites vocabulary test.

RELIABILITY AND VALIDITY: Norms are provided for five age groups, from 5 years to 7 years 6 months, at half-year intervals, with N = 20 for each group. In general, the number of correct responses shows progression with age. Robinowitz (1956, p. 29) also found significant relationships between age of child and ability to learn the relation of opposition.

BIBLIOGRAPHY:

KREEZER, G., and DALLENBACH, K. M. "Learning the Relation of Opposition." *American Journal of Psychology,* 1929, *41,* 432–441.

ROBINOWITZ, R. "Learning the Relation of Opposition as Related to Scores on the Wechsler Intelligence Scale for Children." *Journal of Genetic Psychology,* 1965, *88,* 25–30.

A MEASURE OF PIAGET'S "RECIPROCITY" CONCEPT

AUTHORS: E. L. Hartley and E. I. Gondor

AGE: 5 to 14

VARIABLE: Reciprocity (maturity in social perspective)

TYPE OF MEASURE: Test, individually administered

SOURCE FROM WHICH THE MEASURE MAY BE OBTAINED: Eugene L. Hartley, Univ. of Wisc.-Green Bay, 2413 Nicolet Drive N, Green Bay, Wisconsin 54301

DESCRIPTION OF MEASURE: The examiner presents a series of six pictures to the subject and then proceeds with the interrogation, which for Figure I goes as follows:

Three men were arguing. (Pointing to them in turn) One was American, one was English, one was Chinese. They were talking about flags; which is the prettiest flag. (Pointing) This is the Chinese flag, this is the American flag, and this is the English flag. The three men were Chinese, American, and English. (A) Now what do you think they said? (B) And who was right? (C) Why?

Stage I involves an *absolute* judgment, showing no sensitivity to relative values; stage II involves "symmetrical" responses, with basic sociocentrism maintained; in stage III there is manifested a recognition that others may have motives like ours and derive value judgments from a different perspective. Examples are given of responses that are typical of children in each of the stages I, II, and III. These examples are usable as general scoring criteria.

RELIABILITY AND VALIDITY: None reported.

BIBLIOGRAPHY: None.

MEMORY FOR OBJECTS

AUTHOR: Leon D. Radaker

AGE: Up to 15 (mentally retarded)

VARIABLE: Imagery for concrete objects

TYPE OF MEASURE: Test, individually administered

SOURCE FROM WHICH THE MEASURE MAY BE OBTAINED: See Radaker (1961)

DESCRIPTION OF MEASURE: Sixteen small, common objects are arranged in four rows and put on a white board measuring sixteen inches. The objects are paper clips, girls' hair clips, toy fork, match, and so forth. The board is exposed to the subject for ninety seconds, after which it is removed. The subject is then given the task of recalling objects and their position on the board. A paper form is used to enable the subject to specify their position. If the object is correctly recalled and positioned, the subject is given a score of 2 for that object; therefore, the total possible score for sixteen objects named and positioned is 32.

RELIABILITY AND VALIDITY: A group of fifteen retarded subjects took the test, then repeated it two weeks later. The reliability for this group was .55, significant at the .05 level. Radaker found a low but significant (.05 level) correlation between Memory for Objects and Memory for Word Forms (.38), and between Memory for Objects and Memory for Designs (.41).

BIBLIOGRAPHY:

RADAKER, L. D. "The Visual Imagery of Retarded Children and the Relationship to Memory for Word Forms." *Exceptional Children,* 1961, 27(May), 524–530.

MEMORY FOR WORD FORMS

AUTHOR: Leon D. Radaker

AGE: 10 (mentally retarded)

VARIABLE: Immediate memory for unfamiliar words

TYPE OF MEASURE: Test, individually administered

SOURCE FROM WHICH THE MEASURE MAY BE OBTAINED: See Radaker (1961)

DESCRIPTION OF MEASURE: Items for the Memory for Word Forms are derived from Webster's Unabridged Dictionary and were selected to meet three criteria: unusual in letter pattern; low in frequency; not ordinarily observed in elementary school reading material. Examples of the items are dhu, onyx, phlegm, muzjik. Each word is typewritten in the center of a white 3 × 5 inch card. Each card is exposed to the subject for five seconds, and when the card is removed, the subject is asked to reproduce the word. The score is the total number of words correctly reproduced.

RELIABILITY AND VALIDITY: The test-retest reliability coefficient for this measure administered to fifteen retarded children with a two-week interval was .77, which is significant at the .05 level. Radaker hypothesized that training in visual imagery would improve memory for word forms, as measured by this test. He found significant (.05 level) differences on this test between a group of retarded children trained in visual imagery and an untrained group.

BIBLIOGRAPHY:

RADAKER, L. D. "The Visual Imagery of Retarded Children and the Relationship to Memory for Word Forms." *Exceptional Children,* 1961, 27(May), 524–530.

PROGNOSTIC READING TEST

AUTHOR: Richard W. Woodcock

AGE: Retarded readers in the intermediate grades

VARIABLE: Prognosis for improvement in remedial reading

TYPE OF MEASURE: Test, individually administered

SOURCE FROM WHICH THE MEASURE MAY BE OBTAINED: Dr. Richard Woodcock, George Peabody College for Teachers, Nashville, Tennessee

DESCRIPTION OF MEASURE: The measure consists of five short stories written with pictures and symbols other than the conventional alphabet. The test is, therefore, a measure of the child's ability to master a new reading test, within a short period of time, in a new "language." The measure is an attempt to duplicate the process of learning to read, with a new set of symbols. The stories become progressively more difficult. They are bound in a mimeographed test booklet, and a manual for the test gives specific instructions for the administration of the measure.

Scoring for the measure is relatively simple, involving merely counting the number of errors made by the subject. Some of the symbols used in the test are pictured in an article by Woodcock (1958).

RELIABILITY AND VALIDITY: The measure was administered to a fourth-grade class of twenty-four pupils. The reliability computed by Kuder-Richardson Formula 21 was .91. The corrected split-half reliability was .96 using the same population.

Using the same twenty-four children, the author (1960) found a correlation between the prognostic test scores and the Gates Composite Reading Score of −.95. (The negative value occurs because scores on the prognostic test represent the number of errors.)

Another study described by the author (1960) shows that when fifty-three pairs of children needing remedial reading and matched for age were given the prognostic reading test, the measure was effective in predicting in forty cases which child would improve most with remediation. That is, the child of each pair who did better on the prognostic reading test was more likely to be the child who would improve most with remediation. When the criterion for difference between the two members of the pair was set at two times the standard error, this measure was used to predict correctly thirty-four out of forty-four cases.

In a second predictive validity study using sixteen fourth-grade retarded readers, Woodcock (1960) found that the predictive efficiency of the prognostic reading test ranged from .48 to .92, depending on the size of the difference in scores between members of each pair.

BIBLIOGRAPHY:

WOODCOCK, R. W. *Manual for the Prognostic Reading Test,* Oregon College of Education, 1960.

WOODCOCK, R. W. "An Experimental Prognostic Test for Remedial Readers." *Journal of Educational Psychology,* 1958, *49*(1), 23–27.

WOODCOCK, R. W. *Prognostic Reading Test,* Oregon College of Education, 1960.

SAFIER'S ANIMISM TEST

AUTHOR: Gwen Safier

AGE: 4 to 5, 7 to 8, 10 to 11 years

VARIABLE: Animism

TYPE OF MEASURE: Semistructured interview

SOURCE FROM WHICH THE MEASURE MAY BE OBTAINED: See Safier (1964)

DESCRIPTION OF MEASURE: The Safier Animism Test measures the extent to which a child anthropomorphizes (that is, ascribes human characteristics to non-human objects). Scoring is based on the adult norms that imply that only plants and animals can live and die. Essentially, the scale consists of two parts. In Part I, the child is orally presented ten stimulus words (e.g., dog, ball) consisting of six inanimate objects and four animate objects, with the order of classification presented in random fashion to avoid perseveration. In this part of the examination, the child is asked the following questions about each stimulus word:

Does a (S word) live? Is a (S word) living?
Does a (S word) hurt when hit?
Does a (S word) grow up?
Does a (S word) die?

In scoring the scale at this point, the child receives 1 point for each animistic response with the exception of the stimulus word "ball" for which such a reply receives 2 points. Each object receives both a positive animism score (inanimate objects live), and a negative animism score (inanimate objects die). Further, a total animism score and a death score consisting of the sum of the negative animistic scores are also derived.

In the second part of the examination, the interview attempts to assess the child's reasoning behind his inaccurate responses. Illustrations of the five categories applied here include the temporary nature of life and death (flux) and externality, the idea of an outside agency.

RELIABILITY AND VALIDITY: The author tested ten boys at the three age ranges of 4 to 5, 7 to 8, and 10 to 11 years. No reliability data were reported, but construct validity may be inferred from the findings that, as expected, animism decreased with increasing age and a positive correlation occurred between "animism" and "death" scores.

BIBLIOGRAPHY:

SAFIER, G. "A Study in Relationships between the Life and Death Concepts in Children." *Journal of Genetic Psychology*, 1964, *105*, 283–294.

SPACE CONCEPTUALIZATION SCALE

AUTHORS: Gerald S. Lesser, Gordon Fifer, and Donald H. Clark

AGE: 6 years, 2 months through 7 years, 5 months

VARIABLE: Space conceptualization

TYPE OF MEASURE: Test

SOURCE FROM WHICH THE MEASURE MAY BE OBTAINED: See Lesser et al. (1964)

DESCRIPTION OF MEASURE: This measure consists of two subtests—an Object Completion test in which the subject is requested to identify each of sixteen incomplete familiar objects, and a Perspective test consisting of three large drawings, two of street scenes and one of a children's playground. Each scene contains three or four persons. The subject is asked to identify from four or five options the part of the scene a particular person would be able to see from that person's position in the scene.

The Perspective subtest provides a good spatial measure if one can assume a minimum level reasoning ability. The items were designed to present perspective in its simplest form, directions were simplified as much as possible, and sample items were used to reduce the effect of differences in reasoning ability.

RELIABILITY AND VALIDITY: The reliability coefficient (corrected for attenuation) for Lesser's (1964) entire sample was .85. The reliabilities (corrected for attenuation) ranged from .63 to .86. The reliability coefficient was lowest for middle-class Negro children ($r = .63$). It was also relatively low for middle- and lower-class Jewish children ($r = .74$). The reliability coefficient for lower-class Negroes on this scale was appreciably higher ($r = .81$) than that for middle-class Negro children ($r = .63$). All ethnic groups had high reliabilities for number (.94 to .96) and moderate (.80 to .85) reliabilities for space. The data suggest that the space test, along with the verbal scale, correlates least strongly with other scales (median $r = .54$).

BIBLIOGRAPHY:

LESSER, G. S., FIFER, G., and CLARK, D. H. *Mental Abilities of Children in Different Social and Cultural Groups.* Washington, D.C.: Office of Education, U.S. Department of Health, Education, and Welfare, Comparative Research Project No. 1635, 1964.

DAVIS, F. B., LESSER, G. S., FRENCH, E. G., ET AL. *Identification and Classroom Behavior of Gifted Elementary-School Children.* Cooperative Research Monographs, 1960, No. 2, 19032.

CATEGORY **2**

PERSONALITY AND EMOTIONAL CHARACTERISTICS

Group 2-a

Personality—General

CHILDREN'S INSIGHT TEST

AUTHOR: Mary Engel

AGE: 6 to 12

VARIABLE: Personality

TYPE OF MEASURE: Projective test

SOURCE FROM WHICH THE MEASURE MAY BE OBTAINED: See Engel (1958)

DESCRIPTION OF MEASURE: The Children's Insight Test is a variant of the Sargent Insight Test (Sargent, 1953), adapted for use with children. The test may be conveniently conceptualized along three dimensions. First, a child is pictorially portrayed in an emotionally toned and common everyday problem situation that demands an immediate solution. Second, the examinee's task is to state what the child portrayed might do and how he might feel in this common problem situation which the author designates as an "armature." For example, one armature depicts a child who returned from school and discovered his dog had run away. The examinee is asked to describe the child's probable action and feelings in this situation. Finally, the thirteen armatures deal with a variety of situations and a number of different individuals. The varied content includes mother, father, friend, aggression, and narcissistic injury.

      Scoring of the test is done along three dimensions: A for affect, B for affect-management, and M for maladjustment indicating thought pathology. Expressions of affect are categorized into one of twelve classes. Notations are also made to indicate whether the affect is discharged with the manifest expressions of feeling, by action, or if the response is latent. The twelve scoring categories for the affect dimension are as follows: situation appraisal—frustration; situation appraisal—facilitation; situational reaction—aggression; situational reaction—passivity and dependency; situational reaction—evasion; mood—dysphoria; mood—euphoria; relationship—positive; relationship—negative; stress—anxiety and inadequacy; stress—conflict and confusion; stress—intellectualization. The dimension of affect-management has three categories: evaluation, elaboration, and qualification. The dimension of maladjustment is divided into personal pronoun, irrelevant expressions, subjectivism, unreal solution, no solution, no feeling, and denial. Engel (1958b) gives numerous examples in the use of the scoring categories.

RELIABILITY AND VALIDITY: Interscorer reliability for the three main dimensions of affect, affect-discharge, and maladaptive ideation ranges from .86 to .98, with a median of .91. Split-half reliabilities of thirty-two third-grade pupils were as follows: affect .93, affect-discharge .87, maladaptive ideation .88.

      Test-retest reliability was computed on thirty-four urban Negro children in the third grade by means of a counterbalanced procedure. One half of the armatures was administered to eighteen subjects; the other half was given to the remaining children. Subsequently, each group completed the half of the scale it did not have in the first administration.

The scores from the two separate testings (in separate halves) were then correlated for each group, and the average of the reliability coefficients is as follows: (a) .91, (b) .90, (m) .77 (Engel, 1958).

BIBLIOGRAPHY:

ENGEL, M. "The Development and Application of the Children's Insight Test." *Journal of Projective Techniques,* 1958, 22, 13–25.

ENGEL, M., and RECHENBERG, W. "Studies in the Reliability of the Children's Insight Test." *Journal of Projective Techniques,* 1961, 25, 158–63.

SARGENT, H. D. *The Insight Test.* New York: Grune and Stratton, 1953.

CLASSROOM BEHAVIOR INVENTORY

AUTHORS: Earl S. Schaefer, Leo F. Droppleman, and Alex F. Kalverboer (earlier version); Earl S. Schaefer, May R. Aaronson, and Betty R. Burgoon (current version)

AGE: Junior high and high school

VARIABLE: Personality

TYPE OF MEASURE: Rating scale

SOURCE FROM WHICH THE MEASURE MAY BE OBTAINED: Earl S. Schaefer, National Institute of Mental Health, 5454 Wisconsin Avenue, Chevy Chase, Maryland 20015

DESCRIPTION OF MEASURE: The Classroom Behavior Inventory is based on a hierarchal approach to the organization of behavior based on three levels of generality, including, in ascending order of levels of abstractness, specific observable behaviors, traits, and broad factors. In the initial version, each of the seventeen traits (or subscales) includes from five to nine homogeneous items. Examples of the traits and illustrative items within each subscale are given below:

Dominance—*Will interrupt someone else in order to state his opinion.*
Conscientiousness—*Gets assignments in on time.*
Destructiveness—*Throws books, notebooks, pencils, and other equipment about.*
Gregariousness—*Enters and leaves the class with several companions.*
Cruelty—*Laughs at the mistakes of others.*

A factor analysis of the inventory (earlier version) yields essentially two major factors: positive, loving, social behavior vs. hostility; and extraversion vs. introversion. The factors themselves include both positive and negative poles. Thus, the positive pole for the extraversion vs. introversion factor includes such behaviors as verbal expressiveness, happiness, gregariousness, active helpfulness, friendliness, and leadership. The negative poles subsume the specific behaviors of withdrawal and self-consciousness.

In rating a child's behavior, teachers are directed to indicate whether the behavior is like (L) or not like (NL) that of the ratee. In the interest of greater discrimination of ratings, the current version requires teachers to rate specific item behavior of a child on a four-point scale as follows: very much like, somewhat like, very little like, not at all like (Schaefer, Aaronson, and Burgoon, undated). The specific scoring system is not provided.

RELIABILITY AND VALIDITY: Other than the indications of internal consistency suggested by factor analysis, three sources of statistical data for the scale are evident:

(1) Internal consistency reliability coefficients (Kuder-Richardson Formula 20) based on one teacher's ratings of the same children in the eleventh grade ranged

from .51 (subscale withdrawal) to .95 (subscale conscientiousness), with a median reliability of .86 for a sample of thirty-six boys. For thirty-six girls in the same grade, the reliability coefficients ranged from .51 (subscale considerateness) to .97 (subscale dominance), with a median reliability of .77. The same type of statistics applied to 146 boys in junior high by many teachers yielded a range of reliability coefficients between .70 (subscale kindness) and .92 (subscale conscientiousness), with a median reliability for the seventeen scales of .77.

(2) The test-retest reliabilities by one teacher ranged from .36 (subscale friendliness) to .89 (subscale verbal expressiveness), with a median coefficient of .81 ($N = 33$, junior high boys). As applied to junior high girls ($N = 31$), the range was .22 (subscale conscientiousness) to .77 (subscale destructiveness), with a median coefficient of .50.

(3) Inter-rater reliability coefficients among several raters for 172 pairs of junior high boys ranged from .23 (subscale positive evaluation) to .72 (subscale conscientiousness), with a median reliability coefficient of .50 (Schaefer, Droppleman, and Kalverboer, undated).

BIBLIOGRAPHY: None.

COLUMBUS SENTENCE COMPLETION SCALE

AUTHORS: Jack A. Shaffer and Arthur S. Tamkin

AGE: Preschoolers or adolescents

VARIABLE: Personality

TYPE OF MEASURE: Projective test

SOURCE FROM WHICH THE MEASURE MAY BE OBTAINED: Jack A. Shaffer, Dept. of Psychology, Humboldt State College, Arcata, California 95521. Requests should be accompanied by a business size, addressed, stamped envelope.

DESCRIPTION OF MEASURE: The Columbus Sentence Completion Scale consists of fifty sentence stems selected from a much larger population of sentence stems as those most likely to elicit meaningful psychological material. The authors state that the instrument is useful clinically, especially when administered orally, the examiner recording the responses and latency time. The measure has been used with children as young as age 4, and with adolescents.

Examples of the items follow:

I would like to
At home
My mother
I wish that I
My brother
My secret is

RELIABILITY AND VALIDITY: No data were available on reliability and validity.

BIBLIOGRAPHY: None.

DESPERT FABLES (Fine Revision)

AUTHOR: Reuben Fine

AGE: 3 to upper elementary

VARIABLE: Personality

TYPE OF MEASURE: Projective test

SOURCE FROM WHICH THE MEASURE MAY BE OBTAINED: See Fine (1948)

DESCRIPTION OF MEASURE: The test consists of twenty "fables" each followed by a question to which the subject responds. These responses are the basic data elicited by the fables. An example of one of the fables:

One afternoon a boy comes home from school. The neighbor lady tells him that his mommy has gone away for a while with daddy; she does not know when mommy will come back. What do you suppose he does?

According to Fine (1948) the test measures eight "psychodynamics": dependency, hostility, identification, sibling rivalry, rejection, castration fears, Oedipus complex, fears and wishes. Each fable is considered to tap one of the psychodynamic areas, with varied numbers of fables attached to different areas. For example, the psychodynamics of identification, castration fears, and Oedipus complex are represented by only one fable each. Fears and wishes, another of the psychodynamics, is measured by six of the fables. The measure has been administered individually and in groups. Obviously, the type of administration depends in part on the age of the child. Peixotto (1960) indicates that the measures are most appropriate for children 10 years and younger. As with most projective measures, the scoring is not objective but is determined primarily by the scorer's judgment about the presence or absence of one of the psychodynamics.

RELIABILITY AND VALIDITY: Peixotto (1956) found that reliabilities for 177 children in grades three to eight were significantly above chance level for most stories. She gives some normative data on the frequency of each of the psychodynamic responses to each fable (1957).

With respect to validity, Fine (1948) found significant differences between asthmatics and their siblings on the variables of dependency, hostility to mother, and hostility to father. Peixotto (1960) concluded on the basis of her study of eighty-three child clinic patients compared with normal groups that the fables are unsatisfactory for differential diagnosis because normal and patient groups tend to have similiar responses. There are some significant differences on "popular" responses, but the differences are not high enough for individual diagnosis.

BIBLIOGRAPHY:

DESPERT, J. L. "Psychosomatic Study of Fifty Stuttering Children." *American Journal of Orthopsychiatry,* 1946, *16,* 100–173.

DUS, L. "La Méthode des Fables en Psychoanalyse." *Archives of Psychology,* (Geneva), 1940.

FINE, R. "Use of the Despert Fables (Revised Form) in Diagnostic Work with Children." *Journal of Projective Techniques,* 1948, *12,* 106–118.

PEIXOTTO, H. E. "Reliability of the Despert Fables, a Story Completion Projective Test for Children." *Journal of Clinical Psychology,* 1956, *12,* 75–78.

PEIXOTTO, H. E. "Popular Responses for the Despert Fables." *Journal of Clinical Psychology,* 1957, *13,* 73–79.

PEIXOTTO, H. E. "Use of the Despert Fables wtih Disturbed Children." *Journal of Clinical Psychology,* 1960, *16,* 173–179.

FOLLOW-UP LETTERS

AUTHOR: Elaine Dorfman

AGE: Elementary school children

VARIABLE: Personality (progress in therapy)

TYPE OF MEASURE: Projective

SOURCE FROM WHICH THE MEASURE MAY BE OBTAINED: See Dorfman (1955, 1958)

DESCRIPTION OF MEASURE: As the name of the scale indicates, it provides a means of follow-up evaluation of the progress of children who have undergone psychotherapy. The letters to the children themselves simply ask them to describe memories of their therapeutic sessions and their present social adjustment. A comprehensive manual for analyzing the contents of the letters is available (Dorfman, 1955). In general, however, each letter is classified for therapy memories and reports of present status in terms of three affective categories: positive, negative, or neutral. As an illustration of the scoring categories, the definition of each classification for Therapy Memories follows:

Positive—*expressions of pleasant memories, fun, benefit derived, or that the therapist is missed*

Negative—*expressions of displeasure about the sessions, statements denying their value, or hostile demands for explanations of their purpose*

Neutral—*mere recitals of recalled activities, without statements implying approval or disapproval*

RELIABILITY AND VALIDITY: According to Dorfman (1958), the test has been used on fifteen cases who had been in therapy. The majority of the children were girls who had been rated as maladjusted by their teachers. The subjects also came from prosperous middle-class communities and were at least average in intelligence. The author rated each letter twice within a six-month interval as a reliability check and attained an intrajudge agreement of 100 per cent for therapy memories and 93 per cent for reports of present status. Chance expectation was 33 per cent, since three categories were involved. The obtained agreements differed from chance expectations at the .001 level. Intrajudge reliability ranged between 87 and 93 per cent on therapy memories, and reported status agreements were all 80 per cent. All differed significantly from chance expectancy at the .001 level.

BIBLIOGRAPHY:

DORFMAN, E. "Personality Outcomes of Client-Centered Child Therapy." Unpublished doctoral dissertation, University of Chicago, 1955.

DORFMAN, E. "Personality Outcomes of Client-Centered Child Therapy." *Psychological Monographs*, 1958, 72(3) (Whole No. 456).

IDENTIFICATION FIGURES

AUTHOR: Richard H. Bloomer

AGE: Kindergarten through 12

VARIABLE: Personality

TYPE OF MEASURE: Questionnaire

SOURCE FROM WHICH THE MEASURE MAY BE OBTAINED: See Bloomer (1964)

DESCRIPTION OF MEASURE: The questionnaire consists of just three questions. The child is asked who he would choose to be if he could change places with anyone in the world, who he would dress as if he were going to a masquerade party, and who he would like to be if he were left alone in the jungle. These are described as, respectively, the normal tension situation, the social stress situation, and the survival stress situation.

Scoring is done with an adaptation of Symonds' Teacher Rating scale. Anchored judgments were developed by collecting the identification figures from 632 children in grades one through eight, from which 116 different identification figures were nominated. Thirty-six judges then rated each identification figure on seventeen characteristics using a seven-point scale. These points or scoring criteria are continua, of which the following are examples:

Happy, cheerful, humorous—Unhappy, sad, serious
Active, persevering—Phlegmatic, passive, easily discouraged

Each of the 116 identification figures therefore was given seventeen numbers representing the modal judgment of judges for each point on the seventeen-point scale. The modal ratings became the anchor points for the judgment system. Thus, it is the assumption of this measure that if one knows the figures with whom the child identifies, one can make valid judgments about his needs, conflicts, and type of conflict resolution. Since the child's perception of his identification is not necessarily the same as that of an adult, the children were asked to give their reasons for choosing a particular identification figure. This information helped the judges in assigning scores on each of the seventeen variables to each of the identification figures.

RELIABILITY AND VALIDITY: Bloomer (1964) reports a correlation between judges of .903 resulting from the use of the anchored judgment system.

BIBLIOGRAPHY:

BLOOMER, R. H. "Identification Figures of Boys and Girls under Varying Degree of Implied Stress." *Psychological Reports*, 1964, *15*, 635–642.

KOPPITZ HUMAN FIGURE DRAWINGS AS EMOTIONAL INDICATORS

AUTHOR: Elizabeth Munsterberg Koppitz

AGE: 5 through 12 years old

VARIABLE: Personality (emotional problems)

TYPE OF MEASURE: Projective test

SOURCE FROM WHICH THE MEASURE MAY BE OBTAINED: See Koppitz (1966a)

DESCRIPTION OF MEASURE: Koppitz has developed an objective scoring system for evaluating HFDs among children as emotional indicators. This procedure rests on thirty drawing items that relate to three categories: the quality of the drawings (for example, gross asymmetry of limbs); items usually not included in HFDs of children (for example, hands cut off); omission of eight items frequently found on HFDs of children (for example, no eyes or no arms). Total score was simply the number of these indicators that appeared in the drawing. The test itself was administered individually to the child.

RELIABILITY AND VALIDITY: The author tested seventy-six pairs of public school children matched for age and sex, thirty-two boys and forty-four girls in each group. They ranged in age from 5 to 12. One group consisted of seventy-six children who had been referred to a child guidance clinic. The other group was comprised of children in the same elementary school who had been selected by their teachers as well adjusted emotionally and economically. Both groups were presumedly average or superior in intelligence.

Inter-rater reliability of the scale was reflected by a 95 per cent agreement on all thirty items scored by two psychologists. Several sources of evidence provide validation for the scale: (1) Chi-square analyses revealed that eight items differentiated between the groups at the .05 level or less and four items at the .10 level. (2) Sixteen of the thirty items were present only on the HFDs of the critical group. (3) Koppitz (1966a) found that three quarters of all well-adjusted pupils showed no emotional indicators at all on the measure, while only seven of the clinic patients showed no such signs (chi-square 67.19, P < .001). (4) Finally, the following five emotional indicators have been found to be significantly related to school achievement in the primary grades: poor integration of parts, slanting figures, omission of body, omission of arms, and three or more figures spontaneously drawn (Koppitz, 1966c).

BIBLIOGRAPHY:

KOPPITZ, E. M. "Emotional Indicators on Human Figure Drawings of Children: A Validation Study." *Journal of Clinical Psychology,* 1966, 22(3), 313–315 (a).

KOPPITZ, E. M. "Emotional Indicators on Human Figure Drawings of Shy and Aggressive Children." *Journal of Clinical Psychology,* 1966, 22, 466–469 (b).

KOPPITZ, E. M. "Emotional Indicators on Human Figure Drawings and School Achievement of First and Second Graders." *Journal of Clinical Psychology,* 1966, 22, 481–483 (c).

LERNER-MURPHY FRUSTRATION TEST

AUTHORS: Eugene Lerner and Lois M. Murphy

AGE: Preschool children ranging in age from 2 through $5\frac{1}{2}$ years

VARIABLE: Personality

TYPE OF MEASURE: Situational test

SOURCE FROM WHICH THE MEASURE MAY BE OBTAINED: See Lerner et al. (1941)

DESCRIPTION OF MEASURE: The Lerner-Murphy Frustration Test consists of two blocking techniques in which the experimenter starts from one end of a road made of large play blocks, the subject from the other. The experimenter meets the subject in the area of conflict and asks, "How shall my car (or doll) pass?" Eight repetitions of situations, the first and last three being "car meets car" and the fourth and fifth being "doll meets car," provided the standard experimental situation for each child. This situation might be subjectively characterized as being one of standardized, mild, repeated frustration, the other in which the children do not appear to be more than minimally involved.

In the original publication (Lerner et al., 1941), the authors provided details for the materials needed for the experiment; complete and elaborate descriptions of the blocking techniques, including the order and duration of the play-units; the standard procedures followed for administering the techniques; the preliminary skills necessary for obtaining interrater reliability on observing the actions of preschool children in the play situation; illustrative protocols with interpretations; and the value and aims of the task. No means of scoring were given in the original publication. Otis and McCandless (1955) developed a scoring manual for frequency and intensity of regression and submission responses resulting from reactions to the frustration task by the children.

RELIABILITY AND VALIDITY: In a study by Otis and McCandless (1955), a total of sixty-three subjects was used, consisting of thirty-one boys and thirty-two girls ranging in age from 41 to 65 months. Their concern was with two classes of behaviors: dominant-aggressive (Ag) on the one hand and complacent-submissive (Su) on the other hand. There were also two types of needs investigated: Power-dominance (PD/n) and love-affection (LA/n). PD/n and LA/n were rated by the paired-comparison method by teachers familiar with the children. The reliabilities of the teacher ratings of PD/n for two different groups were respectively .86 and .84; and for LA/n .60 and .63 uncorrected for attenuation. Clinical observers also rated two different groups for total Ag and Su scores. Reliabilities of these observers show Pearson r's from .94 to .97.

BIBLIOGRAPHY:

LERNER, E., MURPHY, L. M., STONE, L. J., and BEYER, E. "Methods for the Study of Personality in Young Children." *Monograph for the Society on Research in Child Development*, 1941, *VI*(4) (Serial No. 30), 3–289.

OTIS, N. B., and MC CANDLESS, B. "Responses to Repeated Frustrations of Young Children Differentiated According to Need Area." *Journal of Abnormal and Social Psychology*, 1955, *50*, 349–353.

LIFE SITUATION PERCEPTION TEST

AUTHOR: A. Ladonko

AGE: Approximately 6

VARIABLE: Personality

TYPE OF MEASURE: Projective test

SOURCE FROM WHICH THE MEASURE MAY BE OBTAINED: See Ladonko (1962)

DESCRIPTION OF MEASURE: This measure is described by the author as a new method of "percept-diagnosis" that provides information supplementary to the Rorschach test, and offers the psychologist a better picture of the subject's situational reactions.

Administration of the measure is simple. The subject is seated comfortably, and the experimenter says, "Now please look around yourself and try to make a description of what you see." The subject has complete freedom to interpret the environment as he chooses.

The psychologist records everything the tested person says as in the Rorschach test. He remains silent until the subject has finished responding or is interrupted in order to end the test. The examiner then says: "This will be enough." If the subject has difficulty after the first answers, the experimenter may ask: "Do you see anything else?" Any response is recorded. The test responses are classified, scored, and interpreted as if it were a Rorschach test (Ladonko, 1962).

Differences between scoring of the Rorschach test and this measure are described and modifications in scoring and interpretation are noted very briefly. Four new types of responses given by subjects taking this test, but not found in Rorschach protocols, are described and exemplified. They are: personal answers; affective answers; subjective answers, "WD" answers. Some personality correlates of each of the four response types are suggested. According to the author, when there are five or more affective responses affect dominates over all other motives.

RELIABILITY AND VALIDITY: None reported.

BIBLIOGRAPHY:

LADONKO, A. "The Life Situation Perception Test." *Journal of Clinical Psychology,* 1962, *XVIII,* 297–299.

MINIATURE SITUATIONS TEST

AUTHOR: Sebastiano Santostefano

AGE: 6 to adulthood

VARIABLE: Personality

TYPE OF MEASURE: Individually administered performance test

SOURCE FROM WHICH THE MEASURE MAY BE OBTAINED: See Santostefano (1957, 1962)

DESCRIPTION OF MEASURE: The Miniature Situations Test (MST) provides an opportunity for the child to act on one of two objects in order to elicit overt, coping responses indicative of personality characteristics. Thus, the child chooses between the following activities, which are examples of the forty-one pairs:

Tearing paper, repairing paper
Driving in a spike, pulling out a spike
Copying a design for speed, copying a design for accuracy
Counting buttons, arranging flowers
Experimenter tells story to subject, subject tells story to experimenter

This method was chosen over a naturalistic observation method because it provides unequivocal responses in a few seconds and equivalent stimuli to all subjects, thus decreasing variance in responses based on uncontrolled stimuli. Criteria for selection of the tasks were: the task can be administered on a desk top; a single act, executed in a few seconds, can complete each task; judges agree on the psychological meaning of the task; the psychological significance of the task is not evident to the subject.

Santostefano's (1960) factor analysis revealed five identifiable factors: overt aggression versus inhibition of aggression; avoidance versus approach of potentially harmful or difficult-to-handle stimuli; verbal self-display versus passive, inconspicuous behavior; symbolic versus overt aggression; and control over versus compliance with the experimenter.

RELIABILITY AND VALIDITY: Santostefano (1965) administered the measure to brain damaged, orphaned, and public school children to determine whether their responses would reflect characteristics generally associated with these groups. Brain damaged children showed more aggression and need for structure. Orphaned children displayed more oral-regressive behavior. None of the data in this study were contrary to expected differences between the groups.

BIBLIOGRAPHY:

SANTOSTEFANO, S. "Forced-Choice Acts as Personality Measures." Unpublished doctoral dissertation, Pennsylvania State University, 1957.

SANTOSTEFANO, S. "An Exploration of Performance Measures of Personality." *Journal of Clinical Psychology*, 1960, *16*, 373–377.

SANTOSTEFANO, S. "Miniature Situations as a Way of Interviewing Children." *Merrill-Palmer Quarterly Behavior Development*, 1962, *8*, 261–269.

SANTOSTEFANO, S. "Construct Validity of the Miniature Situations Test: I. The Performance of Public School, Orphaned and Brain Damaged Children." *Journal of Clinical Psychology*, 1965, *21*, 418–421.

MINNESOTA PERSONALITY PROFILE II

AUTHOR: University of Minnesota Institute of Child Development and Welfare

AGE: Preschool, kindergarten, and elementary school children

VARIABLE: Personality

TYPE OF MEASURE: Teacher rating scale

SOURCE FROM WHICH THE MEASURE MAY BE OBTAINED: Dale B. Harris, Pennsylvania State University, 1 Burrows Building, University Park, Pa. 16802, for research purposes only

DESCRIPTION OF MEASURE: The Minnesota Personality Profile II is a ten-item Likert-type instrument with a five-point designation of behavior for each item in general adjustment, realism, persistence, responsibility, attentiveness, dependency, flexibility, calmness, sensitivity, and compliance. On this scale, adaptive behavior is indicated by a high score. Since the score on each item ranges from 1 to 5, the maximum score may vary between 10 and 50. The array of scores on each item is in scrambled order, possibly to avoid a teacher's set in rating a child's behavior. The PP II is a revision of an earlier scale of twenty items (Anderson and Harris, 1959). Two illustrative items from the scale are presented below:

In my opinion, this child's general adjustment is: *poor—1, fair—2, average—3, good—4, excellent—5.*

How realistic is he? *knows his own faults and good points—5, fairly realistic about himself—4, somewhat realistic—3, doesn't seem to know the score about himself—2, completely unaware of what he is like—1.*

RELIABILITY AND VALIDITY: The PP II has been used for a diversity of predictive purposes with various samples. Two major studies should be consulted for the details on the sampling groups and findings (Anderson and Harris, 1959; Anderson, 1960). Using as subjects seventy-four girls and sixty-five boys who were on the average 11 years old in 1950, in the tenth grade in 1954, and who would normally graduate from high school in 1957, Anderson and Harris (1959) found the following relationships with the PP II (PP II administered 1950; ratings on other variables, 1957):

	Girls	Boys
Combination score	.54	.53
School score (grades)	.52	.56
Informant's score (community reputation)	.44	.40
Participation (in school and community)	.17	.40

BIBLIOGRAPHY:

ANDERSON, J. E. "The Prediction of Adjustment over Time." In Ira Iscoe and H. W. Stevenson (Eds.), *Personality Development in Children.* Austin, Texas: University of Texas Press, 1960, pp. 28–72.

ANDERSON, J. E., and HARRIS, D. B. *A Survey of Children's Adjustment over Time.* Minneapolis, Minnesota: Institute of Child Development and Welfare, University of Minnesota, 1959.

MODIFIED, NONVERBAL ADMINISTRATION OF THE MAPS TEST

AUTHOR: Wilson D. Hess

AGE: Deaf children

VARIABLE: Personality characteristics

TYPE OF MEASURE: Projective test

SOURCE FROM WHICH THE MEASURE MAY BE OBTAINED: Wilson D. Hess, Dean, Graduate School, Gallaudet College, Washington, D.C.

DESCRIPTION OF MEASURE: This is a modification of the MAPS test for use with deaf and severely hard of hearing children. The MAPS test was written by Edwin S. Schneidman and published by the Psychological Corporation. Detailed directions for the modified administration of the test and the recording of responses are given under the following headings: physical arrangements; responses to backgrounds; free-choice sorting of emotions; figures selected as characters; like-dislike sorting; and forced-choice sorting of emotions. Anyone using this modification should be well acquainted with the original MAPS test.

RELIABILITY AND VALIDITY: None reported.

BIBLIOGRAPHY: None.

MOOSEHEART WISHES AND FEARS INVENTORY

AUTHOR: Mooseheart Laboratory for Child Research, Mooseheart, Illinois

AGE: 4 to 16 years

VARIABLE: Personality

TYPE OF MEASURE: Projective test

SOURCE FROM WHICH THE MEASURE MAY BE OBTAINED: Mooseheart Laboratory for Child Research, Child Guidance Clinic, Mooseheart, Illinois 60539

DESCRIPTION OF MEASURE: The information obtained on the Wishes and Fears Inventory is interpreted as a projection of the child's personality. The inventory consists of a series of questions that have no correct answers and hence assume a projective nature. The form of the questions varies, but replies to questions on each of these items and reasons for each of the responses are requested: three wishes; two positive identifications; two negative identifications; two desired activities; two undesired activities; two changes desired (in oneself); two fears; and one earliest recollection. The inventory comes in two forms, Form A designed for younger children, and Form B for older students. In the former, the questions are read verbatim if desired, and the child's responses noted. The child is asked why he chose a response, since the reason for his choice frequently gives the clinician more insight into the child's personality than does the choice itself.

Examples of the questions on this form are given below:

Wishes: *With young children this can be presented as the gifts of a magician. For example, "Do you know what a magician is, a magic man? Today imagine that I am a magician, can give you anything in all the world. Of all the things that a magician can give you, what would you wish for first?"*

Positive Identification: *"I am still a magician who can make you anybody you want to be. Now of all the people you have ever heard of, people you have seen in the movies, in the funny papers, heard on the radio, read about or know them; maybe they are alive or dead, maybe they are real or imaginary, what person would you most want to be like?"*

Negative Identification: *"I am still a magician, and because I like you I don't want to make any mistakes. Of all the people you have ever heard of, know, seen in the movies, if you had to choose someone to be like, who is the last person you would choose? . . . Why would you choose them last?"*

Form B is a record blank and may be used with the questions given on Form A or with simplified questions, such as:

If you could have anything you wished for, what would be your wish? Why? What else would you wish for? (Three answers)
Who would you most like to be like? Why? (Two answers)
Who wouldn't you like to be like? Why? (Two answers)

RELIABILITY AND VALIDITY: The scale has been used with 750 children at the Mooseheart Laboratory for Child Research (Winker, 1949, p. 191). "The Inventory [however] was purely exploratory and . . . no statistics [exist] on reliability and validity."

BIBLIOGRAPHY:

WINKER, J. B. "Age Trends and Sex Differences in the Wishes, Identification, Activities, and Fears of Children." *Child Development,* 1949, *20,* 191–200.

NURSE'S SCALE FOR RATING NEONATES

AUTHOR: Esther Haar, et al.

AGE: Neonates

VARIABLE: Behavioral and personality characteristics

TYPE OF MEASURE: Rating scale

SOURCE FROM WHICH THE MEASURE MAY BE OBTAINED: See Haar, et al. (1964)

DESCRIPTION OF MEASURE: The Nurse's Scale for Rating Premature Neonates consists of sixteen items rated on a four-point scale, two above and two below average. The sixteen forced-choice items cover a broad range of traits possibly manifested by premature neonates. The scale, however, was designed to be used effectively only under natural, long-period observation, rather than short artificially structured observations. The advantage of this requirement is that it avoids measuring transient variations of state.

Examples of the items from the final version of the sixteen-item scale follow:

This baby is usually: *very tense, tense, relaxed, very relaxed.*

This baby is: *very cute, cute, rather unattractive, very unattractive.*

This baby: *cries a great deal, cries somewhat more than others, cries somewhat less than others, is very quiet.*

RELIABILITY AND VALIDITY: Six selected nurses rated one hundred randomly chosen premature babies on the questionnaire, when each baby's weight reached 1,800 grams (4 pounds). Birth weights varied from 1,200 to 2,240 grams, and length of hospitalization ranged from 11 to 77 days. Each nurse was individually instructed on the meaning of each item.

Reliabilities among nurse-raters ranged from .54 to .84 for the group of six nurses, dropping as the reliabilities were estimated for smaller groups of nurses.

Factor analysis revealed two dimensions of the scale:

Factor A (Activity-Inactivity) included six items with factor loadings above .60. Examples of these items were tenseness, irritability, and sensitivity to sound.

Factor HN (Nurse Halo) comprised nine items with factor loadings above .60. Illustrations were cuteness, ease of feeding, contact responsiveness, and general responsiveness to stimuli.

Factor A and Factor HN were significantly but not strongly correlated ($r = .37$).

In summary, the scale appears to have satisfactory reliability, internal consistency, and apparently measures at least two separate dimensions of behavior. The fact that the present form of the scale was based on item analysis also gives additional support to its validity. The significance of the lack of relationship between nurses' ratings of infant behavior and background data has been described by the authors as follows: "Speculations by workers in the field of infant behavior concerning the influence of prenatal factors or birth trauma upon activity or tenseness in the child are not supported by the present findings, since no relationship was found between activity type and either prenatal conditions, cause of prematurity, or difficulty in delivery."

BIBLIOGRAPHY:

HAAR, E., WELKOWITZ, J., BLAU, A., and COHEN, J. "Personality Differentiation of Neonates: A Nurse Rating Scale Method." *American Academy of Child Psychiatry,* 1964, *3,* 330–342.

PETERSON PROBLEM CHECKLIST

AUTHOR: Donald R. Peterson

AGE: Kindergarten through grade six

VARIABLE: Personality and conduct disorders

TYPE OF MEASURE: Checklist

SOURCE FROM WHICH THE MEASURE MAY BE OBTAINED: The rating schedule, correlation matrices, and unrotated centroid factor matrices have been deposited with the American Documentation Institute. Order Document No. 6632 from ADI Auxiliary Publications Project, Photoduplication Service, Library of Congress, Washington, D.C. 20540, remitting in advance $2.00 for microfilm or $3.75 for photocopies. Make checks payable to: Chief, Photoduplication Service, Library of Congress.

DESCRIPTION OF MEASURE: The Peterson Checklist consists of fifty-eight items of behavior that may be completed by a teacher who is familiar with the child and by an interviewer who uses a parent as the informer. The rater or informant is instructed to complete all items and to rate each one in terms of three levels of severity.

The checklist measures two dimensions of behavior—conduct problems and personality problems. Peterson has defined the conduct problem as closely resembling unsocialized aggression, and personality problems as overinhibited behavior (1961).

To obtain a score for conduct problems, the grader is instructed to count 1 point for specifically designated items whether the problem was rated 1 (mild) or 2 (severe). In obtaining these two scores, Peterson has used only those items with the highest loadings on the factors he defined. Examples of items under "Conduct Problem" include the following:

Restlessness, inability to sit still
Attention-seeking, "show-off" behavior
Disruptiveness, tendency to annoy and bother others

The following are examples of items for "Personality Problem."

Doesn't know how to have fun; behaves like a little adult
Self-consciousness; easily embarrassed
Feelings of inferiority (Scoring Instructions)

RELIABILITY AND VALIDITY: When kindergartners were rated by two teachers, interjudge r's of .77 and .75 were found for factors 1 and 2, respectively. The correlations between factors was .18. According to Peterson (1961), these two factors appear uniformly in treatment cases (Hewitt and Jenkins, 1946; Himmelweit, 1953), and similar factors have appeared in the questionnaire behavior of delinquent boys (Peterson, Quay, and Cameron, 1959).

BIBLIOGRAPHY:

BECKER, W. C. "The Relationship of Factors in Parental Ratings of Self and Each Other to the Behavior of Kindergarten Children as Rated by Mothers, Fathers, and Teachers." *Journal of Consulting Psychology,* 1960, *24,* 507–527.

HEWITT, L. E., and JENKINS, R. L. *Fundamental Patterns of Maladjustment: The Dynamics of Their Origin.* Springfield, Ill.: Green, 1946.

HIMMELWEIT, H. T. "A Factorial Study of 'Children's Behavior Problems.' " Cited in J. J. Eysenck, *The Structure of Human Personality.* London: Methuen, 1953.

PETERSON, D. R. "Behavior Problems of Middle Childhood." *Journal of Consulting Psychology,* 1961, *25,* 205–209.

PETERSON, D. R., QUAY, H. C., and CAMERON, G. R. "Personality and Background Factors in Juvenile Delinquency as Inferred from Questionnaire Responses." *Journal of Consulting Psychology,* 1959, *23,* 395–399.

PROJECTIVE INTERVIEW TECHNIQUE

AUTHOR: Richard A. Cutts

AGE: Mentally retarded and primary aged children

VARIABLE: Several personality characteristics (see description of measure)

TYPE OF MEASURE: Projective interview, individually administered

SOURCE FROM WHICH THE MEASURE MAY BE OBTAINED: See Cutts (1956)

DESCRIPTION OF MEASURE: The subject is asked to draw a figure of a person. The measure consists of a series of questions designed to bring out the feelings and attitudes that the subject ascribes to the person that he has drawn. Thus, the subject projects his own means and feelings onto the person he has drawn.

Five areas of "personality development" are measured: home adjustment, school adjustment, social adjustment, ego structure, and ego defenses. Examples of questions under the five areas follow:

Home—relationship with parents: *Does this boy (or girl, or person) that you have drawn have fun with his father?*
School—attitude toward attending school: *Does this boy like school as much now as when he first started?*
Social Adjustment—feelings of belonging and acceptance by peer groups at school: *Is he among the first to be chosen for games by the other kids at school?*
Ego Structure—self-percept: *Would you say that this boy is big and strong, or not so big and strong?*
Ego Defense—fantasy: *When he is alone, does he sometimes like to pretend that he is someplace else or that he is someone else?*

As the author points out, the interview questions he lists are merely examples of questions that he has found useful. The technique is more important than any specific questions used. Each clinician will wish to adapt the questions to his own situation.

RELIABILITY AND VALIDITY: Cutts (1956) administered the measure to eighty-seven retarded children, thirty-four girls and fifty-three boys. In 83.5 per cent of the cases, the child drew a person of his own sex. In approximately 60 per cent of the cases, there was no more than two years' difference between the age of the child and the age which he ascribed to the person he drew. Only 5 per cent of these children drew adult figures.

BIBLIOGRAPHY:

cutts, r. a. "A Projective Interview Technique." *American Journal of Mental Deficiency*, 1956, *61*, 191–197.

RABIN ADAPTATION OF SACKS AND LEVY SENTENCE COMPLETION TEST

AUTHOR: A. I. Rabin

AGE: 9 to 12

VARIABLE: Nine areas of personality and family relations—father, mother, family, friends, abilities, fears, guilt, future, goals

TYPE OF MEASURE: Projective test

SOURCE FROM WHICH THE MEASURE MAY BE OBTAINED: See Rabin (1959)

DESCRIPTION OF MEASURE: This is a thirty-six-item sentence completion test in which four items each deal with the following areas: mother, father, family, friends, future, goals, abilities, fears, and guilt. Examples of items are:

To me the future looks
I would do anything to forget the time I
I believe that I have the ability to
My family treats me like

Rabin (1959) scored some of the items according to several subvariables or "categories." For example: (1) Positive versus nonpositive responses. (2) Responses to items concerning likes and dislikes of people were classified as dependent on the relationship of others to the subject (e.g., "I don't like people who . . . push me"); dependent on others' social attributes and personal relationships; and dependent on others' personality characteristics, especially moral and ethical. (3) Responses to some items could be categorized according to an "internalized guilt . . . versus objective events" involving fear, such as physical injury. (4) Six items were combined to get a measure of self-concept. (5) Goals were classified as "immature" and other.

RELIABILITY AND VALIDITY: Using broad scoring categories (such as "positive," "other") Rabin (1959) found 92.5 per cent interscorer agreement when two scorers other than the author examined fifty-one protocols. He found that Israeli children, compared with Michigan children, idealized the family and mother less; were more suspicious of friends and selected them more on the basis of personal and social qualities rather than their reactions to them; had more internalized guilt; were less optimistic about the future and more mature in their goals; were more critical and less confident.

While the test has been used with children aged 9 to 12, the reading level was found to be high for many of them. The user may wish to apply a readability formula before attempting to use it with children. The measure should be used only by a clinically trained person.

BIBLIOGRAPHY:

RABIN, A. I. "Comparison of American and Israeli Children by Means of a Sentence Completion Technique." *Journal of Social Psychology,* 1959, *59,* 3–12.

RABIN, A. I., and THELEN, M. H. "Some Personality Characteristics and Attitudes of Delinquent Adolescents." *Journal of Offender Therapy,* 1964, *8,* 29–36.

RATING-RANKING SCALES FOR CHILD BEHAVIOR

AUTHORS: Rue L. Cromwell, Dan Davis, and Joan Held

AGE: No age range specified, although appears to apply preschool to adolescence

VARIABLE: Child behavior

TYPE OF MEASURE: Rating scale

SOURCE FROM WHICH THE MEASURE MAY BE OBTAINED: Rue L. Cromwell, Lafayette Clinic, 951 E. Lafayette, Detroit, Mich. 48207

DESCRIPTION OF MEASURE: The measure consists of 125 items, and is designed for use by teachers, counselors, nurses, ward technicians, and other personnel who are in a position to know the children well. The measure is still being developed, and no evidence on item clustering is available. The measure is thus now composed of 125 separate scales, or items. The rater is given a continuum which goes from never to once in a great while to sometimes to frequently to always.

Items are then answered by marking a place, for every child being rated, anywhere along the continuum, not only on the five designated points. Thus, on each item, the judge or rater *rates* every child and consequently *ranks* him with the others on the dimension represented by the item. Examples of items (omitting the continuum, which is the same for all items) are given below:

Attracted to things that require his own action (such as hammering, softball, track, etc.)?
During unstructured activity (free time) expected changes in routine (announced ahead of time) are accepted with ease?
Cries for no appropriate reason?
Does not think he is good enough? Lacks self-confidence?
Is concerned with whether or not adults trust him?
Pouts when he feels mistreated?

RELIABILITY AND VALIDITY: Mean intrajudge reliability of four raters ranged from .78 to .92. Interjudge reliabilities, as indicated by correlation ratios, ranged from .47 to .89, with a mean correlation ratio of .66.

BIBLIOGRAPHY:

CROMWELL, R. L., and DAVIS, D. "Behavior Classification of Emotionally Disturbed Children." Paper read at Council for Exceptional Children, Portland, Oregon, April, 1965.

SCHOOL OBSERVATION SCHEDULE

AUTHORS: Saul Cooper, William Ryan, and B. R. Hutcheson

AGE: Kindergarten and elementary school children

VARIABLE: Personality

TYPE OF MEASURE: Rating scale

SOURCE FROM WHICH THE MEASURE MAY BE OBTAINED: Saul Cooper, Community Mental Health Center, 220 E. Huron, Ann Arbor, Michigan 48108

DESCRIPTION OF MEASURE: The School Observation Scale consists of thirty-seven items for rating a child's behavior. The teacher is simply requested to mark only those items of behavior that apply to the particular child being rated. The score then consists of the total number of items checked. Sample items from the scale follow: irritable, touchy; destructive; negativistic, refuses to comply; sullen, passively hostile; acts noisy, silly.

RELIABILITY AND VALIDITY: Reliability coefficients on this scale between ratings by psychologist-observers and those of teachers were, on two separate occasions, .67 and .86 (with p < .001 in each instance). The validity of this scale rests largely on a highly significant correlation coefficient of .63 (p < .001) with psychiatric diagnosis based on intensive interviewing and its very high efficiency in screening false negatives.

BIBLIOGRAPHY:

COOPER, S., RYAN, W., and HUTCHESON, B. R. "Classroom Screening for Emotional Disturbance." Presentation at the Convention of the American Psychological Association, 1959.

SCHOOL TAT

AUTHOR: Mary Engel

AGE: Elementary school age

VARIABLE: Personality

TYPE OF MEASURE: Projective test

SOURCE FROM WHICH THE MEASURE MAY BE OBTAINED: Mary S. Engel, City College, City University of N.Y., New York, N.Y. 10010. On loan from author for research purposes only.

DESCRIPTION OF MEASURE: This is a picture-story test in which all picture-card stimuli are school-oriented, showing school-age children in various ambiguous situations. The authors constructed a conceptual continuum representing mature and less mature ways of coping with school demands. There are five pictures, four of which have equivalent versions for boys and girls. Everyday school situations are presented—children on a school bus; children in art class; a child at the blackboard, an adult with him; a youngster running down the corridor; and a classroom where all children but one are raising their hands. The examiner classifies the stories into the following categories: rebellion, platitude, constriction, anxiety, punishment, magic solution, never again, problem solving, and fanciful. These categories are described briefly.

RELIABILITY AND VALIDITY: Independent rating of 126 stories by the investigators and a psychologist not associated with the project resulted in an inter-rater reliability coefficient of .81. Two other judges, working from written definitions of the categories, agreed to the extent of r = .83.

BIBLIOGRAPHY:

ENGEL, M., COHEN, R. B., and SANFILIPPO, J. "Children Tell Stories about School—An Exploration of the Differences in the Elementary Grades." Paper read at the convention of the American Psychological Association, Los Angeles, California, 1964.

SONOMA CHECK LIST

AUTHORS: George Domino, Marcel Goldschmid, and Max Kaplan

AGE: Retarded children

VARIABLE: Personality

TYPE OF MEASURE: Checklist

SOURCE FROM WHICH THE MEASURE MAY BE OBTAINED: George Domino, Psychology Department, Fordham University, Bronx, New York 10458

DESCRIPTION OF MEASURE: The SCL consists of a checklist of 210 words modeled on Gough's Adjectives Check List, and derived also from psychological reports on the mentally retarded, nurses' daily log notes, feedback from technicians and aides, and consultations with members of other disciplines concerned with the retarded. The method employed in the use of the checklist simply requested the rater to check those forty words that best described the patient being rated. Each rater was also requested to indicate his degree of familiarity with the patient on a seven-step scale. Sample adjectives from the list include the following: interesting, careful, odd, sad, indifferent, sweet, unteachable, greedy, eager, silent.

RELIABILITY AND VALIDITY: The SCL has been used with fifty-six hospitalized trainable retarded girls, including twenty-one mongoloid patients with an average age of 135 months and a mean IQ on the Stanford-Binet (L-M) of 30. The remainder of the group included thirty-five non-mongoloid patients with an average IQ score on the same test of 35 and a mean age of 125 months.

Rater bias did not influence the results of the measure (Domino et al., 1964). Validity, however, has support from several sources. (1) A considerable number of words correlated beyond the .05 level of probability with the diagnosis of mongolism. The authors assert that the statistically significant adjectives present an internally consistent personality profile of mongoloids. Since this persistent personality pattern substantially agrees with the clinical description, some construct validity for the scale may probably be claimed. (2) The method of developing the adjectives for this scale would appear to give it some content validity. Rater bias did not influence the results, however. (3) Ratings by naive college students on the scale differentiated between mongoloid and non-mongoloid patients at a statistically significant level as measured by the t test.

BIBLIOGRAPHY:

DOMINO, G. "Personality Traits in Institutionalized Mongoloids." *American Journal of Mental Deficiency,* 1965, *69,* 568–570.

DOMINO, G., GOLDSCHMID, M., and KAPLAN, M. "Personality Traits of Institutionalized Mongoloid Girls." *American Journal of Mental Deficiency,* 1964, *68,* 498–502.

STRAUSS-KEPHART BEHAVIOR RATING SCALE

AUTHORS: Alfred A. Strauss and Newell C. Kephart

AGE: Retarded adolescents

VARIABLE: Personality

TYPE OF MEASURE: Checklist type of rating scale

SOURCE FROM WHICH THE MEASURE MAY BE OBTAINED: See Strauss and Lehtinen (1947), and Strauss and Kephart (1940)

DESCRIPTION OF MEASURE: The Strauss-Kephart Diagnostic Behavior Rating Scale consists of fifty-two paired words relating to the behavior of mentally deficient children. The rater is requested to check the pair of words or individual words within the pair according to whether they do or do not describe the behavior of the child. The word pairs relate to the fields of mood, social relations, and activity. The purpose of the scale is to distinguish between endogenous and exogenous types of mental deficiency. The scale itself consists of two parts. Part I includes fifteen items relating to motor activity in general and movements and gestures indicative of emotional states. Part II consists of thirty-seven items, describing the general personality makeup of the child. The rater rates each pair of descriptions in terms of whether one, both, or neither adjective applies. In the original scoring system, the items were weighted from 1 to 3 according to their contribution for differentiating the records of exogenous and endogenous retarded children, but the article by Strauss and Kephart (1940) does not clearly specify the items in question. The score, then, consists of the totals for the items with differential weights. Examples of items from Part I—expressive movements—are: graceful-clumsy; smooth-jerky; normal-peculiar. From Part II—personality: fluctuating-constant; excessive-moderate; daydreaming-present.

RELIABILITY AND VALIDITY: Although the scale was standardized on adolescents, it could easily be applied to younger children because of the descriptive and objective nature of the items that lend themselves to easy and reliable scoring. The authors consider the standardization of the scale not adequate. The number of cases is too small and the sample is limited to high-grade moron and borderline level institutionalized children.

Some content validity may be assumed since the authors chose words descriptive of the organic behavior pattern. Second, the authors retain only those pairs of items that differentiated between the endogenous and exogenous groups as determined by the contingency coefficient. Finally, the comparison of the mean of scores and standard deviations of the two distributions (endogenous and exogenous groups) revealed very little overlapping in scores.

Measure reliability was investigated by the split-half method on odd-even items corrected for attenuation by the Spearman-Brown formula. The resulting reliability coefficient was .918 (Strauss and Kephart, 1940).

BIBLIOGRAPHY:

STRAUSS, A. A., and KEPHART, N. C. "Behavior Differences in Mentally Retarded Children Measured by a New Behavior Rating Scale." *American Journal of Psychiatry,* 1940, *96,* 1117–1123.

STRAUSS, A. A., and LEHTINEN, L. E. *Psychopathology and Education of the Brain Injured Child.* Vol. I. New York: Grune and Stratton, 1947.

THE STRUCTURED INTERVIEW TECHNIQUE

AUTHOR: Pauline G. Vorhaus

AGE: Upper elementary to adult

VARIABLE: Personality-general

TYPE OF MEASURE: Structured interview

SOURCE FROM WHICH THE MEASURE MAY BE OBTAINED: See Harrower, Molly et al. (1960)

DESCRIPTION OF MEASURE: While this measure is not specifically set up for use with children, it and similar structured interview techniques following a short picture projective measure are used by numerous psychologists in working with children. The subject is asked to draw a person. After he has completed his own-sex drawing, he is asked a series of questions concerning his drawing. This is Part I of the structured interview. Part II of the structured interview involves the subject answering the same set of questions about himself.

The measure consists of thirty-two structured interview questions, although some of them are in fact areas of inquiry, for example, relationship to parents, home attitudes, health, appetite. Under "health" there are specific questions such as, "Is he healthy? If not what is wrong? How was his health in childhood?" In general, the questions are designed to bring out the subject's own needs, the pressures impinging on him, his responses to specific types of usually distressful situations. There is no scoring scheme provided for the measure. It is designed to be interpreted clinically, although it would be possible for the researcher to impose a scoring scheme on most of the items.

RELIABILITY AND VALIDITY: There is no evidence given for test validity or reliability. It is suggested that, like the Thematic Apperception Test, this measure gives leads or working hypotheses to be verified by other methods. The discussion of reliability, like that of validation, refers to Murray's Thematic Apperception Manual, and suggests that the same statements of validity and reliability as are made for the TAT can be made for this measure.

BIBLIOGRAPHY:

HARROWER, M., VORHAUS, P., ROMAN, M., and BAUMAN, G. *Creative Variations in the Projective Techniques*. Springfield, Ill.: Charles C Thomas, 1960.

Group 2-b
Personality Variables

ACHIEVEMENT MOTIVATION

AUTHORS: D. C. McClelland, J. W. Atkinson, R. A. Clark, and E. L. Lowell

AGE: The measure appears usable with upper elementary children, especially with modifications such as the use of tape recording of stories

VARIABLE: Achievement motivation

TYPE OF MEASURE: Projective test (McClelland's term is "thought sampling")

SOURCE FROM WHICH THE MEASURE MAY BE OBTAINED: See McClelland, et al. (1953)

DESCRIPTION OF MEASURE: The stimuli for this measure consist of four pictures, two from the Thematic Apperception Test (pictures 7BM and 8BM) and two made up for this measure and reproduced in McClelland, et al. (1953) (Figs. 3.1.A and 3.1.B). Another form of the measure is reported in Atkinson (1950). The instructions used are similar to those used with most picture projective measures, except that this test was administered to a group of students by projecting the stimuli onto a screen. McClelland (1953, p. 98) gives the specific instructions used.

For purposes of measuring achievement motivation, each story is searched for thirteen content categories that are described in detail and exemplified by case protocols, which should be very helpful to the researcher interested in learning the scoring method. The thirteen categories are: unrelated imagery, doubtful imagery, achievement imagery, need, instrumental activity, positive anticipatory goal state, negative anticipatory goal state, personal obstacle, environmental obstacle, positive affective state, negative affective state, nurturant press, and achievement thema. The scoring system was revised twice; intercorrelations of scores using each of the three scoring systems were .95, .90, and .87. The authors state that one and one-half to two minutes is sufficient to score one story, after the scorer has learned the scoring crtieria. Two sets of four pictures each provide alternate forms of the test.

RELIABILITY AND VALIDITY: Interscorer reliability coefficient (experienced scorers scoring one month apart) in one study (N = 30) was .95. An experienced scorer, evaluating protocols of 32 subjects on two occasions, six months apart, found a reliability of .95. When an inexperienced and an experienced scorer evaluated the eight-story records (using both sets of four pictures) of 24 subjects, the rank order correlation was .96. The correlation between scores obtained by subjects on the four original pictures and four new pictures was .48. Test-retest reliabilities tend to be low (see McClelland, 1953, p. 193, for an explanation).

The authors conclude that while the measure is presently unsuitable for prediction of individual n achievement, it has sufficient stability for group comparisons. Further refinements, they feel, should make possible individual prediction.

Numerous validity studies are cited by McClelland et al. (1953) in Chapter 8. The results are mixed, but in general they support the validity of the measure. The interested reader should consult Chapters 8 and 9 for validity data.

BIBLIOGRAPHY:

MC CLELLAND, D. C., ATKINSON, J. W., CLARK, R. A., and LOWELL, E. L. *The Achievement Motive.* New York: Appleton-Century-Crofts, Inc., 1953.

ATKINSON, J. W. "Studies in Projective Measurement of Achievement Motivation, University of Michigan." Abstract in University Microfilms, Vol. X, No. 4.

AFFECTIVITY INTERVIEW BLANK

AUTHOR: Elizabeth Mechem Fuller

AGE: 5 to 12

VARIABLE: Personality (affectivity)

TYPE OF MEASURE: Standard interview

SOURCE FROM WHICH THE MEASURE MAY BE OBTAINED: Child Development Laboratory, University Elementary School, University of Michigan, Ann Arbor, Michigan (University Microfilms).

DESCRIPTION OF MEASURE: The Affectivity Interview Blank is a structured interview schedule consisting of sixty-nine scorable items that attempt to assess the "affective or feeling side" of the child's personality. Two additional items are provided in the interest of establishing rapport with the child. The scoring procedure allocates one point for each favorable response by the child, and a complete key on indices of favorableness for each item has been provided. Since some of the questions require multiple answers, the maximum score possible is 81. In interpreting the test, the primary principle to remember is that the higher scores are related to more desirable affectivity, lower scores to less desirable affectivity. Precautions for the user of the test and suggestions for its use are provided in detail.

Sample items from the scale follow:

How are you getting along this year?
Are there any new children in your room this year? Do you like to have new children there or would you rather the same ones would stay every year?
Which part of your work do you like the best?

RELIABILITY AND VALIDITY: Data available are limited to the use of the scale with a norm sample of sixty-five children in attendance at the University of Michigan Elementary School and a secondary but subsequent sample of thirty elementary school children from the original group. The correlation coefficient for the odd-even items on the original half was .70, with either half used singly. With correction by the Spearman-Brown formula this coefficient increased to .82. In the second sample, the split-half correlation was .58 and the combined reliability value was .74. Over consecutive years, the stability of the scores for a year's interval with the thirty children common to both groups was .70.

In addition to these data on reliability, the interview has some content validity in that the interpretation of a child's response as indicative of a higher level of affectivity was determined on the basis of judgments by experienced clinicians. As an aid in interpreting the scores, a table for converting raw scores to percentile ranks for desirable affectivity level is provided.

BIBLIOGRAPHY:

FULLER, E. M. *Manual for the Affectivity Blank*. Ann Arbor, Michigan: University of
    Michigan, Child Development Laboratories, 1951.
FULLER, E. M. "Affectivity and Growth in Children." *Child Development*, 1943, *14*,
    91–115.
FULLER, E. M. *The Relationship of Affectivity to Various Measures of Growth in
    Children*. Doctoral dissertation, University of Michigan. Ann Arbor, Michi-
    gan: University Microfilms.
FULLER, E. M. "How Do Children Feel about It?" *Childhood Education*, 1946, *23*,
    124–132.

BARBER SUGGESTIBILITY SCALE

AUTHOR: T. X. Barber

AGE: 6 and older

VARIABLE: Suggestibility; hypnotizability

TYPE OF MEASURE: Test, individually administered

SOURCE FROM WHICH THE MEASURE MAY BE OBTAINED: See Barber and Calverley (1963)

DESCRIPTION OF MEASURE: The BSS consists of eight subscales measuring "primary" or "hypnotic-like" suggestibility: arm lowering; arm levitation; hand lock (inability to unclasp hands); thirst hallucination; verbal inhibition (inability to speak name); body immobility; posthypnotic-like response; and selective amnesia. The scale is administered orally on an individual basis as a test of imagination.

For illustrative purposes, the first subscale (arm lowering) is given in full (Barber and Calverley, 1963).

Arm Lowering—*"Hold your right arm straight out in front of you like this." The experimenter guides the subject to extend the right arm directly in front of the body at shoulder height and parallel to the floor. "Concentrate on your arm and listen to me."*

Begin timing. *"Imagine that your right arm is feeling heavier and heavier, and that it's moving down and down. It's becoming heavier and heavier and moving down and down. It weighs a ton! It's getting heavier and heavier. It's moving down and down, more and more, coming down and down, more and more; it's heavier and heavier, coming down and down, more and more, more and more." End 30 seconds.*

"You can relax your arm now!"

Scoring criterion: *1 point for response of 4 inches or more.*

Instructions for administration are given by Barber and Calverley (1963) with some modifications of the instruments for younger children, ages 6 and 7. They also provide detailed scoring instructions. Norms for the scale, together with reliability data, are presented by Barber and Calverley (1962, 1963) and Barber and Glass (1962).

RELIABILITY AND VALIDITY: The test has been administered to 724 students ranging between the ages of 6 and 22. Within this group, test-retest correlations over a six-week period were calculated for subjects of age 7 (N = 12), age 10 (N = 22), and ages 18 to 22 (N = 29). The respective coefficients were .62, .66, and .82. According to Fisher's z transformation, however, these correlations did not differ significantly from each other.

Several studies have shown the following consistent findings on suggestibility with the use of this scale: no sex differences; suggestibility inversely related to age until the adult response level is reached; and suggestibility inversely related to conscious resistance to suggestions. Such consistency in predicted results appears to give the scale some construct validity.

In the interest of improving the value of the scale, the authors have made a number of suggestions for further research, such as a standardized trance induction; instructions for explicit task motivation; and the importance of rapport between examiner and examinee (Barber and Calverley, 1963).

BIBLIOGRAPHY:

BARBER, T. X., and CALVERLEY, D. S. " 'Hypnotic Behavior' as a Function of Task Motivation." *Journal of Psychology,* 1962, *54,* 363–389.

BARBER, T. X., and CALVERLEY, D. S. " 'Hypnotic-like' Suggestibility in Children and Adults." *Journal of Abnormal and Social Psychology,* 1963, *66,* 589–597.

BARBER, T. X., and CALVERLEY, D. S. "Hypnotizability, Suggestibility, and Personality: III, A Study Using Teachers' Ratings of Children's Characteristics." *Journal of Psychology,* 1964, *57,* 275–280.

BARBER, T. X., and GLASS, L. B. "Significant Factors in Hypnotic Behavior." *Journal of Abnormal and Social Psychology,* 1962, *64,* 222–228.

BARBER, T. X., and HAHN, K. W., JR. "Physiological and Subjective Responses to Pain Producing Stimulation under Hypnotically Suggested and Walking-Imagined 'Analgesis.' " *Journal of Abnormal and Social Psychology,* 1962, *65,* 411–418.

BARBER, T. X., and HAHN, K. W., JR. " 'Hypnotic Induction' and 'Relaxation': An Experimental Study." *Archives of General Psychiatry,* 1963, *8,* 295–300.

GLASS, L. B., and BARBER, T. X. "A Note on Hypnotic Behavior, the Definition of the Situation and the Placebo Effect." *Journal of Nervous and Mental Disease,* 1961, *132,* 530–541.

BEHAVIOR UNIT OBSERVATIONS

AUTHORS: Robert R. Sears, Lucy Rau, and Richard Alpert

AGE: Nursery school children

VARIABLE: Behavioral correlates and antecedents of identification among children

TYPE OF MEASURE: Observation rating scale

SOURCE FROM WHICH THE MEASURE MAY BE OBTAINED: See Sears, Rau, and Alpert (1965)

DESCRIPTION OF MEASURE: The BUO consists of a number of subscales, including five measures of dependency, twelve of aggression, and ten of adult role. Formal definitions and behavioral examples have been provided for each subtest, as exemplified by a subscale of the adult role below (Sears et al., 1965):

Real adult mannerisms. *Employing characteristically adult postures, gestures, tone of voice, language, vocabulary, etc.; exhibiting interpretive or indirect imitation, or pseudosophistication.* Examples: *Boy calmly comments to himself, "Jesus Christ." "Clear the area, clear the area," says boy, and motions for all to leave. "I've had 15 minutes here, that's enough," says girl, and shrugs her shoulders and leaves. "Confidentially, Jane," girl whispers coyly into ear of neighbor.*

The observer records the main behavioral category exhibited by the child during each thirty-second observational unit. The subject's final score on each category is derived by dividing the number of half-minute intervals in which that category of behavior occurred by the total number of half-minute intervals he was observed over a specified period of time. These *relative-frequency* measures are the BUO *scores.*

RELIABILITY AND VALIDITY: The general formula for determining level of agreement between any two observers was computed as a per cent value from a ratio of twice the number of agreements to the total number of observations made by the two observers within units of ten-minute intervals. The overall average per cent agreement on 1,723 judgments recorded was .81. For the four major types of behavior, the average agreements were as follows: adult role, 86 per cent; dependency, 78 per cent; antisocial aggression, 70 per cent; prosocial aggression, 61 per cent.

Correlational scores also gave some measure of validity for the BUO. As the authors have emphasized, the various behavior measures were designed to estimate relatively stable trait qualities in the children. Consequently, the BUO measures would be valid insofar as they accomplished this purpose. Since error in observer reliability is also involved, the consistency of a child's score over three time periods is not a "pure" measure of trait disposition; nevertheless, it does give some estimate of this reliability. The correlations for the scores on five major variables on each child for each of the three time periods ranged between .63 (dependency) to

.91 (orality). These were mean correlations based on z transformations but the interested research worker should study the details on the computations in full (Sears et al., 1963, pp. 308–311). The authors have made a number of precautionary statements about trait consistency as measured by these scales.

BIBLIOGRAPHY:

SEARS, R. R., RAU, L., and ALPERT, R. *Identification and Child Rearing.* Stanford, California: Stanford University Press, 1963.

BORKE CATEGORIES FOR QUANTIFYING THE PLAY THERAPY PROCESS

AUTHOR: Helene Borke

AGE: 4 to 12 years

VARIABLE: Children's verbalizations in play therapy

TYPE OF MEASURE: Observation frame of reference

SOURCE FROM WHICH THE MEASURE MAY BE OBTAINED: See Lebo and Lebo (1957)

DESCRIPTION OF MEASURE: The measure consists of twenty-three categories of behavior, with examples. Several of the categories are reproduced below from Lebo and Lebo (1957).

Curiosity about the situation and things present in it. (*Why did you choose me? Anyone else been here? Who owns these toys? Who drew that picture?*)

Simple description, information, and comments about play and playroom. (*This is an army. These are prisoners. More marbles. The room's different.*)

Attempting to shift responsibility to the therapist. (*What should I do next? Is this deep enough? Is this good? Do you like this?*)

Asking for information. (*Do birds have ears? Where is the paint? How does this work?*)

The categories can be used with verbatim notes or with mechanical recordings as the basic data, or as a recording frame of reference for live observation.

RELIABILITY AND VALIDITY: Finke (1947) used five inexperienced judges and found 66 to 77 per cent agreement between her analysis and that of the judges. In one other study, Lebo (1932) found agreement of 71 to 78 per cent between two judges and a criterion judgment. In this study, agreement of the senior author and two judges experienced in play therapy was 77 and 81 per cent. A measure of the similarity of category usage by three judges (Lebo and Lebo, 1957) is the coefficient of concordance of rank order for each category, which was .84.

Lebo and Lebo (1957) found that most of their eleven hypotheses about relationships between age of child, observed aggressiveness, and the Borke categories were supported.

BIBLIOGRAPHY:

FINKE, H. "Change in the Expression of Emotionalized Attitudes in Six Cases of Play Therapy." Unpublished master's thesis, University of Chicago, 1947.

LEBO, D. "The Relationship of Response Categories in Play Therapy." *Journal of Clinical Psychology,* 1946, *2,* 203–213.

LEBO, D., and LEBO, E. "Aggression and Age in Relation to Verbal-Expression in Non-directive Play Therapy." *Psychological Monographs,* 1957, *71,* No. 20 (Whole No. 449).

CAMPOS STORY COMPLETION TECHNIQUE

AUTHOR: Leonard P. Campos

AGE: 9 through 12 (boys only)

VARIABLE: Ability to delay need gratification

TYPE OF MEASURE: Projective test

SOURCE FROM WHICH THE MEASURE MAY BE OBTAINED: See Campos (1963)

DESCRIPTION OF MEASURE: The Story Completion Technique measures the degree to which a subject delays gratifying a need when confronted with a choice situation in which he is free to immediately gratify or defer gratification of a given need. The needs measured include need-acquisition, need-affiliation, need-aggression, need-nurturance and need-achievement. Need is defined as an action tendency, and operational definitions for each type of need are explicit. The scale draws from Murray's system of needs (1938) and McClelland's conceptual schema (1953) on need-achievement. The scale consists of parallel forms (A and B) with each form including a story for each type of need. In each story, a boy named "Johnny" is confronted with a choice of deferring or immediately gratifying the need. As an illustration, the story from Form A measuring need-acquisition follows.

Johnny is passing by the toy store window where there are many interesting toys he can buy which he would like to have. He sees a model airplane he likes very much. But he doesn't have enough money right now to buy it.

The stories are individually presented to each child and the responses in each story are scored on a seven-point scale for ability to delay gratification. Lower scores are in the direction of greater ability for delay in need-gratification.

RELIABILITY AND VALIDITY: Reliability statistics rest on three separate samples: an initial sample of ten boys in an institution between the ages of 10 to 11 (E group); a cross-validation matching sample of twenty-six sixth-grade boys (C group); and a final institutional sample of 103 boys ranging in age between 9 and 12.

Reliability coefficients for Forms A and B were respectively .96 and .84 for the E and C groups. Agreement in scoring between two observers was also quite high with 72 per cent perfect agreement in the E group and 89 per cent perfect agreement in the C group (final form). Test-retest reliability for all ten stories in the E group over a one-month interval was .66 ($p < .05$). Over a three-month interval this coefficient within the same group was still significantly high (r of .56). Similarly, on Form A, test-retest reliability over a five-month interval for group C was .80. In the final form, interscorer reliability of the SCT was .96 between the two independent observers.

Evidence of validity may be inferred from the following. First, the scoring system was derived from the distribution of responses to the story situations within a preliminary sample. Since the adequacy of the scale's scoring was then determined by the judgment of expert clinicians, content validity may be deduced. Secondly, the author has claimed construct validity for the scale in that it correlated significantly with other well-constructed measures of delay capacity in adults, adolescents, and children, including the M-threshold on the Barron-M threshold inkblots (Barron, 1955), the Sutton-Smith and Rosenberg Impulsivity Scale (Sutton-Smith and Rosenberg, 1959), and the monetary expenditure task (Davids and Sidman, 1962).

BIBLIOGRAPHY:

BARRON, F. "Threshold for the Perception of Human Movement in Inkblots." *Journal of Consulting Psychology*, 1955, *19*, 33–38.

CAMPOS, L. P. "The Relationship between Some Factors of Parental Deprivation and Delay of Need-Gratification." Unpublished doctoral dissertation, Michigan State University, 1963.

DAVIDS, A., and SIDMAN, J. "A Pilot Study—Impulsivity, Time Orientation, and Delayed Gratification in Future Scientists and in Underachieving High School Students." *Exceptional Children*, 1962, *29*, 170–174.

MC CLELLAND, D. C., ATKINSON, J. W., CLARK, R. A., and LOWELL, E. L. *The Achievement Motive*. New York: Appleton-Century, 1953.

MURRAY, H. A. *Exploration in Personality*. New York: Oxford University Press, 1938.

SUTTON-SMITH, B., and ROSENBERG, B. G. "A Scale to Identify Impulsive Behavior in Children." *Journal of Genetic Psychology*, 1959, *95*, 211–216.

CHECKLIST OF CHILD'S NERVOUS MANNERISMS AND FEARS

AUTHOR: J. R. Wittenborn

AGE: Kindergarten children and children who have passed the first grade but have not yet attained the preadolescent age level

VARIABLE: Fears and problems

TYPE OF MEASURE: Checklist

SOURCE FROM WHICH THE MEASURE MAY BE OBTAINED: See Wittenborn (1956a)

DESCRIPTION OF MEASURE: This checklist includes sixteen items of nervous and fearful behavior on the part of the child as determined from the Child-Rearing Practices Interview with the mother. The behavioral items are checked only if they are present. The total score would, then, consist of the number of items checked. In addition to the presence of several fears, the checklist includes behavioral items of nail biting, nose picking, hair-pulling, tics, thumb-sucking, and masturbation.

RELIABILITY AND VALIDITY: No data for reliability and validity have been provided.

BIBLIOGRAPHY:

WITTENBORN, J. R. "A Study of Adoptive Children: I. Interviews as a Source of Scores for Children and Their Homes." *Psychological Monographs: General and Applied,* 1956a, *70* (Whole No. 408).

WITTENBORN, J. R. "A Study of Adoptive Children: II. The Predictive Validity of the Yale Developmental Examination of Infant Behavior." *Psychological Monographs: General and Applied,* 1956b, *70* (Whole No. 409).

WITTENBORN, J. R. "A Study of Adoptive Children: III. Relationships Between Some Aspects of Development and Some Aspects of Environment for Adoptive Children." *Psychological Monographs: General and Applied,* 1956c, *70* (Whole No. 410).

CHILD CONFLICT SCALE

AUTHOR: Walter Emmerich

AGE: Preschool children between the ages of 3 years 7 months, to 5 years 1 month

VARIABLE: Personality (emotional conflict)

TYPE OF MEASURE: Rating scale

SOURCE FROM WHICH THE MEASURE MAY BE OBTAINED: See Emmerich (1959)

DESCRIPTION OF MEASURE: The Child Conflict Scale measures a child's conflict about his parental expectations, derived from interview protocols. It is composed of various aspects of behavior signifying that the child is *avoiding* an appropriate response to an item, an "appropriate" response being defined as one that can be scored on the nurturance-control scale.

In scoring the child's responses the following procedure was used: A five-point conflict scale was developed and applied to the child's responses to six mother-child and six father-child test items. The scale ranged from 0 for no conflict to 4 for very strong conflict. Eight conflict categories were set up, including response latency and hesitation, as defined below:

Response latency. *refers to the period following the examiner's presentation of an item before the child gives any response. A "long" response latency is defined as ten seconds or more.*

Hesitation—*the child starts to respond to an item, but needs slight encouragement to complete the item.*

The child's total score on the six items for a parent was used as the index of his conflict about his parent's attitude toward him.

RELIABILITY AND VALIDITY: The scale was administered to the same sample used in the Child Nurturance-Control Scale by Emmerich. Within this sample, both rater reliability and test-retest reliability were derived. In the first case, "the correlation between two judges' independent ratings of a sample of items was +.86." In the latter instance, the test-retest reliability coefficients of twenty-six children "were +.44 for the mother-child items and +.56 for the father-child items" (p. 279).

BIBLIOGRAPHY:

EMMERICH, W. "Parent Identification in Young Children." *Genetic Psychology Monographs*, 1959, *60*, 257–308.

CHILD TRANSITION TEST

AUTHOR: Abraham Blum

AGE: Preschool

VARIABLE: Rigidity-flexibility

TYPE OF MEASURE: Test

SOURCE FROM WHICH THE MEASURE MAY BE OBTAINED: See Blum (1959)

DESCRIPTION OF MEASURE: While there may be some question as to whether or not this measure may be called a test according to the usual criteria, it is the type of item that can be incorporated into a larger measure of the rigidity-flexibility variable.

The CTT was constructed by first drawing the two "end" pictures, a dog and a cat, in a simple line, stylized fashion, and then drawing the transition pictures. The result is a five-card series containing a cat, an "almost" cat, a half-cat-half-dog, an "almost" dog, and a dog. In testing the child is asked to identify the figure on each card, presented one at a time.

An adult version of the same measure, called the Adult Transition Test, is also described by Blum. This version is made up in the same way as the Child Transition Test, except that there are seven pictures in the progression rather than five.

The pictures are reproduced in the Blum article.

RELIABILITY AND VALIDITY: The nature of the task suggests that it would be feasible for use with children. Blum has shown empirically that the measure can be used with preschool children. There is some question whether or not the measure is appropriate for children under 4 years of age. Blum found that these young children in some cases did not shift from cat to dog or vice versa, even when the stimulus had become objectively dog or cat.

BIBLIOGRAPHY:

BLUM, A. "The Relationship between Rigidity-Flexibility in Children and Their Parents." *Child Development,* 1959, *30,* 297–304.

CHILDREN'S OPINION SCALE

AUTHORS: Barbara Long and Edmund H. Henderson

AGE: 6 to 13

VARIABLE: Opinionatedness

TYPE OF MEASURE: Test

SOURCE FROM WHICH THE MEASURE MAY BE OBTAINED: Barbara E. Long, 322 Edgewood Drive, Clayton, Missouri 63105

DESCRIPTION OF MEASURE: The scale consists of thirty opinion statements to which children respond by circling "yes," "no," or "don't know" on the answer sheets. The score consists of the number of "don't know" responses and is presumed to indicate the child's open-mindedness. Examples of items from the test are as follows:

Someday every family will own an airplane.
City children are smarter than country children.
One hundred years from now people will be living on the moon.
French children are more polite than American children.
Canadians are the world's best swimmers.

Test time is fifteen minutes, and it may be administered to groups.

RELIABILITY AND VALIDITY: Corrected split-half reliabilities range from .71 to .84 in samples from grades one to seven. Validity is suggested by the following: scores on this measure were significantly related to scores for fluency, flexibility, and originality from Torrance's Lines Test; scores were significantly related to grade and sex, girls being less opinionated than boys; scores were unrelated to Lorge-Thorndike intelligence test scores and to achievement in reading or math; and scores were significantly related to Rokeach's Dogmatism Scale, to age, class in college, and tendencies for greater predecisional search.

BIBLIOGRAPHY:

HENDERSON, E. H., and LONG, B. H. *An Exploratory Study of Reading-Thinking Styles among Children of Varying Abilities.* Cooperative Research Project, No. 5-8075, Office of Education, 1966.

LONG, B. H., and ZILLER, R. C. "Dogmatism and Predecisional Information Search." *Journal of Applied Psychology,* 1965, *49,* 376–378.

LONG, B. H., and HENDERSON, E. H. "Opinion Formation and Creativity in Elementary School Children." *Psychological Reports,* 1965, *17,* 219–223.

ZILLER, R. C., and LONG, B. H. "Some Correlates of the Don't Know Responses in Opinion Questionnaires." *Journal of Social Psychology,* 1965, *67,* 129–147.

CHILDREN'S SOCIAL DESIRABILITY QUESTIONNAIRE

AUTHORS: Virginia C. Crandall, Vaughn J. Crandall, and Walter Katkovsky

AGE: Grades three, four, five, six, eight, ten, twelve

VARIABLE: Social desirability

TYPE OF MEASURE: Questionnaire

SOURCE FROM WHICH THE MEASURE MAY BE OBTAINED: Order Document No. 8232, remitting $1.25 for microfilm or $1.25 for photocopies, and make checks payable to Chief, Photoduplication Service, Library of Congress, Washington, D.C. 20540.

DESCRIPTION OF MEASURE: Crandall et al. (1965) define social desirability as the tendency to give socially desirable responses. CSD measures this response set by asking the child questions to determine if he behaves according to approved middle-class mores, if he ever behaves in deviating fashion, or if he sometimes thinks or acts in an acceptable manner. Sample items follow:

Sometimes I don't like to share my things with my friends.
When I make a mistake, I always admit I'm wrong.
I never forget to say please or thank you.
I always wash my hands before every meal.

The manner in which the scale is administered varies with the age level of the children. At the sixth-grade level and above, the questionnaire is administered as a true-false scale on a group basis. Below the sixth-grade level, the variations in administration include simplified wording of the items, individual testing, and phrasing of the items so that they may be answered simply as yes or no. At this level, the authors, in the original study at least, recorded the questionnaire items in order to standardize tone, inflection, and rate of presentation.

The scale has a built-in safeguard against the possibility of acquiescence set at both levels. In the group form, this control is obtained by keying the forty-eight items so that approximately half of them require true and half false answers for socially desirable responses. An acquiescent set is much more likely in the younger group because the forty-seven items of the CSD at this level contain twelve items keyed yes and thirty-four no. In either form the score on the scale appears to consist of the total number of items answered in a socially desirable direction as indicated by the key.

The scale has been administered to 336 pupils in grades three, four, and five, and to 620 students at the sixth-grade level and above.

RELIABILITY AND VALIDITY: Reliability data consist of internal consistency and test-retest correlation coefficients. The group form for subsamples of boys and girls at the various age levels shows correlations between .82 to .95, corrected by the Spearman-Brown formula. The test-retest correlations were based on a one-month interval for sixty-three of the younger children and for ninety-eight tenth graders. The respective correlation coefficients were .90 and .85.

The authors cite numerous studies to show that the scale predicts individual differences systematically for a variety of behaviors (Crandall et al., 1965).

BIBLIOGRAPHY:

CRANDALL, V. C., CRANDALL, V. J., and KATKOVSKY, W. "A Children's Social Desirability Questionnaire." *Journal of Consulting Psychology,* 1965, *29,* 27–36.

CROWNE, D. P., and MARLOWE, D. "A New Scale of Social Desirability Independent of Psychopathology." *Journal of Consulting Psychology,* 1960, *24,* 349–354.

DEFENSIVENESS SCALE

AUTHORS: Michael A. Wallach, Leonard R. Green, Paul D. Lipsitt, and Jean B. Minehart

AGE: First grade

VARIABLE: Defensiveness

TYPE OF MEASURE: Questionnaire

SOURCE FROM WHICH THE MEASURE MAY BE OBTAINED: See Wallach et al. (1962)

DESCRIPTION OF MEASURE: The Defensiveness Scale is made up of twenty-eight items, each of which presents the child with two alternatives in a forced-choice situation. The test is individually administered. When the twenty-eight items were administered to 120 first-grade girls, and the resulting data were factor analyzed, a "factorially pure" defensiveness scale of seven items with factor loadings of .35 or greater was derived. The seven items and their factor loadings are given in Wallach et al. (1962, p. 5). Samples of the items are given below:

Do grown-ups ever say you daydream too much, or don't they ever say this?
Does everything go wrong for you sometimes, or are you happy all the time?

RELIABILITY AND VALIDITY: The authors computed an odd-even reliability coefficient for the seven-item Defensiveness Scale, using the Spearman-Brown formula. The reliability coefficient thus obtained was .79.

Evidence for the construct validity of the measure was found by Wallach et al. (1962). They hypothesized the relationships between three dichotomized variables: defensiveness versus non-defensiveness (as measured by the Defensiveness Scale); overt social interaction versus social isolation; and graphic constriction versus graphic expansiveness (as measured by a drawing test). Their hypotheses about the pattern of the interactions among these three variables were supported.

BIBLIOGRAPHY:

WALLACH, M. A., GREEN, L. R., LIPSITT, P. D., and MINEHART, J. B. "Contradiction Between Overt and Projective Personality Indicators as a Function of Defensiveness." *Psychological Monographs*, 1962, *76*, No. 1.

DEPENDENCE PRONENESS SCALE

AUTHORS: Ned A. Flanders, Paul Anderson, and Edmond J. Amidon

AGE: Grades three through six, and eighth grade

VARIABLE: Dependence proneness

TYPE OF MEASURE: Self-rating scale

SOURCE FROM WHICH THE MEASURE MAY BE OBTAINED: See Flanders et al. (1961)

DESCRIPTION OF MEASURE: The Dependence Proneness Scale is a self-administering test in which students are requested to indicate agreement or disagreement with forty-five items that measure the proneness of the students to be dependent on the teacher. The items are keyed for dependence proneness for either answers that agree (A) with the statement or disagree (D) with it. Samples of the items from the original scale with the response indicative of dependence proneness follow (Flanders et al., 1961):

D   *I hesitate to ask for help from others.*
A   *I like to do things with my family.*
D   *It's fun to try out ideas that others think are crazy.*
A   *I enjoy working with students who get good marks.*
A   *Students ought to be allowed to help one another with their school work.*
D   *I don't need my friends' encouragement when I meet with failure.*

Though the method of scoring has not been explicitly described, it apparently consists of totaling the number of responses keyed for dependence proneness.

RELIABILITY AND VALIDITY: The reliability of the forty-five-item scale as measured by the analysis of variance technique suggested by Hoyt (1941) was .68. Validity of the scale may be evaluated from the following: (1) The final forty-five-item scale was developed on the basis of several item analyses. The details of each separate item analysis have been described in full. In the final analysis, the only items retained were those which discriminated fairly well between extreme groups on an original pool of 150 items. (2) On the basis of results from 646 males and 644 females from forty-four eighth-grade classes, the females exhibited significantly higher dependence-prone scores in line with cultural expectations for male independence. For this reason, the authors caution that separate norms be used for different sex groups. (3) Finally, other studies have shown that a high dependence score is associated with failure to take an extreme position on an opinionnaire (Amidon, 1959) and that students scoring high or low on dependence proneness exhibited predicted differences on separate measures of dependence in the classroom (Flanders et al., 1961).

BIBLIOGRAPHY:

AMIDON, E. J. "Dependent-Prone Students in Experimental Learning Situations."
    Unpublished doctoral thesis, University of Minnesota, 1959.

HOYT, C. "Test Reliability Estimated by Analysis of Variance." *Psychometrika,* 1941,
    VI, 153–160.

FLANDERS, N. A., ANDERSON, J. P., and AMIDON, E. J. "Measuring Dependence Prone-
    ness in the Classroom." *Educational and Psychological Measurement,* 1961,
    XXI, 575–587.

SOAR, R. S. "Teacher-Pupil Interaction and Pupil Growth." Paper presented at Amer-
    ican Educational Research Association, February, 1966.

IMPULSIVITY SCALE

AUTHORS: B. Sutton-Smith and B. G. Rosenberg

AGE: Fourth, fifth, and sixth grades

VARIABLE: Personality (impulsivity)

TYPE OF MEASURE: Self-report scale

SOURCE FROM WHICH THE MEASURE MAY BE OBTAINED: See Sutton-Smith and Rosenberg (1959); Hirschfield (1966)

DESCRIPTION OF MEASURE: The original I. S. by Sutton-Smith and Rosenberg (1959) consisted of nineteen self-descriptive statements to be answered "yes" or "no" by the child. A revision by Hirschfield (1966) includes twenty-five self-descriptive statements to be answered "true" or "false" by the child. His revision includes the nineteen items in the original scale. The items are based on the definition of impulsivity by Sutton-Smith and Rosenberg: as a tendency to be restless, to indulge in horseplay, to lose control of feelings, enter activities with overwhelming vigor, and generally lose control in acceptable and unacceptable ways.

Two items from the scale, both of which have a response of "yes" for impulsivity, are as follows (Sutton-Smith and Rosenberg, 1959):

I like to keep moving around.
I like to just "blow off" steam.

Keys have also been provided for all of the items.

RELIABILITY AND VALIDITY: This scale was validated by using teacher ratings with a sample of 171 fourth-, fifth-, and sixth-grade school children. In all comparisons except one, the scale score correlated significantly with these ratings. The test-retest reliability was .85 for an N of 26 (Sutton-Smith and Rosenberg, 1959). In a subsequent study by Sutton-Smith and Rosenberg (1961), the results confirmed the hypothesis that children scoring high on impulsivity would manifest preferences for gaming activities characteristic of the opposite sex.

Finally, a cross-validation study by Hirschfield (1965) revealed the following: (1) The evidence did not indicate that a response set by impulsive children influences their scores. (2) Teachers' ranking of impulsivity and scores on the scale were significantly related. (3) Teachers' rankings were highly correlated to those of Hirschfield based on actual observations of classroom behavior. This agreement served as external validation to the teacher-rankings. The results from Hirschfield were based on a research population of 127 male and female students from two fifth- and three sixth-grade classrooms.

BIBLIOGRAPHY:

HIRSCHFIELD, P. P. "Response Set in Impulsive Children." *Journal of Genetic Psychology,* 1965, *107,* 117–126.

SUTTON-SMITH, B., and ROSENBERG, B. G. "A Scale to Identify Impulsive Behavior in Children." *Journal of Genetic Psychology,* 1959, *95,* 211–216.

SUTTON-SMITH, B., and ROSENBERG, B. G. "Impulsivity and Sex Preference." *Journal of Genetic Psychology,* 1961, *98,* 187–192.

INDEX OF GRAPHIC CONSTRICTION-EXPANSIVENESS

AUTHORS: Michael A. Wallach, Leonard R. Green, Paul D. Lipsitt, and Jean B. Minehart

AGE: First grade

VARIABLE: Graphic expansiveness

TYPE OF MEASURE: Test

SOURCE FROM WHICH THE MEASURE MAY BE OBTAINED: See Wallach et al. (1962)

DESCRIPTION OF MEASURE: This measure can perhaps best be described by giving the gist of the administration and scoring procedures. The child is requested to draw designs on the paper for the examiner. He is instructed that he can draw whatever designs he chooses, but that he is not to draw things like people or houses or animals. He is just to draw designs which he feels like drawing. He is then given an 18 × 12 inch sheet of drawing paper and a red crayon. The examiner begins timing the child as soon as he starts to draw, and after exactly 180 seconds, he removes the crayon from the child's hand. The paper is taken away, and the process repeated a second and third time, except that on the second drawing, 120 seconds are allowed, and 135 seconds for the third drawing.

Scoring is accomplished by using an 18 × 12 inch grid made up of 3-inch squares, twenty-four squares in the whole grid. The scorer simply counts the number of grid squares that have any part of the drawing in it. For each drawing, obviously, the possible score would range from 1 to 24, and for the total measure, from 3 to 72.

RELIABILITY AND VALIDITY: It is possible for two scorers evaluating any one drawing to differ in the number of squares scored from 0-difference to a possible 23. When discrepancies between scorers were 0 to 1 square, they were considered virtual agreements. Differences of two or more squares were considered to be disagreements. When the number of virtual agreements for each drawing was divided by 120 (the number of subjects in this reliability study), the quotients were .99, .97, and .98 for the three drawings, respectively. Reliability of scoring, therefore, was very high.

Test-retest reliability on the first, second, and third drawings was .70 using the first and second drawings, .81 when comparing the second and third drawings, and .69 when comparing the scores on the first and third drawings. This latter measure of reliability is primarily a measure of the stability of the measure.

Evidence for the construct validity of this measure was found by Wallach, et al. (1962). They hypothesized significant relationships among the three variables: defensiveness-nondefensiveness, social interaction-isolation; and graphic constriction-expansiveness. Specifically, they hypothesized that defensive subjects with extensive social ties would be more constricted graphically; defensive subjects who were socially isolated would be more expansive graphically; nondefensive subjects with extensive social ties would be more expansive graphically; and nondefensive subjects who were socially isolated would be more constricted graphically. Whether the data for the three drawings by each subject were combined, or each drawing was treated separately, the analysis of variance interaction effect was highly significant.

BIBLIOGRAPHY:

WALLACH, M. A., GREEN, L. R., LIPSITT, P. D., and MINEHART, J. B. "Contradiction between Overt and Projective Personality Indicators as a Function of Defensiveness." *Psychological Monographs,* 1962, *76,* No. 1.

INTOLERANCE OF AMBIGUITY SCALE

AUTHOR: Rolf E. Muuss

AGE: Sixth grade

VARIABLE: Personality (rigidity)

TYPE OF MEASURE: Self-rating scale

SOURCE FROM WHICH THE MEASURE MAY BE OBTAINED: See Muuss (1959)

DESCRIPTION OF MEASURE: Muuss defines intolerance of ambiguity as a general trait involving need to structure unstructured situations, resort to simplistic solutions, and maintain the status quo. It is closely related to rigidity. The twelve items comprising the Intolerance of Ambiguity Scale reflect the definition of this general trait. The score for the scale simply consists of the total number of items answered in the direction indicative of intolerance of ambiguity. The scale itself has been administered on a group basis by Muuss. Samples of the items from the scale follow. For both, the answer "agree" is scored as indicative of intolerance of ambiguity.

I often wish people would be more definite about things.
I don't like to undertake any project unless I have a pretty good idea as to how it will turn out.

RELIABILITY AND VALIDITY: The scale was administered as part of a series of group tests to 280 sixth-grade pupils in the public schools of a midwestern community of 80,000. Half came from experimental classes emphasizing the dynamics of human behavior, the other half from regular classes.

Though no evidence of reliability is provided for this scale, several indices suggest construct or concurrent validity or both. (1) An r of .41 (N = 232) between the Intolerance of Ambiguity Scale and the Children's Antidemocratic Attitude Scale indicates that the former general trait is positively related to ethnocentrism. (2) Children who score above the mean (Highs) on reliable tests of social and physical causation achieve significantly lower scores on the scale than those who score below the means (Lows). These statistically significant differences hold up even among low and high subjects matched for IQ scores. (3) The correlation between scores on the ambiguity scale and the IQ test was −.07.

BIBLIOGRAPHY:

MUUSS, R. E. "A Comparison of 'High Causally' and 'Low Causally' Oriented Sixth Grade Children on Personality Variables Indicative of Mental Health." *Proceedings of the Iowa Academy of Science*, 1959, *66*, 388–394.

KOOKER'S ACHIEVEMENT-BOREDOM SCALE (AB Scale)

AUTHOR: Earl W. Kooker

AGE: Fifth and sixth grade

VARIABLE: Personality (feelings of achievement and boredom)

TYPE OF MEASURE: Rating scale

SOURCE FROM WHICH THE MEASURE MAY BE OBTAINED: See Kooker (1951)

DESCRIPTION OF MEASURE: Kooker's Achievement-Boredom scale includes seventeen items consisting of a lead sentence followed by a description of the behavior and the situation in which it occurs. In each case, the child is rated by an observer who knows the pupil well. Examples of the items follow:

The child who spends only enough time on his school work to get passing grades. *The child gives the impression of having more ability than he usually displays, for in some isolated phases of work he does much better than usual for him. He makes remarks such as, "I don't see why I have to do this," "I don't see any use in this stuff," etc. The same child seems to get along with others on the playground. Frequently (4.11); fairly often (1.98); seldom (.02).*

The child who "doodles" while working on his lessons, looks out the window, etc. *This refers to situations in which the class is supposed to be studying at their desks. These extraneous activities are not such that they interfere with others' studying. This refers to children who in spite of this "doodling" do at least fair work. Frequently (3.88); fairly often (1.74), seldom (−.36).*

To obtain a score for each child, two scoring schemes may be employed. First, the checked items of "frequently," "fairly often," and "seldom" are assigned the respective scores of 1, 2, and 3. Second, on the basis of successive intervals, scale values that have been assigned to the items may be utilized. The numbers in parentheses are scale values. The larger positive values mean greater insecurity and boredom.

RELIABILITY AND VALIDITY: Rating and rerating by the same raters all approached .90 with three groups of sixth graders and one group of fifth graders, with the size of the samples ranging between eighteen and twenty-six. The mean r for ratings-reratings on the A-B scale was .94. The mean r for between-observer ratings on the A-B scale was .71.

In addition, a large pool of original items was submitted to graduate students and professional judges who were to apply achievement-boredom or security-insecurity categories to each item. The high intrarater (clinical instructors) and interrater agreements (graduate students versus clinical instructors) appear to give the scale some content validity. The system of scoring the items by judges in terms of successive intervals successfully met the test of internal consistency. The intercorrelations between scores on boredom and achievement items were high but in a negative direction. The magnitude of the positive correlations between security-insecurity and achievement-boredom scores brings into question the independence of the two concepts. Each of the intercorrelations included an r of .47 for one school and ranged between .79 to .85 for three schools (Kooker, 1959).

BIBLIOGRAPHY:

KOOKER, E. W. "An Investigation of Security, Insecurity, Achievement, and Boredom in Elementary School Children." Unpublished doctoral dissertation, State University of Iowa, 1951.

KOOKER, E. W. "An Investigation of Security-Insecurity and Achievement-Boredom in Elementary School Children." *Journal of Experimental Education,* 1959, *27,* 333–340.

KOOKER'S SECURITY-INSECURITY SCALE (IS Scale)

AUTHOR: Earl W. Kooker

AGE: Fifth and sixth grade

VARIABLE: Personality (security feelings)

TYPE OF MEASURE: Observer rating scale

SOURCE FROM WHICH THE MEASURE MAY BE OBTAINED: See Kooker (1951)

DESCRIPTION OF MEASURE: Kooker's final Security-Insecurity Scale includes nineteen items consisting of a lead sentence followed by a description of the behavior and the situation in which it occurred. In each case, the behavior of the child is rated by an observer who knows the pupil well (Kooker, 1959). Examples of the items follow:

The child who complains about not being ready for tests. *This refers to situations in which the child when an examination is announced says he's not ready for it even though he had plenty of time, doesn't think he'll be able to do well in it, etc. However, he usually does as well in it as most of the other members in the class and scarcely, if ever, fails an exam. Frequently (1.42); fairly often (.95); seldom (.31).*
The child who, though not accepted by the group, "tags after" a child who is. *This refers to a child with whom others seldom associate, who is chosen last on the playground, etc. The child follows the accepted child around, repeats what he says, asks to be on his side on the playground, etc. The accepted child may become annoyed with this child, tell him to leave him alone, etc. Frequently (1.51); fairly often (1.08); seldom (.55).*

To obtain a score for each child, two scoring schemes are employed. First the checked items of "frequently," "fairly often," and "seldom" are assigned the respective scores of 1, 2, and 3. Secondly, on the basis of successive intervals, scale values which have been assigned to the items (Kooker, 1959) are applicable. The numbers to the left of the items are scale values. The larger positive values mean greater insecurity and boredom. The first value is assigned if "frequently" is checked, the second if "fairly often" is checked and the last if the subject checks "seldom."

RELIABILITY AND VALIDITY: The Kooker IS Scale has been administered to several fifth- and sixth-grade classes ranging in number from eight and fourteen (Kooker, 1959). As part of a battery of tests, however, the scale has been used with large samples of fifth- and sixth-grade children ranging in number between sixty and one hundred. In this investigation, means and standard deviations have been provided for groups high and low in causal thinking (Muuss, 1960).

Though the reliability coefficients of the scales have been derived from smaller samples than Kooker's study (1959), they appear quite satisfactory. Thus, using Fisher's z transformation the mean r for rating-rerating on the IS scale was .92 and the mean for between-observer ratings on the scale was .69.

Validity is based on the following data: (1) Graduate students and clinical instructors evaluated the items for their significance for measuring security-insecurity. This procedure would appear to give the scale some content validity. (2) As predicted, low scoring subjects had significantly poor attendance records (Kooker, 1959) and high causally oriented subjects showed more security (Muuss, 1960; Snider, 1957). (3) The system of scoring the items by judges in terms of successive intervals successfully met the test of internal consistency (Kooker, 1959). (4) High negative and statistically significant negative correlations between security and insecurity scores (−.50 to −.83) suggested the existence of a meaningful continuum for children's feelings of security (Kooker, 1959).

Despite these validating data, quite low intercorrelations have been found between scores on the Children's Manifest Anxiety Scale and the IS (r of .09 to −.20). Muuss (1960) has attributed this finding to the different nature of the two test instruments, the CMAS being a paper-and-pencil test where falsification is more probable, whereas the Kooker scale involves rating by trained observers.

BIBLIOGRAPHY:

KOOKER, E. W. "An Investigation of Security, Insecurity, Achievement, and Boredom in Elementary School Children." Unpublished doctoral dissertation, State University of Iowa, 1951.

KOOKER, E. W. "An Investigation of Security-Insecurity and Achievement-Boredom in Elementary School Children." *Journal of Experimental Education,* 1959, *27,* 333–340.

MUUSS, R. E. "The Relationship between 'Causal' Orientation, Anxiety, and Insecurity in Elementary School Children." *Journal of Educational Psychology,* 1960, *51,* 122–129.

SNIDER, W. D. F. "Relation of Growth in Causal Orientation to Insecurity in Elementary School Children." *Psychological Reports,* 1957, *3,* 631–634.

THE MODIFIED LUCHINS RIGIDITY TEST

AUTHORS: M. L. Kellmer Pringle and I. R. McKenzie

AGE: 11-year-olds

VARIABLE: Rigidity in problem solving

TYPE OF MEASURE: Test

SOURCE FROM WHICH THE MEASURE MAY BE OBTAINED: Adam House, 1, Fitzroy Square, London, W. 1.

DESCRIPTION OF MEASURE: The Modified Luchins Rigidity Test consists of eleven arithmetical items resembling the ingenuity problems on the Terman-Merrill Intelligence Scale, Form L (1937) at year 14, though the questions are very much easier. An example of the first three items that are used in establishing set follows (Pringle and McKenzie, undated):

Now if Jar A holds 7 pints and Jar B holds 4 pints and Jar C holds 2 pints, how can we use them to put exactly 13 pints into the basin?

With the exception of problem 9, the problems may be solved by a "set" solution or a simple alternative. Problem 9, however, cannot be solved by a set formula, so the number of failures on Problem 9 compared with the other ten problems indicates the disrupting effect of set. The results are classified by five categories: three orders of set; no set; and misunderstanding. For example, in a set of the first order, the subject fails item 9 and returns to the "set" solution for items 10 and 11.

The test may be administered on a group basis and the authors recommend ninety seconds per item as a generous time allotment for even the slowest pupil.

RELIABILITY AND VALIDITY: Since only a small number of children misunderstood or failed to grasp what was expected of them, the difficulty level of the scale appears suitable for 11-year-old children. Moreover, the hypothesis that a progressive teaching approach would reduce rigidity was partially verified within the sample of 211 subjects, in that the hypothesis held up for children of low average ability or less but not for bright children (Pringle and McKenzie, 1965).

BIBLIOGRAPHY:

PRINGLE, M. L. K., and MC KENZIE, I. R. "Teaching Method and Rigidity in Problem Solving." *British Journal of Educational Psychology*, 1965, *35*, 50–59.

MORALE SCALE FOR HANDICAPPED CHILDREN

AUTHOR: Harry Dick

AGE: 2 to 18

VARIABLE: Morale

TYPE OF MEASURE: Questionnaire

SOURCE FROM WHICH THE MEASURE MAY BE OBTAINED: See Dick (1964)

DESCRIPTION OF MEASURE: The Morale Scale for Handicapped Children is designed to measure mental well-being, life-satisfaction, and, generally, happiness. In Dick's contention, morale particularly becomes a crucial problem for handicapped children with respect to making decisions about prescriptions for the services and placements they need. He constructed two scales to measure morale. In Scale A, an informant who knows the child well rates him on the relative frequency of specific acts that are presumably positive or negative indices of morale. Below is an example from Scale A:

As far as you know or have been able to observe, during the past month or so, has this child smiled at people? very often (at least once every day), fairly often (almost every day), sometimes (some days), very seldom (maybe once or twice), never (not at all).

Scale B differs from Scale A in that informants were asked to make an evaluative judgment of how much the child enjoyed a series of acts or events, which virtually all children presumably experience on a more or less daily basis. Informants were asked:

During the past month or so, has this child liked or disliked going to school, speech, or other training class? liked it very much, liked it quite a lot, liked it some, hasn't especially liked or disliked it, has not liked it at all.

RELIABILITY AND VALIDITY: Data were subjected to Guttman Scalogram Analysis. All the items on Scale A except items 3, 5, and 7 met the minimum requirements for scalability. The coefficient of reproducibility for Scale B, however, was only .86. The author therefore regards Scale A to be superior to Scale B but cautions that replication on a different population may yield different results. Dick also argues that a scale such as Form A that has a satisfactory coefficient of reproducibility has substantial built-in test-retest reliability.

Dick also considers the high coefficient of reproducibility for Form A as a form of internal validity. The external validity of the scale was checked by correlations between the results of Scale A with the following: Results from Scale B, ratings of children's morale on a seven-point scale by the children's classroom teachers and their preceptors, and three questions asked of the housemothers concerning the children's relative happiness. The questions, the indices of associations used, and the rationale for these statistics are described in full within the article. The correlations with the external variables were as follows: Scale B (.66), for the three questions (.66–.69); classroom teachers' ratings (.36); and preceptors' ratings (.26). Dick attributes the relatively low correlations of the last two variables to the fact that these raters have less day-to-day contact with the child.

BIBLIOGRAPHY:

DICK, H. R. "The Measurement of Morale of Handicapped Children." *Cerebral Palsy Review*, 1964, 25, 12–16.

MUMMERY SCALE OF ASCENDANT BEHAVIOR

AUTHOR: Dorothy V. Mummery

AGE: 3 to 5

VARIABLE: Personality (social acceptability or social maturity)

TYPE OF MEASURE: Rating scale

SOURCE FROM WHICH THE MEASURE MAY BE OBTAINED: See Mummery (1943)

DESCRIPTION OF MEASURE: Mummery's Scale is based on the definition of ascendant behavior as behavior by which an individual attempts to attain, or attains or maintains mastery of a social situation. In the preschooler, it means trying to get things he wants from his peers, directly or indirectly influencing their behavior, defending himself and possessions, and resisting mastery.

The author developed seventy-nine categories of children's behavior classifiable under six headings. The headings and examples of the behavioral categories are given below (Mummery, 1947):

Verbal methods of securing play materials (fifteen items): *The child uses a declarative statement to express a desire for a toy which his companion has, or which lies near his companion: "Want that over there." "Hey, I need that scoop."*

Physical methods of securing play materials (nine items): *Child takes a toy from the possession of his companion; i.e., he immediately picks up a toy which his companion has been using but has just put down: A puts shovel down while he is emptying his dish. B quickly picks it up.*

Verbal methods of directing companion (twenty-one items): *Statements in which he suggests a certain mutual activity by the word "Let's," "We," or similar expressions: "Let's make a road." "Shall we build a bigger hill?"*

Physical methods of directing companion (eight items): *Child attempts to force or inhibit companion's activity by a nonverbal threat of force; e.g., doubles up fists as if to strike: A is making a loud noise which B does not like. B doubles up his fist as if to strike him, but withdraws it.*

Verbal responses (thirteen items): *The child flatly and emphatically refuses to give up the toy or to follow the direction. Differs from [the preceding] mainly in manner and tone; he may even yell or scream: "Stop that!" "No! I won't."*

Physical responses (thirteen items): *A child defends his possession of a toy by calmly taking the toy from the hand of the child who has just succeeded in getting it from him but who is now offering no active resistance; that is, he simply "lifts" it from his now unresisting companion: The moment A puts his shovel down, B picks it up. A takes it from his hand and B lets him, giving no physical sign of resistance whatever.*

The procedure in recording ascendant behavior is to pair children for playing games, record their behavior for a five-minute period in a controlled play situation, and then to complete the record by adding and recording the number of instances falling under each item for each child. The details of conducting the observations, recording the responses, and deriving the two weighted scores and the Jack Score have been described in full. The precise toys used in the controlled play have also been delineated (Mummery, 1943, 1947).

In a later publication (Stott and Mummery, 1956), the 79 categories were regarded as representing three main behavior areas: gaining possession of coveted objects; directing or influencing the activities of another; and defending possessions and activities.

RELIABILITY AND VALIDITY: Test reliability and validity were established on initial scores of forty-two preschool children ranging in age from 42 to 61 months, with a mean of 49 months. The social status of these children was higher than average, and the mean IQ was 119.

Reliabilities varied from .80 to .98, depending upon how the coefficients were computed. In general, the measure appears to have sufficient reliability so it can be used with confidence by the researcher.

According to Mummery (1947), the use of experts to assign scale values to the behavior categories establishes the validity of the weightings for acceptability and unacceptability. Teachers of preschool children rated the child's frequency of attempt to secure possession of toys, to direct his companions' behavior, and to defend himself and his possessions. They also rated his success in getting what he wanted, and the method used. Teachers' ratings of frequency were most closely related to performance on the Mummery Scale, with correlations of .36 to .79. The teachers' ratings on frequency of success correlated .02 to .36 with Mummery Scale scores, and their ratings on method showed insignificant correlation with the Mummery Scale.

BIBLIOGRAPHY:

MUMMERY, D. V. "An Analytical Study of Ascendant Behavior of Preschool Children." Unpublished dissertation, Iowa City, Iowa: State University of Iowa, 1943.

MUMMERY, D. V. "An Analytical Study of Ascendant Behavior of Preschool Children." *Child Development,* 1947, *18,* 40–81.

STOTT, L. H., and MUMMERY, D. V. "Adult Attitudes toward Ascendant Behavior in Young Children." *Merrill-Palmer Quarterly,* 1956, *2,* 110–120.

PARENT-CHILD NEED ASSESSMENT

AUTHORS: Forrest B. Tyler, Bonnie Tyler, and Janet Rafferty

AGE: 2 years 6 months to 5 years

VARIABLE: Five general need categories: recognition-status; protection-dependency; dominance; independence; and love and affection. Need potential of these needs is measured in terms of need value and freedom of movement.

TYPE OF MEASURE: Observation schedule and frame of reference for content analysis

SOURCE FROM WHICH THE MEASURE MAY BE OBTAINED: Forrest B. Tyler, Department of Psychology, University of Maryland, College Park, Maryland 20742

DESCRIPTION OF MEASURE: Parent-interview protocols and child-observation protocols are scored on all the above-listed variables with one exception—the parents are not given scores for protection-dependency or independence. Scoring rationale allows for consideration of the situation or context of the need in assigning importance to it. Need value scores were arrived at by assuming an inverse relationship between the extent of situational structure and the need importance required to elicit a response. Thus, a high need value rating is given if the stimulus situation does not encourage a certain response (for example love), but the response occurs nevertheless. The freedom of movement (expectancy) variable is measured by the constructive-defensive quality of the behavior. Friendly, enthusiastic, outgoing behaviors indicate high expectancy. Tentative behaviors, withdrawal, and the like are thought to indicate low expectancy of freedom of movement. Scores are obtained by rating the variables on seven-point scales. Preliminary scoring-by-example manuals have been developed for ratings. The scoring-by-example manuals are necessary in order to maximize the scoring reliability. Tyler (1960) describes the scoring method for love and affection need value.

RELIABILITY AND VALIDITY: Median inter-rater reliabilities for the scoring manuals have been near .80. The authors report that these reliabilities have remained high when used by competent but inexperienced psychologists. In another study, inter-rater reliability ranged from .68 to .84.

Correlations between parents and children on recognition-status freedom of movement (expectancy) are in the .70's. A total of eleven of twenty-one relationships between parents and children's need values and expectancy measures were significant. There were nine of twenty-six significant intercorrelations among subject groups. Need value and expectancy were found to be specific to the need category under study and to the age and sex of subjects, and were not global in nature.

BIBLIOGRAPHY:

RAFFERTY, J. E., TYLER, B. B., and TYLER, F. B. "Personality Assessment from Free Play Observations." *Child Development,* 1960, *31,* 691–702.

TYLER, F. B. "A Conceptual Model for Assessing Parent-Child Motivations." *Child Development*, 1960, *31*, 807–815.

TYLER, B. B., TYLER, F. B., and RAFFERTY, J. E. "A Systematic Approach to Interviewing as a Method of Personality Assessment." Paper read at American Psychological Association Meeting, Cincinnati, September, 1959.

TYLER, F. B., TYLER, B. B., and RAFFERTY, J. E. "Need Value and Expectancy Interrelations as Assessed from Motivational Patterns of Parents and Their Children." *Journal of Consulting Psychology*, 1961, *25*, 304–311.

TYLER, F. B., TYLER, B. B., and RAFFERTY, J. E. "Relationships among Motivations of Parents and Their Children." *Journal of Genetic Psychology*, 1962, *101*, 69–81.

TYLER, F. B., TYLER, B. B., and RAFFERTY, J. E. "A Threshold Conception of Need Value." *Psychological Monographs: General and Applied*, 1962, *76*, No. 11.

PEER RATING AGGRESSION INSTRUMENT

AUTHORS: Leopold O. Walder, Robert P. Abelson, Leonard D. Eron, Thomas J. Banta, and Jerome H. Laulicht

AGE: Third grade

VARIABLE: Personality (aggression)

TYPE OF MEASURE: "Near sociometric" or peer nomination

SOURCE FROM WHICH THE MEASURE MAY BE OBTAINED: See Walder, et al. (1961)

DESCRIPTION OF MEASURE: The measure of aggression by Walder and his colleagues (1961) is a peer-nomination or guess-who procedure in which each child rates every other child in his class on a series of fourteen items having to do with specific aggressive acts. The questions pertain to items of aggression, defined as acts that injure or irritate others. Originally, an attempt was made to tap different dimensions or patterns of aggression, but it was found that items which fit the above definition accounted for the major portion of the variance of all the aggression items. On the basis of preliminary tryouts, item analysis, and factor analysis, with a large pool of items, the present scale is now reduced to ten principal items, exemplified by the following: Who does not obey the teacher? Who often says, "Give me that!" (Walder, et al., 1961).

In addition, two anxiety-aggression and popularity items are also included. An example of the former is: Who will never forget? (unclassified). An illustration of the latter is: Who would you like to sit next to in class? (Walder et al., 1961).

The scale can be orally administered to a class on a group basis. The major scoring system developed that would be useful to other research workers is a simple percentage figure determined from the ratio of nominations received by a child to the number of nominations possible for that class. Other scoring systems are also developed and instructions for administering the test are outlined (Walder, et al., 1961).

RELIABILITY AND VALIDITY: The scale has been administered in a series of studies to several hundred third-grade children in a primarily rural county in New York State.

The present scale is the outcome of a developmental sequence, beginning with a large pool of original items based on experts' agreement and culminating in its reduced form as a result of preliminary tryouts to test the comprehension of the item, item discrimination analysis, and factor analysis.

Test-retest reliabilities on nine aggressive items from Ns between 73 and 78 range between .70 and .92 over a two-week interval; however, the authors do not consider the scale as valid because replicated results may not be comparable. Nevertheless, they consider the instrument a dependable research tool (Walder et al., 1961).

Lending support to the construct validity of the scale are the findings of

Toigo et al. (1962) that examiner effect on aggression is not significant nor are any of the interactions with the examiner, and that boys receive higher aggression scores. Both of these findings are in accordance with previous results and theoretical expectations. A weak relationship has been found between the social class variable and aggressive behavior as measured by this instrument (Toigo, 1965).

BIBLIOGRAPHY:

ERON, L. D., WALDER, L. O., TOIGO, R., and LEFKOWITZ, M. M. "Social Class, Parental Punishment for Aggression, and Child Aggression." *Child Development,* 1963, *34,* 849–867.

TOIGO, R., WALDER, L. O., ERON, L. D., and LEFKOWITZ, M. M. "Examiner Effect in the Use of a Near Sociometric Procedure in the Third Grade Classroom." *Psychological Reports,* 1962, *11,* 785–790.

TOIGO, R. "Social Status and Schoolroom Aggression in Third-Grade Children." *Genetic Psychology Monographs,* 1965, *71,* 221–268.

WALDER, L. O., ABELSON, R. P., ERON, L. D., BANTA, T. J., and LAULICHT, J. H. *Psychological Reports,* 1961, *9,* 497–556.

PERMISSIVE DOLL-PLAY TEST

AUTHORS: Robert R. Sears, Lucy Rau, and Richard Alpert

AGE: Nursery school children

VARIABLE: Behavioral correlates and antecedents of identification

TYPE OF MEASURE: Rating scale

SOURCE FROM WHICH THE MEASURE MAY BE OBTAINED: See Sears, Rau, and Alpert (1965)

DESCRIPTION OF MEASURE: Like the structured doll-play scale, the permissive doll-play test is used to secure manipulative fantasy behavior from children. Assessment of behavior by this approach includes two twenty-minute sessions in which an experimenter presented a child with five standard doll figures (mother, father, boy, girl, baby) in a standardized open doll house. The child is simply told that he could just show what the family did in the house. Instead of behavioral time units, the child's reactions are recorded in terms of successive behavior units. The frequency of occurrence of a given variable category is divided by the total frequency of behavior units recorded to arrive at a percentage score for each variable. Details on the nature, scoring, and recording of units are provided. Categories are scored by agent and object ($N = 15$), behavior ($N = 19$), and location ($N = 8$).

Examples of the agent and object categories are father doll, mother doll, boy doll, girl doll. Illustrative behavior categories are:

Routine role performance (the largest category in number of responses), as "thematic behavior reproductive of routines carried on in the average home: eating meals, washing dishes, sleeping, bathing, dressing, caring for the baby, sitting in the living room, listening to the radio, father or mother going to work, children going to school, etc. . . ." Also includes casual commands and conversations, and social interaction not affectively toned (e.g., the mother may say, "Go to bed now, children," or the father may say, "I have to go to work").

Male-typed adult work: shop projects, mechanical fixing, other house construction and moving, car activity, going to work.

Exemplifying the location categories are kitchen, toilet, living room, parents' bedroom. These three sets of categories are then combined into thirty-six more general categories, illustrated by activity level: father as routine agent, mother as routine agent, boy as routine agent, girl as routine agent, baby as routine agent, adult as routine agent, child as routine agent, male as routine agent, female as routine agent.

RELIABILITY AND VALIDITY: Though one experimenter did all the doll-play sessions, a measure of inter-rater reliability was made possible by training another person who observed the sessions and scored simultaneously and independently. Scoring was based on per cent agreement between E and O derived from two twenty-minute sessions of doll play for each subject. Agreement on similar behavioral units with respect to total units recorded ranged between 82 and 93 per cent. Agreement was then computed separately for agents, action categories, objects, and locations, and for those actions scored specifically as aggression. The results were: 86 to to 100 per cent for scorers' agent agreements; 74 to 98 per cent for action agreements; 94 to 98 for location agreements; 91 to 100 per cent for object agreements; and 63 to 100 per cent for aggression agreements.

BIBLIOGRAPHY:

SEARS, B. B., RAU, L., and ALPERT, R. *Identification and Child Rearing,* Stanford, California: Stanford University Press, 1965.

PLAYFULNESS SCALE

AUTHOR: Nina J. Lieberman

AGE: Preschool and elementary

VARIABLE: Frequency and quality of playfulness

TYPE OF MEASURE: Rating scale

SOURCE FROM WHICH THE MEASURE MAY BE OBTAINED: See Lieberman (1964, 1965)

DESCRIPTION OF MEASURE: The measure is composed of twelve items—five two-part items and two single items. The A part of the first five items is designed to measure the frequency of playfulness, while the B part is designed to measure the quality of playfulness. An example of one of the items follows. Each part is rated very often (5), often (4), occasionally (3), rarely (2), very rarely (1).

A. How often does the child show joy in or during his play activities? *This may be judged by facial expression such as smiling, by verbal expressions such as saying "I like this" or "This is fun," or by more indirect vocalizing such as singing as an accompaniment of the activity, for instance, "Choo, choo, train, go along." Other behavioral indicators would be repetition of activity, or resumption of activity with clear evidence of enjoyment.*

B. With what freedom of expression does he show his joy? *This may be judged by the intensity or loudness of a chuckle or a singsong as well as the child's ability to repeat or resume his activity by his own choice.*

RELIABILITY AND VALIDITY: When two teachers rated ninety-three kindergarten children, the inter-rater corrected reliability coefficients ranged from .66 to 83.

Lieberman (1965) found a significant relationship between divergent-thinking scores and playfulness as measured by this scale. She raises questions, however, about contamination of this relationship with MA and CA.

BIBLIOGRAPHY:

LIEBERMAN, N. J. Unpublished doctoral dissertation, Columbia University, 1964.
LIEBERMAN, N. J. "Playfulness and Divergent Thinking: An Investigation of Their Relationship at the Kindergarten Level." *The Journal of Genetic Psychology,* 1965, *107,* 219–224.

PROBLEM SITUATIONS TEST

AUTHORS: Ralph H. Ojemann, et al.

AGE: Fourth, fifth, and sixth grades

VARIABLE: Punitiveness

TYPE OF MEASURE: Test

SOURCE FROM WHICH THE MEASURE MAY BE OBTAINED: Ralph H. Ojemann, Educational Research Council of Greater Cleveland, Psychology Department, Rockefeller Building, Cleveland, Ohio 44113, at a cost of $.25 for each manual. "For professional writers in the field."

DESCRIPTION OF MEASURE: The test measures children's willingness to be punitive in situations where no retaliation is likely. It consists of twenty-two multiple-choice items describing interaction between peers, siblings, parents, and teachers, in situations involving aggressive feelings, moral transgression, and personal problems. The subject is required to deal with examples of misbehavior either from the point of view of an authority figure or from his own point of view. Three punitive and three nonpunitive responses are possible. The score for punitiveness is the number of punitive responses to the twenty-two situations. In scoring the PST, the student receives one point for each time he marks a keyed answer. The higher the score the more "non-causal" the child is.

Sample items of the PST are given below:

Betty is sent to the store by her mother and told to come home immediately. On the way home, she meets a friend and they play together for almost an hour. What should Betty's mother do when Betty gets home? (a) Send Betty and her friend together, and play together at Betty's house. (b) Give her a spanking. (c) She should talk to her about it and tell her to come right home and then go play with her friends. (d) Betty's mother should give her a good talking to. (e) She should put her to bed without any dinner. (f) Explain to Betty that she should learn to follow directions.

Mary used to help her mother with the dishes every night. Lately, however, she makes all kinds of excuses to get out of helping. What should Mary's mother do? (a) Ask Mary why she doesn't like to do the dishes. (b) Give her a spanking. (c) Her mother shouldn't let her do some things she wants to do. (d) I think that it's her life, and if she didn't want to help, all right. (e) She should ask her where she is going. (f) She cannot leave her house until she does the dishes.

RELIABILITY AND VALIDITY: The PST has been administered to 154 children in grades four through six. On a rigorous test of reliability with six months' period between test and retest the correlation coefficient was .71. The Kuder-Richardson reliability for the PST has been found to be .77 (Muuss, 1960, p. 481). The PST is related to authoritarianism and parental disciplinary methods, and also to extra-punitiveness and intra-punitiveness as measured by the Rosenzweig Picture-Frustration Study. The correlation between the PST and IQ in fifth-graders was found to be −.29 (Ojemann, et al., 1955). The test has been shown to be sensitive to the effects of a causal teacher training program in that the children of teachers who were exposed to such training had sharply reduced non-causal scores on the Problem Situation Test (Ojemann, et al., 1955).

BIBLIOGRAPHY:

OJEMANN, R. H., LEVITT, E. E., LYLE, W. H., and WHITESIDE, M. F. "The Effects of a 'Causal' Teacher-Training Program and Certain Curricular Changes on Grade School Children." *Journal of Experimental Psychology,* 1955, *XXIV,* 95–114.
MUUSS, R. E. "The Effects of a One- and Two-Year Causal-Learning Program." *Journal of Personality,* 1960, *28,* 479–491.

SOCIAL DESIRABILITY (SD) SCALE FOR CHILDREN

AUTHORS: Patricia W. Lunneborg and Clifford E. Lunneborg

AGE: Grades 4 to 6

VARIABLE: Social desirability

TYPE OF MEASURE: Test—questionnaire

SOURCE FROM WHICH THE MEASURE MAY BE OBTAINED: See Lunneborg and Lunneborg (1964)

DESCRIPTION OF MEASURE: Eighty-nine items from the MMPI, Edwards Personal Preference Schedule, and other sources were rewritten for children in grades four to six. The items as revised now require a clearly socially desirable response, and each item has to vary in the responses given to it by the children. The items have been judged suitable by three elementary school officials and relatively free of anxiety content by ten graduate psychology students. The final scale consists of twenty items.

RELIABILITY AND VALIDITY: The corrected split-half reliability is .83, based on scores of 211 boys and girls in grades four to six. Girls had significantly higher scores than boys, and the scores declined with grade for each sex. The only significant difference for girls and boys combined, however, was between the fourth and the sixth grades.

The authors conclude—from correlations between the SD scale and the Children's Manifest Anxiety Scale (Lie), the General Anxiety Scale for Children (Lie), and the Defensiveness Scale for Children—that the positive correlations between social desirability and other test-taking attitudes support SD as a construct.

BIBLIOGRAPHY:

LUNNEBORG, P. W., and LUNNEBORG, C. E. "The Relationship of Social Desirability to Other Test-Taking Attitudes in Children." *Journal of Clinical Psychology,* 1964, *20,* 473–477.

STORY COMPLETION TEST (Form B)

AUTHOR: Virginia I. Douglas

AGE: Preschool through the sixth grade

VARIABLE: Personality (responses to frustration)

TYPE OF MEASURE: Structured projective test

SOURCE FROM WHICH THE MEASURE MAY BE OBTAINED: Author

DESCRIPTION OF MEASURE: The Story Completion Test, Form B, consists of ten stories in which the desired goal of the hero, a child the same age as the subject, is threatened by an intervening event. The stories are read orally to the child who is directed to provide an ending from among three structured alternatives representing wish fulfillment, pessimism, and compromise. In one story, for example, the desire of the hero (named Mike) to visit the zoo is threatened by a storm and Mike fears that he will not be able to make the visit. The child is asked to select an ending from the three alternatives below, respectively reflecting the responses of compromise, pessimism, and wish fulfillment.

Mike was right, for they could not go. He was very disappointed, but they were able to see the lions on television, which was at least better than not seeing them at all.
Mike was right, the roads were all flooded, and they could not go. Both Mike and his friend were very disappointed.
Mike was quite wrong, they did go, and they had a most exciting day.

In scoring the scale, the child was given a score reflecting the sum for the number of times he selected each type of ending.

RELIABILITY AND VALIDITY: Douglas has provided norms for three samples in terms of means and standard deviation for all three categories of responses. The three samples included fifty-nine boys from the preschool level through the sixth grade from low socioeconomic groups, ninety-one children from grades four to six evenly divided into sex groups and primarily from the middle class, and 111 children from the middle and upper-middle classes.

No statistics on the reliability coefficient for the entire scale or the subscales are presented. At least two types of data in the predicted direction, however, may provide construct validity for the scale. First, in all three samples the correlations between the scores on wish fulfillment and school grades were negative and statistically significant. Second, predicted developmental trends emerged. As one illustration, the tendency for compromise solutions increased with age. As another example, the tendency for wish fulfillment was negatively correlated with age (Douglas, 1965).

BIBLIOGRAPHY:

DOUGLAS, V. I. "Children's Responses to Frustration: A Developmental Study." *Canadian Journal of Psychology*, 1965, *19*, 161–171.

Group 2-c

Personality Adjustment

ADAPTED BILLS, VANCE, AND MC LEAN INDEX OF ADJUSTMENT

AUTHORS: Ronald O. McAfee and Charles C. Cleland

AGE: Mentally retarded males, age 14 to 22, with at least third grade reading ability

VARIABLE: Adjustment

TYPE OF MEASURE: Questionnaire

SOURCE FROM WHICH THE MEASURE MAY BE OBTAINED: Ronald O. McAfee, 1908 Oakhill Road, Bethany, Oklahoma 73008

DESCRIPTION OF MEASURE: The scale is a modified form of the Bills, Vance, and McLean Index (1951), adapted for use with retardates. It is based on the premise that adjustment is determined by the degree of discrepancy between self-concept and ideal-self. In the adaptation process, the five options were reduced to two: Yes or No. Each scale includes forty-nine sentences. Sample items from each scale follow (note similarity of items in Ideal-Self Scale to those in Self-Concept Scale). From the Self-Concept Test:

I am a person who is liked.
I am a person who is right.
I am an alert person.

From the Ideal-Self Test:
I would like to be a person who is liked.
I would like to be a person who is right.
I would like to be an alert person.

RELIABILITY AND VALIDITY: The tests were administered to sixty educable mentally handicapped institutional retardates ranging in age between 14 and 22 and subdivided into two matched groups of adjusted and maladjusted persons. The test-retest reliability coefficients for the subjects over a one-week interval were .66 for the self-concept test, .77 for the ideal-self test, and .54 for the discrepancy scores. Since the discrepancy scores did not differentiate the two groups, the authors concluded that this measure is not applicable to this population.

BIBLIOGRAPHY:

BILLS, R., VANCE, E., and MC LEAN, O. "An Index of Adjustment and Values." *Journal of Consulting Psychology,* 1951, *15,* 257–261.

ADJUSTMENT INVENTORY FOR THE DEAF

AUTHORS: R. Pintner and L. Brunschwig

AGE: Deaf persons between the ages of 9 and 22

VARIABLE: Social adjustment

TYPE OF MEASURE: Self report scale

SOURCE FROM WHICH THE MEASURE MAY BE OBTAINED: See Pintner and Brunschwig (1937)

DESCRIPTION OF MEASURE: The Adjustment Inventory for the Deaf may be administered as a group test or as an individual examination in the intermediate or advanced grades provided that the deaf students have sufficient language skills to comprehend the items. The scale itself consists of sixty-four items with three fixed options in each case. The respondent simply checks the option he regards as the most appropriate for each item. Examples of the items from the scale follow:

Are you strong?   (a) *I am not strong.* (b) *I am the same as my friends.* (c) *I am very, very strong; I am stronger than my friends.*

Do you like to play games?   (a) *I do not like to play games.* (b) *I like to play games a little.* (c) *I like to play games very well.*

Do you like your brothers or sisters?   (a) *I like them a little.* (b) *I do not like them.* (c) *I like them very well.* (d) *I have no brothers and no sisters.*

The scoring procedure outlined makes it possible to derive objective measures in the four areas of general adjustment, social adjustment, school adjustment, and home adjustment. Scoring keys for the four adjustment areas are included, as well as complete directions for administering the scale. Some discussion is also provided for the interpretation of the scale.

RELIABILITY AND VALIDITY: Percentile norms have been provided for each separate sex group, based on the scores of 770 deaf boys and 560 deaf girls. No statistics on reliability are provided. Group differences have revealed consistently superior social adjustment scores for hearing children over deaf pupils of residential schools. Scores on the Adjustment Inventory were related to teachers' judgments of adjustment or maladjustment.

BIBLIOGRAPHY:

PINTNER, R., and BRUNSCHWIG, L. "An Adjustment Inventory for Use in Schools for the Deaf." *American Annals of the Deaf,* 1937, *82,* 152–167.

BEHAVIOR CHECKLIST

AUTHORS: Eli Rubin, Clyde B. Simson, and Marcus L. Betwee

AGE: Kindergarten, first, second, third, and fifth grades

VARIABLE: Classroom behavior

TYPE OF MEASURE: Rating scale

SOURCE FROM WHICH THE MEASURE MAY BE OBTAINED: See Rubin, Simson, and Betwee (1966)

DESCRIPTION OF MEASURE: The Behavior Checklist is a teacher's report of the symptomatic behavior displayed by the child in the classroom. The thirty-nine items or variables can be subsumed under seven major factors according to the factor analytic method. In order of decreasing importance, these are disorientation and maladaptation to the environment; antisocial behavior; unassertive, overconforming behavior; neglect; infantile behavior; immature social behavior; and irresponsible behavior. The meanings of these factors are described in detail by the authors (Rubin et al., 1966). Sample items from Factor I with factor loadings are given below (Rubin et al., 1966).

Misinterprets simple statements	+.70
Disoriented in space	+.70
Daydreams	+.65
Makes odd noises	+.63

In using the scale to rate children, the teacher is directed to indicate the degree to which the item is representative of the child's typical behavior. Thus, two check marks before the item indicate that the behavior is displayed more frequently, while one check indicates that it is representative. The total score, however, consists of the number of items checked.

RELIABILITY AND VALIDITY: Seven factors account for most of the variance in the sample. The factors loading for the group of symptoms representing each cluster of behavior traits range from .41 to .78. Most of these factor loadings were well above .60. A subsequent factor analysis on 2,600 subjects in the first, second, third and fifth grades revealed essentially the same kinds of clusters as on the initial study. These data may be considered evidence in support of the internal consistency of the constructs underlying the scale.

The internal consistency of the scale serves as an index of reliability and construct validity. Moreover, the factors from the Behavior Checklist appear to have low but significant correlations with a variety of measures derived from psychological, neurological, and EEG examinations (Rubin et al., 1966).

BIBLIOGRAPHY:

RUBIN, E. Z., SIMSON, C. B., and BETWEE, M. L. *Emotionally Handicapped Children and the Elementary Schools.* Detroit, Michigan: Wayne State University Press, 1966.

BEHAVIOR DESCRIPTION CHART (BDC)

AUTHORS: Paul H. Bowman, Robert F. DeHaan, John K. Kough, and Gordon P. Liddle

AGE: Upper elementary grades (4 to 6)

VARIABLE: Behavior adjustment

TYPE OF MEASURE: Forced-choice rating scale

SOURCE FROM WHICH MEASURE MAY BE OBTAINED: See Bowman et al. (1956)

DESCRIPTION OF MEASURE: Test scores are derived for social leadership, withdrawn maladjustment, and aggressive maladjustment. An example of one of the items of the BDC is the following (Bowman, et al., 1956):

A.   *Others come to him for help*
B.   *Causes disturbances*
C.   *Lacks confidence in himself*
D.   *Reports those who break the rules*
E.   *Shows emotion in a restrained way*

The judge (the teacher) is instructed to select in each of these pentads the one statement most like the child and the one statement least like the child. In the five items of each pentad one of the statements is descriptive of social leadership (A in the example given above), one of aggressive maladjustment (B, above), and one of withdrawn maladjustment (C, above). The two remaining statements are more nearly neutral in tone and are considered descriptive of an "average" child for whom none of the three weighted statements seem appropriate. The two neutral statements are included so that the judge may not be forced to classify the child into one of the three special groups. The reader should consult the description of the "Who Are They Test" for the definitions of aggressiveness the authors use. The description of this test also gives the standardization group for the present scale, since the same children were tested with both scales.

   After the ratings for each child have been made, the total number of statements selected as *most like* for each of the three dimensions and as *least like* for each of the three dimensions is determined. Thus, there are six basic scores: *most like* leadership, aggressive maladjustment, and withdrawn maladjustment, and *least like* each of these characteristics. The child's final score for each of the three characteristics is then computed by combining the *most like* quantity for the characteristic in question with the two *least like* quantities for the other two characteristics. The *most like* quantity is weighted by multiplying it by 2. A child's leadership score is composed of double his score on *most like* leadership, plus his basic scores for *least like* withdrawn maladjustment and aggressive maladjustment. The basic scores are combined in two other ways to derive scores on masculinity and a maladjustment score without reference to the aggressive or withdrawn dimensions.

RELIABILITY AND VALIDITY: The original test consisted of eighteen pentads or five-statement items. On the basis of item-analysis studies, the revised form consists of ten pentads. Test-retest reliability coefficients were as follows: Leadership, +.63; withdrawn, +.63; aggression, +.54. The authors consider this procedure to be a severe reliability measure since the second ratings a year later were made by different teachers (Bowman et al., 1956).

BIBLIOGRAPHY:

HAVIGHURST, R. J. *A Community Youth Development Program.* Chicago: University of Chicago Press, 1952.

BOWMAN, P. H., ET AL. *Studying Children and Training Counselors in a Community Program.* Chicago: University of Chicago Press, 1953.

BOWMAN, P. H., DE HAAN, R. F., KOUGH, J. K., and LIDDLE, G. P. *Mobilizing Community Resources for Youth.* Chicago: University of Chicago Press, 1956.

DRAW-A-GROUP TEST

AUTHORS: Paul A. Hare, and Rachel T. Hare

AGE: 6 to 10

VARIABLE: Social and personal adjustment of child

TYPE OF MEASURE: Projective drawing test

SOURCE FROM WHICH THE MEASURE MAY BE OBTAINED: See Hare and Hare (1956)

DESCRIPTION OF MEASURE: The Draw-A-Group Test is a group-administered scale that requires children to make drawings in colored crayons describing group activities with children they like as playmates. Essentially, the test is a projective measure of sociometric status within a classroom. The criteria for analyzing the drawings include the usual clinical ones of color preference and range, human activity depicted, size of figures, and the like as well as dimensions of group activities. The scoring is thus done on the basis of subjective clinical impressions, but the authors contend that the nature of the task requirement is such that the results provide clinical analysis of an individual figure test and data on group adjustment as well. The authors have provided directions for administering the scale and detailed and specific examples of case interpretations based on these drawings (Hare and Hare, 1956).

RELIABILITY AND VALIDITY: One hundred and sixty-six children ranging in age from 6 to 10 years were ranked on sociometric standing by clinicians from the test results and by teachers' judgments. Within eight of the ten classes, the correlations were statistically significant (p < .01 or .05), ranging between .47 to .92. A similar rank comparison was made between the extreme groups at the upper and lower one thirds of the distribution. This procedure increased the mean correlation between these two sets of data from .52 to .62. The difference between these mean correlations was statistically significant (Hare and Hare, 1956).

BIBLIOGRAPHY:

HARE, P. A., and HARE, R. T. "The Draw-a-Group Test." *Journal of Genetic Psychology*, 1956, *89*, 51–59.

MITCHELL'S GUESS WHO QUESTIONNAIRE

AUTHOR: James W. Mitchell

AGE: Fourth grade

VARIABLE: Personality adjustment in children

TYPE OF MEASURE: Sociometric questionnaire

SOURCE FROM WHICH THE MEASURE MAY BE OBTAINED: See Mitchell (1956). Also a complete correlation matrix for all possible item pairs has been deposited with the American Documentation Institute. Order Document No. 4802 from American Documentation Institute, 1719 N St. N.W., Washington 6, D.C., remitting $1.25 for 35 mm. microfilm or $1.25 for 6 by 8 inch photocopies.

DESCRIPTION OF MEASURE: This is a sociometric questionnaire administered on a group basis in which children are asked to nominate the leading candidates among their peers for such traits as leadership ability, aggressive maladjustment, withdrawn maladjustment, practical intelligence, and friendship. The total questionnaire, which is a variation of the one previously developed by Bowman (1956), has a total of nineteen items or descriptions of behaviors. These descriptions are subsumed under several behavioral categories. Sample items, with the category given in parentheses, follow:

Who are the boys and girls that make good plans? (leadership ability)

Who are the ones that break rules—rules of the school and rules of games? (aggressive maladjustment)

Who are the ones that seem to understand things most easily, out of school and in school? (practical intelligence)

Who are the boys and girls that stay out of games? They don't like to play hard. (withdrawn maladjustment)

Who are the boys and girls you would like for your best friends? (sole friendship item)

Who are the ones you would not like for your friends? (sole negative friendship item)

The instructions allow the children to list as many names as they want after each description or none at all. As an aid in responding to the sociometric questionnaire, each student receives an alphabetical list of every individual in his class.

A child's score is made up of the number of nominations received for each description.

RELIABILITY AND VALIDITY: Rank-differences correlations, which were computed over a six-month interval for fourth-grade public school students, yielded the respective reliability coefficients of .93, .77, .62, and .78 for leadership, withdrawn maladjustment, aggressive maladjustment, and friendship scores. The results of a teachers' rating scale correlated .66 for leadership, .40 for withdrawn maladjustment, and .52 for aggressive maladjustment.

A factor analysis was performed on responses to all nineteen items for ninety-eight fourth-grade children. Under the Thurstone centroid method, clear-cut and high factor loadings were derived for items representing social skills and those reflecting aggressive tendencies leading to social rejection of the individuals. These factors were designated as "social acceptability" and "aggressive maladjustment." The third factor, which was poorly defined, appeared to be best interpreted as "social isolation" (Mitchell, 1956).

BIBLIOGRAPHY:

BOWMAN, P. H., DE HAAN, R. F., KOUGH, J. K., and LIDDLE, G. P. *Mobilizing Community Resources for Youth.* Chicago: University of Chicago Press, 1956.

MITCHELL, M. V. "The Factor Analysis of a 'Guess-Who' Questionnaire Designed to Identify Significant Behavior Patterns in Children." *Journal of Personality,* 1956, *24,* 376–386.

PITTSBURGH ADJUSTMENT SURVEY SCALES

AUTHORS: Alan O. Ross, Harvey M. Lacy and David A. Parton

AGE: 6- to 12-year-old boys

VARIABLE: Social adjustment

TYPE OF MEASURE: Checklist

SOURCE FROM WHICH THE MEASURE MAY BE OBTAINED: Individuals wishing to use this scale for research purposes may obtain a current version by contacting Alan O. Ross, Pittsburgh Child Guidance Center, 201 DeSota Street, Pittsburgh, Pa. 15213.

DESCRIPTION OF MEASURE: This measure is designed for the objective evaluation of elementary school-age boys' social behavior, using observations by classroom teachers. Scales were developed for aggressive, withdrawn, and prosocial behavior. On the basis of principals' nominations of boys selected upon specific guide lines as well adjusted, aggressive, or withdrawn, the preliminary pool of items was reduced to ninety-four by retaining those that differentiated between extreme groups at the .01 level or less. This group of items was later reduced to seventy-seven on the basis of factor analysis. These items measured aggressive behavior $(N = 26)$, withdrawn $(N = 19)$, prosocial behavior $(N = 20)$, and passive aggressive behavior. The definitions and bases for these scales are presented by the authors. Examples of each in the final scale are as follows:

Aggressive-Behavior Scale (I): *He does things just to attract attention. He tries to get other children into trouble.*

Withdrawn-Behavior Scale (II): *He is afraid of strange adults. He is easily upset by changes in things around him.*

Prosocial-Behavior Scale (III): *He is interested in school work. He volunteers to recite in class.*

Passive-Aggressive-Behavior Scale (IV): *He sulks when things go wrong. He resents even the most gentle criticism of his work.*

In using the scales, the teacher rated the application of each item to describe the child's behavior as follows: O, nondescriptive; 1, somewhat descriptive; 2, definitely descriptive.

RELIABILITY AND VALIDITY: None reported.

BIBLIOGRAPHY:

ROSS, A. O., LACY, H. M., and PARTON, D. A. "The Development of a Behavior Checklist for Boys." *Child Development*, 1965, *36*, 1013–1027.

PSYCHIATRIC FOLLOW-UP CODING

AUTHOR: Eli Rubin

AGE: Kindergarten, first and second grade

VARIABLE: Personality (social and emotional adjustment)

TYPE OF MEASURE: Rating scale

SOURCE FROM WHICH THE MEASURE MAY BE OBTAINED: Eli Z. Rubin, 17000 East Warren, Detroit, Michigan 48224

DESCRIPTION OF MEASURE: These scales provide ratings of the following areas of behavior: spontaneity in the interview situation; cooperativeness; impulsivity; reality-orientation; reality testing; hyperkinetic syndromes—behavioral signs; hyperkinetic syndrome—physical signs; neuropsychiatric symptoms; feelings of self-confidence and self-worth; child's perception of stress in the home; child's perception of stress in school; child's perception of stress in peer relations; emotional maturity; group belongingness; capacity for emotional relationships with others; and overall progress in emotional adjustment. An example of the psychiatric coding is given below (Rubin et al., 1966):

Impulsivity: *This scale evaluates the degree to which the patient has changed in the control of impulsive motor acts, gestures, or behavior as observed in the interview: marked decrease in impulsivity—1; moderate decrease in impulsivity—2; minimal decrease in impulsivity—3; no chance in impulsivity—4; minimal increase in impulsivity—5; moderate increase in impulsivity—6; marked increase in impulsivity —7; no information. Confidence rating.*

RELIABILITY AND VALIDITY: None reported.

BIBLIOGRAPHY:

RUBIN, E. Z., SIMSON, C. B., and BETWEE, M. C. *Emotionally Handicapped Children and the Elementary School.* Detroit: Wayne State University Press, 1966.

ST. LOUIS SYMPTOM INVENTORY

AUTHORS: J. C. Glidewell, Herbert R. Domke, Ivan N. Mensh, and Mildred B. Kantor

AGE: Validating data have been obtained only for white children in the third grade, though the inventory could be readily applied to younger elementary school children

VARIABLE: School adjustment

TYPE OF MEASURE: Symptom inventory, with parents or teachers or both as informants

SOURCE FROM WHICH THE MEASURE MAY BE OBTAINED: See Glidewell et al., 1963

DESCRIPTION OF MEASURE: The information about presenting symptoms of children is collected through a home interview with the child's mother. After collecting some background information, the interviewer asks a series of questions that constitute the symptom inventory. Examples are: Does Johnny have any trouble . . . (eating, sleeping, getting along with other children, etc.)? Affirmative responses were followed by probes into the specific nature of the difficulty, the frequency, the duration, and the severity. Twenty-one areas of difficulty are probed. The range of scores extends from no presenting symptoms to the maximum of 21. The inventory may serve as a screening instrument for emotional disturbance.

RELIABILITY AND VALIDITY: A sample of 184 mothers had about 70 per cent agreement between first- and second-year reports (Glidewell, et al., 1959). The relationship between mothers' reports and teachers' ratings increased as one moved up the social class scale. These correlations were .70 for upper class, .33 for upper middle, .20 for lower middle, and .17 for lower class (Glidewell, et al., 1959).

In a large sample (N = 830), analysis of variance yielded a significant difference between number of symptoms reported by parents and teachers' ratings of adjustment with p < .001. There were no significant differences between sex groups, and the number of symptoms reported by the mother and the analysis of variance held up separately for all social classes (Glidewell, et al., 1963). Glidewell et al. (1963) found that if one wishes to maximize success in predicting both presence and absence of disturbance, the critical cutoff score should be near the middle of the range, that is, after three symptoms.

BIBLIOGRAPHY:

GILDEA, M., DOMKE, H. R., MENSH, I. N., BUCHMUELLER, A. D., GLIDEWELL, J. C., and KANTOR, M. B. "Community Mental Health Research: Findings after Three Years." *American Journal of Psychiatry,* 1958, *CXIV,* 970–976.

GLIDEWELL, J. C., MENSH, I. N., and GILDEA, M. "Behavior Symptoms in Children and Degree of Sickness." *American Journal of Psychiatry,* 1957, *114,* 47–53.

GLIDEWELL, J. C., GILDEA, M. C. L., DOMKE, H. R., and KANTOR, M. B. "Behavior Symptoms in Children and Adjustment in Public School." *Human Organization,* 1959, *18,* 123–130.

GLIDEWELL, J. C., DOMKE, H. R., and KANTOR, M. B. "Screening in Schools for Behavior Disorders: Use of Mothers' Report of Symptoms." *Journal of Educational Research,* 1963, *56,* 508–515.

KANTOR, M. B. "Some Consequences of Residential and Social Mobility for Adjustment of Children." In Mildred B. Kantor (Ed.), *Mobility and Mental Health.* Springfield, Ill.: Charles C Thomas, 1965, pp. 86–122.

SECRET STORIES TEST

AUTHORS: Emory L. Cowen, Mary Ann Trost, Louis D. Izzo, and Sue V. Monjan

AGE: Third-grade children

VARIABLE: Social adjustment

TYPE OF MEASURE: Semi-projective test

SOURCE FROM WHICH THE MEASURE MAY BE OBTAINED: See Cowen, et al. (1964)

DESCRIPTION OF MEASURE: This measure is made up of three incomplete stories, such as the following:

Johnny is an 8 year old boy. One day he was playing in the basement. He had a lot of old boxes that were very good for building a house. He was having fun and he was building a good house. A lot of boxes were scattered around and he was stacking them up to make the house just the way he wanted it. He was very happy. Just about that time his mother came down the stairs. She didn't know that Johnny was there, and at first she didn't see Johnny.

In the other two stories, interruptions of the hero are made by the father and by a friend, respectively.

The test is group administered by the experimenter (this can be the teacher) who reads the story aloud while the children read along from an oversized printed copy. At the point of interruption, the children are asked to close their eyes and to make up an ending for the story. After a short pause, the experimenter asks, "How did Johnny feel—Happy or Mad?" The child then checks, in the appropriate box on his answer sheet, which of the two "feeling qualities" better applies to his secret story. In all, four "feeling" adjectives are used: Happy, Mad, Worried, and Afraid, each paired against all others for a total of six combinations. Next, a similar series of paired comparison choices are posed for four "behavioral" options: (1) Says come play with me, (2) Hides behind the boxes, (3) Say go away, and (4) Does nothing and waits. These too are paired in all six possible combinations, for a grand total of twelve paired comparisons per story. The same procedure is followed for the second and third stories. The twelve paired comparisons serving as options for each story are as follows: happy—mad, mad—worried, worried—afraid, happy—worried, mad—afraid, happy—afraid, play—hide, away—nothing, nothing—play, away—hide, play—away, hide—nothing.

RELIABILITY AND VALIDITY: Chi-square calculations showed a statistically significant choice pattern in thirty of thirty-six paired comparisons, so the test would seem to have some validity in that it appears to indicate preferred choices. The authors present these percentage choices in detail for the twelve paired items, within three classifications: a mother, father, and friend. In a sense they regard these data as preliminary norms (Cowen et al., 1964).

BIBLIOGRAPHY:

COWEN, E. L., TROST, M. A., IZZO, L. D., and MONJAN, S. V. "The Secret Stories Test: A Projective Approach for Young Children." *Journal of Clinical Psychology,* 1964, *XX,* 484–486.

TEACHER'S RATING SCALE

AUTHOR: Eli Rubin

AGE: Kindergarten through second grade

VARIABLE: Social and emotional adjustment in classroom

TYPE OF MEASURE: Rating scale

SOURCE FROM WHICH THE MEASURE MAY BE OBTAINED: Eli Z. Rubin, 17000 East Warren, Detroit, Michigan 48224

DESCRIPTION OF MEASURE: This rating scale is designed to enable teachers to rate social and emotional characteristics of emotionally disturbed children, although the nature of the items suggests that the measure is also applicable to children generally. Many different behaviors are tapped by the seventy-nine items in the scale, each of which is a separate scale. The items each constitute a nine-point scale, where the first, fifth, and ninth reference points are described, and in some cases also the third and seventh points. The rater is instructed that he may use points 2, 4, 6, or 8 if he feels the need to do so.

RELIABILITY AND VALIDITY: Inter-rater reliability coefficients for the seventy-nine scales ranged from .26 to .94. Two-thirds of the inter-rater coefficients were above .75. If the items that show the lowest reliability were eliminated, the coefficients would then range from .60 to .94, with a mean of .78. Rubin states that the scale is useful in the evaluation of change in classroom behavior. "Change" refers to improvement in social and emotional adjustment as a result of placement in a special class for emotionally disturbed children.

BIBLIOGRAPHY:

RUBIN, E. Z. "Rating Guide for Teacher's Rating Scales." Dittoed, 1962.

RUBIN, E. Z., SIMSON, C. B., and BETWEE, M. C. *Emotionally Handicapped Children in the Elementary School.* Detroit, Michigan: Wayne State University Press, 1966.

TORONTO INFANT SECURITY SCALE

AUTHOR: Betty Margaret Flint

AGE: Birth to 2 years of age

VARIABLE: Mental health of infants

TYPE OF MEASURE: Checklist

SOURCE FROM WHICH THE MEASURE MAY BE OBTAINED: University of Toronto Press, University of Toronto, Toronto, Canada

DESCRIPTION OF MEASURE: The scale is based on the theory that the truly secure baby is indicated by the items reflecting dependence on adults and effort in areas where the child has sufficient skill to help himself. A parent as an informant is necessary in order to administer the measure. Scores are available for the acceptance of dependence (D) and the acceptance of effort on the secure items (E) and the rejection of dependence (D) and effort (E) on avoidance mechanisms (deputy agent items and regressive items). Endorsements in each category are expressed in percentages by multiplying the proportion of test items (endorsed) for the total number of applicable items by 100.

The items are grouped according to four age levels, namely 0 to 6 months, 6 to 12 months, 12 to 18 months, and 18 to 24 months. Directions are given for scoring and for the use of the findings from the scale. Administration time is about half an hour. The author recommends that use of the measure be confined to trained clinicians.

RELIABILITY AND VALIDITY: In the process of developing the items for the scale the author used the following sequence. Records of factual behavior for 150 infants who were under care of a local agency were examined. Descriptions of behavior were then listed according to their reflection of security or insecurity. Subsequently agreement with the senior psychologist at the clinic was obtained with respect to the categorization of the majority of items. Lastly, items for the final revision were selected on the following basis: initial adjustment to a new or changing situation; reflections of security; and indications of insecurity. Test-retest reliability coefficients for the four scales range from .46 to .91. The author contends that consistency of results on the same infants over time should not be expected in view of their intense responsiveness to their environment. At present she is attempting to obtain data from inter-rater reliability.

BIBLIOGRAPHY:

FLINT, B. M. *The Security of Infants.* Toronto: University of Toronto Press, 1959.

ULLMANN'S FORCED-CHOICE PUPIL ADJUSTMENT SCALE

AUTHOR: C. A. Ullmann

AGE: Grades four through nine

VARIABLE: Emotional adjustment

TYPE OF MEASURE: Forced-choice rating scale

SOURCE FROM WHICH THE MEASURE MAY BE OBTAINED: See Ullmann (1952)

DESCRIPTION OF MEASURE: The Forced-Choice Pupil Adjustment Scale, otherwise known as the Prince Georges Pupil-Adjustment Chart, consists of eighteen sets of descriptive behavior that were constructed by pairing items and then assembling the pairs into tetrads or hexads. In each set, preference values were kept as nearly uniform as possible. Hexads rather then tetrads were constructed around items of low preference value.

Within each pair of items, one is highly indicative with respect to adjustment, either favorable or unfavorable, while the other, although of equal preference value, has a neutral discriminative value. The discrimination values employed are those which have been obtained from the ratings of clinicians. It is supposed that by using clinician rather than teacher ratings it might be possible to compensate for any tendency on the part of teachers to overvalue conforming behavior.

In each of the eighteen sets, the teacher is requested to select the statement that fits the child's behavior most appropriately. She is also directed to answer every set. Directions to the teacher further state that she should be able to complete the eighteen entries for each child within a five-minute period. Though the method for obtaining the total score is not explicit, presumably it consists of a sum of the weights allowed for each response option within each set. These weights, which range between 0 and 2 for each statement within a set, are based on a preference value which clinicians and teachers placed on the discriminative value of the item.

Examples of the item sets, the preference values used, and the scores are given below:

Sees the bright or funny side of things	165	2
Likes to be praised	139	1
Obedient	176	1
Participates actively in school functions	173	2
Pitches in when things are to be done	187	2
Requires corrections	207	1
Needs much extra help	220	0
Respects rules	191	1

RELIABILITY AND VALIDITY: Normative data on 810 ninth graders have been presented with respect to each sex group and the total sample. Reliability coefficients, based on a sample of 100 boys and 100 girls, were .92 (boys), .87 (girls), and .90 (total).

Teachers rated children whom they had nominated as poorly or well adjusted on a preliminary pool of 144 behavioral items. The items that discriminated between these two extreme groups were then submitted to twenty-two clinical workers who rated the items as indicative of good or poor adjustment. Discriminative items were subsequently correlated with the mean of clinicians' ratings of the items, with a resultant correlation of .86 for the total scores of .69 for favorable items and .50 for unfavorable items.

Pearson-Product coefficients of correlation between the scores on this scale and related variables are as follows: adjustment level as rated by teacher (r of .73 sultant correlation of .86 for the total scores, of .69 for favorable items and .50 for girls).

BIBLIOGRAPHY:

ULLMANN, C. A. *Identification of Maladjusted School Children*. Washington, D.C.: Superintendent of Documents, 1952, 1957.

VISITING TEACHER RATING SCALE

AUTHORS: Eli Z. Rubin, Clyde B. Simson, and Marcus L. Betwee

AGE: Kindergarten through second grade. The scale could probably apply to almost any age school child

VARIABLE: Social adjustment

TYPE OF MEASURE: Combined structured interview and rating scale

SOURCE FROM WHICH THE MEASURE MAY BE OBTAINED: Eli Z. Rubin, 17000 E. Warren, Detroit, Mich. 48224

DESCRIPTION: The Visiting Teacher Rating Scale is a combination of a structured interview and a rating scale. It is a structured interview in that it provides specific directions for the type of data a social worker should seek. On the other hand, the scale requires the social worker to rate the responses on a point scale, ranging from 1 to 9. The scale consists of nine subscales covering the following areas for disturbed children and their families: identification, referral complaint, history of present illness, child's awareness and concern over academic difficulty, academic work habits, speech, personality characteristics of the patient, family history, and developmental history.

Three additional important characteristics of the scale should be mentioned. First, each of the subscales has a number of subsections. For example, the subscale on family history has more than fifty subsections. Second, the scales vary considerably in objectivity, from highly objective to considerably subjective. An example of the former is the identification subscale entitled "Persons Seen by Social Worker." The social worker indicates how many times he has seen the true mother, true father, substitute mother, substitute father, sibling, child himself, other family member, with a point on the scale from 0 to 9 being awarded for each time he has seen one of these people. An example of a much more subjective scale is the subsection from "identification" which measures parents' resistance to previous recommendations for retention: Suggested it to teacher and eager—1; agreed and cooperative—2; noncommittal but cooperative—3; disagreed but cooperative—4; noncommittal and completely passive—5; agreed but uncooperative—6; noncommittal but uncooperative—7; disagreed and uncooperative—8; vehemently opposed and antagonistic—9; no information—0.

Though no explicit scoring directions for obtaining the total are provided, presumably this score is derived from the sum of the individual subscales. Apparently, the higher score is in the direction of greater pathology. The scale appears sufficiently objective to use a number of scoring schemes.

RELIABILITY AND VALIDITY: Eighty-nine per cent of the inter-rater correlations for all subjects were above .75.

BIBLIOGRAPHY:

RUBIN, E. Z., SIMSON, C. B., and BETWEE, M. L. *Emotionally Handicapped Children and the Elementary School.* Detroit: Wayne State University Press, 1966.

ZELIGS' ANNOYANCE TEST

AUTHOR: Rose Zeligs

AGE: Sixth grade

VARIABLE: Adjustment

TYPE OF MEASURE: Questionnaire

SOURCE FROM WHICH THE MEASURE MAY BE OBTAINED: See Zeligs (1962)

DESCRIPTION OF MEASURE: This test is designed to identify the personal, social, and environmental factors annoying to children. The author suggests indirectly that the test may measure adjustment or irritability.

This is actually several measures, each of which measures attitudes toward different aspects of the subject's living. Thus, there are measures of annoyances concerning health and appearance, hobbies and interests, foods, games and amusements, and fears. The numbers of items in the boys' form, for the above-mentioned areas respectively, are: thirty-eight, thirty-seven, thirty-four, seven, and five. There are separate forms for boys and girls for each of these areas of annoyance. The items, with examples from some of the areas mentioned above, are as follows. The weights used for scoring are: like—2; don't mind—4; don't like—6; hate—8; hate much—10.

To take castor oil	*To read boring books*
To get poison ivy	*When I can't get a drink*
Dirty people	*To eat liver*
To have nothing to do	*To have no time for play*

Zeligs (1945) used the same technique previously to measure (using separate forms for the sexes) attitudes toward social situations (forty male items, 100 female); attitudes toward home and family (thirty and twenty-six items, respectively); attitudes toward school situations (twenty-four and thirty items); and attitudes toward personal conduct (twenty-two and seventeen items).

Scoring is accomplished by multiplying the number of items marked "like" by 2, the number marked "don't mind" by 4, and so forth according to the five weights. The totals are added and then divided by 10 to get the score, which is divided by the number of items to arrive at a percentage. A score of 100 per cent means that the respondent marked each item "hate much."

RELIABILITY AND VALIDITY: Some standardization figures are given for sixth grade boys and girls.

BIBLIOGRAPHY:

ZELIGS, R. "Children's Attitudes toward Annoyances." *Journal of Genetic Psychology,* 1962, *101,* 255–266.

ZELIGS, R. "Environmental Factors Annoying to Children." *Sociology & Social Research,* 1941, *25,* 549–556.

ZELIGS, R. "Social Factors Annoying to Children." *Journal of Applied Psychology,* 1945, *29,* 75–82.

Group 2-d

Anxiety

THE ANXIETY SCALE

AUTHOR: Jerry D. Alpern

AGE: Preschool

VARIABLE: Personality-anxiety

TYPE OF MEASURE: Modified interview

SOURCE FROM WHICH THE MEASURE MAY BE OBTAINED: See Alpern (1959)

DESCRIPTION OF MEASURE: The Anxiety Scale is a modified interview consisting of seventy-nine items which the subject responds to by placing a steel ball in one of two boxes, one contiguous to and represented by a "happy" face of a child of the same sex as the subject, the other contiguous to and represented by a "sad" face of the same-sex child. The interview is composed of three types of items: those designed to elicit "happy" responses; those designed to elicit "sad" responses; and those constructed to elicit either a "happy" or "sad" response depending on the experience of the individual. The anxiety scores were derived from this last group of items (ambiguous items). The first ten items of the measure included six "happy" and four "sad" ambiguous items. The other sixty-nine items consisted of alternating ambiguous and unambiguous items, beginning with ambiguous item 11.

In administering the measure, the examiner calls attention to the "happy box" and points out that there is a picture of a happy boy (or girl) by a period. He does the same for the "sad box" and then instructs the child to put the marble in whatever box he wants to after he hears the question.

Four scores are derived from the Anxiety Scale: (1) the total "sad response" score, which is the number of times the child makes a sad response to the ambiguous interview items; (2) the "speed score," which is the child's main latency on the ambiguous items, latency being defined as the time elapsed between the presentation of the item or question and response; (3) "latency score"; a basal response time was determined for each child by getting the average of the latency time on the thirty-four unambiguous items. The latency score, then, is the difference between the mean latency time on the thirty-five ambiguous items and the basal time mentioned above. (4) "Variance score," which is simply the variance of the latency times on the ambiguous items.

While reliabilities are not high and validity is not demonstrated in the form of significant correlations between any of the four anxiety scale scores and either of the two criteria, teachers' ranking of anxiety and a motor task, the test procedure used and the pool of items for the anxiety measure may be of interest to other researchers. Low reliability should be expected in view of the fact that the age range of the subjects was from 3 years 3 months to 5 years 1 month in the original sample.

RELIABILITY AND VALIDITY: Test-retest reliabilities on the four anxiety scores, for the younger group (chronological ages 3 years 3 months to 3 years

11 months) range from − .14 to .46. For the older group, with chronological ages from 3 years 11 months to 5 years 1 month, the reliabilities ranged from .57 to .89. None of the anxiety scale scores correlated significantly with teachers' rankings of anxiety. There was also no significant relationship between performance on a motor task and any of the anxiety scale scores.

BIBLIOGRAPHY:

ALPERN, J. D. "The Relationship of an Objective Measure of Anxiety for Pre-School Aged Children to Two Criterion Measures." Unpublished master's thesis, State University of Iowa, 1959.

CHILDREN'S ANXIETY PICTURES

AUTHOR: Roger J. Callahan

AGE: Borderline retarded children ranging between 11 and 13 and normal children in the sixth grade

VARIABLE: Personality (anxiety)

TYPE OF MEASURE: Projective test

SOURCE FROM WHICH THE MEASURE MAY BE OBTAINED: Roger J. Callahan, Apt. 28D, 340 East 64th Street, New York, N.Y. 10021. Copies of the test are available from Dr. Callahan at $7.00 per set.

DESCRIPTION OF MEASURE: The CAP consists of forty black and white ambiguous figures of varying shapes designed to measure clinical anxiety among children. In the individual administration of the test, the children are asked to tell what each picture looks like to them. As measured on this test, anxiety is defined as the tendency to perceive ambiguous figures as representing threatening types of objects, such as ghosts, monsters, robbers. In scoring the items, each response is assigned a weight from 0 to 3 (Rosenblum and Callahan, 1958). The highest scores are reportedly indicative of a greater level of anxiety. The total score then consists of the sum of the individual scores.

Callahan provides directions for administering and scoring the test, illustrative items indicative of different ways to score items, a rationale for the test, suggestions on its use and limitations, and sample protocols of high and low anxious children.

RELIABILITY AND VALIDITY: Normative data for the scale are presently not available. Nevertheless, the mean, standard deviation, and the ranges of scores for sixty-six 13-year old high-grade retarded boys have been obtained (Manual, undated). Interjudge reliability of the scoring system was found to be .90 for the thirty 11- and 12-year old high-grade retarded children. The test-retest reliability coefficient for thirty-six 13-year-old high-grade retarded boys was .85 for a time interval ranging from four to six weeks (Rosenblum and Callahan, 1958).

Consistent with expectation, children with low Binet digit span scores received significantly higher scores on the CAP (Callahan and Keller, 1957). Children in a psychiatric ward (age range 7 to 15) scored significantly higher on the CAP than a non-hospitalized group from the public schools (Callahan, 1962).

BIBLIOGRAPHY:

CALLAHAN, R. J. "Validity of the Children's Anxiety Pictures." *Perceptual Motor Skills,* 1962, *14,* 166.

CALLAHAN, R. J., and KELLER, J. E. "Digit Span and Anxiety: An Experimental Group Revisited." *American Journal of Mental Deficiency,* 1957, *61,* 581–582.

ROSENBLUM, S., and CALLAHAN, R. J. "The Performance of High-Grade Retarded, Emotionally Disturbed Children on the Children's Manifest Anxiety Scale and Children's Anxiety Pictures." *Journal of Clinical Psychology,* 1958, *14,* 272–275.

CHILDREN'S MANIFEST ANXIETY SCALE

AUTHORS: Alfred Castaneda, Boyd R. McCandless, and David S. Palermo

AGE: 6 to 12

VARIABLE: Personality (manifest anxiety)

TYPE OF MEASURE: Self-report questionnaire

SOURCE FROM WHICH THE MEASURE MAY BE OBTAINED: See Castaneda, et al. (1956)

DESCRIPTION OF MEASURE: The CMAS consists of fifty-three items in which the child indicates agreement (Yes) or disagreement (No) regarding the applicability of the behavior to himself. Among these fifty-three items, forty-two are anxiety items and eleven refer to an L subscale that provides an index of the subject's tendency to falsify his responses. The anxiety score is obtained by summing the number of anxiety items answered "Yes." Sample items from the anxiety scale follow:

It is hard for me to keep my mind on anything.
I get nervous when someone watches me work.

Below two of the L items are cited:

I like everyone I know.
I would rather win than lose in a game.

In the original normative study, the test was administered on a group basis by the classroom teacher (Castaneda, et al., 1956). Adaptations have occurred, however, in the administration of the test to educable mentally handicapped children, including self-administration with explanation of word meanings when necessary (Cochran and Cleland, 1963), small group administration (Feldhusen and Klausmeier, 1962), and oral examination on an individual basis (Feldhusen and Klausmeier, 1962; Carrier and Orton, 1962).

RELIABILITY AND VALIDITY: Means and standard deviations of both scales have been provided for the following groups: (1) 386 white boys and girls in grades four, five, and six (Castaneda, et al., 1956); (2) sixty-one Negro boys and seventy-five Negro girls in the same grades as above (Palermo, 1959); (3) thirty-seven adolescent educable mentally handicapped (EMH) students with a chronological age spread of 13 to 18 and an IQ range of 57 to 60 who had attained a fourth-grade level of achievement (Cochran and Cleland, 1963); and (4) twenty-seven non-institutionalized and seventeen institutionalized educable mentally handicapped children with a mean age of 12 years 11 months (Carrier, et al., 1962).

Reliability coefficients for both scales have included the following results: .90 for the anxiety (A) scale and .70 for the L scale over a one-week interval with white children in grades four, five, and six (Castaneda, et al., 1956); .59 to .91 for Negro children in the same grades for the A scale and .77 to .80 for the L scale over a one-month interval (Palermo, 1959).

In the original study all fifty-three items were checked by school officials for their comprehensibility for the population to be evaluted (Casteneda, et al., 1956).

The intercorrelations between the A and L scales have been found to be quite low, ranging between −.11 to .22. The authors of the scale support the desirability of such a low intercorrelation (Castaneda, et al., 1956).

A number of findings from the use of the scale have been in the expected direction, suggesting construct validity: Children with high CMAS scores make significantly more errors than non-anxious children in a complex learning task (McCandless, et al., 1956). Retarded adolescents achieving a fourth-grade level on a standardized achievement test showed significantly more manifest anxiety than fourth-grade children of normal intelligence (Cochran and Cleland, 1963). Mean scores on the A scales for Negro children in grades four, five, and six were significantly higher than those for white subjects at all grade levels and for both sexes (Palermo, 1959). CMAS correlated highly with Sarason's Score for Anxiety among children of both sexes in grades four, five, and six, with coefficients ranging between .76 to .79 (Grams, et al., 1962).

In contrast to these findings, however, results on CMAS did not correlate significantly with teacher's ratings (Grams, et al., 1962). Moreover, at least one group of workers has reported the possibility of an acquiescent set among EMH children as well as negative correlations betweeen CMAS results and IQ scores. On the basis of these two findings, these authors have urged caution in using the CMAS (Carrier, et al., 1962).

BIBLIOGRAPHY:

CARRIER, N. A., ORTON, K. D., and MALPASS, L. F. "Responses of Bright Normal and EMH Children to an Orally Administered Children's Manifest Anxiety Scale." *Journal of Educational Psychology*, 1962, *53*, 271–274.

CASTANEDA, A., MC CANDLESS, B. R., and PALERMO, D. C. "The Children's Form of the Manifest Anxiety Scale." *Child Development*, 1956, *27*, 317–326.

COCHRAN, I. J., and CLELAND, C. C. "Manifest Anxiety of Retardates and Normals Matched as to Academic Achievement." *American Journal of Mental Deficiencies*, 1963, *67*, 539–542.

GRAMS, A., HAFNER, A. J., and WENTWORTH, Q. "Children's Anxiety as Compared with Parents' Reports and Teachers' Ratings of Adjustment." Presentation at American Psychological Association, August 30, 1962, St. Louis, Missouri.

LIPSITT, L. P. "A Self-Concept Scale for Children and Its Relationship to the Children's Form of the Manifest Anxiety Scale." *Child Development*, 1958, *29*, 463–472.

MALPASS, L., MARK, S., and PALERMO, D. S. "Responses of Retarded Children to the Children's Manifest Anxiety Scale." *Journal of Educational Psychology*, 1960, *51*, 305–308.

MC CANDLESS, B. R., and CASTANEDA, A. "Anxiety in Children, School Achievement, and Intelligence." *Child Development*, 1956, *27*, 379–382.

MC CANDLESS, B. R., CASTANEDA, A., and PALERMO, D. S. "Anxiety in Children and Social Status." *Child Development*, 1956, *27*, 385–391.

PALERMO, D. S. "Racial Comparisons and Additional Normative Data on the Children's Manifest Anxiety Scale." *Child Development*, 1959, *30*, 53–57.

GENERAL ANXIETY SCALE FOR CHILDREN (GASC)

AUTHORS: Seymour Sarason, et al.

AGE: Grades 1 to 9

VARIABLE: Personality—Anxiety

TYPE OF MEASURE: Test—group

SOURCE FROM WHICH THE MEASURE MAY BE OBTAINED: See Sarason (1960)

DESCRIPTION OF MEASURE: The GASC is made up of forty-five items of which thirty-four are designed to measure general anxiety and eleven constitute a lie scale. Examples of items in this scale are as follows:

When you are away from home, do you worry about what might be happening at home?
Are you frightened by lightning and thunderstorms?
When you are home alone and someone knocks on the door, do you get a worried feeling?
Do you worry that you are going to get sick?
Do you worry about whether your father is going to get sick?

RELIABILITY AND VALIDITY: There are no reliability data given for the GASC. Several kinds of data on validity are provided by Sarason. He describes correlations between the Test Anxiety Scale for Children and the General Anxiety Scale for Children from grades one to six in American schools and from one to five in English schools. As might be expected, the correlations between the two measures are lower in the lower grades, probably as a result of lower reliabilities in the first and second grades. The median correlation between TASC and GASC for American boys was .67, and for girls .56. The girls in the study do not show the same pattern of low reliabilities in the lower grades as did the boys, which is probably explainable in terms of sex differences on GASC scores.

Low negative correlations are reported by Sarason between GASC and IQ scores and GASC and mean achievement scores.

According to Sarason, since more of the items of the GASC have to do with possible bodily harm than with developing and maintaining social relations, the measure is more pertinent to the anxieties of boys than of girls.

BIBLIOGRAPHY:

SARASON, S. B., DAVIDSON, K. S., LIGHTHALL, F. F., WAITE, R. R., and RUEBUSH, B. K. *Anxiety in Elementary School Children.* New York: John Wiley & Sons, 1960.

PALMAR SWEAT PRINTS

AUTHOR: Richard K. Lore

AGE: 6 to adult

VARIABLE: Anxiety

TYPE OF MEASURE: Test—physiological

SOURCE FROM WHICH THE MEASURE MAY BE OBTAINED: See Lore (1966)

DESCRIPTION OF MEASURE: Lore (1966) describes the technique for measuring anxiety by painting the surface of the finger with a ferric chloride solution, placing the finger in contact with paper impregnated with tannic acid, and then measuring the amount of ferric tannate remaining on the paper. This last step is facilitated by the use of a densitometer, which measures the relative amount of light passing through the print. High densitometer readings indicate low sweating and vice versa, since the measurement is based on the amount of light transmitted through the print.

RELIABILITY AND VALIDITY: Lore (1966) found test-retest reliability coefficients to range from .54 to .8 for the four fingers over a one-day interval, the subjects being second-grade children. The reliability coefficients over a 15-day time interval for essentially the same group of subjects was .56 to .60. He found interfinger correlations of twenty-six children to range from .73 to .83. Other researchers (Wenger and Gilchrist, 1948; Haywood and Shoemaker, 1963; Brutten, 1959) observed somewhat higher reliability coefficients.

Lore (1966) found significant differences between the palmar sweat prints of two groups of 4- and 5-year-old children divided into two groups of six each. The experimental group heard a presumably mildly anxiety arousing story read by the experimenter while the control group had no known anxiety stimulus. The difference in the densitometer scores of the palmar sweat prints was significant at the .05 level, and in the expected direction, with a higher level of anxiety being shown by the experimental group.

BIBLIOGRAPHY:

BRUTTEN, E. J. "Colormetric Measurement of Anxiety: A Clinical and Experimental Procedure." *Speech Monograph,* 1959, *26,* 282–287.

FERREIRA, A. J., and WINTER, W. D. "The Palmar Sweat Print: A Methodological Study." *Psychosomatic Medicine,* 1963, *25,* 377–383.

HAYWOOD, C. H., and SHOEMAKER, D. J. "Measurement of Palmar Sweating: Effect of Repeated Measurement from the Same Area." *Journal of Psychology,* 1963, *55,* 363–369.

LORE, R. K. "Palmar Sweating and Transitory Anxiety in Children." *Child Development,* 1966, *37,* 115–123.

LOTSOF, E. J., and DOWNING, W. L. "Two Measures of Anxiety." *Journal of Consulting Psychology,* 1956, *22,* 170.

WENGER, M. A., and GILCHRIST, J. C. "A Comparison of Two Indices of Palmar Sweating." *Journal of Experimental Psychology,* 1948, *38,* 757–761.

TEACHER'S RATING SCALE

AUTHORS: Seymour Sarason, et al.

AGE: Elementary school children

VARIABLE: Personality—anxiety

TYPE OF MEASURE: Rating scale

SOURCE FROM WHICH THE MEASURE MAY BE OBTAINED: See Sarason (1960)

DESCRIPTION OF MEASURE: This rating scale, to be used by teachers, is designed to measure anxiety in elementary school children. Each of the seventeen items is rated on a five-point scale, in which a score of 1 means that the behavior described in each item occurs very often. (A child is very often like this; it is very characteristic of him.) A score of 2 means that the behavior occurs fairly often. (The child is frequently like this; it is fairly characteristic of him.) A score of 5 means that the behavior almost never occurs. (The child is hardly ever like this; it is not characteristic of him.)

Examples of the items on which the child is rated using the aforementioned scale are as follows:

Does the child perform less well in school than your evaluation of his intelligence would lead you to expect?
Does the child's voice tremble when he is asked to recite?
Does the child become upset when he is told that the answer which he has given is wrong?
Does the child's illness or physical complaints tend to coincide with test days or class recitations?

RELIABILITY AND VALIDITY: Sarason (1960) correlated scores on the Test Anxiety Scale for Children and the Teaching Rating Scale and found that the correlations ranged from .09 to .34. Most correlations were significant at or beyond the .05 level. Sarason (1960) found fairly high negative correlations between teacher rating scores and mean achievement, with a strong tendency for the magnitude of the correlations to drop as grade level increased. There is also a negative but low correlation between teachers' ratings and IQ.

BIBLIOGRAPHY:

SARASON, S. B., DAVIDSON, K. S., LIGHT, F. F., WAITE, R. R., and RUEBUSH, B. K. *Anxiety in Elementary School Children.* New York: John Wiley & Sons, 1960.

TEST ANXIETY SCALE FOR CHILDREN (TASC)

AUTHORS: S. B. Sarason and others

AGE: Grades one to nine

VARIABLE: Test anxiety

TYPE OF MEASURE: Test—group

SOURCE FROM WHICH THE MEASURE MAY BE OBTAINED: See Sarason (1960)

DESCRIPTION OF MEASURE: The test consists of thirty items that are read to the children, who are instructed to answer by circling either "yes" or "no" (Sarason, 1960).

Do you worry when the teacher says that she is going to ask you questions to find how much you know?

When you are in bed at night, do you sometimes worry about how you are going to do in class the next day?

When you are taking a test, does the hand you write with shake a little?

While you are taking a test do you usually think you are doing poorly?

Feld and Lewis (n.d.) and Dunn (1965) in factor-analytic studies concluded that the TASC does not measure a unidimensional variable. Feld and Lewis have constructed reversed items (where anxious subjects would tend to respond "no") to investigate any effect of acquiescence set on TASC scores (where anxious subjects tend to respond "yes").

RELIABILITY AND VALIDITY: Sarason (1960) devotes much of his book to the task of demonstrating the construct validity of the TASC. The overall evidence for validity is impressive, and is approached in numerous ways. The prospective user of this test should examine the wealth of data presented in Sarason's book, chapter 6, entitled "Initial Validity Studies," in particular. Sarason concludes that the TASC has an encouraging degree of validity, and that it reveals differences among cultures which place differential emphasis on academic achievement.

BIBLIOGRAPHY:

DUNN, J. A. "Stability of the Factor Structure of the Test Anxiety Scale for Children across Age and Sex Groups." *Journal of Consulting Psychology,* 1965, 29, 187.

SARASON, S. B., DAVIDSON, K. S., LIGHTHALL, F. F., WAITE, R. R., and RUEBUSH, B. K. *Anxiety in Elementary School Children.* New York: John Wiley & Sons, 1960.

PERCEPTIONS
OF ENVIRONMENT

Group 3-a: Attitudes Toward Adults

Group 3-b: Attitudes Toward Peers

Group 3-c: Other Factors

Group 3-a

Attitudes Toward Adults

ABOUT MY TEACHER INVENTORY

AUTHOR: William R. Beck

AGE: Sixth-grade children

VARIABLE: Pupils' attitudes toward their teachers

TYPE OF MEASURE: Questionnaire

SOURCE FROM WHICH THE MEASURE MAY BE OBTAINED: See Beck (1964a)

DESCRIPTION OF MEASURE: Beck's original inventory consists of 100 items pertaining to the pupils' perceptions of teacher merit or effectiveness along the five dimensions of affective merit, cognitive merit, disciplinary merit, innovative merit, and motivational merit. The items rotate in the above order throughout the inventory in twenty five-item cycles. The administrative format requires that the test items be read aloud to the children who respond in terms of Yes, No, or a question mark (?) when uncertain. The items from the first cycle of the five categories follow:

Do you like your teacher?
Do you wish your teacher would use more examples to make the lesson clearer?
Do the children behave well for your teacher?
Does your teacher do things in the same old way all the time?
Does your teacher make you want to go to the library?

A shortened and revised form of the test has been developed, consisting of thirty items, with six from each of the five dimensions. Apparently, the prime basis for selecting these items was factor loading (Reiter, 1966).

RELIABILITY AND VALIDITY: Beck has administered the 100-item inventory to a sample of 2,108 sixth-grade pupils. On the basis of this sample, the five factors emerged as described previously. The author selected relevant items from the literature according to his best judgment, submitted them to professionally qualified judges for categorization in the five dimensions, and pretested them for comprehensibility with sixth-grade pupils (Beck, 1964b). Test-retest coefficients for the reliability of class means with intervals over several months averaged between .82 and .86, based on a sample of more than 200 elementary school children (Yee, 1966b, p. 6).

BIBLIOGRAPHY:

BECK, W. R. "Pupil's Perceptions of Teacher Merit: A Factor Analysis of Five Hypothesized Dimensions." Unpublished doctoral dissertation, Stanford University, 1964a.

BECK, W. R. "Pupil's Perceptions of Teacher Merit: A Factor Analysis of Five

Hypothesized Dimensions" Unpublished doctoral dissertation, Stanford University, 1964b (Abstract).

REITER, R. L. "A Revision of the 'About My Teacher' Instrument on Item Factor Loadings." Unpublished master's thesis, the University of Toledo, 1966 (Excerpts, Chapter IV).

YEE, A. H. "Factors Involved in Determining the Relationships between Teacher's and Pupil's Interpersonal Attitudes." Paper read at American Educational Research Association, Chicago, February 17, 1966a.

YEE, A. H. "Factors Involved in Determining the Relationships between Teachers' and Pupils' Attitudes." Research report to the U.S. Office of Education, University of Texas, 1966b.

ADULT-CHILD INTERACTION TEST

AUTHOR: Theron Alexander

AGE: 6 to 65

VARIABLE: Children's perception of adults

TYPE OF MEASURE: Projective test

SOURCE FROM WHICH THE MEASURE MAY BE OBTAINED: See Alexander (1955)

DESCRIPTION OF MEASURE: This is a picture projective test similar to the Thematic Apperception Test. It consists of eight cards, 5 × 8 inches, with black and white drawings that depict children in settings with limited structure, usually in the presence of an adult. The test must be given individually to young children. With older subjects, slides can be used for group presentation.

A "framework for analysis" is given under two broad headings: apperception and reasoning, and motivation and emotion. The apperception and reasoning heading is divided into perceptual approaches, reasoning processes, response to internal and external stimuli, and problem solving approaches. Motivation and emotion is divided into drive and emotion. There are also subcategories in addition to these main categories. An analysis chart is provided on which the examiner can record: the stimuli which are in the card and which are mentioned by the subject, and he can compare them with the stimuli which are added by the subject; the type of problem approach the subject uses; any emotional expressions or actions, positive or negative; and external forces, beneficent or hostile. Again, examples are given of the use of the analysis chart. Two sample protocols are given, with accompanying analysis. The eight stimulus cards are included with the monograph describing the measure. The user of this measure should have appropriate training in clinical psychology and measurement.

RELIABILITY AND VALIDITY: No evidence of reliability is presented. Two cases are presented showing relationships between performances on the ACI Test and, in one case, behavior in psychotherapy, and in the other case, the classroom behavior of the subject (a teacher).

BIBLIOGRAPHY:

ALEXANDER, T. "The Prediction of Teacher-Pupil Interaction with a Projective Test." *Journal of Clinical Psychology,* 1950, *6,* 273–276.

ALEXANDER, T. "Certain Characteristics of the Self as Related to Affection." *Child Development,* 1951, *22,* 285–290.

ALEXANDER, T. "The Adult-Child Interaction Test: A Projective Test for Use in Research." *Monograph of the Society for Research in Child Development,* 1955.

TILLER, P. O. "Father-Separation and Adolescence: A Study of Attitudes and Personality of Adolescent Sailor and Whaler Children." Oslo, Norway: Institute for Social Research, 1961.

ATTITUDES TOWARD AUTHORITY

AUTHOR: Orval G. Johnson

AGE: Upper elementary

VARIABLE: Attitudes toward authority

TYPE OF MEASURE: Individually administered projective test

SOURCE FROM WHICH THE MEASURE MAY BE OBTAINED: See Johnson (1954)

DESCRIPTION OF MEASURE: This is a picture-projective test made up of sixteen line drawings each depicting an adult person talking to a young boy. A statement by the adult is contained in a cartoon type balloon over the adult's head. No facial expression is shown on the figures because the mouth is omitted and no facial lines (such as furrows on the brow) are shown. The stimulus pictures are intended to incorporate three stimulus variables: the sex of the authority figure, the power of the authority figure, and threat, defined in Johnson's study as follows: "The authority figure interferes in some way with the satisfaction of the subject figure's need or needs. There may be open or implicit attack on the individual's self esteem. Threat often involves attempts to interfere with one's freedom and mobility and it frequently implies an attempt at domination of a subject figure by the authority figure" (Johnson, 1954). The stimulus cards are made up using all possible combinations of the three dichotomized variables—sex of authority figure, power of authority figure, and degree of threat in the depicted situation—eight combinations in all. Each combination is represented by two stimulus pictures, making sixteen stimulus pictures in the test in all. For example, one of the stimulus cards is intended to present a male authority figure with low power in a high threat situation. This card shows a grocer saying to a young boy, "I don't want you kids hanging around this store." The stimulus card presenting the pattern of female figure with high power and low threat shows a female librarian saying to a boy who is standing in front of the book stacks, "Do you want me to pick out a book for you to read?"

The responses are scored in terms of the degree of hostility or submissiveness indicated by the response. A five-point scale is used, with scores extending from 0 to 4. A score of 0 means extreme submissiveness. A score of 1 indicates mild submissiveness. A score of 2 means that the response cannot be classified as either submissive or hostile, or the response was unscorable for technical reasons primarily, or that both submissiveness and hostility occur in the same response, and they appear to be about equally strong although in different directions. A score of 3 indicates mild hostility, while 4 means extreme hostility (Johnson, 1954).

Hostility and submissiveness are defined as the presence of certain kinds of behavior which are described in the thesis.

RELIABILITY AND VALIDITY: Interscorer reliability for the sixteen-picture test given to forty boys was .90.

BIBLIOGRAPHY:

JOHNSON, O. G. "Attitudes toward Authority of Delinquent and Non-Delinquent Boys." Unpublished doctoral dissertation, University of Wisconsin, 1954.

BRONFENBRENNER PARENT BEHAVIOR QUESTIONNAIRE

AUTHOR: Urie Bronfenbrenner

AGE: Fourth through sixth grade

VARIABLE: Attitude scale (child's perception of how his parents treat him)

TYPE OF MEASURE: Questionnaire

SOURCE FROM WHICH THE MEASURE MAY BE OBTAINED: See Siegelman (1965)

DESCRIPTION OF MEASURE: The BPBQ requires that the child answer questions about how his parents act toward him. The questionnaire apparently has particular research value from the phenomenological standpoint since this view stresses that only the child's perception of his parent behavior toward him affects his personality development. The questionnaire requires the child to answer forty-five items concerning parental behavior from fixed alternative responses within two sets of statements. In the first set of twenty-five items, the child selects his choices from the following options: in every case, in most cases, sometimes, seldom, never. In the last twenty statements the response choices include: almost every day, about once a week, about once a month, only once or twice a year, never. The scoring ranges from 1 to 5 in every item, with a low score indicating the presence of certain parental behavior (e.g., 1 for almost every day) and a high score denoting its absence (e.g., 5 for never). Moreover, the identical items are used for both parents. Finally, the BPBQ attempts to measure fifteen variables with three items serving as a measure of each one. Accordingly, the range of scores for a single variable is 3 to 15.

Examples of three variables with their representative statements are given below (Siegelman, 1965):

Nurturance: *I can talk with her (him) about everything. Comforts me and helps me when I have troubles. Is there for me when I need her (him).*

Affective Reward: *Says nice things about me to other people. Is very affectionate with me. Praises me when I have done something good.*

Instrumental Companionship: *Teaches me things which I want to learn. Helps me with hobbies or handiwork. Helps me with schoolwork when I don't understand something.*

RELIABILITY AND VALIDITY: Girls (N = 131) and boys (N = 81) from grades four through six have comprised the sample for this test. These children were primarily from lower socioeconomic areas of New York City, and were of the following ethnic groups: 65 per cent Puerto Pican, 25 per cent Negro, and 10 per cent Italian. Extremes in intelligence from both the brightest and slowest children in grades five and six were included in the sample.

On this sample, Kuder-Richardson 20 reliability coefficients ranged from .26 to .83 for male fathers, .23 to .70 for male mothers, .55 to .88 for female fathers, and .32 to .75 for female mothers. The mean reliabilities for all BPB scales were .58 for male fathers, .45 for male mothers, .68 for female fathers, and .51 for female mothers. Siegelman attributes the rather low reliabilities to the very abbreviated nature of the scales since only three items comprise each variable. He has suggested a method of merging scales to increase the reliability of measurement on the BPB. The details of the procedure as well as the statistical justification have been presented in full. In any case, factor score reliabilities based on the merger of scores from several scales ranged from .70 to .91 and internal consistency reliabilities are generally higher than the reliabilities of the individual scales. Since twelve to eighteen items are used to calculate the factor score reliability as opposed to the three items included within any one variable, the improvement in reliability may be attributed to the increased length of the new scale.

BIBLIOGRAPHY:

SIEGELMAN, M. "Evaluation of Bronfenbrenner's Questionnaire for Children Concerning Parental Behavior." *Child Development*, 1965, *36*, 163–174.

CHILDREN'S REPORTS OF PARENTAL BEHAVIOR INVENTORY (CRPBI)

AUTHOR: Earl S. Schaefer

AGE: 12 to 18 years old

VARIABLE: Perception of parental behavior

TYPE OF MEASURE: Questionnaire inventory

SOURCE FROM WHICH MEASURE MAY BE OBTAINED: Dr. Earl S. Schaefer, National Institute of Mental Health, 5454 Wisconsin Ave., Chevy Chase, Md. 20015

DESCRIPTION OF MEASURE: The motivation for the CRPBI by Schaefer comes from the accumulating evidence that children's reports of parental behavior were valid. The inventory itself (earlier version) consists of twenty-six self-administering scales, each including ten items designed to sample a child's perceptions of a particular concept of parental behavior. Each of the ten items within the scale describes relevant, specific, observable parental behavior. The child is instructed to indicate whether the item was "like" or "not like" his parents. Separate but identical forms are provided for each parent. Each of the concepts, in turn, related to molar dimensions of parental behavior which were variants of two dimensions: love versus hostility and autonomy versus control.

Samples of the concepts and illustrative items within each concept are given below (Schaefer, 1965):

Extreme autonomy	*Allows me to go out as often as I please.*
	Lets me go any place I please without asking.
Lax discipline	*Lets me get away without doing work she's (he's) told me to do.*
	Excuses my bad conduct.
Moderate autonomy	*Allows me to pick my own friends.*
	Gives me the choice of what to do whenever possible.
Encouraging sociability	*Helps me give parties for my friends.*
	Enjoys it when I bring friends to my home.
Positive evaluation	*Often praises me.*
	Often speaks of the good things I do.
Sharing	*Enjoys talking things over with me.*
	Enjoys working with me in the house or yard.
Expression of affection	*Almost always speaks to me with a warm and friendly voice.*
	Smiles at me very often.

A later version of the CRPBI consists of eighteen scales with 192 items. This version was developed from an item and factor analysis of the twenty-six-scale, 260-item version. The instructions for scoring this version are: Assign a value of 3 to L (like the parent), 2 to SL (somewhat like the parent) and 1 to NL (not like the parent). The clarity and simplicity of the directions and scoring system lend themselves to appropriate use with a younger age group than Schaefer used.

RELIABILITY AND VALIDITY: The scales were administered to 165 (eighty-five boys, eighty girls) white seventh-grade children in a suburban parochial school, and to eighty-one institutionalized delinquent boys from unbroken homes. The delinquent sample represented a somewhat lower socioeconomic group. All normal children were tested in a single group; the delinquents were tested in groups of approximately thirty each.

Median internal-consistency reliabilities (Kuder-Richardson Formula 20) of groups of scales that were chosen to sample the molar dimensions were: love, .84; hostility, .78; autonomy, .69; and control, .66. Schaefer felt that the effort to develop homogeneous measures for specific components of parental behavior succeeded fairly well. The reliabilities are high enough for research on differences between groups. All statistical data were derived from the earlier version of the scale.

The validity of the scales was based primarily on their discriminative power between the criterion groups of normal versus delinquent children. As illustration of this discriminative power, three general findings may be cited: (1) Among the fifty-two scales (twenty-six for each parental form), the Mann-Whitney Test found twenty-six to be significant beyond the .05 level and fourteen significant beyond the .01 level. (2) Within the delinquent group, correlations between the two parental forms of the scale were lower for twenty-five of the twenty-six scales. (3) An item analysis for individual items revealed even clearer differences between the two groups than was the case for total scores on the scales, with differences between the groups beyond the .001 level (Schaefer, 1965).

BIBLIOGRAPHY:

SCHAEFER, E. S. "Children's Reports of Parental Behavior: An Inventory." *Child Development*, 1956, *36*, 413–424.

EMMERICH'S CHILD NURTURANCE-CONTROL SCALE

AUTHOR: Walter Emmerich

AGE: Children between the ages of three years, seven months, and five years, one month

VARIABLE: Child's identification with the parent

TYPE OF MEASURE: Rating scale of structured interview behavior

SOURCE FROM WHICH THE MEASURE MAY BE OBTAINED: See Emmerich (1959)

DESCRIPTION OF MEASURE: The Nurturance-Control Scale is a structured doll-play interview that is conducted individually with children of preschool age who do not have siblings. The objects used are dolls representing a mother, a father, a baby, and the child himself. The purpose of the scale is to obtain an identification index. In general, a three-step procedure is followed in obtaining this index, consisting of a two-part interview and a derived identification index. The first part of the interview assesses the child's expectations of parental attitudes with eight standard situations. For example, the examiner says:

The mother and the girl are in the store and the girl won't leave. She sees a toy she wants. What does the mother do?

In the second part of the structured interview, the same situations are represented, only with the child and baby dolls as the essential character. The scores for the responses range from +3 for strong nurturance (facilitation) to −3.0 for strong control (interference). A zero score applies either to two separate but diametrically opposed responses for the same situation or to a remark by the child that the doll does nothing. For example, any of the responses below to the above toy episode in the parent-child situations would be scored as +3.0 or strong nurturance (Emmerich, 1959):

Buys several toys.
Reads for a long time.
Prepares special food.
Plays with child.

In the last step, two indices of identification are developed. One refers to the absolute discrepancy in scale values between six child-baby items and six part-child items. Identification increases as the score approaches 0. A second index is based simply on the direction of the discrepancy between the above two sets of scores on the nurturance-control dimension. A positive value here indicates that the child is more nurturant in the same situation than he perceives the parent to be; a negative value suggests that he is more interfering than he expects the parent to be. No attempt is made to determine these values as quantitative absolute.

Detailed information is provided on the methods used in obtaining a child's cooperation, the interview setting and the materials, the examiner's behavior, the order of presentation of items and doll figures, and a complete scoring guide for responses on the Nurturance-Control Scales and the derivation of identification indices. The definitions of nurturance and control and the methodological assumptions of the instruments and scores are described explicitly. The administration of each item requires less than a minute.

RELIABILITY AND VALIDITY: The scale has been used with thirty-one preschool children between the ages of 3 years, 7 months, and 5 years, 1 months. They were predominantly white children of intact middle-class families. The range of scores, the mean, and the standard deviation on the scale for this small sample are presented. The correlation of inter-rater scorings on both parent-child and baby-child items was .97. Test-retest correlations for the six scorable items on the responses of twenty-six children were .69 for mother-child items, .50 for the father-child items, and .73 for the child-baby items.

The findings from the identification indices are in line with research data showing boys to be more aware of sex-appropriate roles than girls. As expected, identification with the same-sex parent occurred more frequently.

BIBLIOGRAPHY:

EMMERICH, W. "Parent Identification in Young Children." *Genetic Psychology Monographs,* 1959, *60,* 257–308.

IMITATION SCHEDULE

AUTHOR: Willard W. Hartup

AGE: 3 to 8

VARIABLE: Identification with like-sex parent

TYPE OF MEASURE: Structured doll-play interview

SOURCE FROM WHICH THE MEASURE MAY BE OBTAINED: Willard W. Hartup, University of Minnesota, Child Development, Minneapolis, Minn. 55455

DESCRIPTION OF MEASURE: The Imitation Schedule is composed of eighteen items, fifteen of which are designed to measure the like-sex parent identification, and three of which are open-ended situations interspersed for relief purposes. Five of the fifteen situations involve alternative routes to a goal as in the following examples:

The people are in the front yard. They want to go and pick flowers in the back yard. Mama goes this way [left]. Daddy goes this way [right]. Which way does the little ———— go, the way daddy goes or the way mama goes [with the examiner indicating direction as he questions the subject]?

Five of the situations involve value judgments, as indicated by the following item:

Now the people are in this yard to pick some flowers. Daddy says, "This is the prettiest flower." Mama says, "This is the prettiest flower." Which flower does the little ———— say is the prettiest, the one mama said was the prettiest or the one daddy said was prettiest?

Five of the situations involve conflicting perceptual judgments, as indicated by the following item:

Here are two pies. Daddy says, "This pie is the biggest." Mama says, "This pie is the biggest." Which pie does the little ———— say is the biggest, the one mama says is the biggest or the one daddy says is the biggest?

The props used in all the items are identical-appearing objects. The situations are presented to the subjects in cyclical order with the alternate route situation presented first, then the "value" situation. The order of presentation is counterbalanced over the entire interview. In the "alternate route" situation involving left and right routes to a goal, the position of the parent dolls is counterbalanced. The score on the measure is the number of times the subject used the child-doll to imitate the like-sex parent doll.

RELIABILITY AND VALIDITY: The corrected odd-even reliability for sixty-three children, ages 3½ to 5½, was .86 (Hartup, 1962). Findings from the same study suggested that femininity, as measured by the IT scale, was related to mother-imitating girls, but for boys, masculinity did not appear to be related to the tendency to imitate the father rather than the mother. Each sex preferred to imitate the parent doll of the same sex. Girls' tendencies to imitate the mother doll in the interview were positively related to the presence of authoritarian, suppressive, punitive attitudes manifested by the mother toward her child and toward other family members.

BIBLIOGRAPHY:

HARTUP, W. W. "Some Correlations of Parental Imitation in Young Children." *Child Development*, 1962, *33*, 85–96.

INDEX OF OVERCRITICAL PERCEPTION BY THE CHILD

AUTHORS: Bernard Farber and William C. Jenné

AGE: Normal children ages 11 to 16 inclusive

VARIABLE: Communication

TYPE OF MEASURE: Questionnaire

SOURCE FROM WHICH THE MEASURE MAY BE OBTAINED: Farber and Jenné (1963)

DESCRIPTION OF MEASURE: The scale is based on the manner in which the child responds to fifty activities after the question:

If your mother (father) could change the following things about you, which of them do you think she (he) would like you to do more often, less—and which do you think she (he) would like you to do as you do now?

In responding, the child checks: "much less, a little less, as I do now, a little more, much more, or does not apply." Parents are also asked to rate their satisfaction with the child's behavior for the same items with the same fixed-alternative responses. With the parents, appropriate changes have been made in the wording for the directions ("If you could change the following activities . . . ," etc.). Sample activity items follow (Farber and Jenné, 1963).

Think about school work.
Help around the house.
Listen to radio and TV programs.

After both sets of data are available, the Index of Overcritical Perception by the Child can be calculated. Essentially, this index may be most easily derived as a two-part operation. First, one should obtain the difference between the number of items on which the child perceives a parent as dissatisfied with his behavior and the number of times the parent actually indicates dissatisfaction. The index then constitutes the ratio between this difference to the total number of items on the activities list. Theoretically, the numerical value of the ratio can range between +1.00 to −1.00, with a positive score indicative of a child's tending to be overcritical; that is, the child perceives the parent as dissatisfied more often than is, in fact, the case.

RELIABILITY AND VALIDITY: None reported.

BIBLIOGRAPHY:

FARBER, B., and JENNÉ, W. C. "Family Organization and Parent-Child Communications." *Monographs of the Society for Research in Child Development,* 1963, *28* (Whole Monograph, No. 7).

LOUIS-HAWKES SCALE

AUTHORS: D. B. Louis and G. R. Hawkes

AGE: Fifth graders

VARIABLE: Child's perception of family control

TYPE OF MEASURE: Questionnaire

SOURCE FROM WHICH THE MEASURE MAY BE OBTAINED: Glen R. Hawkes, Virginia Commonwealth University, 901 West Franklin Street, Richmond, Va. 23220

DESCRIPTION OF MEASURE: There are two forms of this measure, although only one was available at the time of this writing. Twelve judges sorted the items into one of three categories: items relating to the child's view of control of his behavior (his report of limitations imposed upon him or conversely his degree of freedom of behavior within the family setting); items pertaining to his reaction to what he reports; and items that do not fit either of these two categories. Two-thirds agreement of the judges on the placement of an item was required for that item to be considered as part of the scale. Subscores were derived from the items in the first two categories. The instructions are simple and straightforward. Samples of items follow:

Are you allowed to play with other children?   (a) *always,* (b) *often,* (c) *sometimes,*
   (d) *seldom,* (e) *never.*
Do your parents help you when you get "in wrong" with your friends?   (a) *always,*
   (b) *often,* (c) *sometimes,* (d) *seldom,* (e) *never.*
How much do you think you should have to say about what your family plans to do?
   (a) *a great deal,* (b) *much,* (c) *some,* (d) *a little,* (e) *none.*
How much time does your mother spend with you?   (a) *a great deal,* (b) *much,*
   (c) *some,* (d) *a little,* (e) *none.*
Does coaxing help you to get your father to change his mind?   (a) *always,* (b)
   often, (c) *sometimes,* (d) *seldom,* (e) *never.*
Do you think you have too many jobs?   (a) *yes,* (b) *usually,* (c) *no.*
Do you work for all your spending money?   (a) *yes,* (b) *usually,* (c) *no.*

Two weighted scoring systems are provided. In the first system, described as the "Judges' Weights," thirteen judges ranked the responses to each item along a continuum from most to least conducive of healthful control of children's behavior. Weights from 1 to 5 were assigned the responses, higher weights indicating healthful control. Items were excluded if agreement among judges was low. Scoring according to the "Children's Weights" involved giving the scale to a sample (N = 730) of children and using the percentages (rounded to a single whole digit) of children who checked each response as the weight for that response. These scores are considered measures of the children's "typicality" of perception of control.

RELIABILITY AND VALIDITY: When forty-nine children were retested after one week, reliabilities for the subscores using children's weights were .69 and .73 and, for the scores based on judges' weights, were .61 and .74. Total score reliabilities were .85 for each form of the scale. Significant correlations in the expected direction were found between the family relationship score from the Rogers Test of Personality Adjustment and total score on both forms of this scale.

BIBLIOGRAPHY:

HAWKES, G. R., BURCHINAL, L. G., and GARDNER, B. "Measurement of Preadolescents' Views of Family Control of Behavior." *Child Development,* 1957, *28,* 387–392.

MY TEACHER SCALE

AUTHOR: Carroll H. Leeds

AGE: Fourth, fifth, and sixth grades

VARIABLE: Attitude scale

TYPE OF MEASURE: Questionnaire

SOURCE FROM WHICH THE MEASURE MAY BE OBTAINED: Leeds (1950)

DESCRIPTION OF MEASURE: The My Teacher Scale consists of a fifty-item questionnaire in which the child responds to each question by circling yes, no, or a question mark. The My Teacher Scale, which has also been known as the Pupil's Rating Scale, is scored +1 for "yes," −1 for "no." Examples of the items from the My Teacher Scale follow:

Do you like school?
Are there usually flowers and plants in your room?
Does the teacher, whose name is written above, praise you for doing good work?
Does this teacher scold the pupils a lot?
Is this teacher usually cross?

Apparently, the results of the questionnaire can be utilized in several ways: to distinguish teaching methods and traits between good and poor teachers as perceived by all children; to enable classroom teachers to know how their classroom behavior registers in the minds of their pupils; and to help teachers gain knowledge of the emotional impact of specific classroom practices on children.

RELIABILITY AND VALIDITY: The scale has been administered to several hundred pupils in grades four through six (Leeds, 1954). On the basis of these samples, reliability was determined by two principal procedures. First, reliability of odd-even items for 200 randomly selected students was .94. A second procedure involved average ratings for two separate groups of ten children each from 100 teachers. The correlation between these sets of averages was .93 based on the Spearman-Brown correction (Cook, 1947).

Validity was determined by the manner in which the items differentiated at statistically significant levels between very poor and extremely capable teachers (Leeds, 1954) as judged by the Principals' Rating Scale and a Teacher Effectiveness Scale. The fact that both of these scales had respectable split-half reliabilities (respectively .87 and .92) strengthened their case as validating criteria (Cook and Leeds, 1947).

BIBLIOGRAPHY:

COOK, W. W. "Measuring the Teaching Personality." *Educational and Psychological Measurement*, 1947, *7*, 399–410.

LEEDS, C. H. "A Scale for Measuring Teacher-Pupil Attitudes and Teacher-Pupil Rapport." *Psychological Monographs, General and Applied*, 1950, *44*, No. 6 (Whole No. 312). Washington: American Psychological Association.

LEEDS, C. H. "Teacher Behavior Liked *and* Disliked by Pupils." *Education*, 1954, *75*, 29–37.

PALS AND PEN PALS TEST

AUTHOR: Walter C. Williams

AGE: The measure is suitable for self-administration by any child with third-grade reading level

VARIABLE: Child's perception along the dimensions of authority and love

TYPE OF MEASURE: Projective test and questionnaire

SOURCE FROM WHICH THE MEASURE MAY BE OBTAINED: Walter C. Williams, 19945 24th N. W. Seattle, Washington 98177

DESCRIPTION OF MEASURE: Two separate measuring instruments are combined on one scoring sheet. Both tests are designed to measure how children see their parents as sources of authority and love.

The child's Pals test consists of thirty-two items each of which is scored for both authority and love. The child responds simply by checking one of two columns, "Like my father" or "Not like father." The "Father" and "Mother" forms are on opposite sides of the same sheet. Examples of the items are as follows:

Asks other people what to do about things (high love, low authority).
Teaches me how to play games (high authority, high love).
Always says go ask mother—she is the boss (low authority, low love).

The Pen Pals test consists of sixteen situations involving a child and one parent figure. There are two separate forms of the test booklet, one for boys and one for girls. In all of the pictured situations (simple line drawings) the child is saying something to the parent figure, and below the picture are four optional responses that the child is to ascribe to the parent figure. For example, in one situation the boy says to the mother, "Mommy, can I sit on your lap?" The options that the child may choose as the mother's typical response are as follows:

I'm so tired and you are so big now.
Why baby—you know Mommy would just love it!
Of course, dear. Climb up and we will read together.
At your age? You are too big for that. Find your own chair.

The faces of the human figures are blank, so that the child's response to the items cannot be influenced by facial expressions.

The scoring of both tests is straightforward, and the recording and summing of scores is simplified by a special format. The scoring sheet also includes a grid for plotting the summarized scores. The four quadrants of the grid correspond to four personality pattern types as follows: High authority, low love parents who are described as "authoritarian to exploitative." High authority, high love parents who are described as "democratic to overprotective." Low authority, high love parents who are described as "permissive to overindulgent." Low authority, low love parents described as "ignoring to self-centered." When the scores cancel to nearly zero on both axes, the parents are described as "psychologically unknown."

RELIABILITY AND VALIDITY: Williams (1961) studied one hundred acting-out children—fifty boys and fifty girls from child guidance centers, psychiatric centers, and state institutions—and compared their scores on the child's Pals, the Pen Pals, and the combination of the two measures with the scores of 100 matched normal children. When the parental patterns as indicated by the tests were classified as socially desirable versus socially undesirable for each of the children in the study, impressive differences were found between the normal and acting-out boys and between the normal and acting-out girls on the Pals, the Pen Pals, and the combination of both.

BIBLIOGRAPHY:

WILLIAMS, W. C. "The PALS Tests: A Technique for Children to Evaluate Both Parents." *Journal of Consulting Psychology*, 1958, 22(6), 487–495.

WILLIAMS, W. C. "Evaluation of Their Own Fathers and Mothers by Acting-out Children, Using the Parental Authority-Love Statements." Prepared for Presentation at a conference on delinquency, held March 3, 1961, Jones Hall Auditorium, UPS, Tacoma.

PARENTAL PUNITIVENESS SCALE

AUTHORS: Ralph Epstein and S. S. Komorita

AGE: School children between 7 and 15 years of age

VARIABLE: Children's perception of parental child-rearing practices

TYPE OF MEASURE: Rating scale

SOURCE FROM WHICH THE MEASURE MAY BE OBTAINED: See Epstein and Komorita (1965a)

DESCRIPTION OF MEASURE: The PPS represents an attempt to measure children's perceptions of parental discipline toward aggression. The scale consists of forty-five items that assess parental punitiveness toward physical, verbal, and indirect aggression in five major situations: aggression toward parents, teachers, siblings, peers, and inanimate objects. In each item, the child selects his response to a common incident requiring parental discipline from four fixed alternatives. In each case, the subject responds in terms of his perceptions for each paternal reaction, with his thoughts on paternal disciplinary practices first. Each response is weighted from 1 to 4 for its relative severity and the scale is scored separately for each parent. The same fixed alternatives available for responses in each case are weighted as follows: (1) have a long talk with me, (2) take away television, (3) send me to bed without supper, and (4) whip me.

The fixed-alternative responses were randomly ordered for each item. A sample item follows (Epstein and Komorita, 1965a):

If I throw a rock at someone's car, my father (mother) would (a) send me to bed without supper, (b) take away my television, (c) whip me, (d) have a long talk with me.

RELIABILITY AND VALIDITY: The administration of the test to 120 children between 7 and 13 years of age from middle- to upper-middle class families yielded internal consistency reliability coefficients of .93 and .92 respectively for father and mother scales based on the Kuder-Richardson Formula 20. Construct validation of the PPS was attempted by correlating it with ethnocentrism, defined in terms of generalized social distance toward outgroups and measured by Bogardus social distance scales. The relationship between pooled parental punitiveness and ethnocentrism was curvilinear so that the correlation ratio, eta, was used. Based on these data this correlation coefficient was .33 (Epstein and Komorita, 1965a).

BIBLIOGRAPHY:

EPSTEIN, R., and KOMORITA, S. S. "The Development of a Scale of Parental Punitiveness towards Aggression." *Child Development,* 1965a, *36,* 129–242.

EPSTEIN, R., and KOMORITA, S. S. "Parental Discipline, Stimulus Characteristics of Outgroups, and Social Distance in Children." *Journal of Personality and Social Psychology,* 1965b, *2,* 416–420.

EPSTEIN, R., and KOMORITA, S. S. "Childhood Prejudice as a Function of Parental Ethnocentrism, Punitiveness and Out-group Characteristics." *Journal of Personality and Social Psychology,* 1966, *3,* 259–264.

PERCEPTION OF PARENTS

AUTHORS: Jerome Kagan and Judith Lemkin

AGE: 3 years 9 months to 8 years 6 months

VARIABLE: Attitude

TYPE OF MEASURE: Structured interview

SOURCE FROM WHICH THE MEASURE MAY BE OBTAINED: Photostats of the pictures involved in the indirect picture method for the perception of parents are available upon request. The remaining material is described in the article outlining the complete procedure (Kagan and Lemkin, 1960).

DESCRIPTION OF MEASURE: The individual interview devised to elicit children's attitudes or perceptions or both toward parents uses three methods to measure children's perception of parents with respect to nurturance, punitiveness, source of fear, and competence. The procedures involved in each method are:
    Indirect questions: The children are shown line drawings of a mother, father, and child and asked questions pertaining to parental nurturance, competence, punitiveness, and source of fear. Sample questions are: "Who gives the child the most presents?" "Who is the child more scared of?"
    Picture method: The children are shown ten different pictures illustrating a child in situations usually involving a parent, but without showing the parent. The child is asked to designate which parent is missing.
    Direct questions: The child is asked the some thirteen questions as in the indirect method but the questions are phrased in terms of the child and his own parents: for example, "Who gives you the most presents, your mother or your father?" "Who are you more scared of, your mother or your father?"

RELIABILITY AND VALIDITY: The authors tested sixty-seven children, rather closely divided by sex classification, with an age range from 3 years 9 months to 8 years 6 months and a median age of 5 years 6 months. No reliability statistics are presented. Evidence for construct validity of the scale appears in that the findings for all three methods verify previous research results that young children see mothers as more nurturant, less punitive, less fear-arousing, and less competent than fathers. Also, in line with prior research and predictions, girls view the father with more ambivalence than do boys.

BIBLIOGRAPHY:

KAGAN, J., and LEMKIN, J. "The Child's Differential Perception of Parental Attributes." *Journal of Abnormal and Social Psychology,* 1960, *61,* 440–447.

ROLE TAKING QUESTIONNAIRE

AUTHOR: Eleanor E. Maccoby

AGE: Sixth graders

VARIABLE: Parental identification

TYPE OF MEASURE: Questionnaire

SOURCE FROM WHICH THE MEASURE MAY BE OBTAINED: The seven scales and a table presenting their intercorrelations have been deposited with the American Documentation Institute. Order Document No. 6869 from ADI Auxiliary Publications Project, Photoduplication Service, Library of Congress, Washington, D.C. 20540, remitting in advance $1.75 for microfilm or $2.50 for photocopies. Make checks payable to Chief, Photoduplication Service, Library of Congress.

DESCRIPTION OF MEASURE: The RTQ measures the extent to which the child has learned elements of adult role behavior that characterize his parents. The scale consists of thirty-nine items distributed among seven subscales as follows: rule enforcement, acceptance of rule enforcement, give nurturance, accept material help, accept comfort, beg for return of nurturance, and adult-child role choice. The scale is administered on a group basis and the child checks his own choices after silently reading the items. Time limits are difficult to ascertain but none have been prescribed. Most items are two- and three-choice items. The example below from the Rule Enforcement Scale (Maccoby, 1961) not only illustrates this option but also the direction of the scoring.

You are on your way to school. A boy in your class is walking in front of you. He drops a bottle on the sidewalk, and it breaks into many pieces. The boy walks on. What would you do? Say nothing; it's his business, not mine—0; tell the boy to pick up the pieces—1.

In general, the higher score is in the direction of the variable being tested. Although not explicitly stated, the total score for the scale is the sum of the individual item scores. Scoring is facilitated by a key for the various responses, though the subscales are not clearly designated. Nevertheless, close perusal of the items would reveal little difficulty in assigning them to the proper subscale.

RELIABILITY AND VALIDITY: No data on the reliability of the scale appear to be available. Since the subtests were formed on the basis of adequate correlation of each item with the total score on the scale, the scale evidently has internal consistency.

A number of indices are available as validating support for the scale. The intercorrelations among the subscales are very low, suggesting that the subscales do measure somewhat different dimensions of role-taking. For example, the intercorrelations among the girls (N = 264) range between —.11 to .25 (ADI Document 6869). Also, the verification of predictions and previously confirmed hypotheses apparently give the scale some construct validity: (1) It was hypothesized that the degree to which children would enforce rules among their peers violating them would be positively related to parental restrictiveness or punitiveness but negatively related to parental permissiveness, as reported by mothers in earlier interviews. All relationship held for boys but enforcement among girls was related only to maternal punitiveness. (2) Piaget's finding that moral development among girls was not as dependent on developing a reciprocal relationship with peers as it was with boys was verified. (3) Finally, a number of low but statistically significant correlations between scores of adult role-taking functions on this scale and other personality measures indicate that boys and girls who select the role enforcing alternative tend to be well socialized in other respects (Maccoby, 1961).

A significant factor to consider in the use of this scale is that all findings related to it are based on self-report verbal behavior with all of its limitations.

BIBLIOGRAPHY:

MACCOBY, E. E. "The Taking of Adult Roles in Middle Childhood." *Journal of Abnormal and Social Psychology,* 1961, *63,* 403–503.

SEARS' OBSERVER RATING SCALE

AUTHORS: Robert R. Sears, Lucy Rau, and Richard Alpert

AGE: Nursery school children

VARIABLE: Behavioral correlates and antecedents of identification among children

TYPE OF MEASURE: Rating scale

SOURCE FROM WHICH THE MEASURE MAY BE OBTAINED: See Sears, Rau, and Alpert (1965)

DESCRIPTION OF MEASURE: The observer ratings, which are supplementary measures to Sears' Behavioral Unit Observations, should be completed by raters who know the children well. The ratings are based on six five-point scales measuring masculinity-femininity, aggression, physical-contact seeking, attention getting, physical activity, and amount of social interaction. A sample scale for sex typing follows (Sears, et al., 1963):

Masculinity ranges from highly masculine (a "buck") through average, then effeminate, to "sissy." Femininity ranges from "coquette" or "clinging vine" through average, then somewhat boyish, to "tomboy."

RELIABILITY AND VALIDITY: Since there were six subscales within the test, the interobserver reliability coefficients were the averages of the six rs between each observer and each other one, using a z transformation. The mean inter-rater reliability coefficients for five scales ranged between .53 (physical-contact seeking) to .80 (social interaction level). In contrast, the mean intercorrelation for attention getting was .39. On the basis of these data, the authors regarded the reliability coefficients for these scales as quite satisfactory.

Direct measures of concurrent or predictive validity were not evident. The researcher may wish to make some assumptions about content validity since the variables measured were formulated by agreement of a group of highly trained professional workers who did the ratings. Validity of the measures exemplified by this approach depends on the degree to which they measure trait consistency. In the authors' estimation, the scales assess this trait consistency to some extent in that this measurement requires a sampling of constant stimulus conditions from one child to another.

BIBLIOGRAPHY:

SEARS, R. R., RAU, L., and ALPERT, R. *Identification and Child Rearing.* Stanford, California: Stanford University Press, 1963.

SECHREST'S STRUCTURED INTERVIEW SCHEDULE WITH CHILDREN

AUTHOR: Lee B. Sechrest

AGE: Kindergarten through third grade

VARIABLE: Attitudes toward classroom teacher

TYPE OF MEASURE: Structured interview

SOURCE FROM WHICH THE MEASURE MAY BE OBTAINED: See Sechrest (1962)

DESCRIPTION OF MEASURE: This interview, a relatively structured one, attempts to measure the school attitudes of children. The content of the interview consists of twenty questions followed in a two-phase sequence. In the first part, the child is asked ten open-end questions referring to school situations and requiring rather extensive replies. Two examples follow:

When you begin a new lesson at school, what kind of things does your teacher do to get you started?
What does your teacher do that makes it fun to learn new things?

The second phase consists of ten questions relating to specific techniques teachers use for task motivations. These are so worded that the child can reply simply by answering Yes or No. Three illustrative items follow:

Give stars for good work.
Yell at children for misbehaving.
Write nice things on children's papers.

Responses of the children are recorded verbatim for content analysis. These categories, however, apply only to the open-end questions. Examples of the categories, as applied to the first open-end question, are given below:

When you begin a new lesson at school, what kind of things does your teacher do to get you started? *Responses indicating a high pupil-teacher interaction: verbal assistance, explanation; concrete demonstration; general assistance, unexplained. Response indicating low pupil-teacher interaction: simple direction, no mention of assistance.*

RELIABILITY AND VALIDITY: In one study (Sechrest, 1962), teachers were asked to refer representative children in terms of variation in ability and behavioral adjustment. A similar number of boys and girls were interviewed, equally subdivided in number at each grade level. In terms of the content categories, the author gives a complete breakdown on the number of responses to the ten questions by thirty-two children at each of the four grade levels, kindergarten through third. Categorizing responses to three questions, two judges agreed 94 per cent of the time.

BIBLIOGRAPHY:

SECHREST, L. B. "The Motivation in School of Young Children: Some Interview Data." *Journal of Experimental Education,* 1962, *30,* 327–335.

SEX-ROLE ATTITUDE TEST (Child Form)

AUTHOR: G. H. McKay

AGE: 5 and over

VARIABLE: Children's perceptions of parents' attitudes

TYPE OF MEASURE: Structured interview questionnaire

SOURCE FROM WHICH THE MEASURE MAY BE OBTAINED: See McKay (1964)

DESCRIPTION OF MEASURE: The purpose of the SRAT is to tap the child's perception of parental attitudes toward children's sex roles, his judgment of the sex-role choices, and permissiveness of one of his sex peers. The material for the test was mounted in books, one set for boys and another for girls. The stimuli for the measure include first of all a series of nine paired choices taken from the "IT Scale for Children," with one of the pair being a drawing of a toy gun (the masculine choice) and one a drawing of a doll (feminine choice). Other paired drawings are toy tools for building (masculine) and toy things for cooking (feminine); pants and shirt, and a dress; men's shoes to play grown up in, women's shoes to play grown up in. The child is also introduced to three pictures of a father figure and three of a mother figure, with facial expressions to represent three feeling states which are termed "happy," "in between," and "angry." The child is given a line drawing of a child of the same sex and is told, "It's a girl (boy) just like you. She (he) is about your age." During the administration of the test, the subject holds in his or her hand the drawing of the child figure for whom the child is ostensibly responding.

The subject is asked a series of ten questions as follows:

Which would you like to play with the most?
Would you like to play with this tool? (pointing to the rejected option)
Which would your Daddy like you to play with the most?
Which would your Mommy like you to play with the most?
Show me how your Daddy would feel if you wanted to play with both the ——— and the ———.
Show me how your Mommy would feel if you wanted to play with both the ——— and the ———.
Show me how your Daddy would feel if you wanted to play with the ———.
Show me how your Mommy would feel if you wanted to play with the ———.
Show me how your Daddy would feel if you wanted to play with the ———.
Show me how your Mommy would feel if you wanted to play with the ———.

Scoring of the measure is described in detail by McKay (1964), and will not be dealt with here. The scoring system varies among items, but is objective and clearly stated in the McKay reference.

The measure is designed to tap ten variables as follows: the child's preferences; the child's permissiveness in accepting both the same-sex and the cross-sex choices; the child's perception of father's preference of object or activity for the child; the child's perception of mother's preference of object or activity for the child; the child's perception of father's attitude toward permissiveness; the child's perception of mother's attitude toward permissiveness; the child's perception of father's attitude toward a same-sex choice; the child's perception of mother's attitude toward a same-sex choice; the child's perception of father's attitude toward a cross-sex choice; and the child's perception of mother's attitude toward a cross-sex choice.

RELIABILITY AND VALIDITY: McKay (1964) has concluded that some of the items have insufficient variability, that reliability of the measure must be established, and that concordance of children's perceptions with actual parental practices needs to be determined.

BIBLIOGRAPHY:

MC KAY, G. H. "Some Dimensions of Sex-Typing in Kindergarten Children: an Exploratory Study." Unpublished doctoral thesis, Harvard University, 1964.

SEXUAL DIFFERENTIATION SCALE FOR THE D-A-P TEST

AUTHORS: Mary R. Haworth and Cheryl J. Normington

AGE: Children between the ages of 7 and 12

VARIABLE: Psychosexual maturity or sexual identification or both

TYPE OF MEASURE: Semistructured projective technique

SOURCE FROM WHICH THE MEASURE MAY BE OBTAINED: See Haworth and Normington (1961)

DESCRIPTION OF MEASURE: The Sexual Differentiation Scale attempts to measure psychosexual maturity in a child by his ability to differentiate between the sexes in his drawings. The measure of his sexual differentiation occurs through three dimensions: the number of points scored, the levels of differentiation, and the item types.

Levels of differentiation: The figure drawings of the children on the D-A-P are differentiated in terms of increasing psychosexual maturity as (1) no apparent sex differentiation between two figures, (2) minimal differentiation, (3) clear differentiation for one figure, and (4) clear differentiation for both figures.

Types of items: Items are classified into four groups as A, B, C, and D, with only the last three groups of items involved in classification of the levels. The details of the items included within each level are described in full. A Type A item, for example, includes belts, buttons, collars, cuffs, eyelashes, stripes, and solid fill-in. In general, however, a specific level includes certain types of items and omits others. For illustration, a Level I drawing (no apparent sex differentiation) has one B item in one or both figures and disregards all other type items.

Points of items: Since the scale requires each subject to draw a pair of drawings, one for each sex, the points are given according to the differentiation between the two figures. The condition under which the points are given and the items for which credit is allowed are described in detail. The specific items are accredited in terms of the differentiation between the two figures.

Complete directions for scoring the scale are provided. One possible advantage of the scale is that it can be administered on a group basis.

RELIABILITY AND VALIDITY: Reliability of the scale was determined by agreement between the same pair of judges on two separate sets of 100 drawings. Agreements were 90 and 88 per cent. The primary validation of the scale rests on construct validity. The following sources of evidence appear relevant: (1) As expected, sex differentiation improved as a function of age. (2) Sexual differentiation was not related to level of intelligence. It was more closely related to developmental age changes. (3) Consistent with previous findings in literature, girls differentiated between the sexes significantly better than the boys at practically all age levels (differentiation was equal at age 11).

BIBLIOGRAPHY:

HAWORTH, M. R., and NORMINGTON, C. J. "A Sexual Differentiation Scale for the D-A-P Test (for Use with Children)." *Journal of Projective Techniques,* 1961, *25,* 441–448.

STRUCTURED DOLL-PLAY TEST

AUTHORS: Robert R. Sears, Lucy Rau, and Richard Alpert

AGE: Nursery school children

VARIABLE: Behavioral correlates and antecedents of identification among children

TYPE OF MEASURE: Rating scale

SOURCE FROM WHICH THE MEASURE MAY BE OBTAINED: See Sears, Rau, and Alpert (1965)

DESCRIPTION OF MEASURE: The Structured Doll-Play test consists of a single session in which the experimenter uses the doll house to present six incomplete stories that the subject is required to complete. In each case, the story involves a child doll of the same sex as the subject committing a deviant act, something disapproved of in our culture. The stories involve such actions as careless destruction of property, theft, physical aggression, and bedtime disobedience. The story involving property destruction is presented below:

> *Mother in kitchen; father in shop; child in living room; baby in cradle in bedroom. The story: This boy is playing in the living room with a ball. Daddy says, "It's all right to play ball here, but be very careful not to hurt anything," and goes into his shop. The boy is having a lot of fun but he isn't as careful as he should be and the ball hits this floor lamp and knocks it over. Now you take the doll and show me and tell me how the rest of the story goes.*

The essential purpose of the test is to determine the child's tendency to express behavior and feelings related to guilt. Responses are scored in terms of nineteen categories relevant for this purpose. Two such categories are defined below:

> Redefinition minus (R−). *The subject distorts or retells the story stem in such a way as to make the deviation more severe; a story in which there is a repetition of the deviant act is also scored R−.*
> Delay (D). *The subject is unwilling or unable to complete the story without prompting and urging by the examiner, and may use various irrelevant and distracting behaviors to avoid continuing; score D also for long periods of silence.*

The scoring of the responses apparently follows two basic principles. First, all completions are scored regardless of their number. For this reason, more than one category can apply to each completion. Essentially, the score for each category is a percentage figure derived from its fractional part of all the categories used. Thus, if twenty categories are scored and two are physical punishment, the final score for that category would be 10 per cent.

RELIABILITY AND VALIDITY: The authors cite reliability data in the literature for a comparable procedure that yielded 96 per cent agreement on the coding of fifty-five completions. Though the authors repeatedly emphasize the need of their tests to reflect trait consistency among children as an index of their validity, they present no such data for this scale, possibly because it included only one examination session. Since the variables measured and the procedures employed were formulated by agreement among highly trained professionals as to their appropriateness and significance, content validity may be assumed. This conclusion could probably apply to all the scales by these authors measuring identification.

BIBLIOGRAPHY:

SEARS, R. R., RAU, L., and ALPERT, R. *Identification and Child Rearing*. Stanford, California: Stanford University Press, 1965.

Group 3-b

Attitudes Toward Peers

CHILDREN'S PERCEPTIONS OF THEIR CLASSMATES

AUTHORS: Bryce B. Hudgins, Lewis M. Smith, and Thomas J. Johnson

AGE: Grades five through eight

VARIABLE: Perception of academic and social skills in peers

TYPE OF MEASURE: Sociometric questionnaires

SOURCE FROM WHICH THE MEASURE MAY BE OBTAINED: See Hudgins et al. (1962)

DESCRIPTION OF MEASURE: This sociometric questionnaire consists of three tests, each of which includes four questions relating to a child's perceptions of skills among his peers. The three tests measure perceived arithmetic ability and perceived general academic ability (Test I), perceived arithmetic ability and acceptance as arithmetic partner (Test II), and perceived arithmetic and general social acceptance (Test III). Sample items from two of the questionnaires are given below. For Test I:

1. *Who are the three or four pupils in the class who are the best students in arithmetic?*
2. *Who are the three or four pupils in the class who have the most difficulty with arithmetic?*
3. *Who are the three or four pupils in the class who in general are the best students, know the most?*
4. *Who are the three or four pupils in the class who have the most difficulty with their school work, in general?*

For Test II:

1. *Same as in Test I above.*
2. *Same as in Test I above.*
3. *Who are the three or four pupils in the class with whom you would most like to work on arithmetic problems?*
4. *Who are the three or four pupils in the class with whom you would rather not work on arithmetic problems?*

The scoring scheme for the measure is not described explicitly. It appears that the scale tests certain hypotheses on the relationship between perceived arithmetic ability and perceived general ability, acceptance as arithmetic partner, and general social acceptance.

RELIABILITY AND VALIDITY: Hudgins et al. (1962) used the measure with children in grades five through eight, some in large classes (twenty or more students in the same class) and some in small classes (fewer than twenty students). In the large classes, the reliability data included contingency coefficients of .79, .69, and .35, respectively, for the following variables: (a) arithmetic ability versus general; (b) arithmetic ability versus acceptance as arithmetic partner; and (c) arithmetic ability versus general social acceptance. The corresponding values in small classes were .80 and .75 for variables (a) and (b) above.

Split-half reliability coefficients ranged in the large classes (uncorrected) from .34 for the variable (a) to .53 for the variable (b). The range in the small classes was from .56 for variable (a) to .64 for variable (b). With Spearman-Brown corrections, these split-half reliabilities improve considerably. The details of these statistics, as well as the method of determining these values, are described in full by the authors. In addition to these reliability data, the scales verified hypotheses in the predicted direction at statistically significant levels between perceived arithmetic ability and several other variables.

BIBLIOGRAPHY:

HUDGINS, B. B., SMITH, A. M., and JOHNSON, T. J. "The Child's Perception of His Classmates." *Journal of General Psychology*, 1962, *101*, 401–405.

CLASSROOM SOCIAL DISTANCE SCALE

AUTHORS: Ruth Cunningham and associates

AGE: Upper elementary

VARIABLE: Social acceptance-rejection

TYPE OF MEASURE: Nomination questionnaire

SOURCE FROM WHICH THE MEASURE MAY BE OBTAINED: See Cunningham (1951)

DESCRIPTION OF MEASURE: The instructions and method for using this scale are simple and straightforward. Each child rates every other child in the room on a five-point scale as follows:

Would like to have him as one of my best friends.
Would like to have him in my group but not as a close friend.
Would like to be with him once in a while but not often or for long at a time.
Don't mind his being in our room but I don't want to have anything to do with him.
Wish he weren't in our room.

This scale allows for a reaction, on a five-point scale, of each youngster to every other. The instrument is most useful when it is used by a teacher who knows his group. It is possible, by assigning numerical values to the five items on the scale, to arrive at two social distance scores: a self-social-distance score indicating the degree to which an individual accepts or rejects the group, and a group-social distance score, indicating the degree to which the group accepts or rejects an individual.

RELIABILITY AND VALIDITY: Cunningham reports correlations between scores for group-social distance (how others rated him) and chronological age, IQ, and socioeconomic status. She also reports correlations between self-social-distance (how he rated others) and chronological age, IQ, and socioeconomic status. The subjects were thirty-two fourth- and fifth-grade children, and the results were as follows:

Group-social-distance and chronological age	+.036
Intelligence quotient	+.480
Socioeconomic status	−.337
Self-social-distance and chronological age	−.345
Intelligence quotient	−.026
Socioeconomic status	−.09

Cunningham observes that the child with a high group-social distance score tended to be the child who, on the basis of his Social Analysis of the Classroom score, could be described as aggressive, displaying initiative, cheerful, jolly, friendly, and having a sense of humor. Someone who is judged to be timid, untidy, and afraid, frequently sad or unhappy, unfriendly or too bashful and shy, will tend to have a low score on the Classroom Social Distance scale.

BIBLIOGRAPHY:

CUNNINGHAM, R. *Understanding Group Behavior of Boys and Girls.* New York: Teachers College, Columbia University, 1951.

FORCED-CHOICE SOCIOMETRIC INTERVIEW

AUTHOR: Margaret Jenne Dunnington

AGE: Nursery school children

VARIABLE: Social status (acceptance) in classroom

TYPE OF MEASURE: Structured interview

SOURCE FROM WHICH THE MEASURE MAY BE OBTAINED: See Dunnington (1954, 1957a)

DESCRIPTION OF MEASURE: This sociometric interview, which is administered on an individual basis, requires the children to state both positive and negative play preferences to a fixed set of questions. The child is asked to name the peer in his nursery school class whom he considers the most preferable playmate. To secure three choices, the child is asked, "Anyone else? Anyone else?" The same three-choice procedure is followed in securing negative choices. In this case, the original question is "Whom in nursery school don't you like to play with?" As a final step in the interview, a simple yes or no response is obtained from the child regarding his desire to play with each of the other children in the class whom he had not mentioned within the two three-choice procedures. In effect, these latter replies constituted "forced" choices. The verbalizations of the child are recorded in full.

Scoring for each child's choices is done on a weighted numerical system, with 14 points for first choice, 7 for second, 5 for third, and 1 for forced responses. Positive responses are assigned plus values, while negative choices are given minus scores. In the event the child names two peers at any one choice level, each response receives the full value. The total sociometric score for any one child is the algebraic sum of the numerical weights for each response-choice assigned to him by his peers.

RELIABILITY AND VALIDITY: The identical procedure was repeated for fifteen children after sixty days. The test-rest rank order coefficient of correlation was .86. Moreover, the membership status of the three status groups (high, middle, and low) remained constant.

Evidence of the validity of the scale comes from several sources: (1) Almost perfect agreement between the present scoring system and an arbitrarily weighted one would apparently indicate that the interview measures levels of preference. (2) The present form of the interview is far superior in consistency to two other modifications: the use of positive choices only, or the assignment of equal value to all choice levels. (3) Total points assigned to a given child, regardless of algebraic signs (notice score), differentiated status groups. (4) The independent ranking of the children into three status groups by a nursery school teacher showed a 75 per cent agreement with the results of the sociometric test.

BIBLIOGRAPHY:

DUNNINGTON, M. J. "An Exploratory Study of Behavioral Variables Related to Differences in Sociometric Status of Nursery School Children." Unpublished master's thesis, Cornell University, 1954.

DUNNINGTON, M. J. "Investigation of Areas of Disagreement in Sociometric Measurement of Preschool Children." *Child Development,* 1957a, *28,* 93–103.

DUNNINGTON, M. J. "Behavioral Differences of Sociometric Status Groups in a Nursery School." *Child Development,* 1957b, *28,* 103–111.

PICTURE SOCIOMETRIC INTERVIEW

AUTHORS: Shirley Moore and Ruth Updegraff; Boyd R. McCandless and Helen R. Marshall

AGE: Nursery school children

VARIABLE: Social status (acceptance) in classroom

TYPE OF MEASURE: Structured interview

SOURCE FROM WHICH MEASURE MAY BE OBTAINED: See Moore and Updegraff (1964), McCandless and Marshall (1957)

DESCRIPTION OF MEASURE: The picture sociometric test by Moore and Updegraff combines the verbal interview by Dunnington (1957) with the picture board presentation developed by McCandless and Marshall (1957). The child is requested to name each 3 by 3 inch picture of the children in his group. If necessary the examiner helps him name the children. Details on the process of picture taking and the selection of representative photographs are described elsewhere (McCandless and Marshall, 1957). Once it is clear that the child recognizes the photographs of his peers, he is asked to select someone he especially likes at school. For this purpose, pointing is permissible if needed. Subsequently, he is asked to find three other choices he especially likes. The same procedure is followed for children he does not like very much. These four-choice clusters are respectively labeled spontaneous positive and spontaneous negative choices. Finally, the examiner points to each of the remaining unselected classmates, asking the subject, in each case, if this is someone he likes or does not like. These choices are called forced positive and forced negative choices, respectively. The spontaneous choices receive weighted scores of 8, 6, 4, and 3 points in descending order of preference, forced choices receive 1 point. An individual's total sociometric score is the algebraic sum of the points given to him by others in his class.

RELIABILITY AND VALIDITY: Three groups of nursery school children ($N = 18$ in each) were retested one to two weeks after the initial interview. The product-moment correlation coefficients for paired scores were .62 for group 1 ($p < .01$), .52 ($p < .02$) for group 2, and .78 ($p < .01$) for group 3. Though the correlations were statistically significant, the investigators regarded them only as moderate.

The test (Moore and Updegraff, 1964) provides partial confirmation of Marshall and McCandless' data that children's dependency on adults as defined by the total number of adult-child interactions seems to interfere with popularity among groups (McCandless and Marshall, 1957). Age and sex were not related to popularity (Moore and Updegraff, 1964). As predicted, instrumental dependency (the seeking of objective help) was not related to popularity (McCandless and Marshall, 1957).

BIBLIOGRAPHY:

DUNNINGTON, M. J. "Investigation of Areas of Disagreement in Sociometric Measurement of Preschool Children." *Child Development*, 1957, *28*, 93–102.

MARSHALL, H. R., and MC CANDLESS, B. R. "Relationships between Dependence on Adults and Social Acceptance by Peers." *Child Development*, 1957, *28*, 413–419.

MC CANDLESS, B. R., BILOUS, C. B., and BENNETT, H. L. "Peer Popularity and Dependence on Adults in Preschool-Age Socialization." *Child Development*, 1961, *32*, 511–518.

MC CANDLESS, B. R., and MARSHALL, H. R. "A Picture Sociometric Technique for Preschool Children and Its Relation to Teacher Judgments of Friendship." *Child Development*, 1957, *28*, 139–147.

MOORE, S., and UPDEGRAFF, R. "Sociometric Status of Preschool Children Related to Age, Sex, Nurturance-Giving, and Dependency." *Child Development*, 1964, *35*, 519–524.

QUESTIONNAIRE ON THE ABILITIES OF BLIND CHILDREN

AUTHOR: Barbara Bateman

AGE: Grades three to eight

VARIABLE: Sighted children's perceptions of abilities of blind children

TYPE OF MEASURE: Questionnaire

SOURCE FROM WHICH THE MEASURE MAY BE OBTAINED: Barbara D. Bateman, University of Oregon, School of Education, Eugene, Oregon 97403

DESCRIPTION OF MEASURE: This questionnaire lists activities assumed to be within the capablities of sighted children in grade three or above. The subjects are asked whether they think a blind child their age could perform each activity, checking yes, no, or not sure. The scoring is as follows: +1 point for each yes answer; 0 points for not sure; and −1 point for no. Examples of the items on the questionnaire follow:

Do you think a blind child could: *Read a regular newspaper? Listen to the radio? Dress himself or herself for school? Comb his or her own hair? Pour a glass of milk?*

RELIABILITY AND VALIDITY: Bateman (1962) analyzed the responses to the questionnaire by 115 sighted subjects who had not known a blind child and 117 sighted subjects who had known blind children in school. The findings suggested the following: (1) Subjects who had known blind children were more positive in their appraisal of the abilities of blind children than were those who had not known blind children. Within the group who had known blind children, the positiveness of appraisal increased with the number of blind children known. (2) Urban children were more positive in the appraisals than were rural children. (3) Positiveness of appraisal increased with grade level from grades three through eight, most noticeably in grades three through six, with a tendency to level off in grades six through eight.

BIBLIOGRAPHY:

BATEMAN, B. "Sighted Children's Perceptions of Blind Children's Abilities." *Exceptional Child,* 1962, 29, 42–46.

SOCIAL DISCRIMINATION QUESTIONNAIRE

AUTHORS: Louise Centers and Richard Centers

AGE: 5 through 12

VARIABLE: Attitudes toward other children

TYPE OF MEASURE: Sociometric questionnaire

SOURCE FROM WHICH THE MEASURE MAY BE OBTAINED: See Centers and Centers (1963)

DESCRIPTION OF MEASURE: The SDQ was designed to investigate the hypothesis that the presence of amputation represents a threat to the bodily integrity of nonamputees, and this threat is reflected in attitudes of rejection of amputee children by their peers. The scale consists of seventeen items. On ten of the questions the subject could be named by his peers. Five questions present occasions for positive response and five present opportunities for rejection of other children. The following are examples of the items included on the questionnaire:

Who is the best-liked boy in the class?
Who is the best-liked girl in the class?
Who do you think is the happiest child in the class? (*either boy or girl*)

The questionnaire is administered either by personal interview (with younger children) or by having the child write the names of his nominees. Nine items can be scored positively (+1) and eight negatively (−1), and a child's score is the algebraic sum of his item scores from the other children.

RELIABILITY AND VALIDITY: The SDQ was administered to children ages 5 to 12 in twenty-eight public school classes, where 413 children were in classes with children having upper extremity amputations, and 423 were in classes without amputee children.

No reliability or normative data have been provided for the SDQ. However, both raw scores and ranking scores indicate that the data from the questionnaire support the hypothesis that peer group children reject amputees more than they do nonamputee classmates. The differences were statistically significant beyond the .01 level.

BIBLIOGRAPHY:

CENTERS, L., and CENTERS, R. "Peer Group Attitudes toward the Amputee Child." *Journal of Social Psychology*, 1963, *61*, 127–132.

WHO ARE THEY TEST

AUTHORS: Paul H. Bowman, Robert F. DeHaan, John K. Kough, and Gordon P. Liddle

AGE: Upper elementary grades (four to six)

VARIABLE: Social adaptation or adjustment

TYPE OF MEASURE: Sociometric rating scale

SOURCE FROM WHICH THE MEASURE MAY BE OBTAINED: See Bowman et al. (1956)

DESCRIPTION OF MEASURE: The Who Are They Test is a rating scale in which peers rate each other on certain behavioral characteristics. The scale, which consists of a total of fifteen items, measures leadership (six items), aggressiveness (four items), and withdrawn behavior (four items). One item is clearly indicative of a positive friendship choice. The children are directed to write the name of peers under the item that describes their behavior appropriately. The two items below measure leadership qualities (Bowman et al., 1956):

Who are the boys and girls who make good plans?
Who are the good leaders? They are leaders in several things.

Details are provided on a separate weighted scoring system for friendship. All four scores (on leadership, withdrawn behavior, aggressive maladjustment, and friendship) are converted to percentile ranks (Havighurst, 1952).

RELIABILITY AND VALIDITY: Product-moment correlations between two sets of percentile scores over two years (test-retest) yielded the following figures: aggressive maladjustment, .40; withdrawn maladjustment, .47; social leadership, .74; and friendship, .53. A check was made on the possibility that the scores reflected only school adjustment but not neighborhood adjustment. The authors concluded that children were in the same leadership, friendship, and maladjustment situations in their neighborhood as they were at school (Bowman, et al., 1956).

BIBLIOGRAPHY:

BOWMAN, P. H., ET AL. *Studying Children and Training Counselors in a Community Program.* Chicago: University of Chicago Press, 1953.
BOWMAN, P. H., DE HAAN, R. F., KOUGH, J. K., and LIDDLE, G. P. *Mobilizing Community Resources for Youth.* Chicago: University of Chicago Press, 1956.
HAVIGHURST, R. J. *A Community Youth Development Program.* Chicago: University of Chicago Press, 1952.

Group 3 - c

Other Factors

ATTRIBUTION OF RESPONSIBILITY QUESTIONNAIRE (Form E)

AUTHORS: Marvin E. Shaw and Jefferson L. Sulzer

AGE: Second graders

VARIABLE: Attribution of responsibility

TYPE OF MEASURE: Questionnaire

SOURCE FROM WHICH THE MEASURE MAY BE OBTAINED: Marvin E. Shaw, Department of Psychology, University of Florida, Gainesville, Florida 32601

DESCRIPTION OF MEASURE: The AR Questionnaire is designed to measure the degree to which a person uses certain variables in assigning responsibility for his behavior to others in his environment. These variables include the five levels of sophistication described by Heider (1958) plus outcome quality and outcome intensity. The meanings of these terms are described in full (Shaw and Sulzer, 1964). These five levels represent successive stages of development in which the person takes into account an increasing number of variables.

The AR Questionnaire consists of two twenty-item forms, matched as closely as possible. Each form consists of four items at each of the five levels outlined above. A story at a given level incorporates only the minimum factors required to elicit attribution by a person functioning at that level of sophistication. All the stories to which the children respond deal with situations commonly encountered by second-grade children and employ a common character, Perry. Examples of stories with different levels are given below (Shaw and Sulzer, 1964).

A boy hit another child with Perry's toy gun. Is Perry responsible for the child being hit? (Global Association level, negative outcome)

When Perry rang the doorbell it made the baby drop a sharp knife he had picked up when his mother wasn't looking. Is Perry responsible for the baby dropping the knife? (Extended Commission level, negative outcome)

In Global-Association the person is held responsible for any outcome that he is connected with in any way. In the Extended Commission level, the person is held responsible for any outcome that he produced by his actions, even though he could not have predicted the results of his actions.

Administering and scoring the test consist of three interrelated processes. First, the stories are read orally to the children on a group basis. Second, on a response sheet containing a picture representing the story, the children respond by circling yes or no alternatives. Finally, provisions are made to enable the children to respond in terms of a five-point rating scale (Shaw and Sulzer, 1964).

RELIABILITY AND VALIDITY: The test has been administered to approximately 135 pupils in the second grade. Test-retest correlations on separate groups of twenty-six and twenty-two children yielded the respective correlations of .84 and

.81. The correlation coefficient between equivalent forms of the questionnaire was .99.

The responses of children and adults have been in the predicted direction, with children showing much less differentiation in their attribution of responsibility. Also, since independent ratings by three judges have shown complete agreement on item classification, the scale appears to have content validity (Shaw and Sulzer, 1961).

BIBLIOGRAPHY:

HEIDER, F. *The Psychology of Interpersonal Relationships.* New York: Wiley, 1958.
SHAW, M. E., and SULZER, J. L. "An Empirical Test of Heider's Levels in Attribution of Responsibility." *Journal of Abnormal and Social Psychology,* 1964, *69,* 39–46.

CHECK SHEET OF OPPORTUNITY IN HUMAN RELATIONS

AUTHOR: Ruth Cunningham and associates

AGE: Upper elementary and older

VARIABLE: Opportunity to participate in human relations

TYPE OF MEASURE: Questionnaire

SOURCE FROM WHICH THE MEASURE MAY BE OBTAINED: See Cunningham (1951)

DESCRIPTION OF MEASURE: The purposes of this check sheet are to evaluate the range of activities in which an individual engages; the values he places on his activities; his opinion of the degree of adult control over him; whom he would go to for help with personal problems; and his opinion of himself as a group member. The measure consists of forty activities that the subject is to evaluate as to how often he participates in them—[frequently (almost every day), sometimes (once a week or so), seldom or never (not more than once a month), or?—] and how valuable he perceives the experience to be for him—important, O.K., good but not important, unimportant, or?. Samples of items are the following:

Be a member of a team for some sport.
Work or play with people of differing religious belief.
Work or play with people who have considerably less money than my family.
Meet people who come from outside my community.
Discuss boy-girl relations.
Work for pay.

The scale consists of five additional items asking the subject to whom he would go in the family with a personal problem and to whom he would go outside the family with such a problem, how he feels about adult control in his family, and in school, one item having to do with self-evaluation on which he checks words or phrases which he feels describe him, one item in which he describes the three things he wants most to improve about himself; finally he lists the three best friends in his room, home room, group, or section at school. The reading level for this measure is appropriate for the more able upper elementary children and beyond.

RELIABILITY AND VALIDITY: None reported.

BIBLIOGRAPHY:

CUNNINGHAM, R. *Understanding Group Behavior of Boys and Girls.* New York: Teachers College, Columbia University, 1951.

CHILDREN'S LOCUS OF CONTROL SCALE

AUTHORS: Irving Bialer, Rue Cromwell, and James O. Miller

AGE: Grades three through eight

VARIABLE: Children's conception of locus of control

TYPE OF MEASURE: Questionnaire

SOURCE FROM WHICH THE MEASURE MAY BE OBTAINED: See Bialer (1960) and Miller (1961)

DESCRIPTION OF MEASURE: The scale may be described in terms of its rationale, its administration, and its scoring system.

Rationale: This scale is designed to measure locus of evaluation and locus of control. Locus of evaluation is the extent to which a person internalizes a set of standards by which to judge his actions, or is dependent upon an external frame of reference. Locus of control refers to the extent to which an individual perceives himself as being in control of environmental events or at the mercy of external forces.

Administration: The scale can be used with children ages 10 to 13, and has been used successfully with third graders when the examiner has read the items aloud. The scale should be administered individually and orally to retardates. Administration time is twenty to thirty minutes.

Scoring: Two scores are derived, one for locus of evaluation and one for locus of control. The higher the score, the greater the locus in the internal direction.

RELIABILITY AND VALIDITY: The constructs of locus of evaluation and locus of control appear to be relatively independent. Significant but low correlations have been consistently obtained. Reliabilities for normal subjects in the middle elementary grades, using the Guilford adaptation of the Spearman-Brown formula for homogeneous tasks, are in the mid to high 80 range for both constructs.

Using the Bialer scale upon which the present instrument was based, Battle and Rotter (1963) have found external-internal locus of control to vary with socioeconomic status and race and also with mental age and chronological age. Finally, the performance of children with an external or internal frame of reference has been discovered to co-vary on a predictive basis with failure-success experiences; with learning climates (success, failure, or neutral outcome); with inter- and intracue responsiveness; and with the values of significant others (Cromwell, 1963, 1965).

BIBLIOGRAPHY:

BATTLE, E., and ROTTER, J. R. "Children's Feelings of Personal Control as Related to Social Class and Ethnic Group." *Journal of Personality,* 1963, *31,* 482–490.

BIALER, I. "Conceptualization of Success and Failure in Mentally Retarded and Normal Children." Ann Arbor, Michigan: University Microfilms, 1960. Also, *Journal of Personality,* 1961, *29,* 303–320.

CROMWELL, R. L. "A Methodological Approach to Personality Research in Mental Retardation." *American Journal of Mental Deficiency,* 1959, *64,* 333–340.

CROMWELL, R. L., ROSENTHAL, D., SHAKOW, D., and ZAHN, T. P. "Reaction Time, Locus of Control, Choice Behavior, and Descriptions of Parent Behavior in Schizophrenic and Normal Subjects." *Journal of Personality,* 1961, *29,* 363–379.

CROMWELL, R. L. "A Social Learning Approach to Mental Retardation." Chapter 2 in N. Ellis (Ed.), *Handbook of Mental Deficiency.* New York: McGraw-Hill, 1963. Pp. 41–91.

CROMWELL, R. L. "Locus of Control and Symbolic Reinforcements in the Mentally Retarded." Cincinnati, Ohio: Sound Seminars, 1963. Also, *Acta Psychologica,* 1964, *23,* 336–337.

CROMWELL, R. L. "Success-Failure Reactions in Mentally Retarded Children." Paper presented at meetings of the Society for Research on Child Development. Minneapolis, Minnesota, March 24, 1965.

GARDNER, W. I. *Reactions of Intellectually Normal and Retarded Boys after Experimentally Induced Failure: A Social Learning Theory Interpretation.* Ann Arbor, Michigan: University Microfilms, 1958.

JAMES, W. H. *Internal vs. External Control of Reinforcement as a Basic Variable in Learning Theory.* Ann Arbor, Michigan: University Microfilms, 1957.

JAMES, W. H., and ROTTER, J. B. "Partial and One Hundred Per Cent Reinforcement under Chance and Skill Conditions." *Journal of Experimental Psychology,* 1958, *55,* 397–403.

MILLER, M. B. *Locus of Control, Learning Climate, and Climate Shift in Serial Learning with Mental Retardates.* Ann Arbor, Michigan: University Microfilms, 1961.

PHARES, E. J. *Changes in Expectancy in Skill and Chance Situations.* Ann Arbor, Michigan: University Microfilms, 1955.

ROTTER, J. B. *Social Learning and Clinical Psychology.* New York: Prentice-Hall, 1954.

CONCEPTIONS OF RELIGIOUS DENOMINATIONS

AUTHOR: David Elkind

AGE: 6 to 12

VARIABLE: Conception of religious identity

TYPE OF MEASURE: Semiclinical interviews

SOURCE FROM WHICH THE MEASURE MAY BE OBTAINED: See Elkind (1962, 1963, 1964)

DESCRIPTION OF MEASURE: The Conceptions of Religious Denominations consists of six structured questions that explore the child's thinking on religious identity in four areas of conceptualization: the extent of membership in religious groups by humans and infrahuman species; external indices indicative of certain religious membership; abstractions concerning common properties among all religions; and the possibility of simultaneous membership in religious and nonreligious groups.

The method employed is the semistructured interview of Piaget in which predesignated questions are designed to elicit spontaneous thought. For this purpose, the same set of six questions applies to each area of conceptualization. Examples of the items in the interview are the questions dealing with the extent of religious group membership (Elkind, 1964):

Are you a ———*?*
Is your family ———*?*
Are all boys and girls in the world ———*?*
Can a cat or a dog be a ———*?*

Subsequently, the children are asked to explain their affirmative or negative answers. Their responses serve as the basis for the interviews. In line with the discovery of definite stages in the conceptualization of religious identity among children, Elkind (1964) has discussed the implications of these findings for religious education.

RELIABILITY AND VALIDITY: Almost 800 children from three religious denominations (Jewish, Catholic, and Congregational Protestant) were interviewed by the author. In general, Elkind discovered three differentiated stages in a child's conceptualization of religious identity: a vague undifferentiated conception; a differentiated but concrete conception; and a differentiated and abstract conception of their denomination.

The author and a psychologically naive observer were able to reach more than 90 per cent agreement on the categorization of 300 responses into the three stages. The author also tested homogeneity of development in conceptualization within a given age level, a tenet that has been strongly emphasized by Piaget. To determine whether this assumption could be supported by the results, each child was given a homogeneity score. If all his answers (to the four questions that elicited responses categorizable by stages) were at the same stage, he was given an A score.

If all his replies but one were at the same stage, he was given a B score. If two replies were at one stage and two at another, he was given a C score. Finally, if he gave replies at all three stages, he was given a D score. Since the responses of very few children could be classified as C or D scores, the homogeneity of replies was considerable.

BIBLIOGRAPHY:

ELKIND, D. "The Child's Conception of His Religious Denomination: II. The Catholic Child." *Journal of Genetic Psychology,* 1962, *101,* 185–193.

ELKIND, D. "The Child's Conception of His Religious Denomination: III. The Protestant Child." *Journal of Genetic Psychology,* 1963, *103,* 291–304.

ELKIND, D. "The Child's Conception of His Religious Identity." *Lumen Vitae,* 1964, *XIX,* 635–646.

ELEMENTARY SOCIAL CAUSALITY TEST

AUTHORS: Ralph H. Ojemann, E. E. Levitt, Wm. H. Lyle, Jr., and Maxine F. Whiteside

AGE: Fourth through sixth grade

VARIABLE: Children's awareness of causes of behavior

TYPE OF MEASURE: Test

SOURCE FROM WHICH THE MEASURE MAY BE OBTAINED: Research Council of Educational Research Council of Greater Cleveland, Psychology Department, Rockefeller Building, Cleveland, Ohio 44113

DESCRIPTION OF MEASURE: Two forms of the SCT have been developed, an earlier form consisting of thirty true-false items (Ojemann et al., 1955) and a later version including seventy-nine similar items (Manual, Elementary Problem Series, undated). On the shorter scale, the total score is inversely related to a causal orientation, whereas it is directly related in the later version. In general, social causality, as defined by this scale, refers to awareness of the complex factors in human motivation, flexibility in thinking, and the suspension of judgment in the absence of sufficient information (Muuss, 1961, p. 231). A sample item from the first edition of the Elementary Causal Test follows:

Ruth is four years old. She is put to bed every night at seven-thirty. There are two older children in the family. Their bedtime is later. Ruth has a nap each afternoon. She sleeps an hour or more then. As soon as she is in bed, she begins to call. First she wants a drink. A few minutes after the drink she needs a handkerchief or something else. (a) A good talking to might not make Ruth stop, but it wouldn't hurt her any. (b) If I remembered that I had forgotten to give her a handkerchief, I would give her one and that would take care of it. (c) Ruth is just afraid to be alone and that's all there is to it. (d) There is no reason for Ruth acting this way and so I would tell her to keep still.

RELIABILITY AND VALIDITY: In the initial group administration for the early form of the scale, complete records were available for 240 children in grades four through six, with the number of students in each class ranging from sixteen to twenty-five. The results among fifth-grade pupils ($N = 158$) yielded a correlation coefficient with intelligence test scores of only .36; the Kuder-Richardson reliability was .63 (Ojemann et al., 1955). Corresponding statistics for the later version resulted in the respective coefficients of .30 and .77. The authors claim face validity for the scale since the items retained for the scale meet their definition of causal thinking in children. As predicted, children of teachers who have undergone in-service training on the causal approach (experimental group) exhibit a much more causal approach on posttest scores than a control group (Ojemann, et al., 1955).

BIBLIOGRAPHY:

MUUSS, R. E. "The Transfer Effects of a Learning Program in Social Causality on an Understanding of Physical Causality." *Journal of Experimental Education,* 1961, *29,* 231–247.

OJEMANN, R. H., LEVITT, E. E., LYLE, W. H., and WHITESIDE, M. F. "The Effects of a 'Causal' Teacher-Training Program and Certain Curricular Changes on Grade School Children." *Journal of Experimental Education,* 1955, *24,* 95–114.

INTELLECTUAL ACHIEVEMENT RESPONSIBILITY QUESTIONNAIRE

AUTHORS: Virginia C. Crandall, Walter Katkovsky, and Vaughn J. Crandall

AGE: Grades three to six, eight, ten, twelve

VARIABLE: Internal versus external control orientation

TYPE OF MEASURE: Forced-choice questionnaire

SOURCE FROM WHICH THE MEASURE MAY BE OBTAINED: See Crandall, et al. (1965)

DESCRIPTION OF MEASURE: The IAR Questionnaire attempts to measure the child's beliefs on whether he is responsible for his progress or whether external factors beyond his control affect his progress.

The children's IAR scale is composed of thirty-four forced-choice items. Each item stem describes either a positive or a negative achievement experience that routinely occurs in children's daily lives. This stem is followed by one alternative stating that the event was caused by the child and another stating that the event occurred because of the behavior of someone else in the child's immediate environment. Positive-event items are indicated by a plus sign, and negative events by a minus sign following the I. A child's I+ score is obtained by summing all positive events for which he assumes credit, and his I— score is a total of all negative events for which he assumes blame. This total I score (intellectual achievement responsibility) is the sum of his I+ and his I— subscores. Sample items from the scale are given below:

If a teacher passes you to the next grade, would it probably be (a) because she liked you, or (b) because of the work you did?
When you do well on a test at school, is it more likely to be (a) because you studied for it, or (b) because the test was especially easy?

In the original standardization of the scale, its administration varied with the age of the child. Individual, oral presentation was considered desirable for children below the sixth grade. The stimulus questions were tape recorded in order to standardize the examiner's inflections, tone, and rate. The subject's oral responses were recorded by the examiner. The children in grades six, eight, ten, and twelve were administered the scale in written form in group sessions. Complete directions for administering the scale have been provided.

RELIABILITY AND VALIDITY: The IAR Questionnaire has been administered to children in the third, fourth, fifth, and sixth grades with the respective totals of 102, 103, 99, and 166. Data on means, standard deviations, and range of scores are presented according to each sex classification. Results are also provided for the test-retest reliability and internal consistency scale. The test-retest reliability coefficients were based on scores of forty-seven children in grades three, four, and five over a two-month interval. Test-retest correlations were .69 for total I, .66 total I+, and

.74 total I—, all significant at the .001 level. There were no significant sex differences. Split-half reliability coefficients on the random sample of 130 of the younger children were .54 for I+, and .57 for I— after correction with the Spearman-Brown Prophecy formula. Low correlations were found between I+ and I— scores. One possible exception to this low interscale correlation may have occurred in sixth grade where r was .38 (p < .001). Below the sixth grade, interscale correlations range between .11 and .14.

Some other findings bearing on validity are: (1) Older girls give more self-responsible answers than older boys. (2) Slight significant age changes do occur in subscale scores depending on the sex of the child. (3) In the upper grades, IAR scores are moderately and positively related to an ordinal position of first-born child and membership in a small family. According to the authors, both findings are predictable from personality theory and from common observations. (4) IAR scores are positively and significantly related to reading, math, and language subscores and total achievement-test scores, and to report cards in grades three, four, and five. These correlations, however, are moderate, ranging from .34 to .53. The scale shows differential sex predictions for achievement at different age levels and exhibits its most consistent prediction to report-card grades.

BIBLIOGRAPHY:

CRANDALL, V. C., KATKOVSKY, W., and CRANDALL, V. J. "Children's Beliefs in Their Own Control of Reinforcements in Intellectual-Academic Achievement Situations." *Child Development*, 1965, *36*, 91–109.

A SCALE FOR THE CONTENT AND TEMPORAL DIMENSIONS OF LIFE SPACE

AUTHORS: Morris E. Eson and Norman Greenfield

AGE: Older elementary school-age children and adults

VARIABLE: Attitude (content and temporal dimensions of life space)

TYPE OF MEASURE: Semistructured interview

SOURCE FROM WHICH THE MEASURE MAY BE OBTAINED: See Eson (1951)

DESCRIPTION OF MEASURE: The scale is an individually administered semi-structured interview that elicits information from an individual on the content and temporal dimensions of his life space. The scale requires the subject to list his thoughts and conversations of the past week and to evaluate them in terms of three dimensions: (1) He rates each item as to its importance at the time the conversation or thought occurred, on a three-point scale: very important (VI), important (I), or not important (NI). (2) He describes the feeling tone of each item as pleasant (+), unpleasant (−), or indifferent (0). (3) He labels each item on a temporal basis as distant past (DP), near past (NP), near future (NF), or distant future (DF). If the subject selects more than one time limit, he is asked to choose the most appropriate one.

In addition, the content of each item is depicted by eleven categories: health and physical development (HP); personal appearance (PA); personal-psychological (PP); courtship, sex, and marriage (CSM); home and family (HF); education (E); vocational-economic (VE); relationships with people (RP); social-recreational (SR); citizenship, politics, and community (CPC); and morals, ethics, and religion (MER). Two examples of the full descriptions for these categories are given below:

Health and physical development (HP): *This category includes those items that center around thoughts of physical status, illness, deformities, and energy, and also thoughts of physical aspects of the environment (for example, temperature). These thoughts are of a personal nature and do not deal with concerns over those same conditions in others.*

Personal appearance (PA): *Thoughts dealing with personal appearance, exclusive of size, deformity, and other aspects of physical status, are included in this category. Expenditures of money for clothes, cosmetics, and cleanliness are also included.*

The scoring system may be visualized by these responses from 10-year-old children, followed by the scoring code for importance, feeling tone, time division, and content category, respectively.
For 10-year-old males:

Thought about saying my prayers.	I,	+,	NF,	MER
If I talk, I wouldn't get gym at school.	VI,	+,	NF	PP
Don't want to wrestle with a girl.	I,	−,	NP	CSM

For 10-year-old females:

I have been thinking about school and homework.	I,	+,	NP,	E
I was thinking about saving up for my Scout uniform.	VI,	+,	DF,	VE
Talked about having a new dress.	I,	+,	NF,	PA.

Within the twelve feeling tone-time division categories, the responses of VI, I, NI, which the subject ascribes to an item are respectively weighted as 3, 2, or 1 (Eson and Greenfield, 1962).

RELIABILITY AND VALIDITY: Two types of reliability checks on the stability of scores for this scale were used. First, interjudge agreement on the content categories of one hundred randomly selected items was quite high (92 per cent). Then a test-retest method for the interview was used for eleven subjects. The time interval between the two interviews ranged between three weeks and four months. Rank-order correlations for each time and feeling division ranged between .21 and .97 with a median of .71 (Eson and Greenfield, 1962). A high degree of internal consistency (r of .85) has also been found for future references obtained from recent conversations (Teahan, 1957, 1958).

Several findings in accordance with the expected influences of age and sex on the results suggest construct validity. For example, adolescent females placed significantly more emphasis on personal appearance than adult males did, and the latter, in turn, emphasized this aspect more than the younger male age groups.

BIBLIOGRAPHY:

ESON, M. C. "Analysis of Time Perspectives at Five Age Levels." University of Chicago, unpublished doctoral dissertation, 1951.

ESON, M. C., and GREENFIELD, N. "Lifespace: Its Content and Temporal Dimensions." *Journal of Genetic Psychology,* 1962, *100,* 113–128.

TEAHAN, J. E. "Future Time Perspective, Optimism and Academic Achievement." *Journal of Abnormal and Social Psychology,* 1958, *57,* 379–380.

USES TEST

AUTHOR: Wayne Dennis

AGE: 5 to 11

VARIABLE: Children's perceptions of societal values or interests

TYPE OF MEASURE: Structured interview

SOURCE FROM WHICH THE MEASURE MAY BE OBTAINED: See Dennis (1957)

DESCRIPTION OF MEASURE: The Uses Test is administered as a structured interview with individuals or as a questionnaire with groups. The scale uses the simple and universal question "What is ——— for?" Though the question may be asked regarding any plant, animal, class of persons, or part of the body, in the Uses Test it applies to sixteen different stimuli, including such diverse elements as the mouth, hands, mother, father, and gold. The test reportedly is an index of the activities, interests, and values prevailing in a society. According to the author, this technique is universally applicable, apparently regardless of culture.

In scoring the responses, each answer is assigned to only one category, and the scoring process itself consists of tabulating the percentage of responses for each stimulus word. Thus, the two responses of eating and talking to the stimulus word *mouth* made up 100, 96, and 92 per cent of the answers among American, Lebanese, and Sudanese children respectively.

RELIABILITY AND VALIDITY: Findings appear to offer construct validity for the scale in that, as predicted, a considerable number of cultural and age differences among the data appeared. In fact, cultural differences emerged as early as 5 years of age. No data on the reliability of the scale are provided.

BIBLIOGRAPHY:

DENNIS, W. "Uses of Common Objects as Indicators of Cultural Orientations." *Journal of Abnormal and Social Psychology*, 1957, 55, 21–28.

SELF-CONCEPT

ADJECTIVE CHECK LIST

AUTHORS: Helen H. Davidson and Gerhard Lang

AGE: Fourth, fifth, sixth grades and junior high

VARIABLE: Self-concept

TYPE OF MEASURE: Checklist

SOURCE FROM WHICH THE MEASURE MAY BE OBTAINED: See David-son and Lang (1960)

DESCRIPTION OF MEASURE: The Adjective Check List consists of thirty-five behavioral traits that measure the child's perceptions of his teacher's attitude toward him. It also serves as a measure of self-perception. The words in the scale were selected on the basis of established trait lists, appropriate difficulty level, and an equal distribution of negative and positive connotations. Examples of the thirty-five words that have either a favorable (F) or unfavorable (U) rating are as follows: fair (F), a nuisance (U), afraid (U), a hard worker (F), bad (U), a good sport (F). In administering the checklist, children are instructed to rate each trait name on a three-point scale in terms of how the teacher feels toward them. For this purpose, the children choose from three frequency categories: most of the time, half of the time, seldom or almost never. On favorable items, the respective scores for these responses are 3, 2, and 1. On unfavorable items, the scoring procedure is reversed.

The total score or Index of Favorability has a possible range from 1.00 to 3.00, and is obtained by adding the scores of all the words and dividing by the number of words checked. Higher scores mean the child perceives the teacher as feeling positively toward him.

RELIABILITY AND VALIDITY: On the basis of the three criteria described above for selecting items, 135 trait names were originally rated by thirty-five teach-ers and fifty junior high pupils as favorable, unfavorable, or neutral. The final list contained only those words that had been rated as favorable or unfavorable by more than 80 per cent of the members in each scale. These results, then, would provide some evidence that the scale has content validity. A rank-difference correlation coefficient of .85 (p < .001) was obtained for 105 junior high school children, based on two administrations of the checklist four to six weeks apart. Further, a rank cor-relation coefficient of .51 (p < .001) was obtained between a teacher approval score derived from a Guess Who Sociometric Technique in three elementary classes (N = 93) and the Index of Favorability on the checklist. The authors regard this correlation as a measure of empirical and concurrent validity (Davidson and Lang, 1960).

BIBLIOGRAPHY:

DAVIDSON, H. H., and LANG, G. "Children's Perceptions of Their Teachers' Feelings toward Them Related to Self-Perception, School Achievement and Behavior." *Journal of Experimental Education*, 1960, *29*, 107–118.

CHILDREN'S RESPONSIBILITY INVENTORY
(Children's Form)

AUTHOR: Michael Zunich

AGE: Sixth-grade children

VARIABLE: Perception of responsibility

TYPE OF MEASURE: Questionnaire

SOURCE FROM WHICH THE MEASURE MAY BE OBTAINED: See Zunich (1963)

DESCRIPTION OF MEASURE: The CRI (Children's Form) consists of twenty-five items designed to test children's perceptions of the ages at which they could develop responsibility for various tasks, such as care of clothing, cleanliness of self, and household tasks. The children are asked at what age the majority of children could assume responsibility for returning an object one has borrowed unseen from a friend, placing dirty clothes in a hamper without a reminder, and cleaning before a meal without being told. On the basis of responses by 508 sixth-grade pupils, rather evenly divided between sex groups and social classes, median age responses are available for each of the twenty-five items.

RELIABILITY AND VALIDITY: The author (Zunich, 1963) deduces reliability for the scale from his interviews with children in which he attempted to determine the basis for their responses and the possibility of misconceptions of the meanings of the items. Further, test-retest reliability over a one-week period yielded an agreement of 77 per cent for thirty-one pupils. Content validity may be attributed to the scale from the fact that a panel of six university instructors rated the validity of the items.

BIBLIOGRAPHY:

WALTERS, J., STROMBERG, F. I., and LONIAN, G. "Perceptions Concerning Development of Responsibility in Young Children." *Elementary School Journal,* 1957, *57,* 209–216.

ZUNICH, M. "Development of Responsibility Perceptions of Lower and Middle Class Children." *Journal of Educational Research,* 1963, *56,* 497–499.

CHILDREN'S SELF-CONCEPTION TEST

AUTHOR: Marjorie B. Creelman

AGE: 6 to 11

VARIABLE: Self-concept

TYPE OF MEASURE: Test

SOURCE FROM WHICH THE MEASURE MAY BE OBTAINED: A microfilm copy of the complete manuscript is available from the University of Michigan Microfilms, Ann Arbor, Michigan for $3.58. Enlargements 6 × 8 inches are 10¢ per page.

DESCRIPTION OF MEASURE: The C-S-C test may be administered on a group or individual basis. The test itself consists of twenty-four sets of pictures with eight pictures in each set. Four pictures show a boy engaged in an activity common to our culture and an equal number of pictures describe an identical activity for girls. One sequence of pictures, for example, shows a child playing with his father, helping his parents dry dishes, playing independently, and doing the dishes by himself.

The test is administered separately but consecutively for three different purposes. First, on each set, the children are asked to select the picture they like the best and to choose the one they dislike most. Second, they are asked to choose the good and bad pictures within each set. Finally, they are requested to select the pictures most like them and most unlike them. In scoring, each criterion has positive and negative choices. Specific procedures for scoring responses are provided for four types of scores: self-acceptance score, self-rejection score, acceptance of social values, and rejection of social values. The separate scores or combinations of scores provide a measure of self-acceptance or self-rejection, positive or negative self-evaluation, and acceptance and rejection of moral or social standards as the child perceives them. The scoring is objective and the author provides detailed instructions on scoring and administration. The author suggests a time period from two to two and one-half hours for testing groups of twenty to twenty-five young children to allow for frequent rest periods.

RELIABILITY AND VALIDITY: The author provides no data on either test-retest or scorer reliability but emphasizes that the latter should be "perfect" in view of the completely objective nature of the scoring. Creelman claims only face validity for the test (1966). She also contends, however, that the results are consistent enough with theories of self-concept and other theories of child development so that the C-S-C may provide a useful and valid method for investigating the self-conceptions of children and their relationships to adjustment and maladjustment (1955a).

BIBLIOGRAPHY:

CREELMAN, M. B. "The CSC Test: Self Conceptions of Elementary School Children." Unpublished doctoral dissertation, Western Reserve University, 1954.

CREELMAN, M. B. "The CSC Test: Self Conceptions of Elementary School Children." Dissertation Abstracts, 1955a, *15*, No. 10.

CHILDREN'S SOMATIC APPERCEPTION TEST

AUTHORS: Nancy M. Adams and Willard E. Caldwell

AGE: 7 to 14

VARIABLE: Body image

TYPE OF MEASURE: Objective projective technique

SOURCE FROM WHICH THE MEASURE MAY BE OBTAINED: See Adams and Caldwell (1963)

DESCRIPTION OF MEASURE: The test consists of ten wooden figures with removable head, legs, and arms, the complete figures ranging from 11½ to 16 inches tall and differing from the next larger or smaller figure by ½ inch. There is additionally a set of ten heads of the same graduated sizes as the ten figures, and ten sets of each of the four limbs, also graduated in size as with the original figures. The child picks out the one of the ten figures that he feels is most like him, and also his ideal, the figure he would most like to be. He then constructs his ideal from the extra parts. Several scores are obtained: the ratio between the child's actual measurements and his self-drawing; the ratio between actual measurements and choice of body parts; and the difference between perceived and desired body image.

Some norms are given for white males ages 7 to 14, thirty-five normals, thirteen moderately disturbed, ten retarded.

RELIABILITY AND VALIDITY: None reported.

BIBLIOGRAPHY:

ADAMS, N. M., and CALDWELL, W. E. "The Children's Somatic Apperception Test, a Technique for Quantifying Body Image." *Journal of General Psychology,* 1963, *68,* 43–57.

ELEMENTARY SCHOOL INDEX OF ADJUSTMENT AND VALUES

AUTHOR: Robert E. Bills

AGE: Grades three, four, and five

VARIABLE: Personality—self-concept

TYPE OF MEASURE: Rating scale

SOURCE FROM WHICH THE MEASURE MAY BE OBTAINED: Robert E. Bills, Dean, College of Education, University of Alabama, University, Alabama. Cost is $1.50 for ninety-page mimeographed summary of reports on relevant data.

DESCRIPTION OF MEASURE: The ESIAV consists of nineteen descriptive statements describing traits about the self and others. The directions are read aloud and administered on a group basis. A sample item describing the trait of truthfulness follows:

Are you truthful? Do you like the way you are? Would you like to be truthful?

Whether describing behavior about himself or others, the three fixed alternative responses available to the child for each item are yes, no, sometimes; or yes, no, don't care.

     In classifying the responses, there are several scores: a Self Index score that indicates a child's agreement with descriptive statements as they relate to his behavior; an "Others" score in which the children answer the questions as they think most other children would answer; and categorical scores that indicate the agreement between "Self" scores and "Others" scores. Four categorical scores are possible: ++, −+, +−, −−. A ++ person is more accepting of himself than the average and believes that other people are at least as accepting of themselves. Changes in self-concept can be assessed by rating changes in the "Self" scale scores. In the final form of the ESIAV, however, the "Ideal Self" scale has been eliminated.

RELIABILITY AND VALIDITY: Content validity rests on the selection of words with an appropriate difficulty level and on item analysis. The low correlations between the "Self" and "Others" scales support the conclusion of independent measures. Corrected split-half reliabilities of the "Self" form of the ESIAV ($n = 80$) are: Self scales .48, "Ideal" Self scale .69, "Others" scale .72. Because of the low split-half reliabilities, the author recommends caution in applying any of the indexes as individual measures.

BIBLIOGRAPHY:

BILLS, R. E., ET AL. "An Index of Adjustment and Values." *Journal of Consulting Psychology*, 1951, *15*, 257–261.

INSIDE-OF-THE-BODY TEST

AUTHORS: C. Downing Tait, Jr., and Robert C. Ascher

AGE: Sixth grade

VARIABLE: Body image

TYPE OF MEASURE: Projective test

SOURCE FROM WHICH THE MEASURE MAY BE OBTAINED: See Tait and Ascher (1955)

DESCRIPTION OF MEASURE: The instructions to the subject taking this test are straightforward. He is told to draw the inside of the body, including all the organs. He is given three minutes to draw, and an additional minute to label the organs drawn.

RELIABILITY AND VALIDITY: None reported. Tait and Ascher list numerous parts of the body and body systems, and give norms on the frequency with which each of these body parts and systems is named by neuropsychiatric patients, Naval Academy candidates, medical and surgical patients, and sixth graders. The scores on the test were the number of times each organ or system was mentioned.

Offord and Aponte found that groups of congenital heart and normal children did not differ significantly in the number of hearts drawn, but that the congenital heart children drew significantly larger hearts; the normal children drew significantly more internal body parts than the congenital heart children.

BIBLIOGRAPHY:

TAIT, C. DOWNING, JR., and ASCHER, R. C. "Inside-of-the-Body Test," *Psychosomatic Medicine*, 1955, *XVII*(2).

LIPSITT SELF-CONCEPT SCALE FOR CHILDREN

AUTHOR: Lewis P. Lipsitt

AGE: Fourth-, fifth-, and sixth-grade children

VARIABLE: Self-concept

TYPE OF MEASURE: Self-rating Likert-type scale

SOURCE FROM WHICH THE MEASURE MAY BE OBTAINED: See Lipsitt (1958)

DESCRIPTION OF MEASURE: The self-concept scale consists of the following twenty-two trait-descriptive adjectives: friendly, happy, kind, brave, honest, likeable, trusted, good, proud, *lazy,* loyal, cooperative, cheerful, thoughtful, popular, courteous, *jealous,* obedient, polite, *bashful,* clean, helpful. Each of these adjectives is prefaced by the phrase "I am . . ." and is followed by a five-point rating scale. Nineteen of the adjectives may be considered positive or socially desirable attributes, while the three that are italicized may be considered negative. The rating categories, scored from 1 to 5, are entitled not at all, not very often, some of the time, most of the time, and all of the time. A score of 1 is received on an item if the subject checked the first category, a score of 5 if the last category is checked, except in the case of the three negative adjectives, which are scored in inverse fashion. A score on the self-concept scale is obtained for each subject by summing the ratings ascribed to himself on each item. Lower scores are presumed to reflect degree of self-disparagement.

The ideal-self scale contains the same adjectives but here each is prefaced by "I would like to be . . ." Again, the subject rates himself on each item on similar scales. The discrepancy scores (indicating degree of self-dissatisfaction) are obtained by subtracting the total self-concept score from the total ideal-self score.

RELIABILITY AND VALIDITY: The scale was administered to 300 fourth, fifth, and sixth graders on the same day. The sample was subdivided as follows: fourth grade, forty-seven boys and sixty-two girls; fifth grade, fifty boys and sixty-one girls; sixth grade, forty-one boys and thirty-seven girls.

Test-retest reliabilities over a two-week period ranged from .73 to .91 for the self-concept scale and .57 to .72 for the discrepancy score. In the former scale all the correlation coefficients reached statistical significance beyond the .001 level. In the latter scale, four of the six correlations reached significance at the .001 level, and two at the .01 level. No reliable grade or sex differences in mean self-concept scores were evident. The self-concept measure was significantly correlated with performance on the CMAS (Children's Manifest Anxiety Scale), while comparable correlations for the discrepancy scores were somewhat less and in some cases not reliable.

BIBLIOGRAPHY:

LIPSITT, L. P. "A Self-Concept Scale for Children and Its Relationship to the Children's Form of the Manifest Anxiety Scale." *Child Development,* 1958, *29,* 463–472.

MORGAN PUNISHMENT-SITUATIONS INDEX

AUTHOR: Patricia K. Morgan

AGE: Elementary school age children between 9 and 12, and parents

VARIABLE: Personality

TYPE OF MEASURE: Projective test

SOURCE FROM WHICH THE MEASURE MAY BE OBTAINED: See Morgan and Gaier (1956)

DESCRIPTION OF MEASURE: The MPSI, a projective device developed to assess the direction of aggression in situations commonly leading to punishment of the child by parents, consists of ten cartoon-like pictures (one series for boys, another for girls). For example, the pictures depict situations in which the child was apparently lying, stealing, disobedient, or destroying parental property. When the test is administered to both the child and his mother, four classes of perceptions are obtained: the child's conception of himself (CC) and his mother (CM); and the mother's conception of herself (MM) and her child (MC).

The responses to the test are scored using the scoring factors developed by Rosenzweig (1947). Essentially, these reactions in the punishment situation are classified as: obstacle-dominance (O-D), in which the barrier to the goal is emphasized; ego-defense (E-D), in which the ego of the subject predominates; and need-persistence (N-P), where the response is built around a solution of the frustrating problem. Each major category is divided further into three subcategories. For example, under the obstacle-dominance category, the response is scored as E' if the frustrating obstacle is emphasized or as M' if the obstacle is minimized almost to the point of denial.

Morgan and Gaier (1957) present seven questions that should be asked of the child and mother for each picture through individual inquiry. These refer primarily to statements, feelings, and actions by the mother and child for the particular situation. The manual seems to indicate, however, that the test could be administered to children on a group basis since fixed-alternative answers are provided for each cartoon and the directions for administering the test are self-explanatory. A key also provides examples for almost any category of response.

RELIABILITY AND VALIDITY: Since the studies by Morgan and Gaier (1956, 1957) replicated previous findings by Rosenzweig (1944, 1947) regarding the common reactions of children and parents, the scale apparently has some construct validity. No norms or reliability data for the scale are available.

BIBLIOGRAPHY:

MORGAN, P. K., and GAIER, E. L. "The Direction of Aggression in the Mother-Child Punishment Situation." *Child Development*, 1956, 27, 447–457.

MORGAN, P. K., and GAIER, E. L. "Types of Reactions in Punishment Situations in the Mother-Child Relationship." *Child Deveolpment,* 1957, *28,* 161–166.

ROSENZWEIG, S. "An Outline of Frustration Theory." In J. McV. Hunt (Ed.), *Personality and the Behavior Disorders.* New York: Ronald, 1944, Vol. I. Pp. 379–387.

ROSENZWEIG, S., FLEMING, E., and CLARKE, H. J. "Revised Scoring Manual for the Rosenzweig Picture Frustration Study." *Journal of Psychology,* 1947, *24,* 165–208.

PERCEPTION SCORE SHEET

AUTHORS: A. W. Combs and D. W. Soper

AGE: Kindergarten and first grade

VARIABLE: Perceptions of self and perceptions of others

TYPE OF MEASURE: Observation schedule

SOURCE FROM WHICH THE MEASURE MAY BE OBTAINED: See Combs and Soper (1963)

DESCRIPTION OF MEASURE: This frame of reference is to be used by specially trained personnel to evaluate the self-perceptions of children and their perceptions of other significant persons in their environment. There are thirty-nine items or areas on which each child is rated, using a five-point scale. Most items are described and clarified, as in the following example of perceptions of self generally:

Adequate-inadequate: *This category refers to the child's overall feeling of adequacy. It represents a global feeling of being fulfilled, enough, sufficient, as contrasted to feeling ineffectual, lacking, or the like. It should be recognized that it is possible for a child to feel generally adequate while at the same time possibly feeling inadequate with respect to some individual items on our checklist.*

For self as instrument:

This section has to do with various categories describing how the individual perceives himself as an instrument for carrying out his purposes.

The items are grouped as follows: Perception of self—self generally, self as instrument, self with other children, self with adults, self with teachers, self and the school curriculum. Perceptions of others—perception of children, perception of adults, perception of teachers, perception of school. This observation schedule seems appropriate for most elementary school children, although Combs and Soper used it only with kindergarten and first graders.

RELIABILITY AND VALIDITY: Scores of the kindergarten group were factor analyzed. Only six of the thirty-nine items showed communalities of less than .70, indicating a high level of reliability for the scales.

The strongest factor identified was The General Adequacy Factor. This factor included thirty-seven of the thirty-nine items on the schedule, and accounts for 67 per cent of the total variance of the thirty-nine items. The next strongest factor accounts for only 9 per cent of the variance.

BIBLIOGRAPHY:

COMBS, A. W., and SOPER, D. W. "The Relationship of Child Perceptions to Achievement and Behavior in the Early School Years." Cooperative Research Project No. 814. University of Florida, 1963.

SELF-CONCEPT INVENTORY

AUTHOR: Pauline S. Sears

AGE: The test has been used with fifth and sixth graders and with "bright" third graders

VARIABLE: Personality (self-concept)

TYPE OF MEASURE: Self-report questionnaire

SOURCE FROM WHICH THE MEASURE MAY BE OBTAINED: Pauline Sears, 110 Golden Oak Drive, Portola Valley, California 94026. "This inventory . . . is available to qualified research workers and to students working under the supervision of a qualified professor . . . ; anyone wishing to undertake a project which has been carefully conceived for its potential benefits to the students, and carefully protected against possible damage to self-esteem of students, may write me an account of the proposed project" (Sears, memorandum, undated).

DESCRIPTION OF MEASURE: The original scale by Sears includes 100 items measuring the child's self-esteem in several areas assumed to be important in children's self-evaluation: physical ability, attractive appearance, convergent mental ability, social relations with same sex, social virtues, divergent mental ability, work habits, happy qualities, and school subjects. On the scale itself the child was requested to rate himself in terms of the following behavioral dimensions: satisfaction with himself (yes or no); estimation of improvement in the future (some improvement or no change); comparison with peers (very good, better than a good many, better than average, fair, and not very good). Sample items are playing outdoor games after school, learning things rapidly, getting along well with boys.

In a revised forty-eight-item version (1966) suitable for bright third graders, the child is requested to rate himself in terms of five options ranking from excellent to not so good. Sample items from this form of the scale follow (Instructions for self-concept scale, 1966 version, undated): being good at sports, learning things rapidly, making friends easily, with my own sex.

This test may be group administered in about forty minutes. A special score making friends easily with my own sex.

RELIABILITY AND VALIDITY: The Kuder-Richardson reliability coefficients on a population of thirty-two third graders ranged from .56 for happy qualities to .89 for convergent mental ability on the 1966 version. Spaulding (1963, 1964) and Sherman (1964) used a revised and adapted addition of the 100-item inventory with some new items on self-concept for creativity and other areas. Reliabilities were: height of self-concept, .85, and differentiation, .82.

Wtih regard to validity, Gelfand (1962) has found that self-esteem as measured by this scale and persuasibility were negatively correlated. Self-concept measures were highly intercorrelated from one area of ability to another. The degree or "height" of self-concept on this scale, as expected, was found to vary as a result of sex and degree of mental ability. Considerable material also exists on the correlates of self-concept and the contingencies under which they occur (Sears, 1963, mimeographed).

BIBLIOGRAPHY:

GELFAND, D. M. "The Influence of Self-Esteem on Rate of Verbal Conditioning and Social Matching Behavior." *Journal of Abnormal and Social Psychology*, 1962, *64*, 259–265.

SEARS, P. S. "The Effect of Classroom Conditions on the Strength of Achievement Motive and Work Output of Elementary School Children." Palo Alto, Calif.: Stanford University (U.S. Office of Educ. Coop. Res. Project No. 873), 1963. (Mimeographed)

SEARS, P. S. "Memorandum with Respect to Use of the Sears Self-Concept Inventory." Unpublished material (undated).

SHERMAN, V. "Personality Correlates of Differential Performance on Intelligence and Creativity Tests." Unpublished doctoral dissertation, Stanford University, 1964.

SPAULDING, R. *Achievement, Creativity, and Self-Concept Correlates of Teacher-Pupil Transactions in Elementary Schools*. Urbana, Ill.: University of Illinois (U.S. Office of Educ. Coop. Res. Project No. 1352), 1963.

SPAULDING, R. Title as above. Reprinted in Stendler, C. B. (Ed.), *Readings in Child Behavior and Development*, 2nd ed. New York: Harcourt Brace, 1964.

SPAULDING, R. "Affective Dimensions of Creative Processes." *Gifted Child Quarterly*, 1963, *VII*, Winter.

THE SELF-CONCEPT–SELF-REPORT SCALE

AUTHORS: A. W. Combs, D. W. Soper, and C. C. Courson

AGE: Sixth graders

VARIABLE: Self-concept

TYPE OF MEASURE: Rating scale

SOURCE FROM WHICH THE MEASURE MAY BE OBTAINED: See Combs, Soper, and Courson (1963)

DESCRIPTION OF MEASURE: This is a simple scale of eighteen pairs of positive and negative statements about self, arranged on a five-point scale. Examples of the eighteen statements are:

People like to have me around. People don't care if I'm there or not.
Teachers like me pretty well. Teachers don't like me much.
I don't think I'm brave. I think I'm a brave person.
I'm not much good at sports and games. I'm good at sports and games.

Scale items are randomized so that positive and negative statements do not always run in the same direction. No labels or descriptions are placed on the five-point digit spread so that the values invested in the scale are more likely to be personal than externally suggested.

The authors of this measure make a point of distinguishing between the self-report and the self-concept.

RELIABILITY AND VALIDITY: The authors correlated the self-report scores with the self-concept ratings given the subjects by trained observers, for each of the eighteen items for fifty-nine subjects. The eighteen correlations ranged from −.199 to +.336. Also, to arrive at a mean coefficient, the eighteen correlations were converted to z-scores and averaged, resulting in a mean correlation of .114, which was not statistically significant. There was no significant relationship between the inferred self-concepts of these sixth-grade subjects and their self-reports.

BIBLIOGRAPHY:

,COMBS, A. W., SOPER, D. W., and COURSON, C. C. "The Measurement of Self Concept and Self Report." *Educational and Psychological Measurement,* 1963, *XXIII*(3).

,COMBS, A. W., and SOPER, D. W. "The Relationship of Child Perceptions to Achievement and Behavior in the Early School Years." *Cooperative Research Project No. 814,* 1963.

SELF-OTHER ORIENTATION TASKS

AUTHORS: Robert C. Ziller, Barbara H. Long, and Edmund Henderson

AGE: Preschool to adult (four forms)

VARIABLE: Self-concept

TYPE OF MEASURE: Test, individually administered

SOURCE FROM WHICH THE MEASURE MAY BE OBTAINED: Dr. Robert C. Ziller, Department of Psychology, University of Oregon, Eugene, Oregon ($1.00 per copy)

DESCRIPTION OF MEASURE: These tests are in four forms—adult, college student, grades six to twelve, and preschool to fifth grade. The preschool form involves the child in sticking gummed labels on points he chooses, or simply pointing to a circle to indicate his position with respect to a question. The preschool tasks appear intrinsically interesting to children.

The tests measure different variables at different age levels. The sixth- to twelfth-grade form constitutes a measure of self-esteem, identification, social interest, majority identification, power, self centrality, and group identification. The Children's Self-Social Constructs Test, the preschool form, measures dependency, esteem, identification, realism color (realistic assessment of one's own skin color), realism size, and "forced choice," involving a choice among several significant persons in the child's experience.

The preschool form is appropriate for children ages 3 to 8. Administration time is about ten minutes, and it is administered individually. Scoring is objective.

RELIABILITY AND VALIDITY: Reliability of the sixth to twelfth grade form (n = 100) is reported as follows: self-esteem = .80; identification = .78 to .95; social interest = .84; majority identification = .87; power = .65; self centrality = .58; and group identification = .88.

BIBLIOGRAPHY: None.

SELF-SOCIAL SYMBOLS TASKS

AUTHORS: Robert C. Ziller, Barbara H. Long, and Edmund H. Henderson

AGE: About 10 and older

VARIABLE: Conception of self in relation to others

TYPE OF MEASURE: Test

SOURCE FROM WHICH THE MEASURE MAY BE OBTAINED: See Henderson, Long, and Ziller (1965)

DESCRIPTION OF MEASURE: This instrument is designed to measure the following aspects of the self-concept in relation to salient others: esteem, identification (with mother, father, teacher, and friend), group identification, dependency, individuation, power, centrality, and complexity. The test is made up of fifty-six items distributed among the above-mentioned variables as follows, respectively: six, eight, four, six, ten, six, six, ten.

The subject works in a test booklet, selecting and arranging symbols to represent himself with respect to others. For example, item 1 pictures a square with ten circles inside it, and three circles in a row outside and to the right. Six of the inside circles are blank, and four have vertical lines. The three circles outside of the square are respectively blank, horizontally lined, and vertically lined. The instructions to the subject are: "All of the circles within the square stand for other people. Choose any one of the three circles on the right to stand for yourself, and draw one like it anywhere in the square." This is one of the "individuation" items, and a point is scored if the subject chooses a circle different from the majority of circles.

Long, Ziller, and Henderson (undated) describe briefly the rationale for the item types and scoring. Administration time is given as approximately twenty minutes.

RELIABILITY AND VALIDITY: Corrected split-half reliability coefficients for twelve variables (identification is divided into six areas, consequently six scores) ranged from .58 to .95, median .82. The subjects were 420 students, thirty boys and thirty girls, grades six to twelve. The authors found significant effects for grade or sex for the following measures: esteem, dependency, three of the power items, and all five identification measures (Long, Ziller, and Henderson, undated). They provide additional details on validity. Norms for boys and for girls in grades six to twelve, separately, are provided, broken down by subvariable.

BIBLIOGRAPHY:

HENDERSON, E. H., LONG, B. H., and ZILLER, R. C. "Self-Social Constructs of Achieving and Non-Achieving Readers." *The Reading Teacher,* 1965, *19,* 114–118.
KELSO, J. "Self-Social Constructs and Sibling Sex Structure." Unpublished master's thesis, University of Delaware, 1964.

RIDGEWAY, S. "The Relationships among Three Measures of Self-Concept." Unpublished master's thesis, University of Maryland, 1965.

ZILLER, R. C., MEGAS, J., and DECENCIO, D. "Self-Social Constructs of Normals and Acute Neuropsychiatric Patients." *Journal of Consulting Psychology,* 1964, *20,* 50–63.

ZILLER, R. C., and LONG, B. H. "Self-Social Constructs and Geographic Mobility." Paper presented at Eastern Psychological Association meeting, Atlantic City, 1965.

ZELIGS' TEST ON NEW YEAR'S RESOLUTIONS

AUTHOR: Rose Zeligs

AGE: Sixth grade

VARIABLE: Children's worries

TYPE OF MEASURE: Questionnaire

SOURCE FROM WHICH THE MEASURE MAY BE OBTAINED: Rose Zeligs, 14256 Ventura Boulevard, Sherman Oaks, California 91403

DESCRIPTION OF MEASURE: This test measures self-concept by attempting to identify the aspects of a child's behavior that he views negatively. There are thirty-two items in all. The children are asked to put a circle around yes, no, or sometimes describing their true feelings for each item. For example:

I worry about the need to: *obey parents promptly, stop biting my finger nails, get up on time, help my country, help my parents, not chew gum in school.*

Scoring is straightforward: no = 2 points, sometimes = 1 point, and yes = 0 points.

The items were derived by getting sixth-grade children to write their New Year's Resolutions. Thirty-two items accounted for 62 per cent of the resolutions. The items could be classified in the following areas: school, home, parents, conduct, home routines and habits, social relations, health habits, character and personality traits, siblings' food and eating, and patriotism.

RELIABILITY AND VALIDITY: No data were presented.

BIBLIOGRAPHY:

ZELIGS, R. "Children's New Year's Resolutions." Reprinted from *Childhood Education*, 1964, *40*, 244–246.

ZELIGS, R. "Trends in Children's New Year's Resolutions." *Journal of Experimental Education*, 1957, 26(2), pp. 133–150.

CATEGORY 5

ENVIRONMENT

Group 5-a
Quality of Mothering

CHILD-REARING PRACTICES INTERVIEW

AUTHOR: J. R. Wittenborn

AGE: Mothers of kindergarten children and children who have finished the first grade

VARIABLE: Maternal attitudes toward child-rearing practices

TYPE OF MEASURE: Semistructured interview

SOURCE FROM WHICH THE MEASURE MAY BE OBTAINED: See Wittenborn (1956a)

DESCRIPTION OF MEASURE: The Child-Rearing Practices Inventory (CRPI) was part of a battery of tests developed to serve as an external criterion for the predictive validity of the Yale Development Examination of Infant Behavior. The CRPI is a lengthy semistructured interview conducted with the mother concerning her child-rearing practices. Behavioral factors investigated include feeding, independence, toilet training, aggression, cleanliness, sleeping, and sex training, with subfactors within each area. Investigations of the areas begin with a standard set of projective questions, though answers to specific items of behavior are sought in the course of the questioning. These individual bits of behavior are already listed so that the interviewer simply has to record their presence or absence as Yes or No. It is recommended that the interview continue until all the desired information is obtained but that specific questions be reserved until the end of the interview. The interview requires well-trained professional workers.

The area of feeding may be used to illustrate the subfactors checked, the prototypical introductory question used, and the specific items included (Wittenborn, 1956a):

Take the problem of feeding, what happened with ———'s feeding and eating? (1)
Was infant awakened for bottle feeding? (2) Was hungry infant required to wait
for a scheduled bottle feeding? (3) Was infant unable to take milk easily?

The answers to the items in turn have been subsumed under two broad clusters according to their psychological implications and positive intercorrelations. These clusters relate to both the child and parental behavior. The form includes the following for younger children: compulsivity, aggressiveness, phobia, dependence, and suppression of aggression. The cluster for older children is different, including aggressiveness, anxiety, the spoiled child syndrome, control, and dependence. The parental clusters of behavior include eagerness, unsympathetic, severe toilet training, punishment for aggression, overcontrolling (Wittenborn, 1956a). The number of items within each cluster range between seven and eleven, with the exception of dependence, which includes only four items. The range of item numbers for the parental clusters is similar. The items constituting each cluster are described in detail. Frequency of responses for each behavioral item under the major clusters is provided for a sample of kindergarten children (N = 100) and a group of 8-year-old children (N = 50).

RELIABILITY AND VALIDITY: For the children's clusters, split-half correlations corrected for attenuation ranged between .36 (suppression of aggression) to .71 (dependence) for the five major clusters of the younger group. For the five major clusters of the older group, the split-half reliability ranged between .64 (aggressiveness) and .78 (spoiled child and control). With parental clusters, the reliability range was between .33 (unsympathetic parent) and .82 (punishment for aggression). With regard to validity, the psychological meanings of the clusters were interpreted by agreement among social workers, psychologists, and pediatricians, as well as by pretesting.

BIBLIOGRAPHY:

WITTENBORN, J. R. "A Study of Adoptive Children: I. Interviews as a Source of Scores for Children and Their Homes." *Psychological Monographs: General and Applied,* 1956a, *70* (Whole No. 408).

WITTENBORN, J. R. "A Study of Adoptive Children: II. The Predictive Validity of the Yale Developmental Examination of Infant Behavior." *Psychological Monographs: General and Applied,* 1956b, *70* (Whole No. 409).

WITTENBORN, J. R. "A Study of Adoptive Children: III. Relationships Retain Some Aspects of Development and Some Aspects of Environment for Adoptive Children." *Psychological Monographs: General and Applied,* 1956c, *70* (Whole No. 410).

FIFTEEN RATING SCALES OF MATERNAL BEHAVIOR

AUTHOR: Marion Blank

AGE: Mothers of infants

VARIABLE: Quality of maternal care

TYPE OF MEASURE: Rating scale

SOURCE FROM WHICH THE MEASURE MAY BE OBTAINED: Marion Blank, 259-A Hoym Street, Ft. Lee, New Jersey 07024; price $3.00 per set

DESCRIPTION OF MEASURE: Hypothesizing that availability, rate, and manner of maternal stimulation affect the development of the child, Blank developed fifteen rating scales on maternal behavior, including emerging attitudes of the child, affective attitudes between child and mother, extensiveness of the child's contacts with people, quality of care given to the child, pressure on the child to achieve skills, and opportunity for growth and independence available to the child.

The scores designed for the Protectiveness Scale and their meanings are described as follows: *One*—extreme overprotectiveness and projected imagination of hazards; *Two*—mild restrictions and imagination absent; *Three*—maternal allowances for independence are made but no encouragement is given; *Four*—definite encouragement is given by mother who also protects baby from realistic dangers; *Five* —mother deliberately allows baby to cope with some dangers on his own, somewhat underprotective (Blank, 1964). In the Anxiety, Protectiveness and Flexibility scales the usual scoring is reversed.

RELIABILITY AND VALIDITY: The principal sample consisted of forty English infants in excellent health, rather evenly divided by sex classification, and living at home. The mothers of these infants represented a wide range of socioeconomic levels. In addition to this main group, there were also nine institutionalized infants.

Analysis of variance showed eight scales to be significantly related to infants' scores on the Griffiths Developmental Scale. Some concurrent validity can thus be claimed for these eight scales at least (competence, training in independence, attentiveness, flexibility, anxiety, protectiveness, contact with father, and physical freedom). The general lack of interrelationships among the scales suggest that the scales measure relatively independent components of mothering. Since the principle upon which the scales were based was confirmed they would appear to have construct validity. The reference here is to the major finding that maternal behavior can influence maturational processes, such as the development of sensory motor skills (Blank, 1964b).

BIBLIOGRAPHY:

BLANK, M. "The Mother's Role in Infant Development: A Review." *Journal of the American Academy of Child Psychiatry,* 1964a, *3,* 89–105.

BLANK, M. "Some Maternal Influences on Infants' Rates of Sensorimotor Development." *Journal of the American Academy of Child Psychiatry,* 1964b, *3,* 668, 687.

LEVY'S MATERNAL INTEREST INTERVIEW

AUTHOR: David M. Levy

AGE: Mothers

VARIABLE: Maternal behavior

TYPE OF MEASURE: Structured interview questionnaire

SOURCE FROM WHICH THE MEASURE MAY BE OBTAINED: See Levy (1958)

DESCRIPTION OF MEASURE: For the most part, the seven items of this questionnaire are presented orally to the mother. Complete directions for probing further, scoring the responses, variation, and administration are given by Levy (1958). The questions concern affection, interest, and desire for babies, and involve a self-rating of maternal attitudes. Replies are rated as highly maternal, above average, average, below average, or nonmaternal, and numerical values are assigned to the ratings. Some norms are available. The items of the questionnaire were derived originally from studies of mothers who referred their "behavior problem" children. Sample items from the interview follow:

Of the following games with dolls or other children, number in the order of your preference: hospital or doctor, school, house (other than play of being a mother), mother and baby, shopping, nurse, prince and princess, others. What role did you choose in these games?

Score: marked preference for mother-baby play and mother role, 5; mother and baby in first two choices, 4; in first four, 3; below fourth choice, 2; not chosen, 1.

As a child were you a neighborhood mother? Did you voluntarily take care of younger brothers or sisters? Elaborate.

In the interview elaborations are encouraged to get at the feeling involved, especially negative feelings when care of younger siblings was compulsory. Scores are limited to 2, 3, and 5: 2 when negative feelings are clear; 3 when the answer was a mixture of positive and negative feelings about care of siblings or there was no opportunity for care of either sibs or other children; 5 when it was clear that patient was a "neighborhood mother," a voluntary "baby sitter," loved mothering younger sibs.

RELIABILITY AND VALIDITY: Originally, the interview consisted of seventeen items (Levy, 1942). On the basis of questionnaire results from 385 college students and interviews with seventy-two women, the list was reduced to seven items. The criteria for revision have been elaborated by Levy (1958).

No data on the reliability of the interview questionnaire are reported, but at least two possible sources of validity exist. Levy (1942) found a correlation of .58 between maternal behavior and duration of menstrual flow (N = 385). Maternal behavior was derived from the responses to the questionnaire. Second, on a total

N = 15 mothers, the rank correlation coefficient between interview ratings of maternal interest and average scores based on direct observations of the mothers in the breast-feeding situation was .985 (Levy, 1958).

BIBLIOGRAPHY:

LEVY, D. M. "Psychosomatic Studies of Some Aspects of Maternal Behavior." *Psychosomatic Medicine*, 1942, *IV*, 223–227.

LEVY, D. M. *Behavioral Analysis: Analysis of Clinical Observations of Behavior as Applied to Mother-Newborn Relationships*. Springfield, Illinois: Charles C Thomas, 1958.

MATERNAL ATTITUDE TOWARD INDEPENDENCE TRAINING

AUTHOR: June E. Chance

AGE: Not stated; reading level is at least upper elementary

VARIABLE: Parental attitude toward independence training

TYPE OF MEASURE: Questionnaire

SOURCE FROM WHICH THE MEASURE MAY BE OBTAINED: See Chance (1965)

DESCRIPTION OF MEASURE: This measure is an adaptation and extension of Winterbottom's Independence Training Attitude Questionnaire, which asks the mother to tell at what age she would expect her child(ren) to be able to do certain things involving mastery, achievement, and self-help. (To Winterbottom's twenty items, Chance added twenty more.) Item analysis showed thirty-one of the forty items to be predictive of total score; these were used to obtain mother's score. The mother's score is a mean age of independence demands and is called MAIT X. (Chance also found for each mother the standard deviation of her responses around her own mean and treated this score as a measure of her flexibility of attitude. This score is referred to as MAIT.)

Examples of the items are given below. The parent indicates the age at which he would like his child to be able to do the activity indicated and also the range of ages from the earliest at which the parent would expect the child to do the activity to the age at which the parent begins to feel concerned if the child is not doing the activity.

To hold short conversations with grownup friends who come to visit the family.
To visit and to stay overnight with a playmate.
To straighten out most of his difficulties with other children without adult intervention.
To be interested in obtaining good grades in school.

RELIABILITY AND VALIDITY: None reported.

BIBLIOGRAPHY:

CHANCE, J. E. "Independence Training and Children's Achievement." Paper read at Society for Research in Child Development, Minneapolis, March, 1965.

CHANCE, J. E. "Internal Control of Reinforcements and the School Learning Process." Paper read at Society for Research in Child Development, Minneapolis, March, 1965.

WINTERBOTTOM, M. R. "The Relation of Need for Achievement to Learning Experiences in Independence and Mastery." In J. W. Atkinson (Ed.), *Motives in Fantasy, Action, and Society*. Princeton, N.J.: Van Nostrand, 1958.

MATERNAL CARE CHECKLIST

AUTHOR: Harriet Rheingold

AGE: Infancy

VARIABLE: Maternal care, mothering

TYPE OF MEASURE: Observation schedule

SOURCE FROM WHICH THE MEASURE MAY BE OBTAINED: See Rheingold (1960)

DESCRIPTION OF MEASURE: This measure is designed to measure maternal care by observing the operations the mother performs in caring for the infant. The method employs the technique of time-sampling maternal care as it occurs in its natural setting. A checklist based on observation and trial is used, consisting of forty-two items, thirty of which are concerned with mother activities and twelve with infant activities. Six of the mothering activities deal with the location of the child in his environment, four with the number of people in his room, and four with the number of others within 6 feet of him. The other sixteen items are more closely related to mothering, and include "caretaking" (someone is near the subject doing something for him), "N of caretakers" (number of different caretakers in an eight-hour period), "talks" (caretaker talks to anyone within earshot of the subject, including the subject), and "plays" (caretaker plays with child *or* imitates toy play).

The score is the incidence of each item during a specific time period.

RELIABILITY AND VALIDITY: The median percentage of interobserver agreement in scoring all items was 89.8, with a range of 16.7 to 100. Observer agreement was also measured by correlating the frequencies obtained for each item by different observers. The median r was .97, range .35 to 1.00.

Evidence on validity is given by Rheingold's comparison of the maternal care given to five home infants and five infants in an institution. Significant differences were found on twenty-three of the forty-two items. The differences were in what most child researchers would consider the expected direction.

BIBLIOGRAPHY:

RHEINGOLD, H. L. "The Measurement of Maternal Care." *Child Development*, 1960, *31*, 565–575.

MATERNAL VALUES QUESTIONNAIRE

AUTHOR: Henrietta Cox

AGE: Parents

VARIABLE: Maternal values

TYPE OF MEASURE: Likert-type scale, forced-choice scale, and ranked traits

SOURCE FROM WHICH THE MEASURE MAY BE OBTAINED: See Cox (1964)

DESCRIPTION OF MEASURE: This is a measuring instrument with three independent parts: a Likert-type scale, a forced-choice scale, and a list of traits to be ranked. The Likert-type scale consists of five subscales with names and numbers of items in each scale as follows: emotional tone (demonstrativeness or nondemonstrativeness of affection) (six items); autonomy-control of the child's behavior (six items); achievement-orientation in childhood and adult life (six items); mastery of powerlessness over the environment (six items); conceptions of human nature (trust or distrust in interpersonal relations) (six items); and discipline practice (not intended to constitute a scale) (five items). In addition, three items relating to marital adjustment are included, but are not intended to constitute a scale. The items are taken from various other existing scales and combined into new ones as noted above. The subject marks each item by circling either SA (strongly agree), A (agree), D (disagree), or SD (strongly disagree). Examples of items are given below.

Children should be allowed to learn through their own experience rather than being told what to do all the time.

Mothers ought to punish children who misbehave by taking away something they like.

A child should be taught from infancy to take the greatest pride in doing things well.

Parents ought to show their children they love them by hugging, kissing, and playing with them often.

Nowadays the wise parent will teach the child to live for today and let tomorrow take care of itself.

Children should learn that most people can be trusted.

Part II, the forced-choice scale, parallels the Likert scale in content. This scale is given in the appendix of Cox's thesis. A trait list constituted the third scale. These latter two measures are not used in Cox's thesis, so no data on reliability or validity are given for them.

RELIABILITY AND VALIDITY: Each of the five scales discriminated significantly among social classes, but none of the scales discriminate among races or religion, although some of the individual items do. Each of the thirty items (five scales, six items each) in the total scale is analyzed for discriminability between social classes, races, and religions.

BIBLIOGRAPHY:

cox, h. s. "Social Classes as Subcultures: Variations in Value-Orientations in Selected Areas of Mother-Child Behavior." Unpublished Master Thesis. Washington University, St. Louis, Missouri, June, 1964.

MOTHER-CHILD INTERACTION METHOD SCALE

AUTHOR: Lawrence E. Dameron

AGE: Mothers of young preschool children

VARIABLE: Child-rearing practices

TYPE OF MEASURE: Guided interview

SOURCE FROM WHICH THE MEASURE MAY BE OBTAINED: See Dameron (1955)

DESCRIPTION OF MEASURE: The Mother-Child Interaction Method is a guided interview made up of twenty-five items concerned with self-restraint by the child; seven items involving reward-punishment practices by the mother; and information about the family. The items are selected empirically from a pilot study and theoretically from a presumptive basis so that they are characteristic of the culture and cover a wide range of the child's cultural contacts, especially with his mother. Examples of the items used are: not crying, not going out of bounds; not lying (excluding tall tales); not being physically aggressive to adults—hitting, biting, kicking, spitting, and the like as aggressive acts; not taking things belonging to others; not coming to the table with dirty hands and face.

In the guided interview with the mother, three kinds of information are sought for each item: *the expectancy of the mother* in which she is questioned concerning behavior the child ought to control; *the achievement of the child* in which she is queried regarding the actual behavior level of the child; and *training practices* by the parents. In this last area, the mother is asked how she handled training the child. She is asked what she did specifically, and (after responding) if she did anything else. The interview is guided along four major inquiries relating to maternal expectations for control, actual achievement by the child, specific training practices, and questions on training practices of a general nature.

The score within the first three major dimensions of maternal behavior mentioned above is based on counting many specific instances of behavior. For example, in the area of general practices a total number of times physical punishment is mentioned by the mother in connection with the twenty-five items is regarded as a "score." In addition, the statements of the mothers are reduced to appropriate categories in terms of whether or not the item is expected; whether or not control has been achieved; and whether or not physical punishment is used. Other categories are answer unclear (symbolized AU); and, the child has not shown such behavior as yet (symbolized DKH, "he doesn't know how to do it yet").

RELIABILITY AND VALIDITY: Ninety mothers were interviewed, each being questioned about one child who at the time of the interview was between the third and fourth birthdays. All families were within the Chicago city limits and were white native-born Protestants. The social classes represented were slanted intentionally in terms of upper-middle and lower-lower.

Dameron has presented no statistics on the reliability of the maternal responses, but it could be derived readily because of the objectivity of the scoring system. In contrast, several findings involving the use of the scale are in accordance with the literature and theoretical expectations, providing evidence of construct validity for the scale. (1) The rank-difference correlation between items most demanded by mothers and items achieved was .936. (2) The product-moment correlation between expectancy and age was .51 and significant beyond the .01 level. (3) Several relationships between social class and the results were as expected: The middle classes showed significantly higher levels of expectations. The scores of the lower-lower groups on the use of physical punishment were statistically significant in the direction of more magnitude than the results from the middle-class mothers. (4) Middle classes had a significantly higher level of achievement.

BIBLIOGRAPHY:

DAMERON, L. E. "Mother-Child Interaction in the Development of Self-Restraint." *Journal of Genetic Psychology*, 1955, *86,* 289–308.

A SCALE TO MEASURE SOCIAL CLASS DIFFERENCES IN MATERNAL ATTITUDES

AUTHORS: Margaret C. L. Gildea, Herbert R. Domke, Ivan N. Mensh, A. D. Buchmueller, John C. Glidewell, and Mildren B. Kantor

AGE: Mothers of elementary school children

VARIABLE: Maternal attitudes

TYPE OF MEASURE: Questionnaire

SOURCE FROM WHICH THE MEASURE MAY BE OBTAINED: See Gildea, et al. (1958)

DESCRIPTION OF MEASURE: The Scale to Measure Social Differences in Maternal Attitudes consists of seventeen items with which the parents are to indicate agreement or disagreement. All items are indicators of negative maternal attitudes. As examples, two items are given below:

Children have more fun than grown-ups do.
It is hard to know when to make a rule and stick by it.

These items are derived from a pilot study of eighty items identical with Shoben's scale on maternal attitudes (1949). The items deal with such areas as mother's attitude toward discipline and conformity; the comfort and self-confidence or discomfort in the mother-child roles; the ability to handle sexual play or ideas; parental rejection; and maturity levels.

Although the authors are not explicit about the scoring system, the score is evidently the number of times the respondent indicates agreement with the items.

RELIABILITY AND VALIDITY: This seventeen-item attitude schedule was administered to a total sample of 823 third-grade mothers of three criterion groups of children: a well-adjusted group that showed no evidence of disturbance, a group that showed mild emotional disturbance but not of a sufficient degree to necessitate referral to a child guidance clinic, and a group that had been referred to a child guidance clinic. Though the maternal answers did not differentiate between criterion groups, eight of the seventeen items were found to differentiate significantly on the basis of social class at the .05 level of probability or better in chi-square tests. The authors conclude that the mother who feels involved or responsible and also feels able to change things is likely to have the best adjusted child. On the other hand, the mother who does not feel involved or responsible and feels unable to change things is likely to have the least adjusted child.

No reliability data are reported.

BIBLIOGRAPHY:

GILDEA, M. C. L., DOMKE, H. R., MENSH, I. N., BUCHMUELLER, A. D., GLIDEWELL, J. C., and KANTOR, M. B. "Community Mental Health Research: Findings after Three Years." *American Journal of Psychiatry,* 1958, *114,* 970–976.

SHOBEN, E. J., JR. "The Assessment of Parental Attitudes in Relation to Child Adjustment." *Genetic Psychology Monographs,* 1949, *39,* 101–140.

SHOBEN'S PARENT-ATTITUDE SURVEY

AUTHOR: Edward Joseph Shoben, Jr.

AGE: Mothers of elementary school-aged children

VARIABLE: Maternal attitudes

TYPE OF MEASURE: Likert-type scale

SOURCE FROM WHICH THE MEASURE MAY BE OBTAINED: See Shoben (1949)

DESCRIPTION OF MEASURE: The Shoben scale of parental attitudes consists of eighty-five items that differentiate between problem and nonproblem parents at statistically significant levels. Items are weighted in accordance with discrimination of each of four response categories: strongly agree, mildly agree, mildly disagree, and strongly disagree. The items are subsumed under four variables (ignoring, possessive, dominant, and miscellaneous or unclassified). Examples of items from each variable are given below:

Ignoring	A child should be seen and not heard.
Possessive	Parents should sacrifice everything for their children.
Dominating	Children need some of the natural meanness taken out of them.
Unclassified	Children usually know ahead of time whether or not parents will punish them for their actions.

RELIABILITY AND VALIDITY: The original scale was administered to 100 white urban mothers subdivided into two equal groups—mothers of problem children and mothers of nonproblem children. The three criteria used to identify problem children are the presence of maternal complaints, indication of trouble with the law, and evidence of clinical help. The two groups were fairly equivalent with the exception of marital stability, education, and age. On these variables, the mothers of nonproblem children differed sharply from those with problem offspring. Shoben provides the ranges, means, and standard deviations for the total sample and its problem and nonproblem halves.

The reliability of the survey was determined by the split-half method and corrected by the Spearman-Brown formula. The coefficients derived by this method range between .84 for the Ignoring Scale to .95 for the Total Scale. Evidence of validity comes in several forms. First, in classifying the items according to the categories dominant, possessive, ignoring, and miscellaneous, five sophisticated judges were able to reach agreement levels ranging between 85 and 88 per cent, suggesting content validity. When twenty mothers of problem children and twenty mothers of nonproblem children were tested, the validity coefficients were as follows: total scale, .769; dominant, .23; possessive, .721; and ignoring, .624.

Content validity was indicated by the marked extent to which well-trained clinicians were able to agree on the responses of an "ideal" parent.

BIBLIOGRAPHY:

SHOBEN, E. J., JR. "The Assessment of Parental Attitudes in Relation to Child Adjustment." *Genetic Psychology Monographs*, 1949, *39*, 101–140.

TEACHERS' RATING SCALE OF PARENTAL NURTURANCE-CONTROL

AUTHOR: Walter Emmerich

AGE: Mothers of preschool children

VARIABLE: Nurturance-control toward child by mother

TYPE OF MEASURE: Rating scale

SOURCE FROM WHICH THE MEASURE MAY BE OBTAINED: See Emmerich (1959)

DESCRIPTION OF MEASURE: The Teachers' Rating Scale of Parental Nurturance-Control includes two subscales—a scale for rating the mother's nurturance toward the child when he was dependent on her (as the child's "wanting the mother to play with him") and a scale rating the mother's control of the child when he was deviant (as the child's "refusing to go home and continuing to play"). In both cases, the scores range from +3.0 to −3.0. Examples from these subscales are strong nurturance for a child when he is dependent on the mother and strong maternal control when a child is deviant:

+3 Strong Nurturance. *Mother usually facilitates child's accomplishment of a goal to a greater extent than the child requested; for example, mother volunteers to play with the child in several activities.*

−3 Strong Control. *Mother usually strongly interferes with child's goal, for example, scolds or physically punishes the child for making the request.*

RELIABILITY AND VALIDITY: The teachers' ratings consisted of two subscales —the mother's nurturance-control toward the child when he is dependent and the same maternal behavior when he is deviant. The respective teacher agreement reliabilities for these subscales were +.62 and +.41. The correlation between the sum of the teachers' scores on the two subscales with the sum of the mother's nurturance-control scales for the first five questionnaire items was +.51 (p < .01).

BIBLIOGRAPHY:

EMMERICH, W. "Parent Identification in Young Children." *Genetic Psychology Monographs,* 1959, *60,* 257–308.

Group 5-b

Child-Rearing Practices

CHILDREN'S RESPONSIBILITY INVENTORY (Parental Form)

AUTHORS: James Walters, Frances Ireland Stromberg, and Geraldine Lonian

AGE: Parents

VARIABLE: Parental perceptions of children's responsibility for behavior

TYPE OF MEASURE: Questionnaire

SOURCE FROM WHICH THE MEASURE MAY BE OBTAINED: See Walters, et al. (1957)

DESCRIPTION OF MEASURE: On this inventory, parents are requested to indicate the earliest age at which children could assume responsibility for independence of behavior in fifty activities in the areas of self-care and social skill. The scoring system followed in the original design is to determine the median ages for which children could assume responsibility for various acts as indicated by responses of adults. These normative data apply to separate sex groups. The samples for these data included 210 mothers of Negro children in the first grade, 170 mothers of white children in the same grade, and eighty-one single white women enrolled in a university. As an aid in developing norms for evaluating the responses of the parents and students, nineteen experts in child development were also asked to provide the age level they considered most favorable for expecting children to assume the responsibility depicted in each of the fifty items. Examples of the responsibilities adults are asked to rate follow (Walters, et al., 1957):

Washing his hands before each meal without being reminded.
Wiping his nose when needed without being reminded.
Polishing his shoes without adult supervision.
Bathing himself with no adult help after he has been reminded to do so.

RELIABILITY AND VALIDITY: Evidence for reliability comes from three sources of test-retest correlations. The agreements pertained to responses by subsamples of twenty-nine white mothers, twenty-two university students, and twenty-five Negro mothers. The respective agreements were 76 per cent (three-week interval), 71 per cent (one-week interval), and 57 per cent (three-week interval). The investigators rated responses as reflecting disagreement if they differed by more than one year from the initial response.

The authors present evidence for content validity. Six expert judges rated the suitability of an original pool of 150 items in terms of several specific questions (for example, is the question significant?). The only items retained for the final pool are those found acceptable by five of the six judges (Walters et al., 1957).

BIBLIOGRAPHY:

MITTON, B. L., and HARRIS, D. B. "The Development of Responsibility in Children." *Elementary School Journal*, 1954, *LIV*, 268–277.

WALTERS, J., STROMBERG, F. I., and LONIAN, G. "Perceptions Concerning Development of Responsibility in Young Children." *Elementary School Journal*, 1957, *57*, 209–216.

CONDITIONS OF CHILD REARING

AUTHOR: J. R. Wittenborn

AGE: Parents of kindergarten children and those who have passed the first grade

VARIABLE: General atmosphere of home

TYPE OF MEASURE: Semistructured interview

SOURCE FROM WHICH THE MEASURE MAY BE OBTAINED: See Wittenborn (1956a)

DESCRIPTION OF MEASURE: The Conditions of Child Rearing scale consists of a set of interview items asked of the mother about the general organization of the home—its activities, values, recreations, and general living pattern. Though the exact approach to use in administering the twenty-six items making up this scale is not altogether clear, the content of the interview is described in detail. Moreover, the hierarchal desirability of the items is evident and specified in detail, as the example on family incompatibility illustrates:

(a) *The parents have contemplated divorce or trial separation. (b) There is evidence of deep incompatibility between parents but not sufficient to lead to a breakdown of the home. (c) There are minor differences of interest and opinion between parents but they are basically compatible. (d) The parents are harmonious and compatible.*

The CCR contributes items to clusters of behavior. With the younger group of children, the scale partially contributes items to the parental behavioral clusters of ambition, harmonious family relationships, no ambition, rejection, incompatibility, and overprotectiveness. The same clusters apply to the older group. The score for each cluster is the number of component bits of information appearing in the interview record for each child. The scoring is facilitated by full specification of the items within each cluster. Because of the lack of a specific format in asking the questions and its original use by trained workers only, proper application of the scale probably requires some skills and knowledge in interviewing techniques.

RELIABILITY AND VALIDITY: With the younger age group, corrected split-half reliabilities for the clusters ranged between .58 (harmonious family relationship) to .78 (ambition). With the older age group, the range was from .52 (incompatibility) to .77 (ambition). Validity may be assumed from the lack of correlation between clusters, the internal consistency for each cluster marked by positive intercorrelations between items, the item analysis in a pretesting period, and the content validity suggested by grouping items within a cluster with similar behavioral implications as determined by agreement among highly trained mental health workers.

BIBLIOGRAPHY:

WITTENBORN, J. R. "A Study of Adoptive Children: I. Interviews as a Source of Scores for Children and Their Homes." *Psychological Monographs: General and Applied,* 1956a, *70* (Whole No. 408).

WITTENBORN, J. R. "A Study of Adoptive Children: II. The Predictive Validity of the Yale Developmental Examination of Infant Behavior." *Psychological Monographs: General and Applied,* 1956b, *70* (Whole No. 409).

WITTENBORN, J. R. "A Study of Adoptive Children: III. Relationships Retain Some Aspects of Development and Some Aspects of Environment for Adoptive Children." *Psychological Monograph: General and Applied,* 1956c, *70* (Whole No. 410).

EDUCATIONAL ATTITUDE SURVEY

AUTHORS: Roberta M. Bear, Robert H. Hess, and Virginia C. Shipman

AGE: Parents

VARIABLE: Attitude toward school

TYPE OF MEASURE: Likert-type scale

SOURCE FROM WHICH THE MEASURE MAY BE OBTAINED: See Bear, Hess, and Shipman (1966)

DESCRIPTION OF MEASURE: The Educational Attitude Survey (EAS) is a twenty-seven-item Likert-type scale in which mothers answer items about their orientation toward education and the public school system. In its present form, the scale is administered individually to mothers who answer the items as a self-administered test in terms of a five-point scale from strongly agree (score of 1), to a neutral position (don't know, score of 3), to strongly disagree (score of 5). A factor analysis of the items reveals six factor clusters as follows: ES1: futility in dealing with school authorities; ES2: conservatism in school practices; ES3: improvement through formal education; ES4: optimistic and positive attitudes to school; ES5: defensiveness about inadequate formal education; and ES6: negative attitude about public education. Sample items from each factor are given below.

Most children have to be made to learn [ES1].
Most teachers do not want to be bothered by parents coming to see them [ES2].
Most kids who can do the work are able to get to college if they really want to [ES3].
The best way to improve the schools is to integrate them [ES4].
In school there are more important things than getting good grades [ES5].
The classrooms are overcrowded [ES6].

In each case, a low score represents agreement with the central theme of the factor, a high score disagreement. The EAS score is computed by summing the raw scores for the items within each cluster.

RELIABILITY AND VALIDITY: The statistics reported below are based on 163 pairs of Negro nonworking mothers and their 4-year-old children. Within this total sample, the subsamples were rather evenly divided into four socioeconomic groups: upper-middle, upper-lower, and two lower-lower classes. With the exception of the ADC group in the lower-lower classification, the families were intact. All groups had approximately the same number of children of either sex. Intercorrelations among the items within factors range from .368 to .719.

Validity is evidenced in two ways. First, with the exception of ES6, the between-group differences on the EAS are statistically significant in the predicted direction in the majority of cases. Secondly, several of the factors on the EAS (ES1, ES2, ES3, and ES6) are related to the child's general work habits in scholastic tasks and to his cognitive skills. For example, ES3, optimistic striving, is related highly to the child's unwillingness to continue a difficult task. The authors interpret this to mean that mothers considering formal education as the only way of improving one's lot are likely to have children who give up readily.

BIBLIOGRAPHY:

BEAR, R. M., HESS, R. D., and SHIPMAN, V. C. "Social Class Differences in Maternal Attitudes toward School and the Consequence for Cognitive Development in the Young Child." Paper presented at American Educational Research Association, February 19, 1966, Chicago, Illinois.

FARM FAMILY SOCIOECONOMIC STATUS SCALE
(Short Form)

AUTHOR: William H. Sewell

AGE: Families or households, particularly rural ones

VARIABLE: Socioeconomic status

TYPE OF MEASURE: Rating scale

SOURCE FROM WHICH THE MEASURE MAY BE OBTAINED: See Sewell (1943b)

DESCRIPTION OF MEASURE: The Sewell Socioeconomic Scale (Short Form) consists of fourteen questions dealing with material possessions (six items), cultural criteria (six items), and social participation (two items). Two illustrative items (with scores) follow:

Construction of house: Brick, stucco, etc., or painted frame (5); unpainted frame or other (3).

Room-person ratio: numbers of rooms; number of persons. Ratio below 1.00 (3); 1.00–1.99 (5); 2.00 and up (7).

As the illustrative items indicate, the scoring is rather obvious in that each item checked has a certain score. The total score then constitutes the sum of the scores for the individual items checked.

According to Sewell, the scale can be administered accurately in approximately five minutes by a relatively well-trained interviewer. Moreover, the scale can even be administered by interviewing a child or others away from home. Sewell has prepared such a form and is willing to forward it to interested parties (1943b).

RELIABILITY AND VALIDITY: Tentative percentile norms were based on 1062 cases in Oklahoma, 454 in Kansas, and 648 in Louisiana. According to Sewell, the cases in Oklahoma were quite representative of the rural farm population within that state, while the sampling in the latter two states did not follow such strict sampling procedure. Detailed discussions of the norms for the original and longer scale have also been provided by Sewell (1942, 1943a).

Reliability of the test rests on split-half coefficients between odd and even items of the scale. The correlation coefficients were .81, .81, and .87 for Oklahoma, Louisiana, and Kansas respectively (Sewell, 1943b).

Validity rests on the high correlation of test results obtained on the short form with those on the longer and original form. The correlation coefficients were based on comparisons between new scores from the brief scale and the original scores on the longer scales. In both instances, the same families were used. The resulting coefficients range from .94 to .95 for the three states.

BIBLIOGRAPHY:

SEWELL, W. H. "The Development of a Sociometric Scale." *Sociometry,* 1942, *V,* 294–297.

SEWELL, W. H. "The Restandardization of a Sociometric Scale." *Social Forces,* 1943a, *21,* 302–311.

SEWELL, W. H. "A Short Form of the Farm Family Socio-Economic Status Scale." *Rural Sociology,* 1943b, *81,* 161–170.

HOME INDEX INVENTORY

AUTHOR: Harrison G. Gough

AGE: Intermediate and secondary school children

VARIABLE: Social class status

TYPE OF MEASURE: Questionnaire

SOURCE FROM WHICH THE MEASURE MAY BE OBTAINED: See Gough (1949)

DESCRIPTION OF MEASURE: The twenty-one-item Home Index Inventory is practically self-administering, can be quickly completed, speedily scored, and preserves to a large extent the precision of the longer, more complex instruments. The scale is based largely on the Sims Score Cards and the American Home Scale, with the addition of certain original items. Twenty-one items are answered by the examinee in terms of yes or no. The items relate to material possessions in the home, as well as to the activities of the parents and the children.

The score is the number of "yes" responses on the first twenty items plus the score (0–2) on item 21. The author cautions that use of the scale probably should be restricted to persons below the age of 21. Despite the limitations of the index, the author believes that the scale can be administered to upper elementary school children. The principal advantages that Gough perceives this scale to have over the longer, more comprehensive, social status inventories include ease of administration, simplicity in scoring, and accuracy and validity despite the considerably shorter length of the scale.

RELIABILITY AND VALIDITY: The test-retest reliability coefficient based on a sample of fifty-five college students was .989. The Kuder-Richardson coefficient for 252 high school students was .74; this represents a minimum estimate of the scale's internal consistency (Gough, 1949). The intercorrelations of the Home Index with other variables were as follows: .65 with father's occupation; .82 with the Sims Score Cards; and .88 with the American Home Scale. Gough (1949) found that the Home Index had the heaviest loadings of all the measures on the social class status factor.

BIBLIOGRAPHY:

GOUGH, H. G. "A Short Social Status Inventory." *Journal of Educational Psychology,* 1949, *40,* 52–56.

HOME RATING SCALE

AUTHOR: J. R. Wittenborn

AGE: Kindergarten and those who have passed the first grade

VARIABLE: General atmosphere of home

TYPE OF MEASURE: Rating scale

SOURCE FROM WHICH THE MEASURE MAY BE OBTAINED: See Wittenborn (1956a)

DESCRIPTION OF MEASURE: The HRS is part of a battery of tests developed as an external criterion for the predictive validity of the Yale Developmental Examination of Infant Behavior. The scale, which is completed by a professional employee such as a social worker subsequent to a home visit, consists of nine factors with three options as choices for responses for each area. The nine factors include: physical plant, outdoor play space, maintenance of home, ownership of home, neatness, stability of residence, contacts with other children, sociability (visitors), and family group recreation. the options for rating the physical plant of the home are: Home is in every way sufficient for meeting the child's physical needs with respect to warmth, quiet, cleanliness, toilet facility, ventilation, sunlight, and freedom from vermin and hazards; home is fairly sufficient for meeting physical needs but may be lacking in one or two respects; and home is lacking in many requisites for meeting physical needs of child (Wittenborn, 1956a).

Together with the Conditions of Child-Rearing and the Multiple Rating Scale, the HRS provides a basis for forming cluster scores descriptive of the general atmosphere in the home.

RELIABILITY AND VALIDITY: The statistics below on corrected split-half reliabilities refer to clusters of behavior to which the Multiple Rating Scale, the Conditions of Child Rearing Scale, and the Home Rating Scale all contribute items. Consequently, these data only refer to the concurrent use of all the scales. The corrected split-half reliability coefficients for the younger and older age groups respectively were as follows: .73 and .52 for parental incompatibility, .78 and .77 for parental ambition, and .58 and .60 for harmonious family relationships. The validating support for the clusters rests on internal consistency, a lack of relationships between clusters, pretesting, and a consensus of professional workers on the homogeneous behavioral meanings of various clusters of items (Wittenborn, 1956a).

BIBLIOGRAPHY:

WITTENBORN, J. R. "A Study of Adoptive Children: I. Interviews as a Source of Scores for Children and Their Homes." *Psychological Monographs: General and Applied,* 1956a, *70* (Whole No. 408).

WITTENBORN, J. R. "A Study of Adoptive Children: II. The Predictive Validity of the Yale Developmental Examination of Infant Behavior." *Psychological Monographs: General and Applied,* 1956b, *70* (Whole No. 409).

WITTENBORN, J. R. "A Study of Adopted Children: III. Relationships Retain Some Aspects of Development and Some Aspects of Environment for Adoptive Children." *Psychological Monographs: General and Applied,* 1956c, *70* (Whole No. 410).

INDEX OF PARENTAL DISSATISFACTION WITH SOCIAL-EMOTIONAL BEHAVIOR

AUTHORS: Bernard Farber and William C. Jenné

AGE: 11 to 16

VARIABLE: Parental satisfaction-dissatisfaction

TYPE OF MEASURE: Questionnaire

SOURCE FROM WHICH THE MEASURE MAY BE OBTAINED: See Farber and Jenné (1963)

DESCRIPTION OF MEASURE: The social-emotional index measures interactional patterns in the family that express a concern for other members. The separate scales for each parent consist of seven items with the highest factor loadings from an original test of twenty-one items. The items from the father's scale, for example, are as follows (Farber and Jenné, 1963):

Show affection toward father (highest loading) [.71]
Show affection toward mother [.71]
Be friendly to people [.61]
Trust people [.53]
Feel sorry for those in trouble [.44]
Show feelings toward friends [.40]
Show care in picking out friends [.36]

Details are provided on all the items selected to represent the factors, the procedure for determining the weighted factor scores, and the range of the weighted scores (Farber and Jenné, 1963).

Four scores are obtained on the child's perception of mother's and father's satisfaction and the perception of satisfaction by each parent for the child's behavior.

RELIABILITY AND VALIDITY: In the item-selection process, three sociologists chose twenty-one items from fifty activities because they judged them to be related to social-emotional behavior. The final scale was derived from factor analysis. In the final selection of items only those with loadings of .36 or more were retained. The factor loadings ranged between .36 to .71 on the father's scale and .36 to .69 on the mother's scale.

BIBLIOGRAPHY:

FARBER, B., and JENNÉ, W. C. "Family Organization and Parent-Child Communications." *Monographs of the Society for Research in Child Development,* 1963, *28* (Whole Monograph, No. 7).

INDICES OF LEVEL OF PARENTS' DISSATISFACTION AND CHILD'S PERCEPTION OF PARENTS' DISSATISFACTION WITH CHILD'S BEHAVIOR

AUTHORS: Bernard Farber and William C. Jenné

AGE: 11 to 16

VARIABLE: Communication

TYPE OF MEASURE: Questionnaire

SOURCE FROM WHICH THE MEASURE MAY BE OBTAINED: See Farber and Jenné (1963)

DESCRIPTION OF MEASURE: This measure constitutes a subscale of the Index of Effectiveness of Parent-Child Communication. Each parent is requested to check an answer—much less, a little less, as he does now, a little more, much more, does not apply—for fifty activities as follows (Farber and Jenné, 1963):

I wish my son would do this activity: think about school work; help around the house; listen to radio and TV programs; play outdoor games such as baseball, tennis, etc.; visit his friends.

The child is also requested to check each statement in the same manner but the prefatory statement reads "My father (or mother) wishes that I would do this activity."

The index of level of parents' dissatisfaction with the child's behavior is the ratio of items on which the parent expresses dissatisfaction to the total number of acceptable responses. The index of the Child's Perception of Parents' Dissatisfaction with Child's Behavior is calculated in a similar fashion, the score being the ratio of the items on which the child perceives parental dissatisfaction to the total number of acceptable responses. On these scales, the total number of acceptable responses is equal to all of the responses (N = 50) less the number of items in which either the parent or the child does not respond or gives conflicting responses. In both indices, the values can theoretically range between .00 to 1.00, with the higher value being in the direction of dissatisfaction.

RELIABILITY AND VALIDITY: The reproducibility coefficients of the scale for instrumental behavior (fourteen items) ranged between .93 to .97. These coefficients applied to the child's perception of parents' dissatisfaction and the parents' dissatisfaction with child's behavior in three different samples. Hence, the unidimensionality of the scale was demonstrated empirically. On the scale for social-emotional items, seven items with the highest factor loading were derived for the child's perception of father's dissatisfaction and for child's perception of mother's dissatisfaction. The factor loading ranged between .36 to .71 on father's dissatisfaction and between .36 and .69 on mother's dissatisfaction. The calculation of these factor scores has been described in full (Farber and Jenné, 1963).

BIBLIOGRAPHY:

FARBER, B., and JENNÉ, W. C. "Family Organization and Parent-Child Communications." *Monographs of the Society for Research in Child Development,* 1963, *28* (Whole Monograph, No. 7).

MINNESOTA SCALE OF PARENTS' OPINIONS

AUTHOR: Institute of Child Welfare, University of Minnesota

AGE: Parents

VARIABLE: Parental attitudes to child-rearing practices

TYPE OF MEASURE: Rating scale

SOURCE FROM WHICH THE MEASURE MAY BE OBTAINED: A more detailed form of this paper (or extended version, or material supplementary to this article) has been deposited as Document Number 5899 with the ADI Auxiliary Publications Project, Photoduplication Service, Library of Congress, Washington, D.C. 20540. A copy may be secured by citing the document number and by remitting $2.50 for photoprints, or $1.75 for 35 mm. microfilm. Advance payment is required. Make checks or money orders payable to Chief, Photoduplication Service, Library of Congress.

DESCRIPTION OF MEASURE: According to Clifford (1959), this measure consists of two subscales, one relating to home practices, the other to traits the mother desires in children. Each subscale consists of forty items, with each item having a weighted response. Actual examination of the scale reveals three subscales, as follows: Part A: whole practices, sixty items; Part B: desirable traits, forty items; Part C: problem behavior, fifty items.

The scale, which can be self-administered, consists of Likert-type items with five options per answer to each item. Directions for answering are given in full and the responses are recorded on the scale itself. Examples of items from each part are given below. From Part A—Home Practices:

Children under 5 years are too young to go on errands within the home block. *(1) strongly agree, (2) agree, (3) undecided, (4) disagree, (5) strongly disagree.*
A child from 6 to 10 years old should have the experience of spending several days away from home unaccompanied by his parents. *(5) strongly agree, (4) agree, (3) undecided, (2) disagree, (1) strongly disagree.*

From Part B—Desirable Traits:

The child prefers doing things with "grown-ups" rather than with children. *(1) Very desirable, (2) desirable, (3) indifferent, (4) undesirable, (5) very undesirable.*
This child enjoys entertaining and amusing people. *(1) Very desirable, (2) desirable, (3) indifferent, (4) undesirable, (5) very undesirable.*

From Part C—Problem Behavior:

If a child of 9 habitually dallies so that he is a few minutes late for meals, school, etc., it is of *(1) no importance, (2) slight, (3) some, (4) great, (5) extreme importance.*
If a child of 9 habitually breaks or defaces whatever he is playing or working with,

it is of *(1)* *no importance,* *(2)* *slight,* *(3)* *some,* *(4)* *great,* *(5)* *extreme impor-tance.*

RELIABILITY AND VALIDITY: Though precise statistical data are lacking in the publication (Clifford, 1959), some findings are available. The scores the parents have chosen at different age levels are quite similar; thus, the mean scales between parents of children at ages 3, 6, and 9 were not statistically different. Similarly, the mean ratings assigned to the individual items by parents of children at different ages were not significantly different. In the majority of cases, correlations between total group scores on the scale and the frequency of disciplinary acts reported by the parents are not statistically significant, although two correlations (.55 and .63) obtained for this relationship were significant, when the subjects were 9-year-old boys.

BIBLIOGRAPHY:

CLIFFORD, E. "Discipline in the Home: A Controlled Observation Study of Parental Practices." *Journal of Genetic Psychology,* 1959, *95,* 45–82.

MULTIPLE RATING SCALE

AUTHOR: J. R. Wittenborn

AGE: Parents of kindergarten children and those who have passed the first grade

VARIABLE: General atmosphere of home

TYPE OF MEASURE: Rating scale

SOURCE FROM WHICH THE MEASURE MAY BE OBTAINED: See Wittenborn (1956a)

DESCRIPTION OF MEASURE: The MRS deals with items descriptive of many important facets of the home other than child rearing per se. The three measures by Wittenborn—Conditions of Child Rearing, Multiple Rating Scale, and Home Rating Scale—measure the general atmosphere in the home. The seven behavioral variables, which include acceptance of child, solicitousness toward the child, affectionateness of mother, accelerational attempt, flexibility of parents' expectations, mother's enjoyment of child, mother's reaction to child, are rated by both the social worker who visits the home of the adoptive parents and the psychologist who interviews the mothers. The seven items of the scale contribute to the behavioral clusters of parental ambition (one item), harmonious family relationship (two items), and rejection of the child (four items). A sample item from the scale—acceptance of child—follows:

a. *Parents completely accept the adoptive child as their own. They note with pleasure physical or behavioral similarities between the child and members of the adoptive family.*

b. *Parents do not wholeheartedly accept the adoptive child as their own. They may observe a few faults of the child or respects in which he compares unfavorably with family.*

c. *Parents do not accept the adoptive child as their own. They regret the adoption and would, at one time, have liked to have annulled it if possible.*

Judicious use of this scale is necessary because of the lack of a specific format for asking the questions. It seems to require mental health workers with interviewing skills.

RELIABILITY AND VALIDITY: The corrected split-half reliabilities for the three clusters with the younger and older samples respectively were .78 and .77 for ambition (total of eleven items in cluster), .58 and .60 for rejection (total of seven items), and .58 and .60 for harmonious family relationship (total of ten items). Again, as in the other scales by Wittenborn, validating evidence lies in intercorrelations of items within a cluster, low correlations between clusters, and the retention of items within a cluster only if they were consistent with the overall implications of the group.

BIBLIOGRAPHY:

WITTENBORN, J. R. "A Study of Adoptive Children: I. Interviews as a Source of Scores for Children and Their Homes." *Psychological Monographs: General and Applied,* 1956a, *70* (Whole No. 408).

WITTENBORN, J. R. "A Study of Adoptive Children: II. The Predictive Validity of the Yale Developmental Examination of Infant Behavior." *Psychological Monographs: General and Applied,* 1956b, *70* (Whole No. 409).

WITTENBORN, J. R. "A Study of Adoptive Children: III. Relationships Retain Some Aspects of Development and Some Aspects of Environment for Adoptive Children." *Psychological Monographs: General and Applied,* 1956c, *70* (Whole No. 410).

OBSERVATIONAL RECORD OF DISCIPLINE

AUTHOR: Edward Clifford

AGE: 3 to 9

VARIABLE: Developmental trends in behavior among children and parental child-rearing practices

TYPE OF MEASURE: Semistructured observation by parents

SOURCE FROM WHICH THE MEASURE MAY BE OBTAINED: Document Number 5899 with the ADI Auxiliary Publications Project, Photoduplication Service, Library of Congress, Washington, D.C. 20540. A copy may be secured by citing the document number and by remitting $2.50 for photoprints, or $1.75 for 35 mm. microfilm. Advance payment is required. Make checks or money orders payable to: Chief, Photoduplication Service, Library of Congress.

DESCRIPTION OF MEASURE: The ORD is a self-administering instrument designed to obtain consistent observations from parents. It does not treat the desirability of parental disciplinary practices; it is solely concerned with objective descriptions of such behavior. The ORD enables a parent to record a child's behavior in terms of the following variables: (1) time of occurrence; (2) place of occurrence; (3) duration of the disciplinary incident; (4) difficulties that arose; (5) the child-rearing practices the parents used; (6) the persons using the control; (7) the issue involved; (8) the outcome of the incident; (9) the reaction(s) of a child to the discipline; (10) and the deviation of the reaction.

Variables 1, 2, 3, 6, and 10 require rather obviously objective responses. In the other broad variables, specific questions or categories are employed, examples and descriptions of which follow:

Difficulties That Arose: Eleven categories are used to classify parental responses. Two illustrations are sibling relationships and eating.

Sibling Relationships—*quarreling, teasing, fighting and hitting (aggression), sharing possessions, threatening, and general interference with or disturbance of siblings.*

Eating—*refusal to eat, poor appetite, making a mess or playing with food, noise, playing, jumping up and down from table, use of utensils, manners, eating wrong foods or demanding foods, asking for food and refusing to eat it, and leaving table during the meal.*

Methods of Control: Parents are left with a mimeographed list of twenty-six different measures of control and their exact definitions. Illustrations of these measures are appeal to emotions (make mother feel bad); appeal to humor; appeal to self-esteem.

Issues Involved: For many parents these were identical with the difficulties that arose so that the same scoring system could apply in both cases.

Outcome of Discipline: For each disciplinary incident, the parent is requested to check one of seven questions, for example, "did the child give in?" The reactions of the child to discipline were also classified by ten categories, exemplified by the following:

Normal.   *All responses that indicate the child "was just fine," resumed activity, was his "usual self," or "settled down."*
Continuance of behavior.   *All responses that indicate no reaction, or that the child was unimpressed or "casual."*

RELIABILITY AND VALIDITY: Tentative norms of means and standard deviations have been provided for the relationship between age of child and parental discipline, the parental methods, the duration of disciplinary acts, and the reactions of children to disciplinary methods.

No data on reliability of the Record have been reported. The hypothesized age differences in difficulties associated with siblings, eating, sleep, and social interaction problems provide evidence of construct validity for the measure.

BIBLIOGRAPHY:

CLIFFORD, E. "Discipline in the Home: A Controlled Observational Study of Parental Practices." *The Journal of Genetic Psychology,* 1959, *95,* 45–82.

PARENTAL ATTITUDE RESEARCH INSTRUMENT

AUTHORS: Earl S. Schaefer and Richard Q. Bell

AGE: Adults

VARIABLE: Attitude toward child rearing

TYPE OF MEASURE: Likert-type scale

SOURCE FROM WHICH THE MEASURE MAY BE OBTAINED: See Schaefer and Bell (1958)

DESCRIPTION OF MEASURE: This scale evaluates the attitudes of parents toward child rearing. There are twenty-three subscales, each measured by five items, so that the total number of items is 115. The twenty-three subscales are entitled encouraging verbalization, fostering dependency, seclusion of the mother, breaking the will, martyrdom, fear of harming the baby, marital conflict, strictness, irritability, excluding outside influences, deification, suppression of aggression, rejection of homemaking role, equalitarianism, approval of activity, avoidance of communication, inconsiderateness of husband, suppression of sex, ascendance of the mother, intrusiveness, comradeship and sharing, acceleration of development, and dependency of the mother (Zuckerman, 1959).

The items are answered strongly agree, mildly agree, mildly disagree, strongly disagree. The item examples given below are from Schaefer and Bell's Form IV of the measure.

Children should be allowed to disagree with their parents if they feel their own ideas are better.
A good mother should shelter her child from life's little difficulties.
A child will be grateful later on for strict training.
Parents should adjust to the children some rather than always expecting the children to adjust to the parents.
All young mothers are afraid of their awkwardness in handling and holding the baby.
Sometimes it's necessary for a wife to tell off her husband in order to get her rights.
Children and husbands do better when the mother is strong enough to settle most of the problems.
Children need some of the natural meanness taken out of them.

Zuckerman (1959) developed a 100-item form of the PARI designed to control for acquiescence response set.

RELIABILITY AND VALIDITY: Schaefer and Bell (1958) calculated Kuder-Richardson Formula 20 reliabilities for the twenty-three scales, administered to sixty primipara mothers and sixty multipara mothers within four days of birth of a child. The range for the primipara mothers was .34 to .77, median .65; for the multipara mothers the range was .40 to .77, median .68. They also found low negative correlations between PARI scales and educational level. Zuckerman and Oltean (1959) compared PARI factor scores with scores on the California F Scale, the Edwards

Personal Preference Schedule, the Minnesota Multiphasic Personality Inventory, and a measure of self-acceptance devised by Zuckerman. Most of the hypothesized relationships were significant, lending support to the construct validity of the PARI.

BIBLIOGRAPHY:

COOPERSMITH, S. *The Antecedents of Self-Esteem*. San Francisco: W. H. Freeman & Company, 1967.

SCHAEFER, E. S., and BELL, R. Q. "Patterns of Attitudes toward Child Rearing and the Family." *Journal of Abnormal and Social Psychology*, 1957, *54*, 391–395.

SCHAEFER, E. S., and BELL, R. Q. "Development of a Parental Attitude Research Instrument." *Child Development*, 1958, *29*, 339–361.

ZUCKERMAN, M. "Reversed Scales to Control Acquiescence Response Set in the Parental Attitude Research Instrument." *Child Development*, 1959, *30*, 523–532.

ZUCKERMAN, M., and OLTEAN, M. "Some Relationships between Maternal Attitude Factors and Authoritarianism, Personality Needs, Psychopathology, and Self-Acceptance." *Child Development*, 1959, *30*, 27–36.

PARENTAL ATTITUDE SCALE

AUTHORS: Elizabeth Monroe Drews and John E. Teahan

AGE: Parents

VARIABLE: Attitude of parents in treatment of children

TYPE OF MEASURE: Likert-type self-administering scale

SOURCE FROM WHICH THE MEASURE MAY BE OBTAINED: See Drews and Teahan (1957)

DESCRIPTION OF MEASURE: The Parental Attitude Scale consists of thirty items taken from the Parental Attitude Survey (PAS) devised by Shoben. The thirty items in this scale contain an equal number of items (ten of each) assigned to three subscales: a dominating (D) scale, a possessive (P) scale, and an ignoring (I) scale. A high score on the D Scale is associated with agreement with items like "It is wicked for a child to disobey his parents." Possessiveness is manifested by agreement with "Babies are more fun for their parents than older children." Ignoring parents should agree with "Children should not interrupt adult conversation."

RELIABILITY AND VALIDITY: Drews and Teahan hypothesized that parents of high academic achievers would be less permissive than parents of low achievers. Mothers of high achievers, both gifted and average in intelligence, had significantly higher scores on the ignoring (I) scale than did mothers of normal or below achievers.

Shoben (1949), using the 148-item version, found that mothers of problem children had attitudes toward their children that were further from the "mental hygiene norm" than were the attitudes of mothers of nonproblem children.

BIBLIOGRAPHY:

DREWS, E. M., and TEAHAN, J. E. "Parental Attitudes and Academic Achievement." *Journal of Clinical Psychology,* 1957, *13,* 328–332.

SHOBEN, E. J., JR. "The Assessment of Parental Attitudes in Relation to Child Adjustment." *Genetic Psychology Monographs,* 1949, *39,* 103–148.

PARENTAL DEVELOPMENTAL TIMETABLE

AUTHOR: Irving Torgoff

AGE: Adults

VARIABLE: Two variables are measured by this instrument: achievement-inducing (tendency of the parent to "push" the child in certain directions), and independence-granting (the degree of emphasis the parent puts on allowing more self-direction and decision-making on the part of the child).

TYPE OF MEASURE: Questionnaire

SOURCE FROM WHICH THE MEASURE MAY BE OBTAINED: Dr. Torgoff at the Merrill-Palmer Institute in Detroit kindly provided us with a copy of the instrument.

DESCRIPTION OF MEASURE: The measure consists of forty-eight items, twenty-four designed to measure along the achievement-inducing (A) dimension and twenty-four along the independence-granting (I) dimension. The parent is asked to write in the appropriate age at which the average boy and girl can be expected to manage certain difficult situations. Examples of items are the following:

Begin to teach their child not to fight but to first try to reason with other children. (A)
Begin to allow their child to decide for himself when he should go to bed. (I)
Begin to expect that their child may not show an interest in a "good night" kiss. (I)
Begin to teach their child how to use a sharp knife at the dinner table. (A)

On each item, the parent gives an age at which he thinks boys and girls (separately) are ready to undertake that particular activity. For each group of parent subjects, the responses to each item individually are ranked and normalized T-scores are assigned to them. The twenty-four A and the twenty-four I scores are averaged to obtain a final score.

RELIABILITY AND VALIDITY: The odd-even reliability for each of the two subscales was greater than .8. Correlation between the two subscales was .2 (Torgoff, 1960).

The ratio of the A to the I scores is used to ascertain the emphasis the subject places on either of the two dimensions. Torgoff (1960) found a curvilinear relationship between A/I ratio and influence technique behavior of the parents. That is, parents with high A/I ratio tended to use power-assertive control techniques, but parents with low A/I ratio used similar influence techniques. He found furthermore that curiosity of the child varied inversely with A/I ratio of the parent; that is, the more emphasis the parent placed on achievement-inducing as compared to independent-granting, the lower the curiosity of the children.

Torgoff (1961) found that none of the correlations between the parents A/I scores and the child's compliance with the parents, as observed in a day-long situation, were significant for working class parents. All correlations between child compliance and the parent's A/I scores were negative. When the same analysis was done with scores of middle-class parents, however, all correlations were positive, and a number of them were statistically significant. Torgoff and Dreyer (1961) found that when daughters identified with their fathers (measured by similarity of responses to the parental development timetable), their level of aspiration was positively related to the A/I ratio of their fathers.

BIBLIOGRAPHY:

TORGOFF, I. "Synergistic Parental Role Components: Application to Expectancies and Behavior: Consequences for Child's Curiosity." Paper presented at the 1960 American Psychological Association convention, Chicago.

TORGOFF, I. "Parental Developmental Timetable: Parental Field Effects on Children's Compliance." Presented at the 1961 Society for Research in Child Development meetings at Pennsylvania State University, State College, Pennsylvania.

TORGOFF, I., and DREYER, A. S. "Achievement-inducing and Independence-granting—Synergistic Parental Role Components: Relation to Daughters' 'Parental' Role Orientation and Level of Aspiration." Paper presented at the American Psychological Association Meeting, New York City, September, 1961.

PARENTAL NURTURANCE-CONTROL ATTITUDE SCALE

AUTHOR: Walter Emmerich

AGE: Parents of preschool children

VARIABLE: Attitudes

TYPE OF MEASURE: Open-ended questionnaire

SOURCE FROM WHICH THE MEASURE MAY BE OBTAINED: See Emmerich (1959)

DESCRIPTION OF MEASURE: The Parental Nurturance-Control Attitude Scale is based on a projective questionnaire consisting of eight hypothetical situations in which the parents are asked how they would deal with their child. The items contained in the self-administering parental questionnaire resemble those presented to the children in doll-play interview. For example, item one is as follows:

You and your child are in the food store and she won't leave. She sees some candy she wants. What do you do?

The parents' responses are then rated on a nurturance-control scale similar to the scales used to evaluate the children's doll-play interview responses, except that the specific examples of the major scale points are expressed in more adult terms. The scale, then, rates the parental responses with scores ranging from +3.0 (strong nurturance) to −3.0 (strong control). The description of the category strong nurturance is given below:

Parent facilitates child's accomplishment of a goal to a greater extent than the child requested.   (1) *Buys several toys;* (2) *reads for a long time;* (3) *makes special effort to prepare or secure food child wants;* (4) *plays with child or lets him play indefinitely;* (5) *allows child free reign in hitting dog;* (6) *gives child special privileges beyond caring for medical problem;* (7) *lets child stay up indefinitely;* (8) *encourages child to get dirty.*

RELIABILITY AND VALIDITY: Twenty-five mothers and twenty-three fathers completed the questionnaires. Two judges independently rated ninety responses, eighteen for each of the first five items of the scale. Half of the ratings were of mothers' responses, half of fathers'. The correlation between the two judges' ratings was found to be +.87. The responses to questionnaire Items 6, 7, and 8 were so often rated +2.0 on the nurturance-control scale that these items did not discriminate among parents. The parents' nurturance-control scores were based upon the first five items only.

Teachers' ratings of the mothers' nurturance-control toward their children were correlated with the sum of the mothers' nurturance-control scores on the first five questionnaire items. The correlation for twenty-five mothers responding to the questionnaires was +.51 (p < .01).

BIBLIOGRAPHY:

EMMERICH, W. "Parent Identification in Young Children." *Genetic Psychology Monographs,* 1959, *60,* 257–308.

PARENTAL PRACTICES INVENTORY

AUTHOR: Rue L. Cromwell

AGE: Parents

VARIABLE: Child-rearing practices

TYPE OF MEASURE: Self-report

SOURCE FROM WHICH THE MEASURE MAY BE OBTAINED: See Cromwell (1966)

DESCRIPTION OF MEASURE: In this self-report and self-administering inventory of child-rearing practices, parents are requested to complete every item with an answer that is closest to the truth. They are urged to describe actual practices they have used in a specific situation. The inventory itself consists of items in six general areas: (1) Identifying information. The parent is requested to answer such items as her relationship to the child, the number of children in the home, and the names and ordinal positions of the children. The entire section includes four items. (2) Description of all children in the home. Eight items request the parent to list the ordinal position of the child with whom she did the best job in child rearing, the best adjusted child, the child with the closest relationship to her, and the like. (3) Description of my practices as a parent. This part of the inventory includes eleven items. In each of eleven behavioral situations the parent is requested to select the best way of handling it for herself. A sample item follows:

When we parents disagree, this child knows it (*a*) *nearly always,* (*b*) *sometimes,* (*c*) *almost never.* (*We try not to let him know.*)

(4) Description of this child's experiences. The emphasis of this description is to urge parents to respond in terms of the child's usual experience. The subscale consists of twelve items. Sample items are given below:

The person who has done most of the raising of this child is (*a*) *his mother,* (*b*) *his father,* (*c*) *his grandparents,* (*d*) *older children in the family,* (*e*) *a relative,* (*f*) *other (for example).*
When this child is punished the person punishing him is usually (*a*) *angry and upset,* (*b*) *calm and rational.*

(5) Home practices. In this section, parents must answer eleven items relating to child-care practices. Not only must parents complete each blank but they are also directed to check off the alternative responses in terms of priority. A sample item follows:

When this child is punished physically (spanked, slapped, etc.) he (*a*) *cries,* (*b*) *talks back,* (*c*) *clams up,* (*d*) *becomes timid or afraid,* (*e*) *behaves even worse,* (*f*) *tries to correct his action if possible,* (*g*) *says he is sorry but doesn't mean it,* (*h*) *says he is sorry and seems to mean it,* (*i*) *seeks reassurance or love,* (*i*) *acts as though he had never been punished at all.*

(6) Home values. The scale employs a forced-choice technique in which parents must select the response that is most important to them from among sixty pairs of statements. A sample is as follows:

Having him get a good education, or
Having him always be on his best behavior around company.

Following the six scales, the parent is required to answer two questions that serve as a check on validity. First, the parent is requested to react to the extent to which the questions and answers give a true picture of her home and child from among three alternatives (very close, fairly close, not very close). Secondly, she is asked to indicate the proportion of answers on which she was completely objective and frank from among four choices (all, most, about half, and only a few). Cromwell has developed a code book for the inventory with complete directions on the scoring of the variables.

RELIABILITY AND VALIDITY: Two validity questions that follow the inventory have already been described. No data on reliability are given. The instrument is a research tool in its preliminary stages.

BIBLIOGRAPHY:

CROMWELL, R. L. "Parent Practice Inventory." Unpublished paper, Vanderbilt University Hospital, January, 1966. (Mimeographed)

PARENT ATTITUDE INVENTORY

AUTHOR: A. N. Oppenheim

AGE: Parents

VARIABLE: Attitudes about child raising

TYPE OF MEASURE: Likert-type scale

SOURCE FROM WHICH THE MEASURE MAY BE OBTAINED: Dr. A. N. Oppenheim, London School of Economics, Houghton Street, London, W. C. 2

DESCRIPTION OF MEASURE: This attitude inventory consists of fifty-two items, of which the following are typical:

It is difficult for a mother to feel at ease when she does not know exactly what her child is doing.
Looking after children really demands too much of me.
A child should never be punished out of sheer irritation, but only for his own good.
I want my child to be neat and clean at all times.
A mother should try to get her baby to use the pot from birth.

The parent answers the item on a five-point scale—strongly disagree, disagree, uncertain, agree, strongly agree. There are fifty-two items in all, five items measuring on each of ten subscales, and two warm-up items at the beginning. The attitude areas covered by the subscales are overprotection (dominant), overprotection (submissive), democracy, autocracy, acceptance, rejection, strict infant training, strictness concerning habits and manners, strictness about sex play, and objectivity.

Oppenheim (personal correspondence) has also developed a "parent behavior inventory," one form for mothers of girls ages 6 to 12, the other for mothers of boys ages 6 to 12. These measures appear designed to get at nine of the ten subarea variables mentioned above.

RELIABILITY AND VALIDITY: The parent attitude inventory has a reliability of .79 (Pittfield and Oppenheim, 1964). Several factor analyses have identified two dimensions, independent of each other, which might be called a "strictness" factor and an "acceptance/rejection" factor. Pittfield and Oppenheim (1964) compared one hundred mothers of normal children, one hundred mothers of mongoloid children, and one hundred mothers of psychotic children on the ten area subscales. Thirteen of the thirty differences (ten subscales × three classes of mothers) were significant at the .05 level or less.

BIBLIOGRAPHY:

PITTFIELD, M., and OPPENHEIM, A. N. "Child Rearing Attitudes of Mothers of Psychotic Children." *Journal of Child Psychology and Psychiatry,* 1964, *5,* 51–57.

PARENT INTERVIEW SCHEDULE

AUTHORS: R. R. Sears, Eleanor E. Maccoby, and H. Levin

AGE: Adults

VARIABLE: Child-rearing practices

TYPE OF MEASURE: Interview schedule

SOURCE FROM WHICH THE MEASURE MAY BE OBTAINED: See Sears et al. (1957)

DESCRIPTION OF MEASURE: From seventy-two items of the interview schedule, plus 121 optional follow-up questions, 188 scales are derived. The scales are listed by Sears et al. (1957) and some of them are described in detail in the text. They measure five aspects or dimensions of maternal behavior: disciplinary technique, permissiveness, severity, temperamental qualities (of mother), and positive inculcation (by mother) of more mature behavior (in child).

RELIABILITY AND VALIDITY: Each interview was independently rated by two raters; when their ratings differed by more than one scale point, they discussed and reconciled their scores. Final scores represented the pooled judgments of the two raters. During the rating process, the entire group of raters occasionally rated and discussed an interview jointly, and the pairs of raters were rotated so that no pair of raters would develop a frame of reference that deviated from that of the other raters. Specific inter-rater scale reliabilities are given by Sears et al. (1957) but are not repeated here because of space limitations.

BIBLIOGRAPHY:

SEARS, R. R., MACCOBY, E., and LEVIN, H. *Patterns of Child Rearing.* Evanston, Illinois: Row Peterson, 1957.

PORTER PARENTAL ACCEPTANCE SCALE

AUTHOR: Blaine M. Porter

AGE: Parents

VARIABLE: Parental acceptance of children

TYPE OF MEASURE: Self-rating questionnaire

SOURCE FROM WHICH THE MEASURE MAY BE OBTAINED: Blaine M. Porter, 1206 Smith Family Living Center, Brigham Young University, Provo, Utah 84601. Available from author at 10 cents per copy, or a special price is available for large quantity orders.

DESCRIPTION OF MEASURE: This scale is composed of forty five-option multiple-choice items designed to measure parental acceptance. The responses to the items are arbitrarily weighted from 1 to 5, 1 representing low acceptance and 5 meaning high acceptance. Scoring keys with the weights of each item are provided.

The acceptance scale involves four dimensions of acceptance. According to these dimensions, an accepting parent is one who respects the feelings of the child, values his uniqueness, recognizes and encourages his autonomy, and loves him unconditionally. Operational definitions of these dimensions are provided (Porter, 1954). Since the items related to each dimension have been enumerated, subscale scores can be obtained.

Examples from items related to the feelings parents have (items one to ten) and the actions they take (items eleven to forty) are given below. The parents indicate one of these degrees of feeling of affection: much more than usual, a little more than usual, the same, a little less than usual, much less than usual.

When he is obedient
When he is with me

RELIABILITY AND VALIDITY: In a sample of forty-three men and fifty-seven women (Porter, 1954), a corrected reliability correlation coefficient of .865 was obtained on the acceptance scale. In a later study (Hawkes et al., 1956) with a more representative sample (N = 256) systematically selected, the total test reliability was estimated at .80. Porter (1954) reports high agreement among five experienced clinicians ranking the responses from 1 to 5, 1 representing low acceptance and 5 representing high acceptance. In every case at least three of five judges agreed.

Only one of the items failed to discriminate between high and low scoring mothers or fathers at a statistically significant level, which suggests that the scale has internal consistency (Burchinal et al., 1957). However, no significant relationships were found between the parental scores on the Porter Acceptance Scale and the Rogers Test of Personality Adjustment.

BIBLIOGRAPHY:

BURCHINAL, L. G., HAWKES, G. R., and GARDNER, B. "The Relationship Between Parental Acceptance and Adjustment of Children." *Child Development*, 1957, *28*, 65–77.

HAWKES, G. R., BURCHINAL, L. G., GARDNER, B., and PORTER, B. M. "Parents' Acceptance of Their Children." *Journal of Home Economics*, 1956, *48*, 195–200.

PORTER, B. M. "Measurement of Parental Acceptance of Children." *Journal of Home Economics*, 1954, *46*, 176–182.

QUESTIONNAIRE FOR PARENTS OF PRE-SCHOOL HANDICAPPED CHILDREN

AUTHOR: Leroy Larson

AGE: Parents

VARIABLE: Several types of preschool experiences

TYPE OF MEASURE: Questionnaire

SOURCE FROM WHICH THE MEASURE MAY BE OBTAINED: See Larson (1954)

DESCRIPTION OF MEASURE: This is a ninety-five-item questionnaire, of which the following are examples:

Has your child ever spent the night away from home with someone other than a member of his immediate family? (a) *Never,* (b) *once,* (c) *twice,* (d) *three times,* (e) *more than three times.*

How many times has he attended a concert, minstrel show, or a play accompanied by an adult? (a) *None,* (b) *one to two times,* (c) *three to four times,* (d) *five to six times,* (e) *more than six times.*

Does any member of the family (a) *play the piano for the child?* (b) *sing to the child?* (c) *play any other instrument for the child?*

How many of the following toys does he own? *toy telephone; tinker toys; erector set; toy typewriter; Lincoln logs; other types of building blocks; ball and bat; doll or teddy bear; small cars, trucks, planes, trains; toy furniture or utensils; wagon, tricycle, or wheelbarrow; ranch or farm sets; jigsaw puzzles; cowboy pistol or cowboy outfit.*

The items are grouped into five classes labeled socialization, recognition, outside experiences, knowledge and experience (also described by Larson in a personal communication as "enlightenment"), and miscellaneous. Larson (1954) gives the item groupings making up these separate variables.

RELIABILITY AND VALIDITY: Larson (1958) found significant differences on the first four main variables (socialization, recognition, outside experiences, knowledge and experience) between 135 physically handicapped children ages 3 to 6 and 135 physically normal children matched for age, sex, social status, and community background. Sixty-one of the ninety-five items were analyzed separately. On forty-six of these sixty-one items the differences between the handicapped and the non-handicapped group were significant at the .01 level, while on six other items the differences were significant at the .05 level. All differences favored the physically normal group.

BIBLIOGRAPHY:

LARSON, L. "Preschool Experiences of Physically Handicapped Children—Ages Three through Six." Unpublished doctoral dissertation, State University of Iowa, 1954.

LARSON, L. "Preschool Experiences of Physically Handicapped Children." *Exceptional Children,* 1958, *24*(7), 310–312.

SCALE OF PARENTAL DISSATISFACTION WITH INSTRUMENTAL BEHAVIOR

AUTHORS: Bernard Farber and William C. Jenné

AGE: Normal children, ages 11 to 16 inclusive

VARIABLE: Communication

TYPE OF MEASURE: Questionnaire

SOURCE FROM WHICH THE MEASURE MAY BE OBTAINED: See Farber and Jenné (1963)

DESCRIPTION OF MEASURE: Instrumental activities are defined as activities directed to goals external to the family but that are conducive to maintaining the family as a social system. The scale measures behavior along a dimension of external constraint or conventionality versus internalization of norms. More precisely, the scale measures the parents' estimate of the extent to which the child has behaved to the degree expected by them, and the child's estimate regarding the degree to which he has abided by these parental expectations.

In the scale, scores of four contrived items are derived from fourteen subitems. The contrived items include conformity to conventional behavior, definition of his "world" as serious, propensity toward task performance, and performance of specific tasks. Since each contrived item is scored as 0 or 1, the range of the total scores is from 0 to 4. Agreement on a subitem between parental and child's dissatisfaction is scored plus, disagreement as minus. A contrived item is scored as 1 when two or three of the subitems are scored plus. The subitems for the contrived item of conformity to conventional behavior follow (Farber and Jenné, 1963):

Go to church or Sunday School.
Stay out late at night.
Go along with fads (rock 'n' roll, hot rods, and so on).

Four scores are obtained on the child's perception of mother's and father's satisfaction and the perception of satisfaction by each parent for the child's behavior. The child is requested to answer each item in terms of the mother's (or father's) desire to change the frequency of behavior or her(his) satisfaction with its present form. Appropriate changes in wording were made in the directions for parents.

RELIABILITY AND VALIDITY: Reproducibility coefficients for child's dissatisfaction, child's perception of mother's dissatisfaction, father's dissatisfaction with child's behavior, and father's dissatisfaction over three different samples ranged between .93 and .97 (Farber and Jenné, 1963).

BIBLIOGRAPHY:

FARBER, B., and JENNÉ, W. C. "Family Organization and Parent-Child Communications." *Monographs of the Society for Research in Child Development,* 1963, *28* (Whole Monograph No. 7).

SEX-ROLE ATTITUDE TEST (Adult Form)

AUTHOR: Leonard M. Lansky

AGE: Parents

VARIABLE: Attitudes toward sex-role choices

TYPE OF MEASURE: Questionnaire

SOURCE FROM WHICH THE MEASURE MAY BE OBTAINED: See McKay (1964)

DESCRIPTION OF MEASURE: The fifty items of SRAT ask parents to report their feelings about their preschool child's choice of objects or activities. The parent is given three "sets" as follows: Set 1: happy, pleased, delighted, content, proud; Set 2: neutral or in between the feelings of Set 1 and Set 3, that is, neither happy nor unhappy, neither pleased or angry, and so on; Set 3: angry, unhappy, sad, discontent, cross, disappointed. Thus, to each item the parent responds with a choice of one of three points along the variable satisfaction-dissatisfaction. For example, Item 1 from the scale that parents would use to rate a daughter goes as follows:

If a girl had a choice between playing with a toy gun and playing with a doll, how would her mother feel if her daughter wanted to play with both the toy gun and the doll?

The parent then indicates his or her degree of pleasure or displeasure by circling one of the sets. There is a comparable item in the scale for evaluating parents' attitude toward boys' sex-role choices. Each comparable item is similar except for the changing of the sex of the "actor." Items 2 and 3 of the scale are given below as further examples of the type of items used.

If a girl had a choice between dressing up as an Indian princess and dressing up as Indian chief, how would her mother feel if her daughter wanted to dress up as an Indian princess?
If a girl had a choice between playing with toy tools for building and playing with toy things for cooking, which would her mother like her daughter to play with the most? (a) building tools, (b) cooking utensils

There are five pairs of sex-linked activities: playing with a gun or a doll; dressing up as an Indian chief or a princess; playing with toy tools for building or toy things for cooking; playing on swings with some boys or some girls his (her) age; and playing with a toy shaving kit or a toy cosmetic kit. Ten variables are measured. Examples are: father's attitude toward a same-sex choice, mother's attitudes toward a cross-sex choice, and father's permissiveness toward the boy's wish to sometimes enjoy a same-sex and other times an opposite-sex choice. Each item is scored 0, 1, or 2, with 0 meaning that the parent responded favorably to the item.

RELIABILITY AND VALIDITY: No data are given on reliability of the measure. Some evidence on construct validity is provided by one of Lansky's studies (1966).

He found that the attitude of parents toward their preschool boy's preference for same- and cross-sex activities was related to the sex composition of the family. The attitude differed between boy-only families and boy-girl families. Parents having preschool girls also manifested different attitudes toward sex-role choices.

BIBLIOGRAPHY:

LANSKY, L. M. "The Family Structure Also Affects the Model: II. Sex-Role Attitudes in Parents of Preschool Children." Revision of paper read at American Orthopsychiatric Association, San Francisco, 1966.

MC KAY, G. H. "Some Dimensions of Sex-Typing in Kindergarten Children: An Exploratory Study." Unpublished Ed. D. dissertation, 1964, Harvard University.

SOCIAL DEPRIVATION SCALE

AUTHORS: Edward Zigler, Earl D. Butterfield, and Genevieve Goff

AGE: Parents of retarded children with IQ scores of 40 or above

VARIABLE: Social deprivation

TYPE OF MEASURE: Rating scale

SOURCE FROM WHICH THE MEASURE MAY BE OBTAINED: According to the authors, a complete description and instructions for the scale will be provided upon request (Zigler et al., 1966).

DESCRIPTION OF MEASURE: The Social Deprivation Scale consists of seventeen items that are rated on the basis of a child's preinstitutional deprivation. These items are subsumed under the four factor structures of gross, overt, early rejection of the child by his parents; less overt, later rejection of the child by his parents; paternal competence; and maternal competence. The scale requires both subjective and objective ratings of deprivation. Instructions have been provided for making both types of ratings and scoring each individual item. The complete criteria for evaluating a sample item from the scale follow (Zigler et al., 1966). For economic circumstance of family:

Rating	Amount of Income	Source of Income	Judgment of Economic Circumstance
7	≤ 1,500	Irregular employment	Very poor
6	1,600–2,500	Relief, A.D.C. child support	Poor
5	2,600–4,000		Marginal
4	4,100–6,000		Average
3	≥ 6,100		Above average

(Leave the rating blank if there is not enough information in the history upon which to base a judgment of economic circumstances).

Additional sample items of an abbreviated nature from the scale are also presented below:

Item Name	Possible Range of Scores	Examples of Selected Scores
Preinstitutional residences	4 and up	Number of residences 3
Proportion of preinstitutional life spent with biological parents	4–8	4 = Stayed with biological parents from birth to institutionalization 7 = Had two or more residences longer than that with biological parents

RELIABILITY AND VALIDITY: In a cross-validation study, the four factor structures were replicated, which would seem to support the internal consistency of the scale. According to the authors, the final form of the scale consisted of items clearly and reliably rated by even untrained raters as measuring social deprivation. When two clinicians subjectively rated thirty subjects, the correlation of mean item scores with their ratings was .723 ($p < .001$).

The mean of intercorrelations among five raters' subjective ratings of twenty-five randomly selected social histories was .81. The average reliabilities for the early rejection, later rejection, paternal competence, and maternal competence factors were respectively .738, .659, .899, and .833 (Zigler et al., 1966).

BIBLIOGRAPHY:

ZIGLER, E., BUTTERFIELD, E. D., and GOFF, G. "A Measure of Preinstitutional Social Deprivation for Institutionalized Retardates." *American Journal of Mental Deficiency*, 1966, *70*, 873–885.

STANFORD PARENT QUESTIONNAIRE

AUTHORS: C. L. Winder and Lucy Rau

AGE: Parents

VARIABLE: Parental attitudes to child-rearing practices

TYPE OF MEASURE: Questionnaire

SOURCE FROM WHICH THE MEASURE MAY BE OBTAINED: The list of these items has been deposited with the American Documentation Institute. Order Document No. 7091 from ADI Auxiliary Publications Project Photoduplication Service, Library of Congress, Washington, D.C. 20540, remitting in advance $1.25 for microfilm or $1.25 for photocopies. Make check payable to Chief, Photoduplication Service, Library of Congress

DESCRIPTION OF MEASURE: The current version of the SPQ has a separate form for each parent. The maternal form consists of 491 items, the paternal form has 518 items. The majority of the items are identical. One scale, Closeness to Father, applies to the paternal form only. The twenty-eight subscales are subsumed under the six major scales of ambivalence, strictness, aggression and tentativeness, parental adjustment, models, and mastery (Winder and Rau, 1962).

In replying to each item, the parent selects one alternative from strongly agree (SA), agree (A), disagree (D), and strongly disagree (SD). The responses are scored dichotomously for the presence or absence of certain traits (respectively 1 or 0) or continuously. In the continuous system, the scoring depends on whether agreement or disagreement with the item indicates the presence of a certain trait. The continuous scores range over a four-point scale, 0 to 3.

Sample items from the paternal scale follow:

Holding back some of his privileges is the best way I have of disciplining him.
I don't believe in them standing up for themselves by picking on some other kid.
The most effective punishment seems to be when we really take him in tow and either give him a spanking or a long talking to. Taking away some privilege doesn't work nearly as well.

RELIABILITY AND VALIDITY: On the maternal form of the scale, the reliability coefficients for the six major scales range from .48 (models) to .87 (mastery). On the paternal scale, the range is from .61 (models) to .89 (strictness). For all scales in both forms the mean reliability is .58. The authors regard the reliability coefficient for the total score on the scale for models (maternal form) to be quite unsatisfactory in view of its length.

The principal validating procedure for the scale rests on the extent to which relationships were found between the parent attitude scales and four measures of deviancy on a "guess-who" technique (aggression, dependency, withdrawal, and depression), notably the Peer Nomination Inventory (Winder and Wiggins, 1960). This procedure showed significant differences between parents of deviant and nondeviant boys. Thus, the mothers of the popular boys reported high parent adjustment and the fathers gave more favorable evaluations of their sons' competence.

The variables to be measured on the SPQ were based on available studies of parental antecedents of personality development in children and verbatim descriptions of interviews with parents of deviant and normal children (Winder and Rau, 1962). Finally, every item retained under the present form of the scale correlated at least .30 with its total scale score.

BIBLIOGRAPHY:

WINDER, C. L., and RAU, L. "Parental Attitudes Associated with Social Deviance in Pre-adolescent Boys." *Journal of Abnormal and Social Psychology,* 1962, *64,* 418–424.

WINDER, C. L., and WIGGINS, J. S. "Measurement of Social Adjustment in Pre-adolescent Boys." Progress report, November 7, 1960, USPHS Grant M-2745 (C 1).

STOUFFER PARENTAL ATTITUDE SCALE

AUTHOR: George A. W. Stouffer, Jr.

AGE: Parents

VARIABLE: Adults' attitudes toward problems of children

TYPE OF MEASURE: Questionnaire

SOURCE FROM WHICH THE MEASURE MAY BE OBTAINED: Dr. George
A. W. Stouffer, Jr., 79 Shady Dr., Indiana, Pa. 15701

DESCRIPTION OF MEASURE: Parents are asked to rate the seriousness of fifty
behavior traits of children, such as tardiness, resentment, truancy, destruction of
school materials, lying. These traits constitute the five problem areas of dishonesty,
difficulty in school work, problems with authority, aggressiveness and antagonism,
and withdrawal behavior. The parents make their ratings at any point on a cali-
brated scale with twenty equal divisions and an ascending order of seriousness. The
parents are also asked to estimate the effect of the behavior on a child's future development. Sample items from the questionnaire are tardiness, truancy, destroying
school materials, untruthfulness (lying). The ratings are: of no importance at all, of
only slight importance, of considerable importance, of extremely great importance.

RELIABILITY AND VALIDITY: No data on reliability and validity are given.
However, results reveal very little relationship between the ratings of parents and
mental health workers on the ranking concerning the undesirability of the behavioral
traits (Stouffer, 1959).

BIBLIOGRAPHY:

STOUFFER, G. A. W., JR. "Behavior Problems of Children as Viewed by Teachers and
    Mental Hygienists." *Mental Hygiene*, 1952, *36*, 271–285.
STOUFFER, G. A. W., JR. "The Attitude of Secondary School Teachers toward Certain
    Behavior Problems of Children." *School Review*, 1956, *64*, 358–363.
STOUFFER, G. A. W., JR. "The Attitudes of Parents toward Certain Behavioral Prob-
    lems of Children." *State College Bulletin*, 1959, *5*, 11–23.

STRUCTURED PARENTAL INTERVIEW

AUTHOR: Robert R. Sears

AGE: Parents of nursery school children

VARIABLE: Identification (antecedent conditions and behavioral correlates)

TYPE OF MEASURE: Structured interview

SOURCE FROM WHICH THE MEASURE MAY BE OBTAINED: See Sears, Rau, and Alpert (1965)

DESCRIPTION OF MEASURE: The SPI comprises a standard set of open-ended questions for the purpose of obtaining parental perceptions regarding some of their child's in-the-home behavior. The interviews are recorded and transcribed, and cover parental behavior deemed relevant to the development of identification in the child. Interviews covered such parental antecedent conditions as caretaker activities, feeding practices, toilet training, and child-rearing practices for sexual behavior, dependency, aggression, and disobedience. Attitudes relating to management of the child as applied to a wide range of additional behaviors are also covered. One hundred eighty-four parental variables are probed.

With the exception of length, the interviews are rather similar, the mother's being somewhat longer, covering fifty-eight main questions to the father's forty. If the main questions are not answered adequately, a number of probes are suggested for elaboration. Each parent is interviewed on two different occasions separated by a week's interval, with the duration of each session about an hour or a little more. Sample questions from the maternal interview follow (Sears et al., 1965):

What happened in the room just now with X?   (*This question referred to the first mother-child-interaction session.*) (*a*) *How did the games go?* (*b*) *What did X do while you were doing the questionnaire?* (*c*) *How did his behavior in the room compare with his behavior with you at home?* (*d*) *What happened when he played the different roles in the telephone game—you, his daddy, etc.?*

Now let's go back to the beginning.   *Can you remember how things were when you found you were pregnant with X?* (*a*) *Was he planned for?* (*b*) *Was it a good time to have a baby?* (*c*) *How did you feel during the pregnancy?* (*d*) *How did the delivery go?* (*e*) *How much change did it make in your life when X came along?* (*f*) *How did you feel about this pregnancy in relation to your others?*

Since the scoring of the scales is rather involved, the directions should be consulted in full before using the scale (Sears et al., 1965). Nearly all the interview scales were rated on nine-point distributions. This rating procedure was applied to 184 parental variables. Examples of the variables, including some paternal ones (P), included the following:

Severity of child's early separation from mother.
Severity of child's early separation from father.
Severity of child's current separation from father (*P*).
Stability of current home situation (*P*).

RELIABILITY AND VALIDITY: Reliability for the interview ratings was rather straightforward, resting primarily on percentage agreement between two raters. The percentage agreement within one scale point on 159 scales in one study ranged from 78 to 100 per cent, median 98 per cent. Three types of rater reliability were calculated: inter-rater agreement on the rating for each parent, mothers and fathers (N = 40 for each); inter-rater agreement on each mother scale (N = 161); and inter-rater agreement on each father scale (N = 119). Median percentage agreements were 72.5 (mothers), 72.5 (fathers), 67.5 (mother scales), and 72.5 (father scales). These coefficients applied to exact agreements. Reliability data were also provided for two lesser levels of stringency, resulting in much more impressive medium levels of agreement (Sears et al., 1965).

The potential user of the scale should consult the detailed results (Sears et al., 1965) to judge the adequacy of the evidence for the test's validity. The data are too voluminous to be described adequately in a few summarizing statements.

BIBLIOGRAPHY:

SEARS, R. R., RAU, L., and ALPERT, R. *Identification and Child Rearing*. Stanford, California: Stanford University Press, 1965.

THE TRADITIONAL FAMILY IDEOLOGY SCALE

AUTHOR: Phyllis Elaine Huffman

AGE: Parents

VARIABLE: Family ideology

TYPE OF MEASURE: Likert-type scale

SOURCE FROM WHICH THE MEASURE MAY BE OBTAINED: See Huffman (1950)

DESCRIPTION OF MEASURE: The Traditional Family Ideology (TFI) Scale is composed of forty items, divided into six subscales as follows: conventional values (twelve items); overidealization of parents (six items); power relationships (nine items); pseudo-masculinity and femininity (eight items); discipline (seven items); and rejection of id (six items). Some items are included in more than one subscale. There are forty *different* items, of which six are used in two subscales and one is used in three subscales. Examples of the items are as follows:

It helps the child in the long run if he is made to conform to his parents' ideas.
Women can be too bright for their own good.
It is only natural and right for each person to think that his family is better than any other.
The saying, "Mother knows best" still holds more than a grain of truth.
The unmarried mother is morally a greater failure than the unmarried father.

The subject responds as follows: +3 for strong agreement, +2 for moderate agreement, +1 for slight agreement, −1 for slight disagreement, −2 for moderate disagreement, −3 for strong disagreement.

RELIABILIITY AND VALIDITY: Reliability of the scale, based on odd-even correlation corrected by the Spearman-Brown formula, is .84 (Huffman, 1950). Item means and an index of discrimination power are given for each item.

The TFI scale correlated .65 with the Adorno ethnocentrism scale and .73 with the Adorno F (Fascism) scale when given to a group of 109 students in adult evening psychology classes.

There are suggested relationships between TFI scores and religious preference and attendance at church. Persons whose religion and politics were different from those of their parents tended strongly to have lower TFI scores than subjects having the same religion as their parents. There was no apparent relationship with the subject's political affiliation. The relationship between TFI and occupation was suggestive. Additional data are given by Huffman (1950) on TFI scores and projective question responses.

BIBLIOGRAPHY:

ADORNO, T. W., AND OTHERS. *The Authoritarian Personality.* New York: Harper and Brothers, 1950.

HUFFMAN, P. E. "Authoritarian Personality and Family Ideology: A Scale for the Measurement of Traditional Family Ideology." Unpublished master's thesis, Western Reserve University, 1950.

Group 5‑c

Attitudes, Primarily of Parents, Toward School

ATTITUDE SCALE TOWARD THE GIFTED

AUTHOR: Jean L. Wiener

AGE: Teachers of gifted children

VARIABLE: Attitudes of teachers toward gifted children and programs for the gifted

TYPE OF MEASURE: Likert-type questionnaire

SOURCE FROM WHICH THE MEASURE MAY BE OBTAINED: See Wiener (1960)

DESCRIPTION OF MEASURE: This measure consists of twenty-eight items arranged in a Likert form in which the examinee responds in terms of agreement (plus 3 for strongly to plus 1 for mildly agree) or disagreement (minus 3 for strongly disagree to minus 1 for mildly disagree). The total score is the sum of the twenty-eight item scores. Sample items from the scale follow:

Gifted children want to take too much of class time.
There should be a change in the grading system for gifted students in special classes for the gifted.
The aptitude of a given child is the primary consideration in the screening and selection of gifted children.
Gifted children should remain in heterogeneous classes because they will spend their lives with all types of people.

RELIABILITY AND VALIDITY: Several groups of teachers and expert judges have evaluated the adequacy of the items for the purpose of the measure. An item analysis based on the responses of 100 experienced teachers yielded a coefficient of reproducibility of .80 for Form A (fourteen items) and .81 for Form B (fourteen items) (Wiener and O'Shea, 1963).

BIBLIOGRAPHY:

WIENER, J. L. "The Relationships Between Selected Variables and Attitudes of Teachers Toward Gifted Children." Unpublished doctoral dissertation, University of California at Los Angeles, 1960.

WIENER, J. L., and O'SHEA, H. E. "Attitudes of University Faculty, Administrators, Teachers, Supervisors, and University Students toward the Gifted." *Exceptional Children*, 1963, *30*, 163–165.

BLATT'S EVALUATION CHECK LIST FOR CLASSES

AUTHOR: Burton Blatt

AGE: Elementary classes for educable mentally handicapped

VARIABLE: Quality of programs and services in EMH classes

TYPE OF MEASURE: Checklist and questionnaire

SOURCE FROM WHICH THE MEASURE MAY BE OBTAINED: See Blatt (1966)

DESCRIPTION OF MEASURE: The schedule for describing and evaluating special classes for EMH children is a checklist in which an observer or rater checks for the quality or presence of certain features and services available for a given program. Six areas are evaluated as follows, the number in parentheses being the number of items (some multiple choice, some yes-no, some fill-in) in each area: (A) details of observed lesson(s) and general learning (13); (B) summary rating of teacher in learning environments (4); (C) summary rating of children in learning environments (10); (D) summary rating of diagnostic and placement procedures and extent of consultative and supervising practice (15); (E) summary rating of quality of observed lessons(s) and curriculum emphasis (10); (F) percentage of daily distribution of time (teacher's estimate) (15). Space is also provided for the observer to record additional comments and impressions. The first three items from area A are given below for illustrative purposes (Blatt, 1966):

Materials for observed lesson (double check if materials were adequate for lesson):
  (a) none, (b) textbooks, workbooks, and other commercial resources, (c) commercial, teacher prepared materials, and/or teacher-pupil materials.
Teacher preparation for observed lesson (double check if preparation was adequate):
  (a) none or little apparent, (b) minimal, (c) extensive.
Evidence of teacher-pupil planning: (a) there is no or little evidence, (b) the room contains evidence of such planning: teacher prepared charts, children's relevant work, etc., (c) from examination of physical environment, one could clearly determine prior and present activities of class—i.e., charts, pupil's work, exhibits, books, and other materials reflecting the curriculum and its objectives.

RELIABILITY AND VALIDITY: No objective data regarding the standardization, reliability, and validity of the checklist are given. Content validity may be inferred from the criteria the author set up for an evaluation instrument of this type; the culling of items from the literature and professional colleagues; and testing and revising the instrument to simplify it and reduce duplication and ambiguity.

BIBLIOGRAPHY:

BLATT, B. "The Intellectually Disfranchised: Impoverished Learners and Their Teachers." Boston: Department of Mental Health, 1966.

PARENT ATTITUDE TOWARD EDUCATION SCALE

AUTHOR: Gene R. Medinnus

AGE: Parents of 5-year-old children

VARIABLE: Attitudes toward school

TYPE OF MEASURE: Attitude scale

SOURCE FROM WHICH THE MEASURE MAY BE OBTAINED: See Medinnus (1962)

DESCRIPTION OF MEASURE: The scale is self-administering and consists of forty statements to which the subject responds "strongly agree," "somewhat agree," "somewhat disagree" or "strongly disagree." Responses are scored 3, 2, 1, 0 or 0, 1, 2, 3, depending on whether the statement is positive or negative regarding school. A high score, therefore, indicates a favorable attitude toward education. Examples of items are:

Too much nonsense goes on in classrooms these days.
There are times when teachers can't be blamed for losing patience with a pupil.
They're not teaching reading as well as they used to.
Schools are the backbone of American democracy.
The school is often to blame where students don't like school.

RELIABILITY AND VALIDITY: The corrected split-half reliability based on sixty-nine parents of 5-year-olds, of upper-lower and lower-middle class status, was .90.

Medinnus found no social-class difference in attitude toward education, although he apparently did not sample the lower and upper ranges proportionately. The correlation between scores of fathers and mothers was .26. Fathers' and mothers' scores were correlated separately with the teacher's ratings of their attitudes toward education. The correlation of mothers' attitudes with teacher rating was −.07; fathers' attitudes and teacher rating, on the other hand, correlated +.53, significant at the .01 level.

BIBLIOGRAPHY:

MEDINNUS, G. R. "The Development of a Parent Attitude Toward Education Scale." *Journal of Educational Research,* 1962, *56*(2), 100–103.

THE TEACHER AS SEEN BY HIS COLLEAGUES

AUTHOR: Morris L. Cogan

AGE: Supervisory personnel of elementary and secondary school teachers, especially principals

VARIABLE: Teacher-pupil interaction

TYPE OF MEASURE: Rating scale

SOURCE FROM WHICH THE MEASURE MAY BE OBTAINED: See Cogan (1956)

DESCRIPTION OF MEASURE: This thirty-five-item Likert type scale has five options, ranging from almost never, poor, or low (score of 1) to very often, superior, or high (score of 5). The direction of the scores is not uniform, however, since a score of 4 may denote desirable teacher behavior on one item but undesirable behavior on another. For example, the items below respectively illustrate the extremes of the desirable-undesirable poles (Cogan, 1956):

This teacher's ability to motivate pupils, to make the class work seem interesting, worthwhile, challenging is (1) poor, (2) a little below average, (3) average, (4) a little above average, (5) superior.

Frequency with which pupils are ridiculed, subject to sarcasm, made fun of: (1) almost never; (2) few times; (3) sometimes; (4) often; (5) very often.

The principal value of the scale does not derive from the total scores but from the sums of three subscales reflecting preclusive, inclusive, and conjunctive behavior. The items of the scale measuring each variable have been enumerated by Cogan (1956). Sample items representative of each variable are given below:

Frequency with which pupils participate in planning, in making classroom decisions on how some of the work is to be done, who will do it, what kind of projects are to be carried out: (1) almost never, (2) few times, (3) sometimes, (4) often, (5) very often (inclusive teacher behavior).

This teacher's ability to motivate pupils, to make the class work seem interesting, worthwhile, challenging is (1) poor, (2) a little below average, (3) average, (4) a little above average, (5) superior (conjunctive teacher behavior).

Frequency with which pupils are punished by being made to sit apart from other pupils or by being sent from room: (1) almost never, (2) few times, (3) sometimes, (4) often, (5) very often (preclusive teacher behavior).

The score for each subscale is the sum of the responses on the items within the scale.

RELIABILITY AND VALIDITY: As part of a larger study investigating teacher-pupil interaction (Cogan, 1954), four principals completed usable returns on this scale and found it comprehensible.

No direct data on validity or reliability are given. In a study that employed a very similar Principal's Rating Scale on 100 unselected teachers at both the elementary and secondary levels, however, the authors obtained a split-half reliability coefficient of .87. In a group of 100 unselected teachers the correlation of Principal's Rating and an Expert's Rating was .48, whereas the correlation between the pupils' perception of their teachers and principals' perceptions was .33. In both instances, the correlations were at the .01 level of significance (Cook and Leeds, 1947).

BIBLIOGRAPHY:

COGAN, M. L. "The Relation of the Behavior of Teachers to the Productive Behavior of Their Pupils." Unpublished doctoral dissertation, Harvard Graduate School of Education, 1959.

COGAN, M. L. "Theory and Design of a Study of Teacher-Pupil Interaction." *Harvard Education Review*, 1956, *26*, 315–342.

COOK, W. W., and LEEDS, C. H. "Measuring the Teaching Personality." *Educational and Psychological Measurement*, 1947, *7*, 399–410.

MOTOR SKILLS, BRAIN INJURY, AND SENSORY PERCEPTION

Group 6-a

Motor Skills

BOSTON UNIVERSITY SPEECH SOUND DISCRIMINATION-PICTURE TEST

AUTHORS: Wilbert Pronovost and Charles Dumbleton

AGE: Kindergarten and first grade

VARIABLE: Articulatory discrimination

TYPE OF MEASURE: Picture-type sound discrimination test

SOURCE FROM WHICH THE MEASURE MAY BE OBTAINED: See Dumbleton et al. (1952)

DESCRIPTION OF MEASURE: The Boston University Speech Sound Discrimination-Picture Test requires children to identify paired word sounds and to discriminate between unlike sounds. It is essentially a revision of a similar scale originally developed by Mansur (1950) and partially validated by Haroian (1951). Each page includes one unlike pairing and two like pairings (for example, cat-cat, bat-bat, cat-bat). Words are randomly placed to eliminate response sets and the pictures themselves are simple line drawings reproduced by multilith.

The complete test consists of seventy-two paired words. The auditory characteristics of the paired sounds consisted of vowels (pen-pin), semi-vowels and nasals (lock-rock), plosives (cat-bat), fricatives (vase-face), blends (grass-glass), and miscellaneous (pan-sand). The test is orally administered on an individual basis, and there is a manual with complete instructions for scoring and administration. The scale has the added advantage of using familiarization instruction before beginning with the test proper. Though the majority of the children complete the test in ten to fifteen minutes, there is no time limit for administering the scale. The test score is simply the number of correct responses.

RELIABILITY AND VALIDITY: When the measure was given to 434 kindergarten and first-grade children, the split-half correlation coefficient, with correction by the Spearman-Brown formula for attenuation, was .88. Sixty-five items discriminated between the upper and lower quarters, with phi coefficients significant at the .01 level of confidence or better. These coefficients range from .17 to .41 (Pronovost and Dumbleton, 1953). The authors caution, however, that the test is insufficiently discriminative to be used for a normal population and also recommend that the administration of the test be tape recorded under a controlled acoustical environment.

BIBLIOGRAPHY:

DUMBLETON, C., FULTON, L. E., LEARY, M. A., MC NAMARA, A. Y., NAKASHIAN, P. M., SIMMERMAN, A., and WISE, P. K. "An Analysis of the Relationships Between Speech and Reading Abilities of Four Hundred and Twenty-Five First Grade Children." Unpublished master's thesis, Boston University, 1952.

HAROIAN, R. D. "Preliminary Validation of Mansur's Speech Sound Discrimination Test in the Kindergarten and First Grade." Unpublished master's thesis, Boston University, 1951.

MANSUR, R. W. "The Construction of a Picture Test for Speech Sound Discrimination." Unpublished master's thesis, Boston University, 1950.

PRONOVOST, W., and DUMBLETON, C. "A Picture-type Speech Sound Discrimination Test." *Journal of Speech and Hearing Disorders*, 1953, *18*, 258–266.

COMPACT PICTURE ARTICULATION TEST

AUTHORS: Ruth B. Irwin and Barbara W. Musselman

AGE: Preschool and early elementary school age children

VARIABLE: Speech (articulation)

TYPE OF MEASURE: Test

SOURCE FROM WHICH THE MEASURE MAY BE OBTAINED: See Irwin and Musselman (1962)

DESCRIPTION OF MEASURE: The CPAT was devised as a more efficient test of articulation. All of the consonants in both initial and final positions, all of the vowels, and all of the diphthongs (sixty-one phonetic elements in all) were incorporated into twenty-seven words. These words were then represented by line drawings. The authors contend that their original short test took half as much time to administer as more conventional measures.

The children's responses to the pictures were scored "correct" or "incorrect" if any deviancy (omission, substitution, or distortion) was noted.

RELIABILITY AND VALIDITY: The test was administered to fourteen children enrolled for speech therapy at the Ohio State University Speech Clinic. The children were of normal intelligence and did not suffer from organic difficulties or stuttering. Equal numbers of children (N = 14) were tested in face-to-face situations or recorded on tape. In the former situation, the fourteen children ranged from 4 to 8 years; in the latter, the age range was from 5 to 7 years. Eight children were involved in both aspects of the study.

In administering the test, experienced speech clinicians evaluated the children by means of face-to-face testing, using both the original Irwin-Musselman shortened test and a conventional longer scale. Both inexperienced and experienced judges evaluated the taped speech of the children. Each type of judge rated the children for the total number of phonetic errors in each type of testing situation. The rank correlations for the two test forms were .980 for face-to-face testing; .971 for the taped testing by inexperienced judges; and .951 for the taped testing by experienced judges. The degree of agreement between the judges on the same test was also calculated by means of Kendall's coefficient of concordance. The findings indicated no significant differences either between tests or between experienced and inexperienced judges. Such agreement indicates concurrent validity for the scale.

BIBLIOGRAPHY:

IRWIN, R. B., and MUSSELMAN, B. W. "A Compact Picture Articulation Test." *Journal of Speech and Hearing Disorders*, 1962, 27, 36–39.

DAILY ACTIVITY RECORD

AUTHOR: Mary Eleanor Brown

AGE: Disabled persons of any age

VARIABLE: Motor skills

TYPE OF MEASURE: Rating scale

SOURCE FROM WHICH THE MEASURE MAY BE OBTAINED: Reprints available from Mary E. Brown, 50 West 8th Street, New York City, New York 10011. Also see Brown (1950a, 1950b, 1950c, and 1951)

DESCRIPTION OF MEASURE: This measure is designed to evaluate the common motor skills of disabled persons as a basis for a rehabilitation program. Disabled persons with mobility problems are checked on their ability to perform one hundred activities of daily life. These activities consist of neuromuscular movements or motor acts varying in complexity and necessary for successful living. The one hundred activities are classified into twelve major groupings. The groupings with sample items and the time allotment for each item are given below (Brown, 1950a):

Speech	Speech	10 seconds
Bed	Back to right side, bed-lying	20 seconds
Bathing and grooming	Combing hair (motions)	30 seconds
Dressing and undressing	Dressing except for fastening shoes or tying shoestrings and putting on and adjusting necktie	15 seconds
Eating	Cutting meat substitute	20 seconds
Desk	Writing or printing	2 minutes
Wheelchair	Bed to wheelchair	1 minute
Bathtub	Into bathtub	1 minute
Appliance	Putting on appliance(s)	15 minutes
Locomotion, upright	Forward thirty feet, upright	15 seconds
Standing-to-sitting and sitting-to-standing	Wheelchair to standing	1 minute
Traveling, upright	Crossing dummy street on green light, upright	22 seconds
	Public vehicles, upright. Traffic	

The author provides an instructional set for each motor act, including the description of the behavior unit itself, the starting position, and the instruction to the subject. As an example, the instructional set for back to right side, bed-lying, follows (Brown, 1950b):

Starting Position: *Back-lying in middle of bed, all extremities downstretched.*
Instructions to Subject: *Turn onto the right side.*

In a series of three articles (1950a, 1950b, and 1951), Brown has provided complete information on administering and scoring all one hundred items of the inventory, criteria for satisfactory responses, and precautions on its administration and use. Other features of the directions include teaching tips for the use of the results, an equipment list necessary to conduct the inventory, and a complete list of categories for scoring responses.

RELIABILITY AND VALIDITY: The inventory was developed under close and extensive medical supervision and by collaborative efforts among nurses, physicians, physical therapists, and occupational therapists (Brown, 1950a). Since these workers are those primarily involved with patients of atypical movements, the agreement on the nature and value of the items constitutes a form of content or logical validity. The directions on administering and scoring the inventory are sufficiently explicit to facilitate scoring for test-retest or inter-rater reliability coefficients.

BIBLIOGRAPHY:

BROWN, M. E. "Daily Activity Inventory and Progress Record for Those with Atypical Movement," Part I. *American Journal of Occupational Therapy,* 1950a, *IV,* 195–204.

BROWN, M. E. "Daily Activity Inventory and Progress Record for Those with Atypical Movement," Part II. *American Journal of Occupational Therapy,* 1950b, *IV,* 261–272.

BROWN, M. E. *Daily Activity Record.* Schenectady, New York: Eastern New York Orthopedic Hospital, 1950c.

BROWN, M. E. "Daily Activity Inventory and Progress Record for Those with Atypical Movement," Part III. *American Journal of Occupational Therapy,* 1951, *V,* 23–29, 39.

IMPULSE-SCALE

AUTHOR: Arne Trankell

AGE: 7 to 10½

VARIABLE: Laterality

TYPE OF MEASURE: Test, individually administered

SOURCE FROM WHICH THE MEASURE MAY BE OBTAINED: Skandinaviska Testforlaget AB, Oxen Stiersgaten 17, Stockholm NO, Sweden

DESCRIPTION OF MEASURE: This measure makes up part of Trankell's laterality tests, the other two basic parts being the Tracing and the Tapping test. The Impulse-Scale only is described here, since in our judgment the other two measures are typical of such measures and can be constructed or adapted readily by the researcher.

The Impulse-Scale consists of twenty items, of which the following are characteristic: pick up an eraser; catch a ball; cut with scissors; pour water; shoot marbles; use a screwdriver; use a hammer; kick a ball; throw a ball; and hop on one foot. Fifteen of the items involve manual activity, four require foot activity, and one is a measure of eye-dominance. Detailed instructions for each item and for the overall testing procedure are provided. Each item is scored according to the hand or foot used by the subject in executing the task. The author provides norms for children ages 7 and 10½.

RELIABILITY AND VALIDITY: The split-half reliability of the fifteen items of the hand Impulse-Scale, administered to eighty-one 7-year-olds, was .91. When the same children were tested twenty-eight days after the first testing, the test-retest correlation coefficient was .86.

BIBLIOGRAPHY:

TRANKELL, A. *Vänsterhänthet hos barn i skoläldern.* Helsingfors: Forum, 1950.

IRWIN ARTICULATION TEST

AUTHOR: Orvis C. Irwin

AGE: Cerebral palsied children between the ages of 3 and 16

VARIABLE: Phonetic articulation

TYPE OF MEASURE: Individually administered rating scale

SOURCE FROM WHICH THE MEASURE MAY BE OBTAINED: See Irwin (1961)

DESCRIPTION OF MEASURE: The Irwin Articulation Test is designed to measure the phonetic articulatory skills of cerebral palsied children from 3 to 16. It consists of four short consonant scales and one vowel scale. Each scale includes a list of words ranging from fifteen to twenty in number. In the administration of the test, which is done on an individual basis, the word lists are read to the child and he is instructed to repeat the words one by one, as they are pronounced by the examiner. On the consonant scales, provisions are made to check initial, medial, and final sounds. On the vowel list, only initial and medial sounds are checked. The measure provides quantitative scores on articulation ability, usable as indicators of growth and change during therapy, and for comparing groups of children.

Scoring may be done during testing, or later if the therapist uses a tape recorder. Directions for administering and scoring the test are given. The score for each test consists of the number of items the child has pronounced correctly. The recording of the responses requires knowledge of the international phonetic alphabet.

RELIABILITY AND VALIDITY: The individual part tests have been administered to a total of 1,155 cerebral palsied subjects in five separate samples. The standardization data for these groups have already been described by Irwin (1956, 1957, 1958a, 1958b, 1959, 1960). However, the scale as a whole, which includes all five parts-tests, has been administered to 147 cerebral palsied children from 3 to 16 years of age. These children were from speech centers in several midwestern and southern cities. Their IQ distribution was as follows: 19 per cent were normal or above normal, 10 per cent were below 40, 81 per cent were below 90, and 39 per cent were below 70.

Three kinds of test reliability were computed. First, the correlation between parallel forms over a two-week period was .98 for the 147 children. Then, Kuder-Richardson coefficients of reliability were respectively .87 and .89 for the initial and medial positions of vowels, and .65, .97, and .97 for the initial, medial, and final position of consonants. Finally, the author repeatedly checked his agreement with other observers with live transcriptions and by reading from tape recordings. These agreements averaged about 90 per cent.

The validity of the test is primarily established by the method of extreme groups. The extreme groups were classified by medical diagnosis of gross paralytic involvement and by ratings from speech therapists on general speech intelligibility and language ability. The articulation scale differentiated between the scores of the two groups (p = .001).

Irwin (1961) calculated the difficulty range of the items, determined the discriminating power and uniqueness of the items, and demonstrated age progression in the scores.

BIBLIOGRAPHY:

IRWIN, O. C. "A Short Test for Use with Cerebral Palsy Children." *Journal of Speech and Hearing Disorders*, 1956, *21*, 446–449.

IRWIN, O. C. "A Second Short Test for Use with Children Who Have Cerebral Palsy." *Cerebral Palsy Review*, 1957, *18*, 18–19.

IRWIN, O. C. "A Third Short Consonant Test for Use with Children with Cerebral Palsy." *Cerebral Palsy Review*, 1958a, *19*, 8–10.

IRWIN, O. C. "A Fourth Short Consonant Test for Use with Children with Cerebral Palsy." *Cerebral Palsy Review*, 1958b, *19*, 12–14.

IRWIN, O. C. "A Fifth Short Consonant Test for Use with Children with Cerebral Palsy." *Cerebral Palsy Review*, 1959, *20*, 7–9.

IRWIN, O. C. "A Short Vowel Test for Use with Children with Cerebral Palsy." *Cerebral Palsy Review*, 1960, *21*, 3–4.

IRWIN, O. C. "A Manual of Articulation Testing for Use with Children with Cerebral Palsy." *Cerebral Palsy Review*, 1961, *22*, 1–24.

PHYSICAL FITNESS TESTS

AUTHOR: F. J. Hayden

AGE: 8 to 17, retarded

VARIABLE: Physical fitness

TYPE OF MEASURE: Test

SOURCE FROM WHICH THE MEASURE MAY BE OBTAINED: See Hayden (1964)

DESCRIPTION OF MEASURE: These tests are designed to measure physical fitness of the mentally retarded. There are two overall tests and subtests as follows:

Tests of muscular fitness: (1) arms and shoulders, hang for time, medicine ball throw; (2) back, back extension flexibility, speed back lifts; (3) abdomen, speed sit ups; (4) legs, vertical jump, floor touch flexibility.
Test of organic fitness: 300 yard run

The equipment needed, the method of testing, and scoring procedures for each of the tests are described. The equipment is relatively simple. The tests can be completed by three testers for fifteen children in three half-hour sessions.

RELIABILITY AND VALIDITY: Standard scores are available, based on scores for severely retarded children only. Scores of "normal" children are generally much higher. Separate norms are provided for retarded boys and girls ages 8 to 9, 10 to 11, 12 to 13, 14 to 15, and 16 to 17.

BIBLIOGRAPHY:

HAYDEN, F. J. *Physical Fitness for the Mentally Retarded: a Manual for Teachers and Parents.* Ontario: Metropolitan Toronto Association for Retarded Children, 1964.

PREDICTIVE SCREENING TEST OF ARTICULATION

AUTHORS: Charles Van Riper and Robert L. Erickson

AGE: Primary school-age children

VARIABLE: Speech articulation

TYPE OF MEASURE: Rating scale

SOURCE FROM WHICH THE MEASURE MAY BE OBTAINED: Continuing Education Office, Western Michigan University, Kalamazoo, Michigan. Available at cost.

DESCRIPTION OF MEASURE: The basic purpose of the Predictive Screening Test of Articulation (PSTA) is to differentiate children with maturational misarticulations from those who exhibit functional errors in speech that will persist without speech therapy by the time third grade is reached. The test consists of forty-seven items subsumed under nine parts, each containing a range of one to twenty-two elements. Among other factors, the scale tests for single consonant sounds, consonant blends articulated within words, correct repetitions of sentences, and replications of rhythms. Administering the test and recording the answers require knowledge of the phonetic alphabet.

Answers are recorded on a separate answer sheet as correct (1) or incorrect (0). A sample answer sheet is included in the manual and the authors have given permission to duplicate it. The score on the test is the number of correct items. Specific directions for administering the test and scoring each item are provided. The test is administered on an individual basis.

RELIABILITY AND VALIDITY: Considerable statistical data support the reliability and validity of the test. (1) The final forty-seven items were selected on the basis of a comprehensive item analysis based on an original test of 111 items. The only items retained were those that differentiated at a statistically significant level ($p < .05$) first-grade children with normal speech from those requiring clinical help. (2) Two cross-validation studies were conducted with first-grade children who had been classified as having functional speech misarticulations serious enough to warrant speech therapy. The raters were state certified speech clinicians. These same children, whenever possible, were tested again in the third grade. The differences between the "still defective" and "normal" subgroups were of sufficient magnitude to demonstrate predictive validity for the test. (3) The original sample of 297 first-grade children was administered two randomly selected halves of the PSTA. The correlation of these halves, corrected by the Spearman-Brown formula, was .895. Inter-rater reliability among six judges, based on the scores of five children, was also high, with a mean coefficient of .97. (4) No significant sex differences were evident.

In using this scale, the authors regard the use of a cutoff score as crucial, and they make several suggestions: (1) A clinician who may want to establish his own local norms should compare his data with the available norms (Riper and Erickson, 1968). (2) To minimize the possibility of extremely high rates of false positives or false negatives, they suggest a cutoff score of 34 or less as a criterion for referral to speech therapy. (3) Data have been provided that show the effects of various cutoff points on the incidence of false positives or false negatives (Riper and Erickson, 1968). This information would enable the clinician to choose the cutoff point that meets his purpose most effectively.

BIBLIOGRAPHY:

VAN RIPER, C., and ERICKSON, R. *Manual: Predictive Screening Test of Articulation.* Kalamazoo, Michigan: Continuing Education Office, Western Michigan University, 1968.

RIGHT-LEFT DISCRIMINATION

AUTHOR: Arthur L. Benton

AGE: 5 to adult

VARIABLE: Right-left discrimination

TYPE OF MEASURE: Test

SOURCE FROM WHICH THE MEASURE MAY BE OBTAINED: See Benton and Cohen (1955)

DESCRIPTION OF MEASURE: This test measures the ability of children and adults to discriminate between right and left. There are two forms of the test: Form A, with thirty-two items, requires the subject to execute "localizing movements" on command. It assesses six aspects of right-left discrimination, the specific tasks being as follows (Benton and Cohen, 1955):

With the eyes open, pointing to single lateral body parts.
With the eyes open, execution of double crossed and uncrossed commands.
With the eyes closed, pointing to single lateral body parts.
With the eyes closed, execution of double crossed and uncrossed commands.
Pointing to lateral body parts on a schematic, frontview representation of a person.
Execution of double crossed and uncrossed commands involving lateral body parts of
  both the subject and the schematic representation.

Form A requires no verbal responses, and no emphasis is placed on speed.

Form V, with thirty-six items, requires the subject to name lateral body parts. Designed to be the verbal response analogy of Form A, it assesses virtually the same aspects of right-left discrimination, but requires the subject to give a verbal response.

Examples of Form A items follow:

Show me your right eye.
Touch your right knee with your right hand.
Point to the man's left ear.
Put your left hand on the man's right shoulder.
(All of the above are done with the eyes open and with the eyes closed.)
Show me your left leg.
Touch your right eye with your left hand.

Form V of the battery includes items like the following:

With the eyes open, the examiner touches the subject's left hand and says, "Which hand is this?" The examiner then points to a picture and says "Which ear is this?" The examiner places the subject's right hand on the subject's right ear and asks, "Which hand is on which ear?" "Now look at these pictures" (Picture B, for example, shows a person with the right hand on the left eye). "Which hand is on which eye?"

With the eyes closed or blindfolded, the examiner touches the subject's left hand and says "Which hand is this?" With the subject's eyes still closed, the examiner gives the same instructions as previously, placing one of the subject's hands on one of his ears and asking him "Which hand is on which ear?"

The same items are used but in reverse order, presumably to eliminate the possibility of the subject's memorizing the order and correct responses.

RELIABILITY AND VALIDITY: With normal children as subjects, corrected odd-even reliability was .88 to .92. The correlation between scores on equivalent forms, given twenty minutes apart, was .72. When equivalent forms were given ten weeks apart, the correlation coefficient was .67. Immediate practice effect was negligible. Norms are given for children ages 6 through 9 (Benton and Cohen, 1955).

BIBLIOGRAPHY:

BENTON, A. L., and COHEN, B. D. "Right-Left Discrimination and Finger Localization in Normal and Brain-Injured Subjects." *Procedures of the Iowa Academy of Science,* 1955.

Group 6-b

Brain Injury

BURKS' BEHAVIOR RATING SCALE

AUTHOR: Harold F. Burks

AGE: Grades one through six

VARIABLE: Organic brain dysfunction

TYPE OF MEASURE: Rating scale

SOURCE FROM WHICH THE MEASURE MAY BE OBTAINED: Office of the Los Angeles Superintendent of Schools, Division of Research and Guidance, 155 W. Washington Boulevard, Los Angeles, California 90015

DESCRIPTION OF MEASURE: The Behavior Rating Scale consists of twenty-eight items divided into three major categories representing expressions of behavior at different levels: vegetative-autonomic, perceptual-discriminative, and social-emotional. The meanings of these categories are explained in detail. Approximately nine items comprise each of these areas.

The scoring on the Behavior Rating Scale requires the teacher to rate a child's overt behavior on a linear dimension according to the severity exhibited. In order of increasing severity, the teacher rates the child on a particular behavior from 1 for behavior not noticeable at all to 5 for behavior noticed to a very large degree. Sample items of the scale from the vegetative-autonomic area are given below:

Hyperactive and restless
Erratic, flighty, or scattered behavior
Easily distracted, lacks continuity of effort and perseverance

RELIABILITY AND VALIDITY: Burks presents two lines of evidence for reliability and four sources of data for validity. Children in grades one to six were rated on a scale and subsamples of ten from each room were rerated two months later. Not a single teacher showed a significant difference in her scores. Also, on the basis of a sign test, only three items of the 124 ratings for each item showed statistically significant differences on the retest.

With respect to validity, the findings are as follows: (1) The scores on the items do not appear to be influenced by age and sex factors. (2) The items of the scale are highly successful in differentiating between children who show abnormal EEG tracings and those who do not. These findings are based on a cross section of 182 regular classroom children. (3) Conduct disorder groups show a much higher score than control groups without such problems. (4) Finally, it has been found that the vast majority of children who were later shown to suffer abnormal EEG tracings scored in the 60 range and upward. With this cutoff score, approximately 12 per cent were false negative and false positives were zero.

BIBLIOGRAPHY:

BURKS, H. F. "A Study of the Organic Basis for Behavioral Deviations in School Children." Unpublished doctoral dissertation, University of Southern California, 1955.

BURKS, H. F. "Brain Pathology and Its Effect on Learning." *Exceptional Children,* 1957, *24,* 169–172.

BURKS, H. F. "The Hyperkinetic Child." *Exceptional Children,* 1960, *27,* 18–26.

CHILD RATING SCALE (Activity Level)

AUTHORS: Thomas McConnell, Jr., Rue L. Cromwell, and Irving Bialer

AGE: 6 years 2 months through 15 years, 1 month for retarded children, though the scale could be employed with children of almost any age level

VARIABLE: Hyperkinesis

TYPE OF MEASURE: Rating scale

SOURCE FROM WHICH THE MEASURE MAY BE OBTAINED: See McConnell et al. (1964)

DESCRIPTION OF MEASURE: The Child Rating Scale consists of ten descriptive statements about body movements to measure hyperkinesis. The rater is required to check the extent to which each item is typical of a child's behavior by answering in terms of "no, never; infrequently; sometimes; frequently; and yes, all the time." The respective scores for these replies range from 0 to 4. Sample items from the scale follow (McConnell et al., 1964):

Did this child seem to do things without thinking—for no apparent reasons?
Did this child get distracted easily? Did he have trouble concentrating and keepng his mind on one thing?
Did this child seem to move about more than a normal child?

RELIABILITY AND VALIDITY: Data on reliability and validity are based on fifty-seven retarded subjects ranging in age between 6 years, 2 months and 15 years, 1 month and in severity of retardation between profound and mild. Though the sample included only ambulatory patients and excluded all those with convulsive disorders, all but four subjects suffered unspecified organicity (chronic brain syndrome).

Children were rated by four attendants who had responsibility for their care. The ratings occurred on two separate occasions prior to treatment by dexedrine and on three additional occasions after treatment by this drug. The test-retest reliability was .86 over a one-week interval before drug administration. The average correlation among all five ratings was .84. This scale showed a positive correlation with sex of the child (r = .56), with boys rated as more active than girls. The results from the Child Rating Scale were unrelated to medical diagnosis. The average correlation between scores on this measure and electronic measurements of body movement was .20 (McConnel et al., 1964).

BIBLIOGRAPHY:

MC CONNELL, T. R., JR., CROMWELL, R. L., BIALER, I., and SON, C. D. "Studies in Activity Level: VII. Effects of Amphetamine Drug Administration on the Activity Level of Retarded Children." *American Journal of Mental Deficiency,* 1964, *68,* 647–651.

ELLIS VISUAL DESIGN TEST (Goldenberg Version)

AUTHOR: Samuel Goldenberg

AGE: Elementary children with Binet Vocabulary IQ scores of 80 or above

VARIABLE: Organic brain disorder

TYPE OF MEASURE: Test

SOURCE FROM WHICH THE MEASURE MAY BE OBTAINED: See Goldenberg (1955)

DESCRIPTION OF MEASURE: The Goldenberg version of the Ellis Test consists of six visual designs of increasing complexity plus a single square. Each design is presented on a 5 × 5 inch white square to be copied by the child on a similar paper. The objective scoring system and the designs are presented in detail. An illustration showing the application of the scoring system in graphic form is also available. The range of possible scores is from 0 to 7. An example of the scoring system as it applies to the drawing of the diamond follows (Goldenberg, 1955):

1 point: (1) completely correct except for slight irregularities due to lack of motor skill or hasty execution; (2) each of the four angles is well defined—not rounded or having ears, etc.; (3) each pair of angles must be approximately opposite; (4) figure must be more diamond-shaped than square or kite-shaped; long axis vertical; (5) no additions to the figure.
½ point: failure to meet any one of the requirements for full credit.
0 points: two or more errors.

RELIABILITY AND VALIDITY: The scale has been administered as part of a battery of tests to three groups of children with a total N of 90. The groups included children with brain injury (N = 26), emotional disturbance (N = 32), and normal development (N = 32). All children, however, had Binet vocabulary IQ scores of 80 or more. With this sample, the measure had a very high Efficiency Score, a measure that was derived from the ratio between the correct identifications for brain-injured children and false-positives. Also, discriminant function analysis revealed that this scale, along with the Marble Board Test, contributed as much to discrimination as the combined data from all other measures in the battery.

Using the total score on the test as outlined in the scoring system, Goldenberg was able to obtain very high product-moment correlation coefficients between his scorings and those of five judges trained by him. With one exception (r of .69) these coefficients were .90 or greater. In addition, recent work by Goldenberg (1967) suggests a cutoff score of 3.0 or below as most effective for differentiating between brain injured and non-brain injured children between the ages of 7 and 13, provided that vocabulary intellectual levels are at least at the dull-normal level.

BIBLIOGRAPHY:

GOLDENBERG, S. "Appendix I: Scoring Guide to Marble Board Test and Ellis Visual Design Test." In A. A. Strauss and N. C. Kephart (Eds.), *Psychopathology and Education of the Brain-Injured Child*. Vol. 2. *Progress in Theory and Clinic*. New York: Grune & Stratton, 1955, pp. 215–222.

GOLDENBERG, S. "Testing the Brain-Injured Child with Normal IQ." In A. A. Strauss and N. C. Kephart (Eds.), *Psychopathology and Education of the Brain-Injured Child*. Vol 2. *Progress in Theory and Clinic*. New York: Grune & Stratton, 1955a.

GRAHAM BEHAVIOR TEST FOR NEONATES

AUTHOR: Frances K. Graham

AGE: Infants (neonates 1 to 5 days old)

VARIABLE: Trauma from birth injury

TYPE OF MEASURE: Rating scale based on specific reactions to stimuli

SOURCE FROM WHICH THE MEASURE MAY BE OBTAINED: See Graham (1956); Graham et al. (1956)

DESCRIPTION OF MEASURE: The Behavior Test for Neonates has five sub-scales, including a Pain-Threshold Test, a Maturation Scale, a Vision Scale, an Irritability Rating, and a Muscle Tension Rating. An abbreviated description follows for each subscale:

Pain-Threshold Test: The Pain-Threshold Test attempts to measure sensory defect as an index of birth trauma. The intent of the scale is to determine pain sensitivity by the manner in which the infant reacts to shock delivered by an electronic stimulator. Essentially, the aim is to gauge the minimum amount of voltage necessary to elicit a withdrawal response in the lower extremities.

Maturation Scale: The Maturation Scale consists of nine items on which an observer rates motor movements or reactions of the neonate. Credits are given to the neonate on the basis of his response level, with 21 constituting the maximum possible score. Detailed directions on the procedure, scoring methods, and trial runs have been outlined. A record blank is also provided as an aid in scoring. Illustrative of the nine behavioral acts the observer rates are head reaction in a prone position, crawling in a prone position, vigor, grasp, and persistence (Graham, 1956).

Vision Scale: In the Vision Scale, the infant's response to a moving stimulus is observed and categorized on the basis of several dimensions, such as presence or absence of fixation or pursuit, direction of eye movement, extent of eye movement. The items are arranged in an increasing order of difficulty so that passing one of the ten items assumes success for a less difficult performance.

Irritability Rating: The Irritability Rating assesses the sensitivity of the infant to stimulation. For this purpose, a three-point scale of 0, 1, and 2 is used respectively for normal irritability, just-perceptible irritability, and abnormal irritability. A description of each point on the scale of irritability is provided.

Muscle Tension Rating: The Muscle Tension Scale measures the amount of deviation in either increased flaccidity or rigidity. The ratings include the five sub-measures of limb muscle tone in a supine position, resistance to limb displacement, change in muscle tone when being pulled to a sitting position, amount of spontaneous activity, and frequency of trembling of body parts. The ratings are in terms of descriptions rather than numerical value. For example, trembling is described by such classifications as none, mild, moderate, and severe. At the end of the examination, however, an overall numerical rating is made ranging from -2 (flaccid) to $+2$ (marked tension). As an aid in scoring, a recording blank is provided for both the Irritability Rating and the Tension Rating.

The authors provide details on the criteria for classifying the infants as normal or traumatized, special variables to consider in the testing, materials and equipment necessary, and directions on administering and scoring the infants' responses (Graham, 1956).

RELIABILITY AND VALIDITY: Split-half reliabilities for the Pain-Threshold scores for both traumatized and nontraumatized children ranged from .82 to .97. The other subtest scores could not be satisfactorily divided into comparable halves. Test-retest reliabilities for the Pain, Maturation, and Vision scales were from .62 to .69. On the Irritability and Vision scales, the test-retest agreements after twenty-four hours were respectively 75 and 86 per cent of perfect agreement. Statistics on interscorer agreement were as follows: Maturation Scale (r = .97); Vision Scale (r = .90); Irritability Scale (68 per cent perfect agreement). Finally, there was 79 per cent perfect agreement in the Tension Scale (Graham, et al., 1956).

Statistics are provided for differentiating groups and accurate identification of individuals as members of a particular group. Statistically significant differences between the normal and traumatized groups occurred on all five scales based on F test, t test, and Chi square (Graham, 1956).

Normal and traumatized groups, paired for relevant variables, obtained significantly different scores on all tests. When a cutting point at the poorer extreme of the normal distribution was selected, all tests identified some traumatized subjects as abnormal while false positives ranged only from 1 to 3 per cent. The percentage identified as abnormal increased with the seriousness, as rated by pediatricians, of the trauma. The authors recommend a combined abnormality score for the entire scale since the intercorrelations of the five tests were low. Cross-validation of the cutoff scores, however, has not occurred (Graham, et al., 1956).

BIBLIOGRAPHY:

GRAHAM, F. K. "Behavioral Differences between Normal and Traumatized Newborns: I. The Test Procedures." *Psychological Monographs*, 1956, *70* (20, Whole No. 427).

GRAHAM, F. K., MATARAZZO, R. G., and CALDWELL, B. M. "Behavioral Differences between Normal and Traumatized Newborns: II. Standardization, Reliability, and Validity." *Psychological Monographs*, 1956, *70* (21, Whole No. 428).

LIPSITT, L. P., and LEVY, N. "Electrotactual Threshold in the Neonate." *Child Development*, 1956, *30*, 547–554.

ROSENBLITH, J. F. "Neonatal Assessment." *Psychological Reports*, 1959, *5*, 791.

ROSENBLITH, J. F., and LIPSITT, L. P. "Interscorer Agreement for the Graham Behavior Test for Neonates." *Journal of Pediatrics*, 1959, *54*, 200–205.

GRAHAM-ERNHART BLOCK-SORT OR CONCEPTS TEST

AUTHORS: Frances K. Graham and Claire B. Ernhart

AGE: Preschool

VARIABLE: Brain injury

TYPE OF MEASURE: Test

SOURCE FROM WHICH THE MEASURE MAY BE OBTAINED: There is a limited supply of Appendix C which includes forty-nine pages of standard score tables and scoring forms so they can be made available only to individuals planning extensive use of the test procedures. Address inquiries to: Frances K. Graham, University of Wisconsin, School of Medicine, 2927 Howard Drive, Madison, Wisconsin 53705. Additional information about the procedures may be found in several references (Graham et al., 1960, 1962, 1963).

DESCRIPTION OF MEASURE: The test consists of twenty-six blocks in combinations of three colors, three forms, and three sizes. Detailed descriptions of the combinations, the dimensions, hue, and numbers of the various materials are provided, as well as the form and sequence of the test's administration. The scale involves four difficulty levels. In Level I, the subject merely places blocks in the form boards. Level II involves matching, and Levels III and IV require sorting. The Level III task is to sort six blocks into like groups when the blocks differ first only in color, then in size, then in form. The maximum score possible on the test is 27 points. The conditions under which credits can be assigned automatically, and some scoring examples, are given.

RELIABILITY AND VALIDITY: The children tested with this measure were a balanced sample and a cross-validation sample drawn from essentially normal children. In the former, the children ranged in age from 2½ to 5½ years. Within this age range, groups were divided by half-year steps and each group included nine boys and nine girls, of whom three of each sex were Negro and six were white. The white subjects, in turn, were subdivided into two equal groups—under private medical care and under clinic care. Subjects from the most deprived socioeconomic level were not obtained. The totals for the balanced sample consisted of 108 children with eighteen in each of six groups. Additional children from an even larger group were examined as a cross-validation sample. The age, sex, and clinic status of the combined normal groups have been outlined in detail (Graham et al., 1963). Extensive tables on standard scores have been developed.

Test-retest reliabilities over a six-month period for both raw and standard score were respectively .70 and .61 for a group of thirty-seven children between the ages of 3 and 5½ (Graham et al., 1963).

With respect to validity, children selected as brain-damaged by a neurologist (N = 71) did significantly poorer on the test than their normal counterparts (N = 185). These differences held up even when they were adjusted for covariance with the Vocabulary score on the Binet scale, indicating significant impairment revealed by the tests beyond that also measured by the vocabulary test (Graham et al., 1963).

BIBLIOGRAPHY:

GRAHAM, F. K., BERMAN, P. W., and ERNHART, C. B. "Development in Preschool Children of the Ability to Copy Forms." *Child Development,* 1960, *31,* 339–359.

GRAHAM, F. K., ERNHART, C. B., THURSTON, B., and CRAFT, M. "Development Three Years after Perinatal Anoxia and Other Potentially Damaging Newborn Experiences." *Psychological Monographs,* 1962, *76,* 1–53.

GRAHAM, F. K., ERNHART, C. B., CRAFT, M., and BERMAN, P. W. "Brain Injury in the Preschool Child: Some Developmental Considerations." *Psychological Monographs,* 1963, *77,* 1–33.

GRAHAM-ERNHART COPY-FORMS TEST

AUTHORS: Frances K. Graham and Claire B. Ernhart

AGE: Preschool

VARIABLE: Brain injury

TYPE OF MEASURE: Test

SOURCE FROM WHICH THE MEASURE MAY BE OBTAINED: (Limited distribution) Frances K. Graham, University of Wisconsin, School of Medicine, 2927 Howard Drive, Madison, Wisconsin 53705

DESCRIPTION OF MEASURE: The test requires the subject to copy eighteen forms drawn in black ink on 5 × 8 inch cards, with each individual card presenting only one form. The forms themselves range in complexity from a straight line to a diamond. Incomplete geometric designs are also included. Drawings are scored in terms of several categories, including the organization of parts, the size relationships, and the intersection of parts (Graham et al., 1963). Some data are also provided for scaling the relative difficulty of the parts and scoring for accuracy in reproduction (Graham, Berman, and Ernhart, 1960). Details on materials, scoring, and administering the tests are available, including specific criteria for scoring and a sample record form (Graham and Ernhart, *Test Procedures,* Appendix A).

RELIABILITY AND VALIDITY: The reader should consult the review of the Graham-Ernhart Block-Sort Test for details on the samples used. The authors have provided data on both split-half and test-retest reliabilities for this test. In the former case, the r was .97 for a sample of fifty subjects distributed equally among five age groups. In the latter instance, r was .86 for raw scores and .61 for standard scores (N = 33). The performance of sixty brain-injured children was inferior to that of 126 normal children, at a statistically significant level.

BIBLIOGRAPHY:

GRAHAM, F. K., BERMAN, P. W., and ERNHART, C. B. "Development in Preschool Children of the Ability to Copy Forms." *Child Development,* 1960, *31,* 339–359.

GRAHAM, F. K., ERNHART, C. B., THURSTON, B., and CRAFT, M. "Development Three Years after Perinatal Anoxia and Other Potentially Damaging Newborn Experiences." *Psychological Monographs,* 1962, *76,* 1–53.

GRAHAM, F. K., ERNHART, C. B., CRAFT, M., and BERMAN, P. W. "Brain Injury in the Preschool Child: Some Developmental Considerations." *Psychological Monographs,* 1963, *77,* 1–33.

GRAHAM-ERNHART PARENTAL QUESTIONNAIRE

AUTHORS: Frances K. Graham and Claire B. Ernhart

AGE: Preschool brain-injured children but primarily 3-year-olds

VARIABLE: Personality traits

TYPE OF MEASURE: Questionnaire (rating scale)

SOURCE FROM WHICH THE MEASURE MAY BE OBTAINED: There is a limited supply of Appendix C which includes forty-nine pages of standard score tables and scoring forms so they can be made available only to individuals planning extensive use of the test procedures. Address inquiries to: Frances K. Graham, University of Wisconsin, School of Medicine, 2927 Howard Drive, Madison, Wisconsin 53705. Additional information about the procedures may be found in several references (Graham et al., 1960; Graham, et al., 1962; and Graham et al., 1963).

DESCRIPTION OF MEASURE: The PQ includes 209 items printed on individual cards describing a wide range of activities among preschool children relating primarily to behavior expected from brain-injured or maladjusted children. In describing his child's behavior, the parent is asked to sort the items as being like, unlike, or questionably like his child. An alternate form, which has been used to obtain test records by mail, is also available.

Though the test primarily measures two broad dimensions of behavior, it also includes fourteen subscales. These include one subscale that provides a check on general factors determining test responses by parents, six Brain-Injury scales, and seven Maladjustment scales. The first two items from each of the subscales are presented as examples:

Brain-Injury scale, Hyperactivity subscale: *(1) too active, (2) always on the go.*

Brain-Injury scale, Aggressiveness subscale: *(1) gets mad easily, (2) hits other children.*

Brain-Injury scale, Emotionality subscale: *(1) gets upset by any little thing, (2) gives up if can't do something right away.*

Brain-Injury scale, Demandingness subscale: *(1) always shows off when people come to the house, (2) has to have his (or her) own way.*

Brain-Injury scale, Unpredictability subscale: *(1) sometimes feel you can't do anything with him (or her), (2) never know what he (or she) is going to do next.*

Brain-Injury scale, Temperateness subscale: *(1) can depend on him (or her), (2) can play well by himself (or herself).*

Maladjustment scale, Inactivity subscale: *(1) moves slowly, (2) not very active.*

Maladjustment scale, Infantilism subscale: *(1) clings to mother, (2) is pretty much of a baby still.*

Maladjustment scale, Negativism subscale: *(1) wants to do the opposite of what he (or she) is asked, (2) is stubborn.*

Maladjustment scale, Compulsiveness subscale: *(1) can't stand to be dirty, (2) always wants things just so.*

Maladjustment scale, Fearfulness subscale: (*1*) *is afraid of almost everything*, (*2*) *is afraid of dogs.*

Maladjustment scale, Inwardness subscale: (*1*) *acts nervous*, (*2*) *worries me a lot.*

Independence subscale: (*1*) *pretty independent for his (or her) age*, (*2*) *dresses himself (or herself) pretty well.*

Buffer subscale: (*1*) *loves his (or her) mother*, (*2*) *loves his (or her) father.*

In scoring the responses, 1 point is given for "true" responses and ½ point for each "not true" response. The item points for each subscale are summed.

RELIABILITY AND VALIDITY: The same comments regarding the sample and the tables of standard scores apply here as they did to the Block-Sort or Concepts Test. The range of split-half reliability coefficients for the Brain-Injury subscale was from .77 to .81 and for the Maladjustment scale from .54 to .77. These data were based on a mean of 100 brain-injured children between the ages of 2½ and 5½. For brain-injured children, test-retest reliabilities for the Brain-Injury subscale range from .69 to .84 for raw scores and .69 to .80 for standard scores. The coefficients for the Maladjustment subscales range between .64 to .84, regardless of the scoring system used. In both instances, N = 46.

Within the Brain-Injury scales, the subscale of unpredictability differentiated the mean performances of brain-injured and normal groups at a statistically significant level. On the Maladjustment scale, the brain-injured children did significantly poorer on the scores for the entire scale and on all of the subscales except Fearfulness (Graham et al., 1963).

BIBLIOGRAPHY:

GRAHAM, F. K., BERMAN, P. W., and ERNHART, C. B. "Development in Preschool Children of the Ability to Copy Forms." *Child Development*, 1960, *31*, 339–359.

GRAHAM, F. K., ERNHART, C. B., THURSTONE, B., and CRAFT, M. "Development Three Years after Perinatal Anoxia and Other Potentially Damaging Newborn Experiences." *Psychological Monographs*, 1962, *76*, 1–53.

GRAHAM, F. K., ERNHART, C. B., CRAFT, M., and BERMAN, P. W. "Brain Injury in the Preschool Child: Some Developmental Considerations." *Psychological Monographs*, 1963, *77*, 1–33.

PERCEPTUAL-MOTOR BATTERY

AUTHORS: Frances K. Graham and Claire B. Ernhart

AGE: Preschool children

VARIABLE: Brain injury

TYPE OF MEASURE: Test

SOURCE FROM WHICH THE MEASURE MAY BE OBTAINED: See Graham and Ernhart (1963)

DESCRIPTION OF MEASURE: The Perceptual-Motor Battery, which has been described in some detail by the authors (Graham et al., 1963), includes the Figure-Ground subtest, the Tactual-Localization subtest, Mark-the-Cars subtest, and the Peripheral-Distraction subtest.

The Figure-Ground subtest closely resembles the test developed by Strauss and Lehtinen (1947) for use with older brain-injured children. On this scale, the examiner requires the subject to identify thirty-five objects from the Binet Picture Vocabulary when these are embedded in distracting backgrounds. The stimuli are presented individually in two sessions, with no time limit set on the responses. The set of thirty-five cards is administered in two ways: as the original cards with no distracting stimuli, and as reproductions embedded in distracting backgrounds. The scoring consists of the number of incorrect identifications on the embedded procedure that had been marked as correct under nondistracting conditions.

The Tactual-Localization subtest is essentially similar to the Face-Hand test (Fink and Bender, 1953).

The Mark-the-Cars subscale is similar to the Figure-Ground subtest in that the subject is to identify ten drawings of cars embedded in distracting background figures. Two trials are given and two scores are recorded—one for accuracy in marking the cars (Mark-Car Accuracy score) and one for the maturity of the markings themselves (Mark-Car Mark score).

The Peripheral-Distraction subtest requires the subject to place a vase of flowers in the center of a sheet of white paper, under four conditions of distraction. Details are available on the necessary materials, administration of the scale, method of scoring, and examples of scoring.

RELIABILITY AND VALIDITY: When the scores for the entire battery are considered, the standard score test-retest correlation for a six-month period (N = 34) was .58. The subscale correlations for comparable groups generally ranged from .32 to .41. On the Figure-Ground subscale, however, the test-retest correlation was so low (r = 12) that the authors are considering eliminating it from the battery.

In samples of 175 to 184 normal children and sixty-one to sixty-eight brain-injured subjects, the latter group exhibited statistically significant inferior mean performances on the entire battery and on all the subscales with the exception of the Distraction-CE subtest.

BIBLIOGRAPHY:

ERNHART, C. B., GRAHAM, F. K., EICHMAN, P. L., MARSHALL, J. M., and THURSTON, B. "Brain-Injury in the Preschool Child; Some Developmental Considerations. II. Comparison of Brain-Injured and Normal Children." *Psychological Monographs,* 1963, *77,* 17–33.

FINK, M., and BENDER, M. B. "Perception of Simultaneous Tactile Stimuli in Normal Children." *Neurology,* 1953, *3,* 27–34.

GRAHAM, F. K., BERMAN, P. W., and ERNHART, C. B. "Development in Preschool Children of the Ability to Copy Forms." *Child Development,* 1960, *31,* 339–359.

STRAUSS, A. A., and LEHTINEN, L. E. *Psychopathology and Education of the Brain-Injured Child.* New York: Grune & Stratton, 1947.

STRAUSS-WERNER MARBLE BOARD TEST
(Goldenberg Version)

AUTHOR: Samuel Goldenberg

AGE: Elementary school age children

VARIABLE: Organic brain disorders

TYPE OF MEASURE: Test

SOURCE FROM WHICH THE MEASURE MAY BE OBTAINED: See Goldenberg (1955)

DESCRIPTION OF MEASURE: The Marble Board Test, which measures the reproduction of visually perceived stimuli, requires two identical square boards having ten rows of ten holes. The examiner makes a design on one board by putting marbles in some of the holes; the subject reproduces the design on his board. The examiner records the location and sequence of placements for each pattern. Directions for these boards are given by Strauss and Lehtinen (1947).

In his version of the Strauss-Werner Marble Board Test, Goldenberg presents an objective scoring system on the variables of accuracy, method of approach, and organization. Examples and definitions of each scoring procedure are provided.

RELIABILITY AND VALIDITY: The Marble Board Test was administered as part of a battery of tests to twenty-six children with clear diagnosis of brain injuries, thirty-two emotionally disturbed children, and thirty-two normal children. All had Binet vocabulary IQ scores of 80 or above.

Discriminant function analysis reveals that the "approach" aspect of the Marble Board Test differentiated brain-injured children as well as did the Ellis Visual Designs, which contributed most of the discrimination obtainable with the nine test measures included. The Ellis Visual Designs and the Marble Board Test were the most effective combinations for diagnosis of brain injury in children (Goldenberg, 1955).

Two experienced clinical psychologists, specially trained in the use of the scoring rules, scored independently 104 performances on the Marble Board produced by thirteen subjects. They and Goldenberg agreed completely in 88 per cent of the cases involving the scoring of "method"; in scoring "accuracy" there was 91 per cent complete agreement, and 75 per cent complete agreement in scoring "organization."

BIBLIOGRAPHY:

GOLDENBERG, S. "Appendix I: Scoring Guide to Marble Board Test and Ellis Visual Design Test." In A. A. Strauss and N. C. Kephart (Eds.), *Psychopathology and Education of the Brain-injured Child.* Vol. 2. *Progress in Theory and Clinic.* New York: Grune & Stratton, 1955. Pp. 215–222.

STRAUSS, A. A., and LEHTINEN, L. *Psychopathology and Education of the Brain-Injured Child.* New York: Grune & Stratton, 1957.

Group 6-c

Sensory Perception

AUDITORY-VISUAL PATTERN TEST

AUTHORS: Herbert G. Birch and Lillian Belmont

AGE: 9 years 4 months to 10 years 4 months (boys only)

VARIABLE: Auditory-visual integration

TYPE OF MEASURE: Test

SOURCE FROM WHICH THE MEASURE MAY BE OBTAINED: See Birch and Belmont (1964)

DESCRIPTION OF MEASURE: The test, which is administered individually, consists of matching auditory tap patterns with corresponding visual configurations. Details on the content of the test, the sequence of administration, and the scoring are provided. The entire scale consists of three sample items and ten in the test proper. On the sample items, the examiner provides the correct response in the event of error by the examinee. In the test proper, only first choices are accepted but responses and scoring are facilitated by a multiple-choice format.

The score is the number of correct matchings between auditory-tap patterns and visual stimuli. In interpreting the uses and value of the test, the authors point out that the instrument may serve as a significant index of reading readiness. They also contend that the findings are unaffected by any impairments in hearing or vision among the children. They suggest caution in using poor performance on the test for determining etiology of poor reading.

RELIABILITY AND VALIDITY: The authors hypothesized that retarded readers would do more poorly on the test than normal age-mate controls. The samples chosen to test this hypothesis included 150 boys who had scored at the lowest 10 per cent on three of four reading tests and a comparison group of fifty boys matched for age and school class but not in the lowest 10 per cent of readers. Both groups, which included only children with IQ scores greater than 80, were drawn from Aberdeen, Scotland. The hypothesis was verified on all four of the reading tests used ($p < .001$).

Though normal readers had a significantly higher mean IQ score than did the poor readers ($p < .001$), children with lower auditory-visual performance tended to have lower reading scores *within* the two groups. Moreover, the differences in performance on the test continued to be statistically significant, even after the elimination of children with low normal IQ scores (Birch and Belmont, 1964).

BIBLIOGRAPHY:

BIRCH, H. G., and BELMONT, L. "Auditory-Visual Integration in Normal and Retarded Readers." *American Journal of Orthopsychiatry,* 1964, *34,* 852–861.

CHILDREN'S VISUAL ACHIEVEMENT FORM

AUTHOR: Winter Haven Lions Club

AGE: Preschool and primary school age

VARIABLE: Perceptual maturity (eye-hand-motor skills)

TYPE OF MEASURE: Test

SOURCE FROM WHICH THE MEASURE MAY BE OBTAINED: Winter Haven Lions Publication, Committee, Box 1045, Winter Haven, Florida

DESCRIPTION OF MEASURE: This measure is part of a combination diagnostic and training program to measure and promote an aspect of perceptual maturity. Testing and training procedure manuals are available. There are two testing procedures that can be administered in either group or individual form. The first form, the Perceptual Forms Procedure, consists of seven mostly familiar geometric forms, in booklet presentation for individual testing. Group Test Cards are mentioned (Sutphin, 1964, p. 27), but they are not further described in the Handbook or in the Teachers Manual (Winter Haven Lions Club, 1963). The children are instructed to copy the forms, presented one at a time, and the testing can be completed in a few minutes.

The group scoring for this procedure is not clear from the materials available to us. The scoring method for individual administration of the test assigns score points for specific characteristics of the drawings. For example, the drawing of the horizontal diamond is scored as follows: straight lines, no "elbows," 4; points closed and sharp, 3; all sides equal in length, 2; and vertical orientation, 3 (total of 12 points). The individual scoring procedure is given in both the Manual and the Handbook, although the two sources differ in method of scoring the divided rectangle.

The second procedure, the Incomplete Forms Procedure, presents the subject with portions of the seven figures used in the Perceptual Forms Procedure, and he is to complete the figures. No scoring method is given, the only statement being, "All of the records are judged on the completion of the Incomplete Forms" (Sutphin, 1964).

Manas (1961) developed the revision of the scoring method used for the individual administration of the CVAF. He presents both the original and the revised scoring method.

Eleven sample cases are illustrated in the Handbook, with reproduction of the original protocols accompanied by the suggested scoring for each.

RELIABILITY AND VALIDITY: No evidence is given for reliability of either procedure. The Handbook quotes Lowder (1956) as finding a significant relationship between perceptual ability and school achievement.

BIBLIOGRAPHY:

MANAS, L. "A New Method of Scoring the Children's Visual Achievement Forms." *Journal of American Optometrist Association,* April 1961, 713–718.

SUTPHIN, F. E. *A Perceptual Testing-Training Handbook for First Grade Teachers.* Winter Haven Lions Club, October, 1964.

WINTER HAVEN LIONS PUBLICATION COMMITTEE. *Teacher's Test Manual.* Winter Haven Lions Club, 1963.

ELKIND'S AMBIGUOUS PICTURES

AUTHOR: David Elkind

AGE: 6 to 11

VARIABLE: Perceptual development

TYPE OF MEASURE: Test, individually administered

SOURCE FROM WHICH THE MEASURE MAY BE OBTAINED: Photoprints of each of the pictures have been deposited with the American Documentation Institute. Order Document No. 8154 from ADI Auxiliary Publications Project, Photoduplication Service, Library of Congress, Washington, D.C. 20540, remitting in advance $1.25 for photoprints or $1.25 for 35 mm. microfilm. Make checks payable to Chief, Photoduplication Service, Library of Congress.

DESCRIPTION OF MEASURE: The Ambiguous Pictures Test consists of two sets (A and B) of seven black and white ambiguous pictures mounted on 8 × 11½ inch tag board sheets. For one set of pictures shields are available which, when placed over the picture, make the object clearly recognizable. The objects are common ones like cat, tree, leaf, face, and so on. Standardized directions are available for the administration of the test, its scoring, timing, and sequence of presentation (Elkind, 1964). The test is individually administered in a fixed order and the child is required to state what he sees in each card. The scoring is quite straightforward in that the child receives one point for each picture identified correctly.

RELIABILITY AND VALIDITY: On a sample of 135 children, ranging in age from 6 to 11, the two sets have shown comparable means and variance scores at each age level. There was a progressive increase in score with greater chronological age, as well as consistency between the two forms, with coefficients ranging between .32 to .71 for the two forms (Elkind, 1964). Scores on the scale distinguish between poor and average readers in the expected direction (Elkind et al., 1965b). Further, though special training in perceptual skills did improve performance considerably among children in the 6 to 8 age range, initial differences between age groups were still apparent (Elkind, et al., 1962). According to the authors, these data show the extremely important role of maturation in breaking away from the influence of the dominant pattern of an object in determining perception and hence provide construct validity for Piaget's notion on decentration (Elkind, et al., 1965b).

BIBLIOGRAPHY:

ELKIND, D. "Ambiguous Pictures for Study of Perceptual Development and Learning." *Child Development*, 1964, *35*, 1391–1396.

ELKIND, D., KOEGLER, R. R., and GO, E. "Effects of Perceptual Training at Three Age Levels." *Science*, 1962, *137*, 755–756.

ELKIND, D., KOEGLER, R. R., GO, E., and VAN DOORNINCK, W. "Effects of Perceptual Training on Unmatched Samples of Brain-Injured and Familial Retarded Children." *Journal of Abnormal Psychology*, 1965a, *70*, 107–110.

ELKIND, D., LARSON, M., and VAN DOORNINCK, W. "Perceptual Decentration Learning and Performance in Slow and Average Readers." *Journal of Educational Psychology*, 1965b, *56*, 50–56.

FINGER LOCALIZATION TEST

AUTHOR: Arthur L. Benton

AGE: Approximately 5 to adult

VARIABLE: Finger localization

TYPE OF MEASURE: Test

SOURCE FROM WHICH THE MEASURE MAY BE OBTAINED: See Benton and Cohen (1955)

DESCRIPTION OF MEASURE: Finger localization may be evaluated by simply asking the subject to show his little finger, his ring finger, until all the fingers have been identified, usually in random order. The test deals with three types of performance in finger localization, in which the subject identifies the fingers that were stimulated individually, with his hand visible to him; individually, with his hand hidden from his view; and in pairs, simultaneously, with his hand hidden from his view. The test thus consists of sixty items, ten items for each of three types of performance for each hand. A schematic drawing of the right or left hand with the digits numbered from 1 to 5 is provided, enabling the subject to respond by pointing or naming the number of the finger, without the necessity of a verbal response.

Items are scored either right or wrong. Norms are given for 6-, 7-, 8-, and 9-year-old children tested by Benton and Cohen (1955) and for children ages 6 through 12 tested by Wake (1957). Numbers of localization errors for each finger on each hand are given for a sample of one hundred children.

RELIABILITY AND VALIDITY: Using a test battery of fifty items similar to those described above, Benton and Cohen (1955) found the corrected split-half reliability of the battery to be .91 (N = 158). Reliabilities of localization (identification of finger) under the following conditions were: twenty items, with the aid of vision: .91; thirty items, without the aid of vision: .90; twenty items, single fingers, without vision: .86; ten items, pairs of fingers, simultaneous stimulation: .72. Practice effect, measured by gain in mean score of equivalent forms given twenty minutes apart, was negligible.

BIBLIOGRAPHY:

BENTON, A. L., and COHEN, B. D. "Right-Left Discrimination and Finger Localization in Normal and Brain-Injured Subjects." *Proceedings of Iowa Academy of Science,* 1955, *62,* 447–451.

MATTHEWS, C. G., and FOLK, E. D. "Finger Localization, Intelligence, and Arithmetic in Mentally Retarded Subjects." *American Journal of Mental Deficiency,* 1964, *69*(1).

WAKE, F. R. "Finger Localization in Canadian School Children." Paper read at Canadian Psychological Association, Ottawa, June, 1956.

WAKE, F. R. "Finger Localization Scores in Defective Children." Paper read at Canadian Psychological Association, Toronto, June, 1957.

HIDDEN FIGURES TEST

AUTHOR: Leonard Cobrinik

AGE: 6 to 11

VARIABLE: Figure-ground discrimination

TYPE OF MEASURE: Test, individually administered

SOURCE FROM WHICH THE MEASURE MAY BE OBTAINED: The pictures are adapted from picture-puzzles published in *Children's Activities,* a publication of the Child Training Association, Inc. Dr. Cobrinik provided us with copies of his adaptation of the original figures.

DESCRIPTION OF MEASURE: There are three sets of ten stimulus figures, plus one or two samples for each set. One set is called picture puzzles, and is the usual type of hidden-figure puzzles seen in children's magazines. The second set of ten is the overlapping type of picture in which figures and background share points rather than contours. The third type of item, called nonoverlapping, involves shared contours of figure and background. On the overlapping and nonoverlapping the subject was told to find one of four pictured objects within the masked condition. The picture-puzzle tasks were to find the given object within the picture.

RELIABILITY AND VALIDITY: Cobrinik (1959) found that performance on this test was affected by variations in age, type of tasks employed, and group. Intelligence test scores were not significantly related to scores on this measure, although the samples of subjects on which this finding was made stayed within a relatively narrow IQ range. Hidden-figures test scores were significantly related to degree of motor impairment.

BIBLIOGRAPHY:

COBRINIK, L. "The Performance of Brain-Injured Children on Hidden-Figure Tests."
    The American Journal of Psychology, 1959, *LXXII,* 566–571.

IRWIN-JENSEN SOUND DISCRIMINATION TEST

AUTHORS: Orvis C. Irwin and Paul J. Jensen

AGE: 6 to 17 for two groups of exceptional children: cerebral palsied and educable mentally retarded

VARIABLE: Sound discrimination

TYPE OF MEASURE: Individually administered rating scale

SOURCE FROM WHICH THE MEASURE MAY BE OBTAINED: See Irwin and Jensen (1963a, 1963b)

DESCRIPTION OF MEASURE: The Irwin-Jensen Sound Discrimination Test consists of thirty pairs of words that are orally presented to the child by the examiner one by one. The child is asked if the words are the same or different. Three possible scores are available: the total number of correct responses, the total number of errors, and the number of no responses. In calculating the scores, five item pairs of identical words should not be included; they merely indicate if the child is listening. The twenty-five word-pairs, then, are unlike words.

In administering the test, two precautions should be taken. First, the child should be tested for hearing. Also, the examiner should determine if the child is mature enough to understand the difference between "same" and "different." A parallel form (Form B) with adequate reliability and validity has also been developed (Irwin and Jensen, 1963b).

RELIABILITY AND VALIDITY: Forms A and B have been administered to both cerebral palsied and mentally retarded children. Form A was administered to 153 cerebral palsied children ages 6 to 16, mean chronological age 10.3, mean mental age 6.5. Form B was administered to 260 cerebral palsied children with chronological age range from 6 to 17, mean 10.9 years. The mean mental age was 6.8 years. Two observers who recorded the responses of sixty-five cerebral palsied children with speech defects were able to obtain a mean overall agreement of 96 per cent (Form A). No significant differences between sex groups have been found for either form. The reliability of Form A by means of a Kuder-Richardson Formula was .87. The Kuder-Richardson coefficient of reliability for Form B was nearly identical with Form A (r of .88). Parallel form reliability is indicated by an r of .90, with homogeneous means and variances (Irwin and Jensen, 1963b).

Form A and Form B differentiated between extreme groups classified as to chronological age, mental age, and educational status (educable and trainable children). The correlations of Form A and Form B with the Templin Sound Discrimination Test were respectively .83 and .73 ($p = .01$). Again, with both forms, Kuder-Richardson reliability coefficients were very similar to those found for cerebral palsied children. Irwin and Hammill (1965c) have done an item analysis of Form A with mentally retarded children.

BIBLIOGRAPHY:

IRWIN, O. C., and JENSEN, P. J. "A Test of Sound Discrimination for Use with Cerebral Palsied Children." *Cerebral Palsy Review*, 1963a, *24*, 5–13.

IRWIN, O. C., and JENSEN, P. J. "A Parallel Test of Sound Discrimination for Use with Cerebral Palsied Children." *Cerebral Palsy Review*, 1963b, *24*, 3–10.

IRWIN, O. C., and HAMMILL, D. D. "A Comparison of Sound Discrimination of Mentally Retarded and Cerebral Palsied Children. Form A." *Cerebral Palsy Review*, 1965a, *26*, 3–6.

IRWIN, O. C., and HAMMILL, D. D. "A Second Comparison of Sound Discrimination of Cerebral Palsied and Mentally Retarded Children. Form B." *Cerebral Palsy Review*, 1965b, *26*, 3–6.

IRWIN, O. C., and HAMMILL, D. D. "An Item Analysis of a Sound Discrimination Test, Form A, for Use with Mentally Retarded Children." *Cerebral Palsy Journal*, 1965c, *26*, 9–11.

STEREOGNOSTIC TEST

AUTHORS: Arthur L. Benton and Leonard M. Schultz

AGE: 3 to 5

VARIABLE: Stereognosis (tactual form perception)

TYPE OF MEASURE: Test

SOURCE FROM WHICH THE MEASURE MAY BE OBTAINED: See Benton and Schultz (1949)

DESCRIPTION OF MEASURE: The Stereognostic Test is an attempt to assess skills in stereognosis, the ability to recognize objects solely by touch. After reviewing the neurological literature, the authors concluded that astereognosis or the impairment of stereognostic capacity usually indicates a central nervous system lesion. The test consists of two forms with eight objects with equivalence in difficulty value. The test is administered individually in two phases. In the first part, the child is requested to name each object as a check on his familiarity with them. In the second phase, the objects are hidden in a wooden box and the child is requested to feel the test object and name it. Both forms of the test are presented. Items from Form A include:

A rubber ball about 2½ inches in diameter
A metal table fork of the usual size
A sharpened pencil about 5 inches in length

Items from Form B include:

A metal teaspoon of the usual size
A plastic comb about 7 inches in length
A metal table knife of the usual size

The scoring for each form is the number of correct identifications made. Thus, the possible range of scores on each scale is 0 to 8.

RELIABILITY AND VALIDITY: Tentative norms and critical cutoff scores have been established for 3-, 4-, and 5-year old children from the results on 156 subjects. Sloan and Bensberg (1951) attempted to determine if the results of the test would show differences in performance among mentally retarded children and adults classified as familial, brain-injured, and undifferentiated, but matched for mental and chronological ages. Analysis of variance revealed no significant differences among the classifications in performance, but only for mental age level, irrespective of nosology.

BIBLIOGRAPHY:

BENTON, A. L., and SCHULTZ, L. M. "Observations on Tactual Form (Stereognosis) in Preschool Children." *Journal of Clinical Psychology*, 1949, 5, 359–364.

SLOAN, W., and BENSBERG, G. J. "The Stereognostic Capacity of Brain Injured as Compared with Familial Mental Defectives." *Journal of Clinical Psychology*, 1951, 7, 154–156.

CATEGORY 7

PHYSICAL ATTRIBUTES

APGAR SCALE

AUTHOR: Virginia Apgar

AGE: Neonates

VARIABLE: Physical condition

TYPE OF MEASURE: Observation frame of reference

SOURCE FROM WHICH THE MEASURE MAY BE OBTAINED: See Apgar (1953)

DESCRIPTION OF MEASURE: This technique is usable only by someone who is present at the time of delivery, usually and preferably the anesthesiologist or nurse anesthetist. The observations are made sixty seconds after both the top of the head and the bottoms of the feet are visible. Five "signs" or variables are observed: heart rate, respiratory effort, reflex irritability, muscle tone, and color. These signs are rated on a three-point scale of 0, 1, or 2, so the possible score range is 0 to 10, with 10 being the most desirable. Heart rate is the most important of the diagnostic signs, while color is the least satisfactory and probably the least reliable. Heart rate is the only one of the signs on which the scoring is based on specific, easily identifiable numerical values. Thus, 100 to 140 is scored 2, under 100 is scored 1, and if no heart beat can be seen, felt, or heard the score is 0.

RELIABILITY AND VALIDITY: Apgar (1953) found that regional obstetric anesthesia, as compared with general anesthesia, was associated with babies' higher scores on the measure. She found furthermore that type of delivery was related to Apgar score, with the more difficult deliveries being associated with lower scores. Scores of infants delivered vaginally were higher than scores of caesarian deliveries, when both groups of mothers (N = 38 for each group) had normal pregnancies. Mortality of infants receiving various scores was as follows: 0, 1, or 2—14 per cent; 3, 4, 5, 6, or 7—1.1 per cent; 8, 9, or 10—0.13 per cent. Apgar and James (1962) found a clear-cut relationship between survival and Apgar score.

BIBLIOGRAPHY:

APGAR, V. "A Proposal for a New Method of Evaluation of the Newborn Infant." *Current Researches in Anesthesia and Analgesia,* July–August 1953, 260–267.
APGAR, V., and JAMES, L. S. "Progress in Pediatrics: Further Observations on the Newborn Scoring System." *American Journal of Diseases of Children,* 1962, *104,* 419–428.

BICYCLE SAFETY—Performance and Skills Test

AUTHOR: B. W. Miller

AGE: Elementary school

VARIABLE: Bicycle skill

TYPE OF MEASURE: Performance

SOURCE FROM WHICH THE MEASURE MAY BE OBTAINED: See Miller (1962), or write: National Safety Council, 425 North Michigan Avenue, Chicago, Illinois 60611

DESCRIPTION OF MEASURE: The author describes twelve tests that measure specific bicycling skills such as balance, pedaling, braking, hand signaling, dismounting, and fine control. The twelve tests are: balance test (straight line); pedaling and braking; straight line test; signaling, mounting, and dismounting; single obstacle test; double obstacle test; double zig-zag obstacle test; figure eight steering; figure eight balance test; turning around; emergency turn and stop; and cruising test.

An example of one of the tests is Test 1, Balance Test (Straight Line), the purpose of which is to test the delicate balance of the rider. There is a diagram showing the length and width of the pathway the cyclist must negotiate. The rider starts from a standstill and very slowly rides through the lane, in not less than thirty seconds, without touching the lines on either side. Success is indicated by (Miller, 1962):

Touching neither foot to the ground.
Going distance in more than thirty seconds.
Having neither wheel touch either line.
Not using brake excessively.
Expending not more than average amount of energy.

Several diagrams give the layout of obstacle courses and other skill tests. Scoring may be either pass-fail for an item, or a point system can be easily devised.

Miller states or shows in his summary score sheet on the last page of his article a possible point total of 70. It appears that this should be 75, since in his summary score sheet he gives a total possible of 15 for the final test, the cruising test, whereas in the description of that test he has a total possible of 20. This would make the total possible score on this test 75.

RELIABILITY AND VALIDITY: None reported.

BIBLIOGRAPHY:

MILLER, B. W. "Skill Tests for Pedal Pushers." *Safety Council Magazine,* 1962.

IRRITABILITY SCALE

AUTHORS: Frances K. Graham, Ruth G. Matarazzo, and Bettye M. Caldwell

AGE: Infants (neonates 1 to 5 days old)

VARIABLE: Physiological irritability

TYPE OF MEASURE: Rating scale

SOURCE FROM WHICH THE MEASURE MAY BE OBTAINED: Frances K. Graham, University of Wisconsin, School of Medicine, 2927 Howard Drive, Madison, Wisconsin 53705

DESCRIPTION OF MEASURE: Several factors contributing to rating of irritability include the intensity of stimuli that evoke crying; the state of the infant; the cry of the infant; and the ease of quieting. Irritability is rated on a three-point scale, with numerical values of 0, 1, and 2. A score of 0 represents normal irritability, 1 represents just perceptible abnormal behavior, and 2, extreme abnormal behavior. The definition for each point classification includes crying in response only to intense and external stimulation for normal irritability; crying or fussing in response to mild stimulation for just-perceptible irritability; and crying in response to many mild stimuli for abnormal irritability.

RELIABILITY AND VALIDITY: The test-retest agreement after twenty-four hours was 75 per cent. Interscorer agreement was 68 per cent.

BIBLIOGRAPHY:

GRAHAM, F. K., MATARAZZO, R. G., and CALDWELL, B. M. "Behavioral Differences Between Normal and Traumatized Newborns . . . ." *Psychological Monographs,* 1956, *70*(20) (Whole No. 428).

BODY MEASUREMENTS OF AMERICAN BOYS AND GIRLS

AUTHORS: Ruth O'Brien, Meyer A. Girshick, and Eleanor P. Hunt

AGE: 4 to 17

VARIABLE: Body measurements

TYPE OF MEASURE: Anthropometric measurements

SOURCE FROM WHICH THE MEASURE MAY BE OBTAINED: See O'Brien, Girshick, and Hunt (1941)

DESCRIPTION OF MEASURE: Thirty-six different body measurements useful in garment making are described. Complete and elaborate details are provided on how to make the measurements and the necessary equipment. The method may be useful to researchers interested in relating physical measurements to other variables.

RELIABILITY AND VALIDITY: Reliability of the different measurements was high, as determined by finding the standard deviation of the differences between scores of the same scorer at different times on the same subject, and between scorers and the persons who instructed them in making the measurements.

BIBLIOGRAPHY:

O'BRIEN, R., GIRSHICK, M. A., and HUNT, E. P. *Body Measurements of American Boys and Girls for Garment and Pattern Construction.* Washington, D.C.: U.S. Government Printing Office, 1941.

WHITEACRE, J., and GRIMES, E. T. "Some Body Measurements of Native-Born White Children of Seven to Fourteen Years in Different Climatic Regions of Texas." *Child Development,* 1959, *30,* 177–209.

MATURATION SCALE

AUTHORS: Frances K. Graham, Ruth G. Matarazzo, and Bettye M. Caldwell

AGE: Infants (neonates 1 to 5 days old)

VARIABLE: Physical maturation

TYPE OF MEASURE: Rating scale

SOURCE FROM WHICH THE MEASURE MAY BE OBTAINED: Frances K. Graham, University of Wisconsin, School of Medicine, 2927 Howard Drive, Madison, Wisconsin 53705

DESCRIPTION OF MEASURE: There are nine items in the scale, measuring prone head position; crawling in a prone position; pushing of feet (supine); auditory reaction to a rattle; reaction of infant (supine) to cotton placed on the nostrils, barely touching the lip; reactions to cellophane paper under the same conditions as the cotton; persistence or the number of times the infant is responding to Items 5 and 6; the *vigor* of the infant's responses throughout the trial; and the *grasp* of the infant for a stirrup that is rubbed against his palm (Graham et al., 1956).

     A Maturation Scale record facilitates scoring of the responses. The range in scores for each response is from 1 to 3 with a maximum score of 21 possible for the entire scale.

RELIABILITY AND VALIDITY: Test-retest reliability for the Maturation scale was in the 60's. Interscorer agreement correlation was .97. Normal and traumatized groups differed significantly on this measure (Graham, 1956).

BIBLIOGRAPHY:

GRAHAM, F. K., MATARAZZO, R. G., and CALDWELL, B. M. "Behavioral Differences between Normal and Traumatized Newborns . . . ." *Psychological Monographs,* 1956, *70*(20) (Whole No. 428).

MEASUREMENT OF HEIGHT AND WEIGHT

AUTHOR: Wilton Mation Krogman

AGE: Birth to 20

VARIABLE: Body measurements

TYPE OF MEASURE: Anthropometric

SOURCE FROM WHICH THE MEASURE MAY BE OBTAINED: See Krogman (1948)

DESCRIPTION OF MEASURE: A careful, detailed description is given of ways physical measurements of height and weight should be made to maximize the reliability of the measurements. Some variables contributing to error of measurement are pointed out. Research concerned with these physical measures would be helped greatly by the suggestions for standardizing the measures.

RELIABILITY AND VALIDITY: None.

BIBLIOGRAPHY:

KROGMAN, W. M. "A Handbook of the Measurement and Interpretation of Height and Weight in the Growing Child." *Monographs of the Society for Research in Child Development*, 1948, *13*(3).

WHITEACRE, J., and GRIMES, E. T. "Some Body Measurements of Native-born White Children of Seven to Fourteen Years in Different Climatic Regions of Texas." *Child Development*, 1959, *30*, 177–209.

MUSCLE TENSION SCALE

AUTHORS: Frances K. Graham, Ruth G. Matarazzo, and Bettye M. Caldwell

AGE: Infants (neonates 1 to 5 days old)

VARIABLE: Muscle tonus and rigidity

TYPE OF MEASURE: Rating scale

SOURCE FROM WHICH THE MEASURE MAY BE OBTAINED: Frances K. Graham, University of Wisconsin, School of Medicine, 2927 Howard Drive, Madison, Wisconsin 53705

DESCRIPTION OF MEASURE: This scale is designed to measure along the rigidity-flaccidity dimension. Five submeasures make up the scale: nature (flexed or extended) of the supine position the legs assumed spontaneously; resistance to limb displacement; change in muscle tone in response to being pulled to a sitting posture; amount of spontaneous activity; and frequency of trembling of body parts and the stimuli evoking this response. Rating is done on a five-point scale, with numerical values from +2 to −2. Zero represents the behavior of a normal infant, and +2 and −2 represent the extremes of flaccidity and rigidity. The +1 and −1 points represent a "just perceptible" form of abnormal behavior.

A composite record sheet for rating muscle tension facilitates the scoring for the scale (Graham et al., 1956).

RELIABILITY AND VALIDITY: There was 79 per cent interscorer agreement on the Tension Scale (Graham et al., 1956). Significant differences between normal and traumatized groups of children occurred on the scale.

BIBLIOGRAPHY:

GRAHAM, F. K., MATARAZZO, R. G., and CALDWELL, B. M. "Behavioral Differences Between Normal and Traumatized Newborns . . . ." *Psychological Monographs,* 1956, *70*(20) (Whole No. 428).

PAIN THRESHOLD TEST

AUTHORS: Frances K. Graham, Ruth G. Matarazzo, and Bettye M. Caldwell

AGE: Infants (neonates 1 to 5 days old)

VARIABLE: Sensitivity to pain stimuli

TYPE OF MEASURE: Rating scale

SOURCE FROM WHICH THE MEASURE MAY BE OBTAINED: Frances K. Graham, University of Wisconsin, School of Medicine, 2927 Howard Drive, Madison, Wisconsin 53705

DESCRIPTION OF MEASURE: This scale measures an infant's reaction to an electronic stimulator. The shock consists of a two-second impulse at a frequency of 14 per second that can be varied in intensity from 50 to 530 volts. The electrical stimulus is applied to the children, sometimes in ascending and sometimes in descending order of magnitude. The threshold level is determined by averaging the scores (voltages) at which a response is first manifested (for ascending order of magnitude) and at which any response disappears (descending order of magnitude).

RELIABILITY AND VALIDITY: Split-half reliabilities for the pain threshold scores for both traumatized and nontraumatized ranged from .82 to .97. Test-retest reliability for the pain threshold scale was in the .60's.

BIBLIOGRAPHY:

GRAHAM, F. K., MATARAZZO, R. G., and CALDWELL, B. M. "Behavioral Differences Between Normal and Traumatized Newborns . . . ." *Psychological Monographs*, 1956, *70*(20) (Whole No. 428).

SCHOOL SURVEY FORM

AUTHORS: Maurice H. Fouracre, M. Leigh Rooke, and Perry Botwin

AGE: Handicapped children of school age

VARIABLE: Prevalence of handicapped children

TYPE OF MEASURE: Questionnaires

SOURCE FROM WHICH THE MEASURE MAY BE OBTAINED: See Fouracre, et al. (1959)

DESCRIPTION OF MEASURE: The School Survey Form is designed to obtain the prevalence of school-aged children with any one of the following handicaps: crippling conditions, visual impairment, speech or hearing impairment, mental retardation, emotional disorder, and special health problems. Each set of questions is grouped according to types of disabilities. Moreover, the questions are designed for nonmedically trained persons. With the exception of identifying data for the child rated, the questions require only yes or no responses. The set of questions for verification of visual impairment is as follows (Fouracre, et al., 1959):

Is there a noticeable eye defect, that is, strabismus (crossed eyes), nystagmus (excessive eye movement), and the like?
Is the child blind (20/200 vision in better eye with maximum correction)?
Does the child have usable vision (between 20/200 and 20/70 with maximum correction)?
If answer to the above is "yes," does the child wear glasses?
If the child wears glasses, can he read ordinary print and see objects at reasonable distance with his glasses?
Does the child have only one usable eye?

The authors raise some questions about teachers' understanding of some terms in the questionnaire, but they feel that the availability of nurses for consultation compensates for this lack.

RELIABILITY AND VALIDITY: The questionnaire has been revised twice, and the questions were designed for use by nonmedically trained persons. They were grouped according to types of disabilities.

BIBLIOGRAPHY:

FOURACRE, M. H., ROOKE, M. L., and BOTWIN, P. *The Report of the Study on the Educational Needs of Physically Handicapped Children in Pittsburgh, Pennsylvania 1958–1959.* Pittsburgh, University of Pittsburgh School of Education, 1959.

CATEGORY **8**

MISCELLANEOUS ATTITUDES AND INTERESTS

A CHILD ATTITUDE INVENTORY FOR PROBLEM SOLVING (CAPS)

AUTHORS: Richard S. Crutchfield and Martin L. Covington

AGE: Fifth and sixth grades

VARIABLE: Attitudes toward thinking, problem solving

TYPE OF MEASURE: Group administered paper and pencil inventory

SOURCE FROM WHICH THE MEASURE MAY BE OBTAINED: Richard S. Crutchfield, Dept. of Psychology, University of California, Berkeley, California 94700

DESCRIPTION OF MEASURE: The CAPS includes two scales, the first of which assesses children's beliefs and attitudes about problem solving. It consists of thirty true-false items measuring variables like a child's attitude toward expressing unusual ideas, the child's conception of the innateness of problem-solving ability, and the wisdom of persisting at difficult problems on which others have failed. Scale II has thirty true-false items treating the child's feeling about his own problem-solving ability. Questions regarding sources of anxiety about thinking are included. Examples from Scale I follow:

A problem like the one about the TV cable and the pipe is probably too hard for anyone in the 5th grade to solve.
There is probably only one answer to a problem like this one.

From Scale II:

Do you feel that other children in class know more about what to do in working on a problem like this than you do?
Would you like to work on a problem like this one?

RELIABILITY AND VALIDITY: When the CAPS was administered twice to fifth and sixth graders, five weeks apart, the reliability coefficients were as follows:

	Scale	
Grade	I	II
5	.70	.65
6	.67	.64

(1) On the basis of item analyses on an earlier form of CAPS, the present version of the scales includes highly differentiating revised items. (2) A positive but modest correlation between the two subscales (r of .35 for 325 subjects) indicates that the amount of overlap is small and that the two tests measure independent functions. (3) The scale scores show a significant and positive correlation with the IQ results on the California Mental Maturity Scale (r of .33, p < .01) but negative correlations exist between these scales and two anxiety measures by Sarason—Test Anxiety Scale for Children and General Anxiety Scale for Children.

BIBLIOGRAPHY: None.

CHILDREN'S KNOWLEDGE ABOUT OCCUPATIONS TEST

AUTHOR: Richard C. Nelson

AGE: Grades three, five, seven, nine, and eleven

VARIABLE: Children's knowledge and interest in selected occupational groups

TYPE OF MEASURE: Structured interview approach at the third-grade level and below. Above that level, the measure consisted of a self-administered scale

SOURCE FROM WHICH THE MEASURE MAY BE OBTAINED: Duplicates of the sixteen slides may be obtained from Dr. Richard Nelson, Education Department, Purdue University, Lafayette, Indiana, for $5.00.

DESCRIPTION OF MEASURE: The scale consists of sixteen color slides of occupations and a questionnaire designed to measure the child's knowledge of the occupation and his interest in it. In administering the questionnaire, the child is requested to identify the occupation, describe it, indicate his interest in it, and explain the basis for his interest or lack of it (Nelson, 1963). A sample item from the questionnaire follows:

First picture shows a ———. *On this job a person* ———. *Would you like this to be your full time job when through school? Yes, no, not sure, why or why not?*

In order of presentation the sixteen slides are: janitor, laborer, assembler (female), bookkeeper, carpenter, manager, teacher (female), farmer, engineer, sales clerk (female), truck driver, doctor, warehouseman, secretary (female), mechanic, and telephone lineman.

In the third grade, children are interviewed individually and the interviewer records the responses. Above this level, the scale is administered on a group basis and the children record their own responses. If one eighth or more of the responses on this group scale are inadequate, Nelson suggests a follow-up individual interview.

The responses to titles and descriptions of the occupations are assigned four values ranging from 3 to 0, 3 indicating an exact title or an insightful description, while 0 indicates an incorrect, impossible, or immature response.

RELIABILITY AND VALIDITY: Nelson (1963) gave the measure to 599 students from the five grade levels given above under "AGE." Details on the composition of the sample have been provided. In determining the reliability of the scale, a subsample of approximately 10 per cent was used (fifty-nine students). The test-retest reliability coefficients over a three- to four-month period were respectively .74 for titling and describing and .58 for interest in occupations. Both of these coefficients were significant at the 1 per cent level of significance (Nelson, 1963).

Responses on the scale are apparently highly related to the variables of sex, socioeconomic levels, intelligence, and urban-rural residences. Since many of these findings were in the predicted direction (for example, older children were consistently superior to younger students in accuracy of job descriptions), the scale appears to have concurrent and construct validity (Nelson, 1963).

BIBLIOGRAPHY:

NELSON, R. C. "Knowledge and Interest Concerning Sixteen Occupations among Elementary and Secondary School Students." *Educational and Psychological Measurement*, 1963, *XXIII*, 741–754.

DOLL-PLAY INTERVIEW

AUTHORS: R. B. Ammons and H. S. Ammons

AGE: 2 to 6

VARIABLE: Interracial feelings

TYPE OF MEASURE: Projective interview

SOURCE FROM WHICH THE MEASURE MAY BE OBTAINED: See Ammons (1950)

DESCRIPTION OF MEASURE: The materials consist of a miniature equipped playground and two 5-inch dolls, one Negro and one white. A further description of the dolls and playground can be found in Ammons (1950). The tester or observer calls attention to the two dolls on the playground. Then the subject is presented with the fifteen stimulus projective questions, nine of which have more than one part, so that there is a total of more than fifteen questions. Examples of the questions are given below:

Here are two little boys who would like to play on this playground. *Do they look the same? How are they different?*

This (white) boy's mother comes along and sees the boys playing. *What does she say?*

This (white) boy hits this (colored) boy. *What does he do? What does he say?*

They play with this big balloon for awhile, then they drop it and it breaks. *Who broke it? The teacher comes up and hits one of them. Whom does she hit? Why?*

Two types of scoring are described for the two types of items, the alternative type item and the objective type item.

RELIABILITY AND VALIDITY: The interscorer reliability varies considerably from one type of item to another. There are essentially two main types of responses, one of which can be scored relatively objectively. The other type of item, calling for qualitative verbal expression, tends to have lower reliability. When two persons scored all of the records in the Ammons (1950) study, independently, they agreed 97 and 99 per cent of the time in two separate sessions on the object-type items (the yes-no answer items); for another set of objective-type items, there was .95 and 94 per cent scoring agreement; and where the responses were scored either unfavorable, noncommittal, or favorable the interscorer agreement was 88 per cent for two testing sessions. When relevance of response was the interscoring criterion, percentage of agreement dropped to 80 per cent in session one and 78 per cent in session two. The Ammons article gives the items on which these reliabilities were based.

Ammons found a decreasing number of refusals to respond as age increased. He found an increase in the number of words per response for those responses calling for more than a single-word answer. Relevance of response, however, did not increase as would be expected with increasing age. No direct evidence for the validity of the measure as a measure of interracial feelings is provided.

BIBLIOGRAPHY:

AMMONS, R. B. "Reactions in a Projective Doll-Play Interview of White Males Two to Six Years of Age to Differences in Skin Color and Facial Features." *The Journal of Genetic Psychology*, 1950, 76, 323–341.

GAMES AND ACTIVITIES PREFERENCE LIST

AUTHOR: Monroe M. Lefkowitz

AGE: Third and fourth grade

VARIABLE: Sex role preference

TYPE OF MEASURE: Alternate choice checklist

SOURCE FROM WHICH THE MEASURE MAY BE OBTAINED: See Lefkowitz (1962)

DESCRIPTION OF MEASURE: There are eleven item pairs, selected from an original pool of twenty-two pairs. Nine items constitute the measure of sex-role preference for boys, seven for girls, with five items common to the two sexes. Items were selected if 90 per cent of either sex agreed in choice of an activity or game. The first column of figures gives percentages for boys, the second for girls.

Girls:			
	Go shooting	44	4
	Go bowling	56	96
Boys:			
	Play darts	93	37
	Play jacks	7	63
Both sexes:			
	Use lipstick and powder	2	99
	Use a razor and shaving cream	98	1

The children are instructed simply to draw a circle around the game or activity they would prefer.

RELIABILITY AND VALIDITY: The item-test correlations for all eleven items were significant at the .01 level. Lefkowitz divided the children into two classes, deviant and nondeviant, a deviant child being one who made at least one deviant response. Thus, the 4 per cent of the girls (item 1) who preferred going shooting to going bowling were classed as deviant, along with deviants on other items. He found the following significant relationships between the GAP and other variables: More parents of nondeviant boys (as against parents of deviant boys) say that both parents take responsibility for the child's discipline. More parents of deviant boys report that mothers are mainly responsible for discipline. Mothers of nondeviant boys are more nurturant than mothers of deviant boys. Fathers of nondeviant boys have lower average occupational ratings than fathers of deviant boys. Nondeviant boys have higher mean IQ's. On the Draw-A-Person test, more deviant than non-deviant boys drew a female figure first. There was no relationship between GAP score and aggression (measured by peer ratings).

BIBLIOGRAPHY:

LEFKOWITZ, M. M. "Some Relationships Between Sex Role Preference of Children and Other Parent and Child Variables." *Psychological Reports*, 1962, *10*, 43–53.

GOUGH, HARRIS, MARTIN, AND EDWARDS PREJUDICE INDEX

AUTHORS: Harrison G. Gough, Dale B. Harris, William E. Martin, and Marcia Edwards

AGE: Third, fourth, fifth, and sixth grades

VARIABLE: Racial or ethnic prejudice

TYPE OF MEASURE: Questionnaire

SOURCE FROM WHICH THE MEASURE MAY BE OBTAINED: See Gough et al. (1950)

DESCRIPTION OF MEASURE: The GHME-Index consists of eighteen statements that could be applied to any minority group, six statements being unfavorable and twelve favorable. The items are read aloud to the children who are requested to express their agreement or disagreement with each item. In general, the child receives one point for each favorable statement with which he agrees and for each unfavorable statement with which he disagrees. It is clear that the lower the score the greater the prejudice toward a specified minority group. Examples of items from the scale, as they have been applied to Negroes, include the following (Gough et al., 1950):

They work hard.
They make good teachers.
I would like to live next door to them.
I do not like them.

RELIABILITY AND VALIDITY: The scale has content validity from at least two sources. First, only items have been retained that cover a range of opinions from favorable to unfavorable as judged by children themselves. Second, pretesting eliminated items that children do not comprehend readily. In addition, the final scale of eighteen items was developed as a comprehensive item analysis differentiating between high and low scorers on the scale. Estimated reliability on this eighteen-item scale is .78 by the Kuder-Richardson formula.

Scale scores were found to be related to generalized reactions of tolerance and intolerance, to personality inventory items (Gough et al., 1950), and to feelings of satisfaction or dissatisfaction with the self (Tabachnick, 1962).

BIBLIOGRAPHY:

GOUGH, H. G., HARRIS, D. B., MARTIN, W. E., and EDWARDS, M. "Children's Ethnic Attitudes: I. Relationships to Certain Personality Factors." *Child Development*, 1950, *21*, 83–91.

TABACHNICK, B. R. "Some Correlates of Prejudice toward Negroes in Elementary Age Children." *Journal of Genetic Psychology*, 1962, *100*, 193–203.

HOW WOULD YOU FINISH IT?

AUTHOR: John E. Anderson

AGE: Upper-elementary school children (9 to 12)

VARIABLE: Child's attitude toward his experience

TYPE OF MEASURE: Structured sentence completion test

SOURCE FROM WHICH THE MEASURE MAY BE OBTAINED: See Anderson (1952); Anderson et al. (1959); Smith (1958)

DESCRIPTION OF MEASURE: This ten-item sentence completion test is scored according to the affectivity of the response—positive, negative, or neutral. Essentially, the test reveals the child's attitude toward his experience. It has usually been administered orally to classes of children on a group basis. Though Smith has given no exact scoring procedure for the test, an earlier version by Anderson (1952) did provide this information. Under Anderson's scheme, neutral statements were ignored. An "Affective Index" was calculated by dividing the score for positive responses by the score for negative responses. Examples of two items from the scale follow:

I like people who
Most boys are

RELIABILITY AND VALIDITY: Smith (1958) used a sample of 245 sixth-grade boys who were classified as well adjusted, adjusted, or maladjusted. The groups differed in the expected direction ($p < .05$). When differences in reading achievements and parental occupation were eliminated by the analysis of covariance, however, the former F value dropped below the .05 level of significance. The test has proved ineffective for long-term prediction (Anderson and Harris, 1959).

BIBLIOGRAPHY:

ANDERSON, J. "The Relation of Attitude to Adjustment." *Education*, 1952, *73*, 210–218.

ANDERSON, J., and HARRIS, D. B. *A Survey of Children's Adjustment over Time.* Minneapolis, Minnesota: Institute of Child Development and Welfare, University of Minnesota, 1959.

SMITH, L. M. "The Concurrent Validity of Six Personality and Adjustment Tests for Children." *Psychological Monographs*, 1958, *72* (Whole No. 457), 1–28.

INTERVIEW SCHEDULE

AUTHOR: Eugene A. Weinstein

AGE: 5 to 12 years

VARIABLE: Concept of flag and sense of national identity

TYPE OF MEASURE: Interview schedule

SOURCE FROM WHICH THE MEASURE MAY BE OBTAINED: See Weinstein (1957)

DESCRIPTION OF MEASURE: The measure consists of twenty-two questions (in some cases question clusters) selected from an originally larger battery, after attrition from ambiguity or lack of discriminability. Examples of items are:

Suppose someone came to you and said that they had never seen an American flag and asked you what it was like. What would you tell him? What colors is it made of?

Do all countries have a flag? Which flag is best? Why?

Does a country always have the same flag or does it change it sometimes? When and why?

Why does the flag fly on a holiday? Do other countries put up their flag when they have a holiday?

Each response is categorized into one of ten scale types or stages of development. For example, in the first stage (5 to 6 years) the child typically associates the flag with certain colors and stars, thinks there is only one flag, and associates it largely with singing and celebration. The stages described by the author increase in sophistication from stage 1 to stage 10. Arbitrary weights are assigned to each of the ten levels, and a summary of the weights on the twenty-two items constitutes an individual's score.

RELIABILITY AND VALIDITY: The correlation between age of child in months and total score on the interview was .76. There were no significant sex differences on the measure. The hypothesis that the concept of flag and national identity develops in a generally systematic, stable pattern for each child (regardless of the rate at which they develop) was supported.

BIBLIOGRAPHY:

WEINSTEIN, E. A. "Development of the Concept of Flag and the Sense of National Identity." *Child Development*, 1957, 28(2).

KUTNER'S ETHNIC ATTITUDE TEST

AUTHOR: Bernard Kutner

AGE: Second grade

VARIABLE: Ethnic attitude

TYPE OF MEASURE: Structured projective questionnaire

SOURCE FROM WHICH THE MEASURE MAY BE OBTAINED: See Kutner (1958)

DESCRIPTION OF MEASURE: In the EAT, prejudice refers to a response readiness for an inflexible generalization that places some individual or group at a disadvantage. Ethnocentrism refers to a response readiness for a faulty generalization that gives individuals or groups an advantage. The test measures these two attitudes. The scale itself consists of nine statements referring to seven different ethnic groups —statements reportedly made by a third party. These statements are couched in prejudicial or ethnocentric terms. In administering the measure, the examiner notes agreement or disagreement with the statements and the child's spontaneous rationale for the support of his beliefs. Since these statements are primarily derogatory in nature, the degree of prejudice is measured by the extent of the child's agreements with the statements. Illustrative statements from the EAT follow (Kutner, 1958, p. 48):

There are city people and there are people who live in the country on farms. Some city people say that the farmers are pretty dumb and they laugh at farmers. What do you think about that? How do you feel about farmers?

Some children learn slowly and some children learn fast. The fast children say that the slow ones are stupid or dumb. They don't like to make friends with slow children. What about children who learn slowly?

The questionnaire is administerd on an individual basis and requires about twenty minutes. The responses are then analyzed in terms of agreement and the intensity of prejudice expressed. Eleven categories are used to classify the manner of agreement or disagreement. For example, agreements or disagreements may be classified an unconditional, conditional, or partial. Intensity of the prejudice expressed is measured on a four-point scale as very unprejudiced, somewhat unprejudiced, somewhat prejudiced, and prejudiced. In the original study by Kutner, however, he classified the first two categories as less prejudiced groups and the last two categories as the more prejudiced groups (Kutner, 1958).

RELIABILITY AND VALIDITY: The original sample included sixty children, involving both sex groups with an average age of approximately 7 years. The majority of the children were primarily from middle-class Jewish families. Though Kutner (1958) admits that ethnic background has a striking relationship to attitude structure, his rationale was that he was attempting to measure functions common to all ethnically prejudiced persons.

In terms of reliability support for the scale, at least two findings have emerged. First, the Pearson r between the author and another rater on the four classifications of prejudice was .62. Then two judges were able to differentiate the more prejudiced group ($p < .001$) (Kutner, 1958). However, the author claims only face validity for the scale and regards it as a relatively untested technique for eliciting ethnic attitudes.

BIBLIOGRAPHY:

KUTNER, B. "Patterns of Mental Functioning Associated with Prejudice in Children." *Psychological Monographs,* 1958, 72(7) (Whole No. 460).

ROLE-DISTRIBUTION—Children's Series

AUTHORS: Ruth E. Hartley and F. P. Hardesty

AGE: 5 to 11

VARIABLE: Children's concept of sex roles

TYPE OF MEASURE: Group test

SOURCE FROM WHICH THE MEASURE MAY BE OBTAINED: See Hartley and Hardesty (1964)

DESCRIPTION OF MEASURE: The stimulus materials for this measure consist of pictures of objects, locales, scenes, and so on that sample aspects of children's experience in play, peer contacts, parental activities, chores, intrafamily relationships, and cultural activities. The child is then asked to tell whether the stimulus picture is more closely related to boys' or girls' activities, or both (the "egalitarian" response).

The instructions, and examples of some of the fifty-six pictures, are as follows:

I am going to show you some pictures of places where boys and girls play (things boys and girls play with; things boys and girls do). As I show you each picture I want you to tell me who mostly plays there (plays with it; does it), boys, or girls— or both or neither.

The pictures are presented in sequence, with a verbal description for each; for example:

This is a park—who mostly plays there?
Here are some marbles—who mostly plays with them?
Here is a man fixing a ceiling—who mostly would help him?

Hartley used a different instrument, called the Role Situations series, in one study (1961b), also involving responses to picture stimuli. She measured girls' identification of women with 135 different pictured activities, such as relaxing in a comfortable chair, going window shopping, playing tennis, washing dishes, and so on.

RELIABILITY AND VALIDITY: Reliability data are provided for the "egalitarian" responses, where the corrected split-half reliability is .84 (Hartley, 1964).

Of the fifty-six items administered to 131 children, forty-six could be assigned to boys, girls, or either. On ten items there was no consensus. In general, children distinguished clearly between boys' and girls' sex-role activities. Hartley investigated the effect of four variables—sex of respondent, age, working status of the mother, and social status—on sex role distribution. None of these were statistically significant, the closest approximation being social status, with $p = .20$.

BIBLIOGRAPHY:

HARTLEY, R. E. "Sex-Roles and Urban Youth: Some Developmental Perspectives." *Bulletin of Family Development,* 1961, *2*(1).

HARTLEY, R. E. "Current Patterns in Sex Roles: Children's Perspectives." *Journal of the National Association of Women Deans and Counselors,* 1961, *25*(1).

HARTLEY, R. E., and HARDESTY, F. P. "Children's Perceptions of Sex Roles in Childhood." *Journal of Genetic Psychology,* 1964, *105,* 43–51.

SOCIAL ATTITUDES SCALE (SAS)

AUTHOR: Dale B. Harris

AGE: Upper elementary through junior high school (grades seven and eight)

VARIABLE: Attitude toward social responsibility

TYPE OF MEASURE: Questionnaire

SOURCE FROM WHICH THE MEASURE MAY BE OBTAINED: See Harris (1957)

DESCRIPTION OF MEASURE: The Social Attitudes Scale consists of fifty items pertaining to responsibility, defined as a general attitude reflecting reliable, accountable, loyal, or effective behavior. The scale consists of two classes of items— personal reference items and nonpersonal reference items. In completing the test, the child answers each item as "agree" or "disagree." The score consists of the number of "rights" the child has marked; that is, responses indicating a degree of responsibility. In the elementary grades the test items should be read individually item by item. With pupils in the seventh grade or above, the recommendation is that the examiner read the directions aloud while the children read them silently. From this point, it becomes a self-administering scale for this group. Sample items from the scale follow (Harris, 1957):

It is always very important to finish anything one has started.
At school, it is easy to find things to do when the teacher doesn't give us enough work.
Police cars should be especially marked so that you can always see them coming.

RELIABILITY AND VALIDITY: The test has been standardized on Ns of 184 for 10-year-old children, 193 for 12-year-old children, 185 for both 14- and 16-year-old children. Means and standard deviations for each sex classification within each age level are provided for the total score, personal reference items, and nonpersonal reference items. Reliability statistics are also provided for the same classifications as described above for the norms. Total score retest reliabilities over a four-month interval range from .60 to .70 for several groups of eighth- and tenth-grade children.

The estimates of reliability were .47 and .63 respectively for the subscale of eighteen personal reference items and for the thirty-two nonpersonal reference items, based on a sample of fifty 12-year-old girls.

The principal validating procedure was obtained by an item analysis of a preliminary pool of items. The final scale of fifty items was derived from items that differentiated criterion groups of more responsible versus less responsible children as determined by sociometric choices by peers. An effort was made to retain only those items that had construct validity. Finally, some concurrent validation for the test may be claimed because of the moderate positive correlations between the results of the scale and adjustment measures. These correlations are approximately in the order of .40 and better (Harris, 1957).

BIBLIOGRAPHY:

HARRIS, D. B. "A Scale for Measuring Attitudes of Social Responsibility in Children." *Journal of Abnormal and Social Psychology,* 1957, *55,* 322–326.

HOYT, C. J. "Test Reliability Estimated by Analysis of Variance." *Psychometrika,* 1941, *3,* 153–160.

THINGS I LIKE TO DO

AUTHOR: John E. Anderson

AGE: Upper elementary grade school children

VARIABLE: Attitude

TYPE OF MEASURE: Questionnaire

SOURCE FROM WHICH THE MEASURE MAY BE OBTAINED: See Anderson (1952); Anderson et al. (1959); Smith (1958)

DESCRIPTION OF MEASURE: This is a measure of attitudes toward various activities in a child's everyday life. It consists of forty items and requires the child to underline his response from two fixed alternatives—like or dislike. The measure is orally administered on a group basis.

Two scoring methods have been devised for this test. In Smith's study (1958), the scale was scored in terms of total number of likes. In the investigation by Anderson (1952), an affective ratio was obtained by dividing the likes by the dislikes. Examples of items follow:

Go to the movies.
Chew gum.

RELIABILITY AND VALIDITY: The same sample described in the How Would You Finish It test applies here. Anderson (1952) found that the ratio of likes to dislikes was significantly different for the well-adjusted and the poorly adjusted groups. The difference between the average adjusted and the poorly adjusted was also consistently in the predicted direction, although it did not reach the 5 per cent level (Anderson, 1952).

BIBLIOGRAPHY:

ANDERSON, J. "The Relation of Attitude to Adjustment." *Education,* 1952, *73,* 210–218.

ANDERSON, J., and HARRIS, D. B. *A Survey of Children's Adjustment over Time.* Minneapolis, Minnesota: Institute of Child Development and Welfare, University of Minnesota, 1959.

SMITH, L. M. "The Concurrent Validity of Six Personality and Adjustment Tests for Children." *Psychological Monographs,* 1958, *72* (Whole No. 457), 1–28.

THURSTONE SENTENCE COMPLETION FORM (TSCF)

AUTHOR: John R. Thurstone

AGE: Children in grades three, six, and nine, and parents of exceptional children

VARIABLE: Attitudes

TYPE OF MEASURE: Semiprojective technique

SOURCE FROM WHICH THE MEASURE MAY BE OBTAINED: See Thurstone (1959)

DESCRIPTION OF MEASURE: The TSCF specifically samples attitudes and emotional reactions of parents of handicapped children in seven significant areas relating to concerns, the satisfaction-discomfiture dimension, sibling reactions, community and neighborhood reactions, attitudes to institutions, parental expectations, and general attitudes. Specific instructions for administering the earlier form of the test and categorizing the forty-five items into seven scales are provided. The items belonging to each scale are enumerated and illustrative interpretations of responses are described. In this early form of the scale, responses are classified on a qualitative basis. Illustrative items for the fourth category (reactions of community, friends, and neighbors) follow (Thurstone, 1959):

The thing I'd like to see my community do for the handicapped is
When people know you have a handicapped child, they

In a subsequent revised form of the scale, a quantitative scoring system is provided that uses differential weights of 3, 2, and 1 for each response. These scores respectively refer to characteristic responses that differentiated maladjusted children from adjusted ones, answers that failed to differentiate the two groups, and replies characteristic of adjusted children. Sample items follow for third-grade males:

I like (3) to hunt; hunting. (2) to have an Army suit; candy; you; animals; to go for rides; to play with you; school; to do arithmetic in school. (1) to play ball; parents; to play or watch a ball game; my father.
I want to know (3) more about schoolwork: how to spell; more in school; more about arithmetic; more about chemistry; how to do my work. (2) ice skate; how to play ball; how you feel; what's said; how to make an atomic furnace; about boys. (1) (none).

The TSCF may be mailed to the parent or given orally or in written form at the time of a visit. One edition is developed for use with handicapped individuals themselves (Thurstone, 1959). Adaptations of the original TSCF include those by Appell and Fishell (1964), by Condell (1966), and by Thurstone and his colleagues (1964).

RELIABILITY AND VALIDITY: The TSCF has been administered to 213 parents of institutionalized cerebral palsied patients (Thurstone, 1959), to twenty-one mothers of retarded children (Appell and Fishell, 1964), to sixty-seven parents of retarded children living in a rural setting (Condell, 1966), and to 192 children nominated as adjusted by their teachers, as well as to an equal number designated as behavior problems by their teachers. In this last sample, the children were in grades three, six, and nine, and the TSCF was administered to both the children and both parents of each child. It is only in this last-mentioned study that any norms have been provided.

Reliability statistics are supplied for a twenty-item revision of the TSCF scored under the objective system of the Behavior Rating Scale. The statistics are based on three independent scorings on ten randomly selected tests from each of grades three, six, and nine. Thus, each scorer rated thirty records. The Pearson Product-Moment correlations for these three pairs of scorings were .70, .77, and .79.

In the original version of the TSCF (Thurstone, 1959) items were selected on the basis of their relevance as judged by numerous professional workers (content validity).

In the study that developed the Behavior Rating Scale, statistically significant differences in scores on the Behavior Rating found between maladjusted and adjusted children were confirmed in a follow-up cross-validation study. The results confirmed some prior predictions that had been made.

Categories of responses by parents of handicapped children appear to indicate some rather insistent trends (concurrent validity on the basis of clinical impressions). These trends related particularly to the manner in which parents first react to knowledge of the handicap and to parental acceptance of the disability (Thurstone, 1960).

BIBLIOGRAPHY:

AFFETT, V., SOURHARD, R., and THURSTONE, J. R. "A Sheltered Workshop for the Handicapped of a Small Community." *Journal of Rehabilitation,* 1963, *4,* 35–37.

APPELL, M., WILLIAMS, C. M., and FISHELL, K. N. "Changes in Attitudes of Parents of Retarded Children Effected through Group Counseling." *American Journal of Mental Deficiency,* 1964, *68,* 807–812.

CONDELL, J. F. "Parental Attitudes toward Mental Retardation." *American Journal of Mental Deficiency,* 1966, *71,* 85–92.

THURSTONE, J. R. "Counseling the Parents of Mentally Retarded Children." *Training School Bulletin,* 1963, *60,* 113–117.

THURSTONE, J. R. "The Slow Learner: Too Close to Normalcy." *The Clearing House,* 1964, *38,* 296–298.

THURSTONE, J. R. "Counseling the Parents of the Severely Handicapped." In J. H. Rothstein (Ed.), *Mental Retardation: Readings and Resources.* New York: Holt, Rinehart, and Winston, 1961. Pp. 461–467.

THURSTONE, J. R. "Attitudes and Emotional Reactions of Parents of Institutionalized Cerebral Palsied, Retarded Patients." *American Journal of Mental Deficiency,* 1960, *65,* 227–235.

THURSTONE, J. R. "A Procedure for Evaluating Parental Attitudes toward the Handicapped." *American Journal of Mental Deficiency,* 1959, *63,* 148–155.

CATEGORY 9

SOCIAL BEHAVIOR

AFFECTIONAL AND AGGRESSIVE OBSERVATION CHECK SHEET

AUTHORS: James Walters, et al.

AGE: Nursery and kindergarten children

VARIABLE: Affective behavior

TYPE OF MEASURE: Frame of reference for observation

SOURCE FROM WHICH THE MEASURE MAY BE OBTAINED: See Walters et al. (1957)

DESCRIPTION OF MEASURE: This is a frame of reference for measuring affectional and aggressive behavior of nursery school and kindergarten children. There are four overall behavior categories: physical affection, verbal affection, physical aggression, and verbal aggression. Under each overall category there are subcategories that help define the overall category or make it operational. For example, under physical affection there are six subcategories: compliant, that is, conforms to another's desire or request; kisses; pats, fondles, hugs; smiles, laughs with someone; helpful, shares, that is, gives assistance to another, divides materials with others; sympathetic. There are five subcategories under verbal affection, eight under physical aggression, and ten under verbal aggression. The score for any one child for any one category of behavior is the number of times during a specified observation period that such behavior is observed.

RELIABILITY AND VALIDITY: Walters et al. (1957), reporting percentages of agreement between observers (there were three observers), indicate that the average percentage of agreement was .85. It is unclear from their table whether they are reporting percentages or reliability coefficients. While no direct evidence of validity is given, some of the data from the Walters study are suggestive. For example, physical aggression of boys at all four age levels (2, 3, 4, and 5) was higher than for girls. Verbal aggression, however, was about equal for boys and girls at the 3-, 4-, and 5-year levels.

BIBLIOGRAPHY:

WALTERS, J., PEARCE, D., and DAHMS, L. "Affectional and Aggressive Behavior of Preschool Children." *Child Development*, 1957, *28*, 1–25.

AGGRESSION SCALE

AUTHOR: Robert R. Sears

AGE: 12 years

VARIABLE: Aggressive behavior

TYPE OF MEASURE: Self-report rating scale

SOURCE FROM WHICH MEASURE MAY BE OBTAINED: A keyed copy of the test blank, together with a table showing proportion of each sex in the 1958 Classmates group who scored at each of the five points on each of the sixty items, and a complete table of interitem correlations calculated separately by sex has been deposited with the American Documentation Institute. Order Document No. 6870 from ADI Auxiliary Publications Project, Photoduplication Service, Library of Congress Washington, D.C. 20540, remitting in advance $2.25 for microfilm or $5.00 for photocopies. Make checks payable to Chief, Photoduplication Service, Library of Congress.

DESCRIPTION OF MEASURE: The aggression scale is a self-report of attitudes measuring five aspects of aggression: aggression anxiety, projected aggression, self-aggression, prosocial aggression, and antisocial aggression. A score of 5 is given to either extreme attitudinal position, "strongly agree" or "strongly disagree." The total score for each subscale is the sum of the scores for the individual items. The five subscales, their meanings, and the number of items in each measure follow: aggression anxiety (twelve items) measures feelings of fear and other unpleasant reactions to aggression; projected aggression (fourteen items) measures the tendency to attribute aggression to sources other than oneself; self-aggression (five items) assesses punishment to oneself; prosocial aggression (eight items) refers to socially acceptable aggressive behavior; and antisocial aggression (nine items) assesses unacceptable aggressive behavior (Sears, 1961). Illustrative items from the aggression anxiety subscale follow:

It upsets me to think some thoughtless word or crack of mine might hurt someone's feelings.
It makes me uncomfortable to see two of my friends fighting.
If someone gets hurt in an accident, I usually try to get a good view of what happened.

RELIABILITY AND VALIDITY: The statistics for this scale are based, to a large extent, on 160 "originals" who had previously been subjects of an experiment by Sears and his colleagues (1957). In terms of demographic features, the follow-up sample "is a surprisingly close representation of the total original group from which it was drawn" (Sears, 1961, pp. 467–468). This finding should give greater credence to the statistics in the reliability and validity of the scale.

With the exception of the self-aggression subscale, the corrected reliability coefficients (Spearman-Brown) on odd-even items for all scales were .6 or better.

These data were based on samples well in excess of 300 cases. The corrected reliability coefficient for the self-aggression scale was .15.

In the area of validating evidence, several findings appear to give construct validity to the scale. The following results are only illustrative of this statistical support. The potential consumer of this scale should consult the extended discussion of the results to obtain the full perspective on its values and limitations (Sears, 1961).

Predictable sex differences in the findings were obtained. For example, girls exhibited statistically significant greater mean scores on the scales of aggression anxiety and prosocial aggression, while the boys' mean scores on antisocial aggression were significantly higher than those of girls.

Results on the aggression scales were correlated with data on the same children from interviews dealing with mothers' child-rearing practices or attitudes. The posited relationships were low, but all were in the expected direction.

An expected results of antisocial aggression correlated negatively at statistically significant levels with data from the scales of prosocial aggression and aggression anxiety.

BIBLIOGRAPHY:

SEARS, R. R. "Relation of Early Socialization Experiences to Aggression in Middle Childhood." *Journal of Abnormal and Social Psychology,* 1961, *63,* 466–492.
SEARS, R. R., MACCOBY, E. R., and LEVIN, H. *Patterns of Child-Rearing.* Evanston, Illinois: Row, Peterson, 1957.

BELLER'S CHILD DEPENDENCE ON ADULT SCALE

AUTHOR: Emanuel K. Beller

AGE: 2½ to 6

VARIABLE: Dependency of a child on the teacher

TYPE OF MEASURE: Rating scale

SOURCE FROM WHICH THE MEASURE MAY BE OBTAINED: See Beller (1957)

DESCRIPTION OF MEASURE: Beller's scale measures dependency of the child on the teacher. The scale includes five subscales, including measures of dependency striving and the frequency with which the child seeks recognition, physical contact, attention, and proximity to the teachers or peers.

In the scoring process, each scale has seven points and the two criteria of frequency and persistence of behavior apply in the definition of these points. If both criteria apply equally, the exact division points are to be used (7, 6, 5, 4, 3, 2, 1). If differences between these criteria hold, the scoring is done in an intermediary position. A sample subscale—dependency striving—follows (Beller, 1957):

How often does the child seek help? *By help is meant any form of assistance from another person, for example, doing something for the child like dressing, washing, finding a toy for him, pushing him in the swing, protecting him against another child when he is attacked or something is taken away from him; giving instructions and guidance, like demonstrating how to build, play, paint; giving what he asks for —a toy to play with, color to paint, and the like.*

The scoring is: very often and very persistently, often and persistently, occasionally and with little persistence, very rarely and without persistence. In the initial use of the scale, Beller provided prior training to nursery school teachers. The procedures to be used in this training are outlined in a previous study (Beller, 1955).

RELIABILITY AND VALIDITY: The scale has been used in a university preschool classroom involving fifty-two children ranging in age from 28 to 74 months. Pairs of teachers rated the same group of ten children over an interval of a week. In addition, each teacher rated the groups at least three times annually. With eleven teachers participating, the product moment coefficients for the five subscales between these workers ranged between .62 to .84 with a median reliability of .78.

Since this scale was developed simultaneously with five other scales of autonomous striving, an attempt was made to check the independence of these measures. The findings show that the majority of correlations within each scale were statistically significant, whereas most intercorrelations between scales failed to reach statistical significance. The data thus show that the scales measure independent functions (Beller, 1957). A previous study by Beller (1955) also provides data in support of the reliability for the two scales of dependency and autonomy. In addition, the fact that the scales differentiated between children at significant levels suggests concurrent validity.

BIBLIOGRAPHY:

BELLER, E. K. "Dependency and Independence in Young Children." *Journal of Genetic Psychology,* 1955, *87,* 25–35.

BELLER, E. K. "Dependency and Autonomous Achievement Striving Related to Orality and Anality in Early Childhood." *Child Development,* 1957, *28,* 287–315.

BELLER, E. K. "Exploratory Studies of Dependency." *Transaction of the New York Academy of Science,* 1959, *21,* 414–426.

EMMERICH, W. "Continuity and Stability in Early Social Development: II. Teacher Rating." *Child Development,* 1966, *37,* 17–27.

LEBO, D. "Aggressiveness and Expansiveness in Children." *Journal of Genetic Psychology,* 1962, *100,* 227–249.

LEBO, D., and LEBO, E. "Aggression and Age in Relation to Verbal Expression in Nondirective Play Therapy." *Psychological Monographs,* 1957, *71,* 1–12.

BELLER'S SCALE OF INDEPENDENCE OR AUTONOMY AMONG CHILDREN

AUTHOR: Emanuel K. Beller

AGE: 2½ to 6

VARIABLE: Independence or autonomy

TYPE OF MEASURE: Rating scale

SOURCE FROM WHICH THE MEASURE MAY BE OBTAINED: See Beller (1957)

DESCRIPTION OF MEASURE: Each item of this measure is rated on a seven-point scale. The five subscales measure such components of behavior as work satisfaction, independence in carrying out routine tasks, skills in overcoming environmental obstacles, initiative in independent activities, and ability to complete initiated tasks. A sample subscale—for autonomous achievement striving—follows (Beller, 1957):

How often does the child derive satisfaction from his work? *This can be judged from the following behavior: The child finishes its activity—painting, building, play, and so on—without asking teacher for comment; without making derogatory comments on the work of other children; or without showing disturbance or irritation by bullying other children, dashing off wildly, destroying one's own work, but instead moving away from a completed activity and getting ready for a new period.*

RELIABILITY AND VALIDITY: Pairs of teachers rated the same group of ten children over an interval of a week. In addition, each teacher rated the groups at least three times annually. Eleven teachers participated in the ratings. The product moment correlations ranged from .67 to .80 with a median of .75. Rho coefficients for summated ratings from teacher pairs ranged between .69 to .93 with a median of .83. The children's relative position over time did not change appreciably on the scale.

BIBLIOGRAPHY:

BELLER, E. K. "Dependency and Independence in Young Children." *Journal of Genetic Psychology*, 1955, *87*, 23–35.

BELLER, E. K. "Dependency and Autonomous Achievement Striving Related to Orality and Anality in Early Childhood." *Child Development*, 1957, *28*, 287–315.

BELLER, E. K. "Exploratory Studies of Dependency." *Transactions of the New York Academy of Science*, 1959, *21*, 414–426.

EMMERICH, W. "Continuity and Stability in Early Social Development: II. Teacher Rating." *Child Development*, 1966, *37*, 17–27.

LEBO, D. "Aggressiveness and Expansiveness in Children." *Journal of Genetic Psychology*, 1962, *100*, 227–240.

LEBO, D., and LEBO, E. "Aggression and Age in Relation to Verbal Expression in Nondirective Play Therapy." *Psychological Monographs*, 1957, *71*, 1–12.

CATEGORIES FOR MEASURING INTERACTION BEHAVIOR IN NONVERBAL PSYCHOTIC CHILDREN

AUTHORS: Ira M. Steisel, I. Hyman Weiland, Kirby J. Smith, Joseph Denny, Janice Schulman, and Nina Chaiken

AGE: The measure has been used with normal and deviant subjects ranging from preschool age to adulthood. Its primary use, however, has been for psychotic children.

VARIABLE: Social interaction

TYPE OF MEASURE: Rating scale

SOURCE FROM WHICH THE MEASURE MAY BE OBTAINED: See Steisel et al. (1960). Specific instructions for the experimenter and mimeographed copies of the rating scales are available from the senior author: Ira M. Steisel, St. Christopher's Hospital for Children, 2603 North 5th St., Philadelphia, Pennsylvania 19133.

DESCRIPTION OF MEASURE: The interactive categories serve as a procedure especially tailored to the nonverbal child for measuring one dimension of social or emotional behavior. The procedure consists essentially of a structured three-phase play situation involving a child and an experimenter. The situation is geared to assess the child's ability to relate or interact with others. In the three phases, the experimenter solicits interaction, rejects interaction by the child, neither rejects nor solicits such behavior but does respond to interactive attempts by the child. The authors carefully and specifically delineate the activity of the experimenter in all three periods.

The child's behavior is rated on seven five-point scales: paying attention to the experimenter or instructions (not scored during rejection period); paying attention to the tasks or objects; following instructions: complying, cooperating (omitted during the last two phases); initiating or instigating interaction (not scored when adult solicits interaction); willingness: degree of investment in interaction; communicative sounds; and response to experimenter's interactive efforts (not rated during the period the child was being rejected). The scores range from 1 to 5 in order of decreasing pathology. Thus, 1 reflects severe impairment, whereas a score of 5 represents a maximum of the attribute being assessed. The other three intermediary scores suggest inconsistencies in behavior or behavioral tendencies only (Steisel et al., 1961).

RELIABILITY AND VALIDITY: The categories for interaction behavior have been used in at least two samples. An earlier sample included nine normal children ranging in age from 48 to 91 months with a mean age of 68 months; a group of twenty-four organic brain-damaged or mentally retarded subjects in an institution (Woods Schools), with an age range from 61 to 130 months, a mean age of 92 months; eighteen inpatient schizophrenic children with ages ranging from 58 to 127 months and an average life age of 99 months (Steisel et al., 1961). In a later sample, the test was given to twenty-eight phenylketonuric (PKU) subjects, ranging in age from 5 to 17 years, with a mean age of 8 years.

Reliability for the rating scale, based on observer agreements, varies widely with the type of child (normal versus psychotic versus brain-damaged versus retarded) being observed (Steisel et al., 1961).

In an attempt to assess the validity of the procedures, judges other than the experimenters were requested to rank each child for his interactions with peers and adults. Interjudge agreement was evaluated by Kendall's W. In the psychotic group, the W values were respectively .55 for adult interaction and 0.66 for peer interaction, both significant beyond the .001 level. The judges from the Woods Schools were able to obtain rank order correlations of .77 (interaction with adults) and 0.64 (interaction with peers), $p < .01$ in both cases (Steisel et al., 1961).

There was a close parallel between the rating scale data and clinical impressions: the interaction scores for the psychotics were lowest; those for the retarded or brain-damaged group were next lowest; whereas those for the normal control were highest (Steisel et al., 1961). Interaction scores of PKU subjects ranked between psychotics and normal and retarded groups.

BIBLIOGRAPHY:

STEISEL, I. M., WEILAND, I. H., DENNY, J., SMITH, K., and CHAIKEN, N. "Measuring Interaction in Nonverbal Psychotic Children." *American Journal of Orthopsychiatry*, 1960, *XXX*, 405–411.

STEISEL, I. M., WEILAND, I. H., SMITH, K., and SCHULMAN, J. "Interaction in Nonverbal Psychotic Children." *Archives of General Psychiatry*, 1961, *5*, 141–145.

CATEGORIES OF INTERPERSONAL COGNITION

AUTHORS: Sanford M. Dornbusch, Albert H. Hastorf, Stephan A. Richardson, Robert E. Muzzy, and Rebecca S. Vreeland

AGE: 9 to 11

VARIABLE: Social perception; person cognition

TYPE OF MEASURE: System of categories for content analysis

SOURCE FROM WHICH THE MEASURE MAY BE OBTAINED: The Coding Manual can be obtained from the American Documentation Institute by ordering Document No. 8014 from ADI Auxiliary Publications Project, Photoduplication Service, Library of Congress, Washington, D.C. 20540. Checks should be made payable to Chief, Photoduplication Service, Library of Congress, in the amount of $1.75 for microfilm or $2.50 for photocopies. A simple listing of the first order categories is given in the article by Dornbusch et al. (1965).

DESCRIPTION OF MEASURE: In the Dornbusch et al. (1965) study, the child is instructed "Tell me about Johnny Doe," and his description is tape-recorded. The subject's description or comments about Johnny Doe are then classified according to one of sixty-nine content categories that make up the First Order Code. The sixty-nine categories are grouped into demographic variables, organic variables, recreational variables, aggression, quality of interaction, frequency of interaction, interpersonal relations, group status, modes of interaction, moods of interaction, total personality, abilities, norms, and miscellaneous. Examples of some of the categories from the First Order Coding Manual are as follows:

Verbal aggression: *This category includes any mention of calling names, telling people to shut up, laughing at someone, and gossip.*
Relations with siblings: *"He has a mother"* or *"My mother helps me tie my shoes."*
Inclusion or exclusion by others in a group: *This category refers to statements specifically indicating that a person is accepted or rejected from membership in a specific collective.*
Competition: *This category refers to statements such as: "He won the race." "He found the most counselors in the counselor hunt." "He tried out for Little League."*

There is also a second coding scheme, consisting of nineteen categories, described by the authors as more abstract than the First Order Code. All the data given herein refer to the First Order Code.

RELIABILITY AND VALIDITY: The authors state that the reliability of the coding is high. Even using the strictest criterion results in a reliability of 86.4 per cent, meaning that in interscorer reliability, when one interviewer coded in a specific category, more than seventeen out of twenty times the other scorer checked the same category.

The authors suggest that the proportion of the residual (nonclassifiable) statements gives some indication of the relevance (and consequently, validity) of the code. The average residual was 11.8 per cent of the number of idea units categorized.

BIBLIOGRAPHY:

DORNBUSCH, S. M., HASTORF, A. H., RICHARDSON, S. A., MUZZY, R. E., and VREELAND, R. S. "The Perceiver and the Perceived: Their Relative Influence on the Categories of Interpersonal Cognition." *Journal of Personality and Social Psychology,* 1965, *1* (5).

CHILD SCALE

AUTHOR: Ralph Rothstein

AGE: Children of any age

VARIABLE: Numerous aspects of child behavior

TYPE OF MEASURE: Rating scale

SOURCE FROM WHICH THE MEASURE MAY BE OBTAINED: Ralph Rothstein, 275 Belmont Street, Worcester, Massachusetts 01600

DESCRIPTION OF MEASURE: The purpose of the Child Scale appears to be to provide a rating scheme for children's behavior without concentrating on any specific aspect of behavior. There are twenty-six items each representing a facet of behavior. For example, the first item is illustrated below:

Comfort: *Relaxed, comfortable and at ease in situations; seems spontaneous and natural in surroundings; does not appear tense, anxious or depressed.* (a) *Not at all characteristic,* (b) *minimally characteristic,* (c) *moderately characteristic,* (d) *strongly characteristic,* (e) *maximally characteristic.*

The other items for which the format is the same (except for the last item), are the following: verbalization, coordination, manipulative skill, relatedness, involvement in situation and tasks, emotional excitability, affective involvement in relationship, curiosity, enjoyment, initiative in relating, goal direction, negativism, hypermotility, preoccupation with body, immaturity, assertiveness, withdrawal from relationship, dependent, communication disturbance, symptomatic mannerisms, marked inappropriateness of behavior, seeking stimulation in physical closeness, interest in body of parent, appealingness of child, and preferred modality of communication.

EVIDENCE OF RELIABILITY: The reliability of the rating scales based on inter-rater agreement is described as moderate to good, coefficients of correlation ranging from .5 to .8.

BIBLIOGRAPHY: None.

CHILDREN'S BEHAVIOR CHECK LIST

AUTHOR: Leland H. Stott

AGE: 3 to 12

VARIABLE: Social interaction

TYPE OF MEASURE: Checklist

SOURCE FROM WHICH THE MEASURE MAY BE OBTAINED: The rotated factor matrix has been deposited as Document number 7093 with the ADI Auxiliary Publications Project, Photoduplication Service, Library of Congress, Washington, D.C. 20540. A copy may be secured by citing the document number and by remitting $1.25 for photoprints, or $1.25 for 35 mm. microfilm. Advance payment is required. Make checks or money orders payable to Chief, Photoduplication Service, Library of Congress.

DESCRIPTION OF MEASURE: Stott's original behavior checklist consists of 220 behavioral items selected from an original pool of 320 items (Stott, 1962). The 220 items were those most likely to provide pertinent personality data by trained raters from an original checklist of 384 behavioral items relating to the behavior of sixty-three nursery school children on the basis of a minimum of four sets of data by teachers. The most recent version consists of 166 items.

On the basis of tetrachoric intercorrelations between items, the early version included fifty-one clusters with varying numbers of items based on findings from sixty-three preschool subjects. Factor analysis, based on intercorrelations of the cluster scores, resulted in fourteen factors. The nature of the factors and their explicit meanings have been described in full by Stott (1962). As an example, Factor I (personal responsibility versus irresponsible impulsiveness) is presented below with a sample of its clusters and its cluster loadings (Stott, 1962).

Compliant Behavior—*cooperative and responsible; does not lag in following suggestions; responds without delay to authority; adjusts immediately to daily routine; responds readily to directions in the day's routine; always goes through the daily procedures willingly* (.81).

Dependable Behavior—*takes good care of his own possessions; seldom quarrels with other children over trivial matters; does not try to get even with a child with whom he is angry; even-tempered; meets situations in a quiet, matter-of-fact manner; not restless or dissatisfied with his own activity* (.77).

Irresponsible Behavior—*attention from other children leads him to "show off" or act silly; haphazard methods of work or play; easily led into mischief by other children; hurts other children, often through carelessness* (−.98).

Evasive Behavior—*tries to get a task done by the person who suggests it; takes a long time to adjust to the daily routine; does not concentrate his energy to accomplish a difficult task; quarrels with other children, often over trivial things; does not put things away carefully* (−.81).

Lusty, Nondeliberative Behavior—*rough and ready; often "shows off" or acts silly; brimming over with ideas for activity* (−.64).

In the most recent version of 166 items, the raw score is the number of items that agree with the key for each factor.

RELIABILITY AND VALIDITY: Internal consistency of the scale rests on cluster and factor analysis based on the records of sixty-three nursery children rated on the original checklist of 220 items. Based on the intercorrelations of these original behavioral dispositions, Stott has reduced the factors to eight. Test-retest reliability data based on scores of 340 preschool children yielded coefficients ranging between .37 and .74. Though these coefficients are statistically significant at a level of confidence greater than .01, Stott concedes that they are quite low. However, the ratings were done six to eight months apart by teachers who had not renewed contact with the children.

BIBLIOGRAPHY:

STOTT, L. H. "Personality at Age Four." *Child Development,* 1962, *33,* 287–311.
STOTT, L. H., and BALL, R. S. "Consistency and Change in Ascendance Submission in the Social Interaction of Children." *Child Development,* 1957, *28,* 259–272.

CHILDREN'S MINIMAL SOCIAL BEHAVIOR SCALE

AUTHORS: Raymond A. Ulmer and Martha Lieberman

AGE: Childhood generally

VARIABLE: Social behavior

TYPE OF MEASURE: Structured interview

SOURCE FROM WHICH THE MEASURE MAY BE OBTAINED: Raymond A. Ulmer, 1632 North Laurel Avenue, Apartment 238, Los Angeles, California 90046

DESCRIPTION OF MEASURE: This measure is a highly structured interview in which the behavior of the examiner is ritualized in order to present the same stimulus to each child. Thirty-one items are presented orally to the subject, some of them ordinary social stimuli like "How are you?" Each response is scored pass (score of 1) or fail (score of 0). There is a total score, which is derived from three subscores: a motor score for those items that require only muscular movements; a verbal score for items requiring speech only; and a motor-verbal score for items involving both. There is also a time score, that being the reciprocal of the total number of seconds needed to complete five of the items. The performance score is the total of all items passed, while the total score is the sum of the time score and the three performance scores mentioned above. The first six items, with instructions, are reproduced below:

The child is brought to the door and introduced to the examiner. The examiner stands up and says, "Hello ———." (1) Score + if the subject enters and approaches the examiner. (2) Score + if any discriminable response to greeting, not necessarily verbal. (3) Score + if response is verbal and appropriate.
The examiner says, "Won't you have a seat?" (4) Score + if the subject sits down without further urging.
The examiner sits and says, "How are you?" (5) Score + any discriminable response to this question. (6) Score + if response is verbal and appropriate.

RELIABILITY AND VALIDITY: Interexaminer reliability for subtest and total scores is high, with coefficients of .97 to .99 for subtest and total scores.

The CMSBS was administered to eighty-one children ages 9 to 11—thirty-two normal (IQ 80 to 139), thirty-two retarded (IQ 13 to 63), and seventeen schizophrenic. Analysis of variance of the total scores showed that this measure significantly differentiated these three groups. There was a significant interaction effect between sex and group, apparently related to large differences between means of male and female retardates. This difference may be based on differences in criteria for admission of males and females to institutions for the retarded. Some of the items having high diagnostic power among the three groups are discussed by Ulmer (1968).

BIBLIOGRAPHY:

ULMER, R. A., and LIEBERMAN, M. "Children's Minimal Social Behavior Scale: A Short, Objective Measure of Personality Functioning (10-Year Level)." *Psychological Reports*, 1968, 22, 283–286.

CRISPIN SYSTEM OF INTERACTIONAL ANALYSIS

AUTHOR: David Crispin

AGE: Though the Crispin system was applied primarily to sixth-grade classes in a pilot study, the nature of the interactional analysis is such that it probably could be used with almost any grade level

VARIABLE: Social interaction in classrooms

TYPE OF MEASURE: Involved rating system

SOURCE FROM WHICH THE MEASURE MAY BE OBTAINED: David Crispin, Indiana State University, Department of Education and Psychology, Terre Haute, Indiana 47809

DESCRIPTION OF MEASURE: The Crispin System of Interactional Analysis offers an objective measure for three kinds of activities within a classroom: teacher behavior, teacher-student behavior, and student-student interaction. The Crispin system measures interactional analysis in terms of modes of behavior, classroom climate, types, and categories as follows:

Mode: Mode refers to the style of dichotomous behavioral acts by teachers and students. It refers primarily to the degree of directiveness by the teacher in guiding classroom activities or to the extent or manner of support the student provides to them.

Climate: Climate is the emotional climate in the class measured by the ratio of indirect to direct behavior on the teacher's part (ID ratio) or supportive to nonsupportive behavior on the student's part.

Types: Types are reportedly used to describe specific acts of both teachers and pupils. The seven types are: authority, criticism, discipline, feelings, nonteaching and nonlearning, subject matter, and values and controversial issues.

Categories: Categories consist of both a type of behavior and the mode in which it is carried out. An example follows for authoritative teacher behavior:

Indirect Mode: *"Where shall we begin today?" "Do you think we should have a test on this material?"*

Direct Mode: *"Take out your books—turn to page ten." "Be ready for the test tomorrow."*

In the application of the system within the classroom, observations are taken every three seconds and recorded according to prescribed procedures including symbols described in detail by Crispin. As a preliminary step, Crispin recommends that the mode and climates of the classroom be checked by two or more observers. He cautions that the rest of the system should not be used until it can be demonstrated that the two observers can reach a very high rate of agreement, preferably at a statistically significant level.

RELIABILITY AND VALIDITY: Crispin claims only face validity for his system in the sense that the classifications were developed on the basis of a clinician's judgment as to whether or not they met predetermined definitions of behavior. However, a pilot study of male teachers in fifth and sixth grade revealed individual differences between teachers and intra-individual differences on the Discipline Category.

BIBLIOGRAPHY: None.

FEEDING RATING SCALE

AUTHOR: Irene H. Wiemers

AGE: 4 to 8 months

VARIABLE: Feeding behavior

TYPE OF MEASURE: Rating scale

SOURCE FROM WHICH THE MEASURE MAY BE OBTAINED: See Wiemers (1960)

DESCRIPTION OF MEASURE: In using this scale, the infant's feeding behavior is rated as either very unsatisfactory, unsatisfactory, satisfactory, very satisfactory, highly satisfactory. Under each of these broad classes, more specific aspects of feeding behavior are evaluated by the scorer: satiation, participation, sucking, coordination, mechanics, relaxation-tension, handling, physical contact, and interaction. The specific category "mechanics" will serve as an example. Mechanics are considered very unsatisfactory if the "feeding process [is] mechanically inadequate." Mechanics is rated as unsatisfactory if "[the mechanics] may be grossly inadequate in some respect." It is considered satisfactory if the "feeding process in general [is] mechanically adequate." Mechanics is given a "very satisfactory" rating if "feeding proceeds smoothly." Mechanics of feeding is considered highly satisfactory if the "feeding [is] conspicuously smooth." There is a description for each specific aspect of feeding behavior mentioned above for each level of satisfactoriness. In Wiemer's (1960) study, the scale is not used in actual feeding situations with the scorers present, but instead the scorers evaluate the feeding behavior from detailed observation and records compiled for another study.

RELIABILITY AND VALIDITY: When two psychologists rated the feeding observations of ten infants, the rank order correlation between their rankings of the ten infants on satisfactoriness of feeding was .92. With respect to validity of the scale, there was no significant relationship between the feeding rating score and other variables such as intelligence test scores, developmental scores, and physiological measures.

BIBLIOGRAPHY:

WIEMERS, I. H. "Evaluating Adequacy of Adjustment in Normal Infants." Unpublished doctoral dissertation, University of Utah, 1960.

FIRST ORDER CODING MANUAL

AUTHORS: Stephen A. Richardson, Albert H. Hastorf, and Sanford M. Dornbusch

AGE: 9 to 11

VARIABLE: (See description of measure below)

TYPE OF MEASURE: Frame of reference for content analysis

SOURCE FROM WHICH THE MEASURE MAY BE OBTAINED: The complete coding manual with the full set of definitions has been deposited as Document 8014 with the ADI Auxiliary Publications Project, Photoduplication Service, Library of Congress, Washington, D.C., 20540. A copy may be secured by citing the document number and by remitting $2.50 for photoprints or $1.75 for 35 mm. microfilm. Advance payment is required. Make checks payable or money orders payable to Chief, Photoduplication Service, Library of Congress.

DESCRIPTION OF MEASURE: The coding manual consists of sixty-nine content categories that are grouped under broader variable categories. The broad categories are as follows (with the content categories composing the first five as examples):

Demographic variables: *spatial location, age, race, ethnicity, religion.*
Organic variables: *handicap, health, physical description, physical attractiveness.*
Recreational variables: *physical recreation, nonphysical recreation.*
Aggression: *physical aggression, verbal aggression, general aggression.*
Quality of interaction: *described* to *describer* (*He likes me*), *others and described* to *describer* (*They like me*), *described* to *others and describer* (*He likes us*), *others and described* to *others and describer* (*They like us*), *describer* to *described* (*I like him*), *describer* to *others and described* (*I like them*), *others and describer* to *described* (*We like him*), *others and describer* to *others and described* (*We like them*), *others* to *described* (*They like him*), *others* to *others and described* (*They like them*) or (*He likes them*), *described* to *others* (*He likes them*), *others and described* to *others* (*They like him*), *described and describer* to *others* (*We like them*), *described and describer and others* to *others* (*We like them*), *others* to *described and describer* (*They like us*), *others* to *described and describer and others* (*They like us*); *reciprocal relationships.*

Examples of the categories and the variables to which they are assigned are as follows:

Recreational variables: *physical recreation, nonphysical recreation, reciprocal relationships, physical ability.*

There is a second order code, which is included in the manual, that is on a higher level of abstraction than the first order code. While the codes were used by the author for making a content analysis of interview material, the codes appear readily adaptable for the analysis of written materials.

RELIABILITY AND VALIDITY: Richardson et al. (1964) randomly selected interviews for coding by the two coders in their study. The coders agreed 86.4 per cent of the time when the "residual" category was not used, and the reliability increased to over 90 per cent when this category was included in the reliability study.

BIBLIOGRAPHY:

RICHARDSON, S. A., HASTORF, A. H., and DORNBUSCH, S. M. "Effects of Physical Disability on a Child's Description of Himself." *Child Development,* 1964, *35,* 893–907.

"GUESS WHO" TECHNIQUE

AUTHOR: Gerald Lesser

AGE: Fifth and sixth grade

VARIABLE: Aggressive behavior

TYPE OF MEASURE: A modified sociometric technique

SOURCE FROM WHICH THE MEASURE MAY BE OBTAINED: See Lesser (1959)

DESCRIPTION OF MEASURE: This is a modified sociometric technique with a "Guess Who" format in which the subjects are asked to identify descriptive characterization by naming one or more classmates who fit the verbal pictures or statements. The test measures five classifications of overt aggression. Definitions of the five categories of aggressive activity, and sample items for each category follow:

Provoked Physical Aggression: *to physically attack or injure provocation. Here is a boy who will fight, but only if someone picks on him first.*

Outburst Aggression: *to display uncontrolled, temper tantrum aggressive behavior. Here is a boy who gets so mad at times that he doesn't know what he is doing.*

Unprovoked Physical Aggression: *to physically attack or injure without provocation. This boy starts a fight over nothing.*

Verbal Aggression: *to verbally attack or injure. This boy often threatens other boys.*

Indirect Aggression: *to attack or injure indirectly through another person or object. This boy tattles to the teacher about what other boys do.*

There are twenty items, thirteen to measure the various forms of aggression and seven filler items. Lesser's scale was originally in a booklet form including the seven filler items. The source of the test merely gives the items employed in the measure but does not contain the filler items.

RELIABILITY AND VALIDITY: The scale has been administered to ages 10 years to 13 years 4 months in grades five and six. (1) For the two different forms of the item measuring Unprovoked Physical Aggression and Verbal Aggression, respectively, tetrachoric correlation coefficients for five classrooms averaged +.90 and +.88. (2) Biserial correlation coefficients between peer and teacher judgments for the five aggressive variables ranged from +.80 to +.72. (3) Correlations between aggression and popularity scores were generally negative ones. One exception was the relationship between provoked physical aggression and popularity that yielded a positive correlation coefficient of .31.

BIBLIOGRAPHY:

LESSER, G. S. "The Relationships Between Various Forms of Aggression and Popularity among Lower-Class Children." *Journal of Educational Psychology*, 1959, *50*, 20–25.

LESSER, G. S. "Conflict Analysis of Fantasy Aggression." *Journal of Personality*, 1958, *26*, 29–41.

G-W METHOD OF PAIRED DIRECT AND PROJECTIVE QUESTIONNAIRE

AUTHORS: J. W. Getzels and J. J. Walsh

AGE: Ages 8 to 13

VARIABLE: Attitude structure and socialization

TYPE OF MEASURE: Incomplete sentences test

SOURCE FROM WHICH THE MEASURE MAY BE OBTAINED: See Getzels and Walsh (1958)

DESCRIPTION OF MEASURE: The scale is based on a twofold view of socialization—the suppression of socially unacceptable behaviors, and conformity with societal expectations for acceptable behavior. The principal measure of socialization is the Index of Differentiation, computed by the formula $ID = P - D/P$ where P represents the number of negative completions on the projective questionnaire and D the same scores on the direct questions. The items of the scale are designed to meet three requirements: social acceptability or unacceptability (negative items); freedom from affectively loaded words (good, bad, angry); and differential discrimination for varying subsections of the population (sex and ethnic groups).

The test consists of forty incomplete sentences. The direct form uses items phrased in the first person, while the projective format uses the third person. Separate forms are administered to boys and girls. In the original use of the scale, the projective instrument was administered first followed by the direct form after a two-week interval. Subsequently, the children completed a personal data sheet with various variables. Examples of items on the direct and projective forms of the scale follow:

I think that most bosses are
Beverly thinks that most bosses are
Chuck thinks that most bosses are

RELIABILITY AND VALIDITY: The interscorer reliability ranges were respectively .97 to .98 for the direct scores, .95 to 96 for the projective scores, and .90 to .95 for the discrepancy scores. The outcomes of the mean index of differentiation were in the predicted directions for the variables of age, sex, family position, and social class status.

BIBLIOGRAPHY:

GETZELS, J. W., and WALSH, J. J. "The Method of Paired Direct and Projective Questionnaires in the Study of Attitude Structure and Socialization." *Psychological Monographs*, 1958, 72(1) (Whole No. 454).

IMPULSE CONTROL CATEGORIZATION INSTRUMENT (ICCI)

AUTHOR: John Matsushima

AGE: Fourth-, fifth-, and sixth-grade boys

VARIABLE: Impulse control

TYPE OF MEASURE: Self-report rating scale

SOURCE FROM WHICH THE MEASURE MAY BE OBTAINED: The complete twenty-four item ICCI has been deposited with the American Documentation Institute. Order Document No. 7755 from ADI Auxiliary Publications Project, Photoduplication Service, Library of Congress, Washington, D.C. 20540. Remit in advance $1.25 for microfilm or $1.25 for photocopies and make checks payable to Chief, Photoduplication Service, Library of Congress.

DESCRIPTION OF MEASURE: The ICCI was designed for use in a study of impulse control among latency age boys (Matsushima, 1963). The measure classified subjects as high or low in self-control over immediate aggressive action when aroused. Collectively administered to thirty or forty boys at a time, the test consists of twenty-four sentence-situations in which subjects state degrees of choice between spontaneously aggressive or nonaggressive behavior. Some of the ICCI items are:

If a boy spit in my face, I would hit him right away.
If I were very angry, I would break up tables and chairs.
If a boy smashes my models, I complain but do nothing.
I get mad right away.
When a boy swears at me, I walk away.
When a boy shoves me, I knock his teeth out.

Each item is answered by circling one of four responses, YES, yes, no, or NO. Perceptual variations in small and large type provide for degrees of emphasis in answers. It is assumed that boys in this age range can more conveniently differentiate levels of abstraction according to type size rather than word content. Subjects have reported that all of the situations are familiar predicaments, and that emphases in responses are especially simple to register.

Each sentence is scored from 1 to 4 points, depending on express tendency to immediate outburst of aggressive behavior. With four responses possible in each situation, 1, 2, 3, or 4 points are scored for a total of twenty-four items. The minimum possible score is twenty-four points, the maximum, 96 points. Higher scores are in the direction of low impulse control.

RELIABILITY AND VALIDITY: Two samples of forty each took the measure, all being boys from the fourth, fifth, and sixth grades, between the ages of 9 and 12. The corrected odd-even reliabilities were .932 and .931. Item analysis showed that all items except one discriminated between the highest and lowest quartile distribution for the total scale at or beyond the .02 level. The author recommends that the one item that failed to discriminate be omitted in the future.

Further validating data for the instrument were provided by an interview schedule, subsequent to test performance in which each boy stated his reactions to the thirty-minute task. The interview schedule consisted of twelve items evenly divided among three measures: self-reported pressure toward impulsivity; self-reported pressure to leave the task; self-reported cohesiveness. In all instances, the differences were in the predicted direction beyond the .01 level of significance. Finally, task persistence shown by the two extreme groups provided partial validating data. Of the thirty-two boys classified by the ICCI as HI C (scoring 50 points or less), none left the task during the thirty-minute period, while eleven of the thirty-two LO C (70 points or more) boys left abruptly to use play materials.

BIBLIOGRAPHY:

MATSUSHIMA, J. "An Instrument for Classifying Impulse Control among Boys." *Journal of Consulting Psychology*, 1964, *28*, 87–90.

INDEX OF EFFECTIVENESS OF PARENT-CHILD COMMUNICATION

AUTHORS: Bernard Farber and William C. Jenné

AGE: Normal children, ages 11 to 16 inclusive

VARIABLE: Communication

TYPE OF MEASURE: Questionnaire

SOURCE FROM WHICH THE MEASURE MAY BE OBTAINED: See Farber and Jenné (1963)

DESCRIPTION OF MEASURE: In this subscale, each parent is requested to check an answer—much less, a little less, as he does now, a little more, much, does not apply—for fifty activities as follows (Farber and Jenné, 1963):

I wish my son would do this activity: *think about school work; help around the house; listen to radio and TV programs; play outdoor games such as baseball or tennis; visit his friends.*

The child is also requested to check each statement in the same manner but the prefatory statement reads "My father wishes that I would do this activity."

The scoring for the measure then consists of four elements: the number of items on which the child accurately perceives parental satisfaction (A); the number of times the child accurately perceives parental dissatisfaction (B); the number of items in which either parent or the child (or both) does not respond or gives conflicting answers (G); and the total number of items (N = 50). The index of effectiveness of parent-child communication is, then, $(A + B)/(N - G)$. The index of effectiveness, then, is the ratio of accurate perceptions by the child to the total number of acceptable responses. Theoretically, the numerical values of scores can range from .00 to 1.00.

RELIABILITY AND VALIDITY: The internal consistency of the scale is indicated by the fact that items with factor loadings of less than .36 were not included. Accuracy on the child's perceptions of father's dissatisfaction ranged between factor loadings of .40 (show feelings toward friends) and .71 (show affection toward father). Accuracy on the child's perceptions of the mother's dissatisfaction yielded a very similar range, though not for the same items. On three different samples, moreover, reproducibility coefficients for the child's perception of parents' dissatisfaction with his behavior ranged between .93 and .97. These data suggest the unidimensionality of the scale.

BIBLIOGRAPHY:

FARBER, B., and JENNÉ, W. C. "Family Organization and Parent-Child Communications." *Monographs of the Society for Research in Child Development,* 1963, *28* (Whole Monograph, No. 7).

MEDINNUS FIRST GRADE ADJUSTMENT SCALE

AUTHOR: G. R. Medinnus

AGE: First grade

VARIABLE: Social adjustment in classrooms

TYPE OF MEASURE: Rating scale

SOURCE FROM WHICH THE MEASURE MAY BE OBTAINED: See Medinnus (1961a)

DESCRIPTION OF MEASURE: The Medinnus Scale consists of fifty-four items (fifty-two items according to Medinnus, 1961a) developed from interviews with twenty-five first-grade teachers. The items are rated on a five-point scale in which 3 = average adjustment, 1 = poor adjustment, and 5 = good adjustment. The classification of the five area groupings and the number of items in each area are as follows: physical status and motor behavior (four items); social behavior (fourteen items); emotional behavior (ten items); intellectual abilities and behavior (seven items); and adjustment to classroom membership and requirements (nineteen items). In the interest of saving space, the article that contains the scale (Medinnus, 1961a) lists only the end points, 1 and 5. In the scale manual, however, each scale item is diagrammed on a horizontal line with 1 and 5 appearing at opposite ends of the line, and the numbers 2, 3, and 4 equally spaced along the line. Examples of items from each area are listed below (Medinnus, 1961a):

Physical status and motor behavior, physical condition and health: (1) weak physical system, poor health, tires easily; (5) excellent physical condition, healthy.
Social behavior, leadership: (1) is lacking in leadership qualities; (5) possesses good leadership qualities.
Emotional behavior, happiness, cheerfulness: [(1)] unhappy, gloomy disposition, whiny, pouts; (5) happy, cheerful.
Intellectual abilities and behavior, language development: (1) immature language development, unable to express self adequately, poor vocabulary; (5) mature language development, able to talk in simple, accurate sentences, large vocabulary for age level.
Adjustment to classroom membership and requirements, ability to listen: (1) inattentive, dreamer, in a world of his own; (5) is a good listener, gives rapt attention.

RELIABILITY AND VALIDITY: Thirty-five first graders, nineteen boys and sixteen girls with mean IQ of 112 were tested. The socioeconomic status of the children's families was approximately evenly divided between the upper-lower and lower-middle classes according to Warner's Index of Status Characteristics. The inter-rater reliability coefficients for the five sections of the scale range from .70 to .78. The reliability coefficient for the full scale was .77.

The development of the items was based on interviews with twenty-five first-grade teachers. Only those items were selected that had a minimal amount of consensus. A correlation of −.52 was obtained between first-grade adjustment ratings and Haggerty-Olson-Wickman ratings of the same children made in the kindergarten year. The correlation is in the expected direction since higher Haggerty-Olson-Wickman scores indicate poor adjustment (Medinnus, 1961a). For mothers only, several Fels Scales in the Dependence vs. Independence Encouraging Factor differentiated the home environments of the well- and poorly adjusted first graders at .05 level or beyond (Medinnus, 1961b).

BIBLIOGRAPHY:

MEDINNUS, G. R. "The Development of a First-Grade Adjustment Scale." *Journal of Experimental Psychology,* 1961a, *30,* 243–248.
MEDINNUS, G. R. "The Relation Between Several Parent Measures and the Child's Early Adjustment to School." *Journal of Educational Psychology,* 1961b, *52,* 153–156.

MOTHER-CHILD INTERACTION TEST

AUTHOR: M. Zunich

AGE: Nursery school age

VARIABLE: Mothers' behavior toward children

TYPE OF MEASURE: Observation frame of reference

SOURCE FROM WHICH THE MEASURE MAY BE OBTAINED: See Zunich (1962)

DESCRIPTION OF MEASURE: This is a frame of reference for use in observing mother-child "interaction," although the seventeen categories refer primarily to the behavior of the mother toward the child, and involve little if any reciprocal behavior on the part of the child. Each category has a name, a short description of the kind of behavior to be observed, and an example. Thus, the first category is "Being Un-cooperative—for example, Mother ignores the child's stimulation. Example: Mother continues to read magazine when child addresses her." Other categories are "Giving Permission—for example, Mother consents to child's proposed activity. Example: 'Yes, you may use the towel.'" "Observing Attentively—for example, Mother noticeably directs her attention to the child or the child's activity by silently watching. Example: Mother watches child as the child plays with the stove." The total list of categories used is: being uncooperative, contacting, criticizing, directing, giving permission, giving praise or affection, helping, interfering, interfering by structurizing, lending cooperation, observing attentively, playing interactively, reassuring, remaining out of contact, restricting, structurizing, teaching.

RELIABILITY AND VALIDITY: Two observers were trained to reach a certain level of agreement in their simultaneous observations before actually beginning any collection of data. Forty mothers and their children were observed in five thirty-minute observation periods by two observers, and the percentage of agreement between the observers for the seventeen categories ranged from 81 to 100 per cent, with the median agreement percentage of 88 per cent. Correlations were computed between the mother's attitudes, as measured by the Parent Attitude Research Instrument (PARI), and their observed behavior toward their children in the seventeen categories mentioned. Twelve of the 272 correlations were significant at the .05 level or beyond. The author points out, in view of the large number of correlations done and the possibility of a number of them being significant by chance, that the interpretation of these statistical relationships should be undertaken with caution.

BIBLIOGRAPHY:

ZUNICH, M. "Relationship Between Maternal Behavior and Attitudes toward Children." *Journal of Genetic Psychology*, 1962, *100*, 155–165.

OBJECTIVE METHOD FOR THE
ANALYSIS OF CHILD-ADULT INTERACTION

AUTHORS: Clark E. Moustakas, Irving E. Siegel, and Henry D. Schalock

AGE: Parents, adults, and preschool children

VARIABLE: Child-adult interaction

TYPE OF MEASURE: Observation schedule

SOURCE FROM WHICH THE MEASURE MAY BE OBTAINED: See Moustakas et al. (1956)

DESCRIPTION OF MEASURE: This is a complex observation schedule that concentrates on verbal behavior. The observation schedule includes eighty-nine adult and eighty-two child categories, as well as anxiety-hostility ratings. The anxiety-hostility ratings go along with each interactive category in the schedule. The numerous categories are then subsumed under seven general broader categories, which are attention; stimulus; orienting and directing; criticism, discipline, and rejection; approval or reward; cooperation, compliance, and noncooperation; and interpretation.

As an example of the broader categories, attention includes nonattention in which no interaction between child and adult is observable and attention in which such interaction is observed—for example, the adult watches the child play in the sand. Stimulus categories involve those in which either the adult or the child attempts to elicit a particular type of response from the other as illustrated by the adult's questions concerning personal information about the child.

The scoring procedure, the symbols used for coding observations, the sample recording cells and protocols are abundantly illustrated. Special recording procedures are also described fully. Essentially, however, the scoring of the categories consists of a frequency count. The following scoring plan is utilized for the anxiety-hostility ratings: $0 =$ little or no anxiety or hostility apparent, $- =$ indication of some anxiety or hostility, and $- - =$ indication of much anxiety or hostility.

RELIABILITY AND VALIDITY: The sample for the observational schedule consisted of time samplings of two forty-five-minute periods of observation in each of three adult-child interactive situations, with behavioral categories recorded within five-second intervals. These three adult-child situations included a therapist and a child in a playroom, the mother and child in the same locale, and the mother and child in the home.

The authors define category reliability as the agreement between two observers on the identification of observed behaviors within the time sample previously described. The majority of the agreements were above 80 per cent. Observer reliability was determined by the ratio between the number of agreements and the sum of agreements and disagreements. These observer agreements pertained to three different situations: mother and child in home, mother and child in the playroom, and comparisons of these observations with those of therapist and child. Reliability for the combined behavioral categories was 92.15; for the anxiety-hostility ratings, 99.10; and for the ratings within each time period, 88.51.

BIBLIOGRAPHY:

MOUSTAKAS, C. E., SIEGEL, I. E., and SCHALOCK, H. D. "An Objective Method for the Measurement and Analysis of Child-Adult Interaction." *Child Development,* 1956, *27,* 111–134.

SLOBODIAN READING OBSERVATION RECORD (ROR)

AUTHOR: June Jenkinson Slobodian

AGE: Teachers of elementary school children

VARIABLE: Teacher-pupil interaction in the setting of the reading group

TYPE OF MEASURE: Structured observation schedule

SOURCE FROM WHICH THE MEASURE MAY BE OBTAINED: See Slobodian (1966)

DESCRIPTION OF MEASURE: The ROR is a frame of reference for observing teacher-pupil verbal interactions in the context of reading instructions. It provides data on amount of time spent on five different instructional categories: readiness, guiding reading, oral reading, skill development, and extending activities. More stress is laid, however, on the classification and sequencing of behavior units. The major headings under which verbal interaction is classified are: talk; calls on/questions; responds; interruption; action (acts); quiet activities. Definitions of some of the headings are given below:

Talk—*Presentation of information, structuring by use of statements, possibly leading or transferring to questioning. Literally any statement that is not in response to a question or in response to teacher request for information falls in the "talk" category.*

Calls on/Questions—*A teacher or student asking a question or requiring by command a response from a student or teacher is marked in this column.*

Responds—*Answers given to questions or replies made when called on are indicated by marking the appropriate box under this column.*

Interruption—*A sudden change of topic that occurs before the appropriate series of actions to choose the unit of action is complete. Entrance into the reading group for information by a student outside the group. Teacher stopping the chain of discussion to speak to child either inside or outside the group for purposes of maintaining order or giving direction. Correcting of oral reading by supplying word missed, or by making the student reread for self-correction.*

RELIABILITY AND VALIDITY: On two different occasions, inter-rater agreement on classification for the observation made reached a level of 95 per cent. In one case, agreement was between the author and an assistant with no training in rating (Slobodian, 1966b). In another instance, five experienced special reading teachers were trained as observers for a specific study, and all reached 95 per cent agreement on all observations made during training. No data on norms or direct evidence of validity are provided.

BIBLIOGRAPHY:

DAVIS, O. L., JR., and SLOBODIAN, J. J. "Teacher Behavior toward Boys and Girls in First Grade Reading Instruction." Paper presented at American Educational Research Association, Chicago, February, 1966.

SLOBODIAN, J. J. "An Analysis of Certain Dimensions of Teacher Behavior during Reading Instruction in the First Grade." Unpublished doctoral dissertation, Kent State University, 1966.

SOCIAL ANALYSIS OF THE CLASSROOM

AUTHOR: Ruth Cunningham

AGE: Elementary school age

VARIABLE: Social behavior

TYPE OF MEASURE: Nomination questionnaire

SOURCE FROM WHICH THE MEASURE MAY BE OBTAINED: See Cunningham (1951)

DESCRIPTION OF MEASURE: This measure is composed of thirty-seven descriptions of behavior that each pupil can apply to as many or as few of his classmates as he wishes. The children are instructed to read each statement and write down the names of the persons whom the descriptions fit. He is to write "myself" if he thinks the description fits him. Some sample items from the measure are given below.

Here is someone who finds it hard to sit still in class; he (or she) moves around in his (or her) seat or gets up and walks around.

Here is someone who doesn't like to talk very much, is very quiet, even when nearly everyone is talking.

This is someone who never seems to have a good time, who never seems to enjoy very much anything he (or she) does.

This is someone who is always cheerful, jolly, and good-natured, who laughs and smiles a good deal.

Here is someone who can enjoy a joke and see the fun in it even when the joke is on himself (or herself).

The reading level of this measure suggests that it is more appropriate for upper level elementary children and older.

RELIABILITY AND VALIDITY: Some items of this measure seem to describe those who received high Group Social Distance scores, but those items were never used to describe subjects having the five lowest scores on this scale (Cunningham, 1951).

BIBLIOGRAPHY:

CUNNINGHAM, R. *Understanding Group Behavior of Boys and Girls.* New York: Teachers College, Columbia University, 1951.

SOCIAL REACTION INTERVIEW (SRI)

AUTHOR: J. R. Wittenborn

AGE: Kindergarten children and those who have completed the first grade

VARIABLE: Parental attitude toward children's behavior

TYPE OF MEASURE: Semistructured interview

SOURCE FROM WHICH THE MEASURE MAY BE OBTAINED: See Wittenborn (1956a)

DESCRIPTION OF MEASURE: The SRI consists of a series of questions asking the child what he would do in a hypothetical standard social situation. The question is asked by the examiner and the child's response is classified under preestablished fixed alternatives. In cases where the child's replies do not fit the prepared alternatives, they are classified under "remarks." A sample item is given below, which is part of the "dependence on adults" cluster:

Let's pretend you just got up in the morning and want to get dressed, what do you do? (a) dress self, (b) tell adult, (c) ask what to wear, (d) wait, (e) get washed, (f) remarks.

A child's cluster score is simply the number of bits of information associated with the cluster appearing in his interview record. For kindergartners, the clusters include dependence on adults, aggression, socialized compliance, taking an adult role, weakness-avoidance, and constructive approach. For older children (age 8) the clusters include: goody-goody behavior, responsible attitude, and cooperation with authority.

RELIABILITY AND VALIDITY: With the younger group, split-half reliability coefficients for the clusters after correction ranged between .58 (aggression) and .88 (dependence on adults). In the older group, corrected split-half reliabilities for the clusters were respectively .41, .52, and .59 for cooperation with authority, responsible attitude, and goody-goody behavior. Validity of the clusters rested on internal consistency, content validity, and a lack of relationship between clusters (Wittenborn, 1956a).

BIBLIOGRAPHY:

WITTENBORN, J. R. "A Study of Adoptive Children: I. Interviews as a Source of Scores for Children and Their Homes." *Psychological Monographs: General and Applied,* 1956a, *70* (Whole No. 408).

WITTENBORN, J. R. "A Study of Adoptive Children: II. The Predictive Validity of the Yale Developmental Examination of Infant Behavior." *Psychological Monographs: General and Applied,* 1956b, *70* (Whole No. 409).

WITTENBORN, J. R. "A Study of Adoptive Children: III. Relationships Retain Some Aspects of Development and Some Aspects of Environment for Adoptive Children." *Psychological Monographs: General and Applied,* 1956c, *70* (Whole No. 410).

SOCIALIZATION SCALE

AUTHOR: James W. Bommarito

AGE: Kindergarten

VARIABLE: Social adjustment within the classroom

TYPE OF MEASURE: Teacher behavior rating check list

SOURCE FROM WHICH THE MEASURE MAY BE OBTAINED: See Bommarito (1964)

DESCRIPTION OF MEASURE: The Socialization Scale is a behavior rating instrument that directs teachers to check items relating to the behavior of specific children within their classroom. The forty-five items of the scale are slanted in an undesirable or negative direction, with the child's score consisting of the total number of items checked. Teachers are requested to rate only those children whom they have known for at least two months. The scale itself includes behavioral items relating to patterns of aggression, social maladjustment, educational maladjustment, and behavior suggesting internal unhappiness, the four most common types of psychological problems coming to the attention of mental health personnel in the schools. Sample items from the scale follow (Bommarito, 1964):

Watches others play; seldom plays by himself.
Plays alone most of the time.
Cries without seeming provocation.
Seeks attention excessively.

RELIABILITY AND VALIDITY: The author presents no evidence for reliability on the scale. The statistical evidence rests primarily on validity data. First, the items of the scale are based primarily on the theory that children with supportive and satisfying social reinforcement histories have learned to depend on adults and hence attempt to please them. According to this learning theory, children should be willing to please adults, control their responses, and conform to the situation of the kindergarten. In short, they should be socialized and be susceptible to further socialization. The items for the Socialization Scale primarily fit this theory.

In addition to this construct validation, the scale receives statistical support from two sources of content validity. First, the final scale of forty-five items is based on an original checklist of eighty-three items collated from the literature. Since the scale is to be used by kindergarten teachers, this original Socialization Scale of eighty-three items was submitted to twenty-seven kindergarten teachers in a large suburban school district. The return was 100 per cent. Teachers were asked to rate each item in terms of its importance as an indicator of a child's adjustment in a kindergarten class. Each item was to be rated as very important (score 4), important (score 3), little importance (score 2), and not important (score 1). The final scale consists of only those items that had an average rating of 3 or above.

The second source of content validity rests on the independent ratings of the significance of these items by three well-trained psychologists. The inter-rater reli-bility for these three psychologists was .87. Moreover the ratings pertaining to the individual items of the scale by the kindergarten teachers were unrelated to years of teaching experience, years of experience in teaching kindergarten, and number of semester hours in psychology. The scale has been used only with 200 randomly selected kindergarten children. The measure is essentially a research tool at this stage of its development.

BIBLIOGRAPHY:

BOMMARITO, J. W. "Conditioning by Mild Verbal Punishment as a Predictor of Ad-justment in Kindergarten." Unpublished doctoral dissertation, Wayne State University, 1964.

STEVENSON'S BEHAVIORAL UNIT OBSERVATIONAL PROCEDURE

AUTHORS: Harold W. Stevenson and Nancy G. Stevenson

AGE: Preschool children

VARIABLE: Social behavior

TYPE OF MEASURE: Controlled observation procedure

SOURCE FROM WHICH THE MEASURE MAY BE OBTAINED: See Stevenson (1953)

DESCRIPTION OF MEASURE: Stevenson's behavioral observational procedure includes three components: the method of analysis or the behavioral unit (BU), the definition of variables, and the procedure for simultaneous observation and ratings. At the core of the method is the behavioral unit (BU) which deals with molar responses, such as swinging, as opposed to molecular responses, such as finger movement.

Three conditions create BUs: an observable environmental change, preceding change in the subject's behavior (Jimmy hits the subject and the subject hits back); an observable environmental change without observable change in the subject's behavior (Jimmy hits the subject and the subject continues playing as before); and no change in environment followed by observable change in the subject's behavior (the subject hits Bill without provocation).

BUs may be rated for any number of behavioral categories. As an example, Stevenson and Stevenson (1961) operationally defined Social Participation (SP) and contact with adults (A). A BU is rated for SP on three levels of interaction. In level 1, the child interacts physically or verbally with another child. Level 2 roughly approximates parallel play. Level 3 refers to solitary or isolate activity. The second category (A) includes all behavior involving the child's contact with an adult, such as when a subject asks an adult for help. To use this procedure, the authors recommend experience in observing children, the division of written observations into BUs, and operational definitions of the behavior being studied. They also find a checklist of the categories and their levels useful. The procedure also entails predetermined time units of observation and a recording method.

RELIABILITY AND VALIDITY: A sample consisted of nine children in a preschool class within a university setting, including five boys and four girls with a range in age from 3 years 5 months to 4 years 7 months. In determining the reliability of the method, Kendall's coefficient of concordance (W) was used for total BUs, the three BUs under SP, and BU of A. The values of W among the three observers for each category ranged between .80 and .94 (Stevenson and Stevenson, 1961).

BIBLIOGRAPHY:

STEVENSON, N. G. "A Method of Analyzing Observational Records." Unpublished master's thesis, Stanford University, 1953.

STEVENSON, H. W., and STEVENSON, N. G. "A Method for Simultaneous Observation and Analysis of Children's Behavior." *The Journal of Genetic Psychology,* 1961, *99,* 253–260.

TEST REACTION SCALE (TRS)

AUTHOR: J. R. Wittenborn

AGE: Kindergarten children and those who have passed the first grade

VARIABLE: Social adaptation

TYPE OF MEASURE: Rating scale

SOURCE FROM WHICH THE MEASURE MAY BE OBTAINED: See Wittenborn (1956)

DESCRIPTION OF MEASURE: The TRS is part of a battery of tests developed to serve as an external criterion for the predictive validity of the Yale Developmental Examination of Infant Behavior. It consists of adult ratings for thirteen areas of a child's behavior, including mother-child relationship as observed by examiner, attention, activity, sociability, belligerence, maintenance, reaction to failure, sensitivity to failure, male versus female examiner, modesty, thumb sucking, fine motor ability, and speech defect. These ratings are made by an evaluation of the child's behavior during psychological and pediatric examinations. Though no definite scoring system is described, the hierarchical order of the behaviors to be rated from most to least desirable is easily discernible within the three to five items comprising each area. The area of the mother-child relationship serves as an example of this hierarchy and the content (Wittenborn, 1956):

Child was not at all hesitant about leaving mother, scarcely said goodbye and went with examiner readily. He showed no concern for mother during examination and was extremely casual about seeing his mother again at close of examination.

Child was somewhat hesitant at leaving mother, said goodbye and looked to see where she would wait, and showed pleasure at seeing her again at close of examination.

Child was extremely reluctant to leave mother, held on to her hand, may have cried, wanted her to come with him, needed to be reassured that she would wait for him. He asked about her several times during the examination. He seemed very much relieved to see her again.

RELIABILITY AND VALIDITY: No statistics on the reliability of the data are as yet available. Perhaps some content validity for the scale may be assumed in that the items were developed by agreement among psychologists, pediatricians, and social workers.

BIBLIOGRAPHY:

WITTENBORN, J. R. "A Study of Adoptive Children: II. The Predictive Validity of the Yale Developmental Examination of Infant Behavior." *Psychological Monographs: General and Applied,* 1956, 70 (Whole No. 409).

WRIGHTSTONE'S CONTROLLED OBSERVATION SCALE

AUTHOR: J. Wayne Wrightstone

AGE: Classroom teachers of elementary school children

VARIABLE: Teacher-child interaction

TYPE OF MEASURE: Controlled-observation instrument

SOURCE FROM WHICH THE MEASURE MAY BE OBTAINED: See Wrightstone (1934)

DESCRIPTION OF MEASURE: Wrightstone's Controlled Observation Scale is an instrument designed to measure teacher conduct of class discussion. Eleven classes of behavior units constitute the system for classifying teacher conduct of class discussion. Examples are: permitting voluntary contributions; encouraging a child to contribute to class discussion; posing a question; and referring a child to a data source. The categories are defined, and a code is assigned so that the observer can record the behavior readily.

The total score for a child is the sum of the total number of entered code numbers. If the teacher wishes to make direct comparisons of scores, the author cautions that the observational period be held constant.

RELIABILITY AND VALIDITY: The reliability of the code rests in observations of children in ten elementary schools. The measure of internal consistency derived from the Spearman-Brown formula yielded a split-half reliability coefficient of .83. Inter-rater agreement among several trained observers with a week's experience in the use of the instrument was 88 to 90 per cent.

The author took pains to ensure that the codes described representative teacher behavior in the classroom. As expected, significant differences among the behavior of teachers were found.

BIBLIOGRAPHY:

WRIGHTSTONE. J. W. "Measuring Teacher Conduct of Class Discussion." *Elementary School Journal,* 1934, *34,* 454–460.

CATEGORY 10

UNCLASSIFIED

COLORADO BRAILLE BATTERY (CBB)

AUTHORS: Richard Woodcock and Stanley E. Bourgeault

AGE: The battery is appropriate for both blind children and adults but the manual should be consulted for details on the appropriate age level for the various subscales

VARIABLE: Braille skills

TYPE OF MEASURE: Test

SOURCE FROM WHICH THE MEASURE MAY BE OBTAINED: Cooperative Research Project 1650, entitled "Construction and Standardization of a Battery of Braille Skill Tests," U.S. Office of Education, Dept. of Health, Education, and Welfare, Washington, D.C.

DESCRIPTION OF MEASURE: The CBB essentially tests the blind person's ability to read or do number work in braille. It samples skills in the Grade 2 Literary Code and the Nemeth Code for mathematics. Seven scales of the battery measure achievement in the former, four in the latter. In addition, pretests are available for screening purposes. All subscales are administered orally on a group basis, with time limits determined only by the judgment of the examiner. All questions are multiple-choice five-alternative items given in braille. Complete directions are available for administering, scoring, and interpreting the battery. Parallel forms exist for the Nemeth test at all levels (Woodcock and Bourgeault, 1964a). Sample items from the Literary Code Test are given below (Woodcock and Bourgeault, 1964b, p. 61):

Put your finger on the place which says "Number 1." [Check to see that all subjects have found "Number 1."] There are five answers in row number one. These answers are M, P, N, V, and Q. Look at all five answers and then mark the letter M. Raise your hand if you need any help.

Put your finger on the place which says "Number 1." [Check to see that all subjects have found "Number 1."] There are five answers in row number one. These answers are V, Q, Y, R, and N. Look at all five answers and then mark the letter R. Raise your hand if you need any help.

RELIABILITY AND VALIDITY: The standardization group included more than 2,000 blind students from residential and public school classes. Within this sample, 10,000 tests were administered. Both grade and percentile norms are available (Woodcock and Bourgeault, 1964a).

Internal consistency coefficients calculated by the Kuder-Richardson 20 formula ranged from .68 to .87 on subscales of the Literary Code test, from .68 to .87 on subscales of the Nemeth Code test, and from .75 to .98 for the entire Literary Code test (Woodcock and Bourgeault, 1964b). In addition, Pearson product moment correlation coefficients on parallel forms ranged from .64 to .94 on the subtests of the Literary Code test (Woodcock and Bourgeault, 1964b) and from .58 to .93 on the subscales of the Nemeth Code test (Woodcock and Bourgeault, 1964c).

The authors claim that the battery has content validity on the basis of the procedure by which they selected the test items from relevant publications (Woodcock and Bourgeault, 1964b).

BIBLIOGRAPHY:

WOODCOCK, R. W., and BOURGEAULT, S. E. *Construction and Standardization of a Battery of Braille Skill Tests*. Greeley: Colorado State College, 1964a.

WOODCOCK, R. W., and BOURGEAULT, S. E. *Colorado Braille Battery: Manual of Directions for Literary Code Tests, Grade 2 Braille*. Greeley: Colorado State College, 1964b.

DALE-CHALL READABILITY FORMULA

AUTHORS: Edgar Dale and Jeanne Chall

AGE: Children and adults

VARIABLE: Readability of printed matter

TYPE OF MEASURE: Index of reading difficulty

SOURCE FROM WHICH THE MEASURE MAY BE OBTAINED: See Dale and Chall (1948)

DESCRIPTION OF MEASURE: The formula appears to serve two purposes: It serves as a check on the comprehension level of reading material, and it also serves as an aid to text simplification. Scoring of the reading materials by this formula rests on the two factors of vocabulary load and average sentence length. Vocabulary load is determined by the number of words not included in the Dale list of 3,000 words. The score can be computed, or the calculations can be abbreviated considerably by the use of prepared tables (Klare, 1952). In any case, the authors present detailed directions for selecting samples, labeling the work sheet, counting the number of words, counting the number of sentences, counting the number of unfamiliar words, and completing the work sheet (Dale and Chall, pp. 11–16).

RELIABILITY AND VALIDITY: The authors present no data for reliability and standardization. Because of the objectivity of the scoring system, it appears that potential users of this scale could determine its test-retest reliability with relative ease. Data on validity are of several types. The correlation between the grade equivalents of the McCall-Crabbs Standard Test in Reading, which served as the external validating criterion, and the grade equivalents as determined by the Dale list was .6833. This correlation was computed from an analysis of all the 376 passages in these lessons that are graded in difficulty, based on the comprehensibility of questions at the end of each passage.

The correlation of the second factor in the formula, average sentence length, with the criterion was .4681. A two-factor formula also predicted difficulty level of reading materials other than the McCall-Crabbs reading passages, correlating .92 with the judgments of readability experts, and .90 with reading grades of children and adults.

On seventy-eight passages on foreign affairs from current-events magazines and newspapers, the correlation between the predictions of the formula and judgments of difficulty by expert teachers in the social studies was .90 (Dale and Chall, 1948).

BIBLIOGRAPHY:

DALE, E., and CHALL, J. "A Formula for Predicting Readability." Columbus, Ohio: Bureau of Educational Research, Ohio State University. Reprint from *The Educational Research Bulletin,* 1948, *XXVII,* 11–20 and 37–54.
KLARE, G. R. "A Table for Rapid Determination of Dale-Chall Readability Scores." Columbus, Ohio: Bureau of Educational Research, Ohio State University. Reprinted from *The Educational Research Bulletin,* 1952, *XXI*(2), 43–47.

FACTS ABOUT MENTAL DEFICIENCY TEST

AUTHORS: L. N. Yepsen and James A. Bitter

AGE: Parents of mentally retarded children

VARIABLE: Knowledge of mental deficiency

TYPE OF MEASURE: Questionnaire

SOURCE FROM WHICH THE MEASURE MAY BE OBTAINED: The majority of the items can be found in Yepsen's previous text (1956)

DESCRIPTION OF MEASURE: The Facts about Mental Deficiency Test is a self-administering scale consisting of fifty true-false statements about the syndrome. Some examples of items from this measure are given below (Yepsen, 1956):

*"Mentally deficient" refers to children who are classified, for educational purposes, as
"trainable" mentally retarded rather than "educable" mentally retarded.
As a baby, first evidences of mental retardation are that the child is slow to notice
things, slow to sit up unsupported, retarded in walking and talking.
Mental deficiency and mental illness are not the same.*

The scale itself has been used (Bitter, 1963) to assess change in parental attitudes following group discussions. Though the author does not give specific directions for scoring, the most desirable answers seem explicit enough. Many of the correct answers are available in Yepsen's pamphlet (1956).

RELIABILITY AND VALIDITY: To our knowledge, this scale has been used only with sixteen parents (eleven mothers and five fathers) of trainable children (Bitter, 1962). As yet, no statistics on reliability are available. Perhaps some content validity may be assumed from the fact that the majority of the items were developed by Yepsen who has had extensive experience and training in mental retardation.

BIBLIOGRAPHY:

BITTER, J. A. "Attitude Change by Parents of Trainable Mentally Retarded Children
     as a Result of Group Discussion." *Exceptional Children,* 1963, *30,* 173–177.
YEPSEN, L. N. *Facts and Fancies about Mental Deficiency.* Trenton, New Jersey:
     New Jersey State Department of Institutions and Agencies, 1956.

SPATIAL CHARACTERISTICS TEST

AUTHOR: Hilda P. Lewis

AGE: Kindergarten through eighth grade

VARIABLE: Spatial representation

TYPE OF MEASURE: Test

SOURCE FROM WHICH THE MEASURE MAY BE OBTAINED: See Lewis (1963a)

DESCRIPTION OF MEASURE: The Spatial Characteristics Test attempts to assess the skills of children in depicting a three-dimensional space relationship within the limits of a two-dimensional medium. The test has been given to 776 children within the three ranges of middle-class status (lower-middle, middle-middle, and upper-middle) with a wide range of intellectual ability. The test, which is administered on a group basis, requires the children to draw three objects that are presented individually: a glass globe, a four-sided, flat-roofed toy house, and a diorama of a landscape. Details of each object are described in full. After each object presentation the child has fifteen minutes to complete his drawing with wax crayons. The drawings are then scored on a 1 to 5 basis depending on the level of three-dimensional representativeness displayed. Graphic representations for each object at every level of scoring are presented in complete detail (Lewis, 1963a).

RELIABILITY AND VALIDITY: Overall agreement between the author's scoring and that by two independent investigators on 768 drawings was 91.4 per cent. The validating evidence for the scale appears to rest primarily upon construct validity in that the data supported predicted findings relating primarily to the relationship between grade-level of pupils and the skills in the drawings, to preferences among children in drawings, and to the lack of significant sex differences in performance (Lewis, 1963a, 1963b).

BIBLIOGRAPHY:

LEWIS, H. P. "Spatial Representation in Drawing as a Correlate of Development and a Basis for Picture Preference." *Journal of Genetic Psychology*, 1963a, *102*, 95–107.

LEWIS, H. P. "The Relationship of Picture Preference to Developmental Status in Drawing." *Journal of Educational Research*, 1963b, *57*, 43–46.

TRI-MODAL IMAGERY SCALE (TIS)

AUTHORS: John R. Bergan and Gloria Macchiavello

AGE: Fourth-grade children

VARIABLE: Visual imagery

TYPE OF MEASURE: Rating scale

SOURCE FROM WHICH THE MEASURE MAY BE OBTAINED: John R. Bergan, University of Arizona, Tucson, Arizona 85721

DESCRIPTION OF MEASURE: The TIS is composed of 148 items, assessing visual, kinesthetic, and auditory experiences in a wide variety of situations. Each situation chosen is represented in all three imagery modes. For example, a subject will be asked to imagine seeing the letter X, to imagine hearing someone say X, and to imagine his hand movement in drawing an X. The test, which is administered orally on a group basis, requires a child to rate his imagery on a five-point scale, ranging from 1 for no imagery to 5 for an image as clear as the real object. The total score then consists of the sum for the individual items. In the major study describing the scale (Bergan and Macchiavello, 1966), only the fifty items relating to visual imagery were scored. T-scores were derived from the mean and standard deviation of each subject's ratings for all items on the TIS. According to the authors, the comparison of external visual stimuli with internal standards representing these stimuli is crucial to the reading process.

RELIABILITY AND VALIDITY: Reliabilities for the TIS, as computed by the Roulon method for odd-even splits for both raw scores and T scores, were respectively .97 and .67 based on a sample of fifty-one children. The correlation between the results on the TIS and reading achievement as measured by the Paragraph Meaning section of the Stanford Achievement Battery was .44 on the same sample previously described. The correlation was significant at the .01 level of confidence. Sixteen items of the TIS showed correlations of .30 or higher with the reading achievement criterion.

BIBLIOGRAPHY:

BERGAN, J. R., and MACCHIAVELLO, G. "Visual Imagery and Reading Achievement." Paper presented at the 50th Annual Meeting of the American Educational Research Association in Chicago, Illinois, on February 17, 1966.

VISUAL IMAGERY INDEX

AUTHOR: Leon D. Radaker

AGE: 10 to 15 (mentally retarded)

VARIABLE: Imagery

TYPE OF MEASURE: Test

SOURCE FROM WHICH THE MEASURE MAY BE OBTAINED: See Radaker (1961)

DESCRIPTION OF MEASURE: This presents an attempt to objectify the assessment of visual imagery. The subject is to visualize the words "come," "front," and "schism." The subject's image of each word is rated on six dimensions: brightness, conformity, boldness, duration, stability, and arousal interval. The first three dimensions must be scored by the subject, and the last three can be scored by the examiner. Models constructed in the first three dimensions help the subject to objectify his responses on the dimensions brightness, conformity, and boldness. Brightness has to do with the glossiness of the stimulus word. Therefore, the stimulus words were constructed out of "paint chips" according to the following scale (score and model):

5	black gloss	2	dark gray flat
4	black semigloss	1	light gray flat
3	black flat	0	no image

Conformity refers to the extent to which the image conforms to the contour of the stimulus word. The following six-point scale was used for scoring:

5	good letter contour, white background
4	slightly irregular contour, white background
3	good letter contour, gray background
2	slightly irregular contour, gray background
1	pronounced irregular contour, gray background
0	no image

Boldness refers to the relative widths of the letters in the image. Thus, the following scoring systems was devised:

5	$\frac{1}{2}$ inch	2	$\frac{1}{16}$ inch
4	$\frac{3}{16}$ inch	1	hairline
3	$\frac{1}{8}$ inch	0	no image

Duration means the length of time the image was retained, while stability concerns the frequency of image fluctuations (in size, color, or intensity). Arousal interval is the latency period between presentation of the stimulus word and the achievement of an image equivalent to the stimulus. Each of the three variables, as with glossiness, conformity, and boldness, is scaled on a six-point scale (Radaker, 1961). The total possible range of scores on this measure is 0 to 90, where the maximum is made up as follows: three stimulus words $\times$ six subvariables $\times$ five (highest possible item score).

RELIABILITY AND VALIDITY: Three groups of fifteen children, age 10 to 15, took the measure. One was a control group, and two were experimental in that they were trained in visual imagery, one group for two sessions and the other for six sessions. Test-retest reliability of the control groups was .98, over a period of two weeks. The hypothesis that visual imagery can be improved by training was supported (Radaker, 1961).

BIBLIOGRAPHY:

RADAKER, L. D. "The Visual Imagery of Retarded Children and the Relationship to Memory for Word Forms." *Exceptional Children,* 1961, 27.

Journals in Which Measures Appear

Academy of Child Psychiatry (Journal of the)

Acta Psychologica

American Journal of Mental Deficiency

American Journal of Orthopsychiatry

American Journal of Psychiatry

American Journal of Psychology

American Journal of Sociology

American Psychologist

Australian Journal of Psychology

Behavioral Science

British Journal of Educational Psychology

British Journal of Educational Studies

British Journal of Psychology

British Journal of Social and Clinical Psychology

Canadian Education and Research Digest

Canadian Journal of Psychology

Child Development

Childhood Education

Education

Educational & Psychological Measurement

Educational Research (British)

Educational Research Bulletin

Elementary School Journal

Exceptional Children

Genetic Psychology Monographs

Indian Journal of Social Work

Japanese Psychological Research

Journal of Abnormal Psychology

Journal of Abnormal and Social Psychology

Journal of Clinical Psychology

Journal of Consulting Psychology

Journal of Counseling Psychology

Journal of Educational Measurement

Journal of Educational Psychology

Journal of Educational Research

Journal of Educational Sociology

Journal of the Experimental Analysis of Behavior

Journal of Experimental Education

Journal of Experimental Psychology

Journal of General Psychology

Journal of Genetic Psychology

Journal of Health and Human Behavior

Journal of Humanistic Psychology

Journal of Mathematical Psychology

Journal of Personality

Journal of Personality and Social Psychology

Journal of Psychological Studies

Journal of Psychology

Journal of Social Psychology

Journal of Verbal Learning and Verbal Behavior

Language Learning

Mental Hygiene

Merrill-Palmer Quarterly

Psychological Bulletin

Psychological Reports

Research Relating to Children

Smith College Studies in Social Work

Index of Authors
of Measures

Index of Measures

Subject Index

General Index

518

Q

Q-technique, 9
Questionnaires, 6

S

Sacks and Levy Sentence Completion Test, 165
Sarason's Score for Anxiety, 242
Sargent Insight Test, 143
School, parents' attitudes toward, 19
School readiness measures, classification of, 14–15, 27
Scoring criteria, 5–6, 11
Search procedure, 4–5
Selection of measures, 5–6
Self-concept measures, classification of, 9, 18
Semantic differential techniques, 9
Sensory perception measures, classification of, 20
SHAW, M. E., 8
Shoben's Scale on Maternal Attitudes, 335
SIMON, A., 8
Sims Score Cards, 345
Smith Vocabulary Test, 77
SNIDER, J. G., 9
Social behavior measures, classification of, 18, 20–21
Sociometric-type measures, 18
Stanford-Binet tests, 28–29, 36, 41, 49, 59, 67, 75, 92–94, 169; Terman and Merrill's revision of, 67, 201
STEPHENSON, W., 9
SUCI, G. J., 9

Sutton-Smith and Rosenberg Impulsivity Scale, 183
Symonds' Teacher Rating Scale, 151

T

TANNENBAUM, P. H., 9
Tasks, measurement of, 5
Terman-Merrill Intelligence Scale, 67, 201
Test, definition of, 5
Test Collection Bulletin, 8
Tests in Print, 7
Thematic Apperception Test, 168, 172, 174, 251
Time period covered in book, 4
Torrance's Lines Test, 187

V

Validity of measures, 5–6, 11
Variables, identifying, 6, 10
Vineland Social Maturity Scale, 43, 67, 76

W

WARBURTON, F. W., 7
Warner's Index of Status Characteristics, 475
WEBB, E. J., 8
Wechsler Intelligence Scale for Children (WISC), 29, 41, 45, 65, 73, 122
Winterbottom's Independence Training Attitude Questionnaire, 330
WRIGHT, J. M., 8
WYLIE, R. C., 12

Y

Yale Developmental Examination of Infant Behavior, 325, 346, 482, 486